MW01641555

THE STORY OF GOD'S LOVE

The Story of God's Love

A SUMMARY OF THE HOLY BIBLE

NORTHWESTERN PUBLISHING HOUSE
Milwaukee, Wisconsin

The Evangelical Heritage Version is part of the Wartburg Bible series.

The Wartburg Bible Series
A Summary of the Holy Bible
EHV Text: © 2021 the Wartburg Project
Published by Northwestern Publishing House
ISBN 978-0-8100-3003-9

In the EHV logo, the circle of light or the rainbow radiating from the cross is divided into three parts to symbolize the three solas of the Reformation: by grace alone, by faith alone, and by Scripture alone. This semi-circle, together with the base, forms the Latin letter D, which means 500 and honors the 500th anniversary of the Reformation in 2017, the year in which the first partial edition of the EHV was published.

21 22 23 24 25 26 27 28 29 30 10 9 8 7 6 5 4 3 2 1

Contents and Outline

The Old Testament

PART 1: THE PATRIARCHS (GENESIS) (JOB)

PART 3: THE JUDGES (JUDGES AND 1 SAMUEL)

PART 4: THE UNITED MONARCHY (1 AND 2 SAMUEL, 1 KINGS) (SELECTIONS FROM PSALMS, PROVERBS, SONG OF SOLOMON, AND ECCLESIASTES)

PART 7: THE RETURN FROM EXILE
(EZRA, NEHEMIAH, ESTHER, SELECTED PROPHETS)

THE NEW TESTAMENT

PART 1: THE EARLY LIFE OF CHRIST (THE FOUR GOSPELS)

PART 2: CHRIST'S PUBLIC MINISTRY (THE FOUR GOSPELS)

PART 3: CHRIST'S DEATH AND RESURRECTION (THE FOUR GOSPELS)

PART 4: THE EARLY CHURCH IN ISRAEL (ACTS)

PART 5: TO THE ENDS OF THE EARTH (ACTS AND THE EPISTLES)

PART 6: JOHN'S VISIONS (REVELATION)

MAPS

FOREWORD

This book started out as a Bible History text for schools, and it still can be used for that purpose, but it developed into something much more. It could be called a condensed or abbreviated Bible. Each section is an excerpt from the EHV translation of the Holy Bible. The sections are not edited or simplified summaries of the biblical text, but retain the wording of the EHV text.

Reading this book is like reading the whole Bible in chronological order. Selections from the prophets, the epistles, and some of the psalms are inserted at the point where they fit into the historical narrative. This abbreviated Bible does not include material like the genealogies, the ceremonial laws, and long descriptions. It does not include all of the historical sections of the Bible, but those that are included were selected to summarize the whole plan of salvation from Eden to eternity.

Besides serving as a Bible History book, this book can be used as a simplified Bible for many instructional purposes. It is recommended for use by first-time Bible readers who want to get a summary of the Bible before tackling all the details. Long-time Bible readers will appreciate it as a summary of the highlights of the Bible. It is recommended for distribution in institutional ministries and outreach. It could be used as a text book for high school or college surveys of the Bible.

In addition to the biblical text, each section has an introduction to help the reader make the connection with the biblical context. Each section concludes with a brief prayer which gives an application to each lesson to the plan of salvation and to Christian life. Throughout, the emphasis is on tracing the revelation and the progress of the gospel.

THE OLD TESTAMENT

PART 1

THE PATRIARCHS (GENESIS) (JOB)

God created a perfect world, but it did not last long. The first people, Adam and Eve, quickly ruined it by their sin. But God immediately promised a Savior who would provide a remedy for their sin and the problems it caused. Many people in this ancient world rejected God and his promise, but God always kept at least one family as his own. The leaders of this family were known as the patriarchs—famous men of faith such as Noah, Abraham, Isaac, and Jacob. These men were not perfect. They were sinners just like everyone else. But they trusted in God, and God always kept his promises to them and to the whole world. As believers they trusted that God would keep his promises—promises of a homeland and of a Savior—even though they would not live to see these promises being fulfilled.

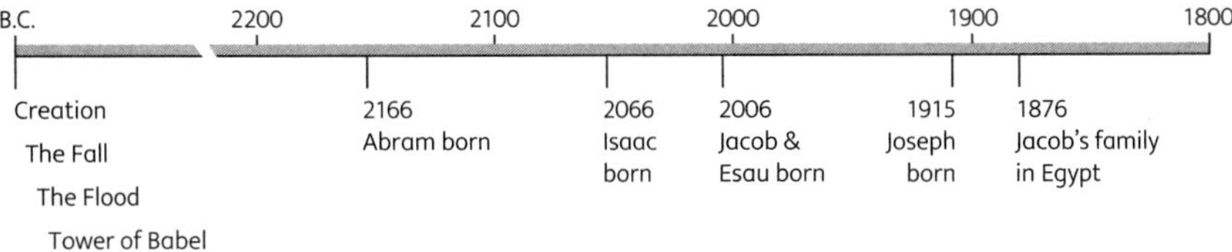

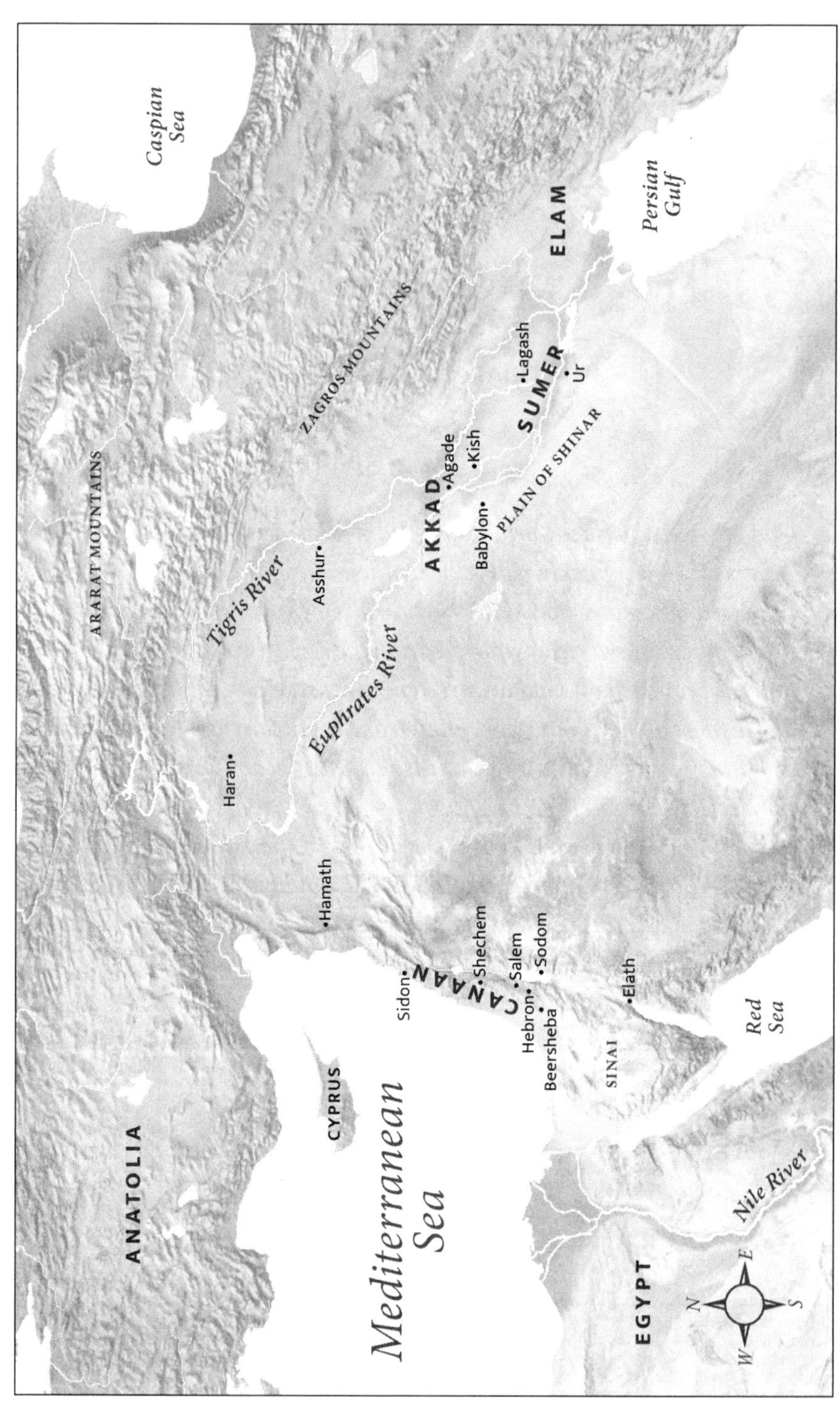

THE ANCIENT MIDDLE EAST

1. THE CREATION OF THE WORLD (GENESIS 1-2)

In seven days God creates a perfect world out of nothing, using his word, and he gives it to mankind, the crown of his creation.

In the beginning, God created the heavens and the earth. The earth was undeveloped and empty. Darkness covered the surface of the deep, and the Spirit of God was hovering over the surface of the waters.

God said, "Let there be light," and there was light. God saw that the light was good. He separated the light from the darkness. God called the light "day," and the darkness he called "night." There was evening and there was morning—the first day.

God said, "Let there be an expanse between the waters, and let it separate the water from the water." God made the expanse, and he separated the water that was below the expanse from the water that was above the expanse, and it was so. God called the expanse "sky." There was evening and there was morning—the second day.

God said, "Let the waters under the sky be gathered together to one place, and let the dry land appear," and it was so. The waters under the sky gathered to their own places, and the dry land appeared. God called the dry ground "land," and the gathering places of the waters he called "seas." God saw that it was good. God said, "Let the earth produce plants, each according to its own kind," and it was so. The earth brought forth plants, each according to its own kind, and God saw that it was good. There was evening and there was morning—the third day.

God said, "Let there be lights in the expanse of the sky to divide the day from the night, and let them serve as markers to indicate seasons, days, and years. Let them serve as lights in the expanse of the sky to give light to the earth," and it was so. God made the two great lights: the greater light to rule the day, and the lesser light to rule the night. He also made the stars. God set these lights in place in the expanse of the sky to provide light for the earth, to rule over the day and over the night, and to divide the light from the darkness. God saw that it was good. There was evening and there was morning—the fourth day.

God said, "Let the waters swarm with living creatures, and let birds and other winged creatures fly above the earth in the open expanse of the sky." God created the sea creatures according to their own kind and every winged bird according to its own kind. God saw that it was good. God blessed them when he said, "Be fruitful and multiply. Fill the waters of the seas, and let birds multiply on the earth." There was evening and there was morning—the fifth day.

God said, "Let the earth produce living creatures according to their own kind, livestock, creeping things, and wild animals according to their own kind," and it was so. God made the wild animals according to their own kind, and the livestock according to their own kind, and everything that creeps on the ground according to its own kind. God saw that it was good.

God said, "Let us make man in our image, according to our likeness, and let them have dominion over all the earth." God created the man in his own image. In the image of God he created him. Male and female he created them.

God blessed them and said to them, "Be fruitful, multiply, fill the earth, and subdue it. Have dominion over every living thing." God said, "Look, I have given you every plant. It will be your food. To every animal in which there is the breath of life I have given every green plant for food." And it was so.

God saw everything that he had made, and indeed, it was very good. There was evening and there was morning—the sixth day.

The heavens and the earth were finished, along with everything in them. On the seventh day God had finished his work that he had done, and he rested on the seventh day from all his work that he had been doing. God blessed the seventh day and set it apart as holy, because on it he rested from all his work of creation that he had done.

Lord God, we praise you for this wonderful world that you have created by your word. Help us to care for your creation, and continue to use your almighty power to bless and care for us. Amen.

2. THE CREATION OF MAN AND WOMAN (GENESIS 2)

Here is a closer look at Day 6 of creation, when God creates man and woman and establishes marriage.

The LORD God formed the man from the dust of the ground and breathed into his nostrils the breath of life, and the man became a living being. The LORD God planted a garden in Eden in the east, and there he put the man whom he had formed. Out of the ground the LORD God made every kind of tree grow—trees that are pleasant to look at and good for food, including the Tree of Life in the middle of the garden and the Tree of the Knowledge of Good and Evil.

The LORD God took the man and settled him in the Garden of Eden to work it and to take care of it. The LORD God gave a command to the man. He said, "You may freely eat from every tree in the garden, but you shall not eat from the Tree of the Knowledge of Good and Evil, for on the day that you eat from it, you will certainly die."

The LORD God said, "It is not good for the man to be alone. I will make a helper who is a suitable partner for him." Out of the soil the LORD God had formed every wild animal and every bird of the sky, and he brought them to the man to see what he would call them. Whatever the man called every living creature, that became its name. The man gave names to all the livestock, and to the birds of the sky, and to every wild animal, but for Adam no helper was found who was a suitable partner for him. The LORD God caused the man to fall into a deep sleep. As the man slept, the LORD God took a rib and closed up the flesh where it had been. The LORD God built a woman from the rib that he had taken from the man and brought her to the man.

The man said, "Now this one is bone of my bones and flesh of my flesh. She will be called 'woman', because she was taken out of man. For this reason a man will leave his father and his mother and will remain united with his wife, and they will become one flesh."

They were both naked, the man and his wife, and they were not ashamed.

Lord God, we thank you for the blessings that you provide through marriage and family. Grant that all husbands and wives love each other. Amen.

3. THE FALL INTO SIN (GENESIS 3)

By giving in to the Devil's temptation and falling into sin, the human race loses God's image and will die, but God immediately promises to send a Savior.

Now the serpent was more clever than any wild animal which the LORD God had made. He said to the woman, "Has God really said, 'You shall not eat from any tree in the garden'?"

The woman said to the serpent, "We may eat fruit from the trees of the garden, but not from the fruit of the tree that is in the middle of the garden. God has said, 'You shall not eat from it. You shall not touch it, or else you will die.'"

The serpent said to the woman, "You certainly will not die. In fact, God knows that the day you eat from it, your eyes will be opened, and you will be like God, knowing good and evil."

When the woman saw that the tree was good for food, and that it was appealing to the eyes, and that the tree was desirable to make one wise, she took some of its fruit and ate. She gave some also to her husband, who was with her, and he ate it. The eyes of both of them were opened, and they realized that they were naked. They sewed fig leaves together and made coverings for their waists. They heard the voice of the LORD God, who was walking around in the garden during the cooler part of the day, and the man and his wife hid themselves from the presence of the LORD God among the trees of the garden.

The LORD God called to the man and said to him, "Where are you?"

The man said, "I heard your voice in the garden, and I was afraid, because I was naked, so I hid myself."

God said, "Who told you that you were naked? Have you eaten from the tree from which I commanded you not to eat?"

The man said, "The woman you gave to be with me—she gave me fruit from the tree, and I ate it."

The LORD God said to the woman, "What have you done?"

The woman said, "The serpent deceived me, and I ate."

The LORD God said to the serpent, "Because you have done this, you are cursed. You shall crawl on your belly, and you shall eat dust all the days of your life. I will put hostility between you and the woman, and between your seed and her seed. He will crush your head, and you will crush his heel."

To the woman he said, "I will greatly increase your pain in childbearing. With painful labor you will give birth to children. Your desire will be for your husband, but he will rule over you."

To Adam he said, "Because you listened to your wife's voice and ate from the tree about which I commanded you, 'You shall not eat from it,' the soil is cursed on account of you. You will eat from it with painful labor all the days of your life. Thorns and thistles will spring up from the ground for you, but you will eat the crops of the field. By the sweat of your face you will eat bread until you return to the soil, for out of it you were taken. For you are dust, and to dust you shall return."

The man named his wife Eve because she would be the mother of all the living. The LORD God made clothing of animal skins for Adam and for his wife and clothed them.

The LORD God said, "Look, the man has become like one of us, knowing good and evil. Now, so that he does not reach out his hand and also take from the Tree of Life and eat and live forever—" the LORD God sent him out from the garden of Eden to work the soil from which he had been taken. So he drove the man out, and in front of the Garden of Eden he stationed cherubim and a flaming sword, which turned in every direction to guard the way to the Tree of Life.

Lord God, we confess that we have sinned against you, just as our first parents Adam and Eve did. We thank you that you sent your Son Jesus as our substitute, to destroy the Devil's work and save us from our sin. Give us, your redeemed people, the strength to fight against the Devil's temptations. Amen.

4. CAIN AND ABEL (GENESIS 4-5)

The sin which has now entered into the world is immediately clear to see, as one of Adam and Eve's sons murders another of their sons.

Eve gave birth to Cain. She also gave birth to Cain's brother Abel. Abel tended sheep, but Cain worked the ground. As time passed, one day Cain brought an offering to the LORD from the fruit of the soil. Abel also brought some of the firstborn of his flock and their fat portions. The LORD looked favorably on Abel and his offering, but he did not look favorably on Cain and his offering. Cain was very angry, and his face showed it.

The LORD said to Cain, "Why are you angry? Why do you have that angry look on your face? If you do good, will you not be lifted up? If you do not do good, sin is crouching at the door. It has a strong desire for you, but you must rule over it."

Cain said to Abel, his brother, "Let's go into the field." When they were in the field, Cain attacked Abel, his brother, and killed him.

The LORD said to Cain, "Where is Abel, your brother?"

He said, "I don't know. Am I my brother's keeper?"

The LORD said, "What have you done? The voice of your brother's blood is crying to me from the soil. Now you are cursed and sent away from the soil which has opened its mouth to receive your brother's blood from your hand. When you work the soil, it will no longer give its strength to you. You shall be a fugitive and a wanderer on the earth."

Cain said to the LORD, "My punishment is too great for me to bear. Look, today you have driven me away from the soil. I will be hidden from your face, and I will be a fugitive and a wanderer on the earth. And whoever finds me will kill me."

The LORD said to him, "No! If anyone kills Cain, he will face sevenfold revenge." And the LORD appointed a sign for Cain, so that anyone who found him would not strike him down.

In the day that God created man, he made him in the likeness of God. Adam became the father of a son in his own likeness, according to his own image, and he named him Seth. All the days that Adam lived were 930 years. Then he died.

Lord God, forgive us the sins we have committed against those close to us, whether in what we think or say or do. Work in our hearts with your Word so that in everything we do, we may be motivated by faith to serve you, our loving Savior. Amen.

5. THE FLOOD (GENESIS 6-9)

God destroys the sinful, unbelieving world in a flood, but he saves believing Noah and his family in an ark.

This is what happened when mankind began to multiply on the face of the earth. The LORD saw that the wickedness of mankind was great on the earth, and that all the thoughts and plans they formed in their hearts were only evil every day. The LORD said, "I will wipe out mankind from the face of the earth, along with the animals." But Noah found favor in the eyes of the LORD. Noah was a righteous man. Noah became the father of three sons: Shem, Ham, and Japheth.

God said to Noah, "Make an ark. The length of the ark is to be 450 feet, its width 75 feet, and its height 45 feet. I am about to bring a flood. Everything that is on the earth will die, but you shall come into the ark—you, your sons, your wife, and your sons' wives with you. You shall bring a pair (male and female) of every kind of living flesh into the ark with you to keep them alive." So that is what Noah did. Noah went into the ark with his sons, his wife, and his sons' wives. Animals went into the ark with Noah two by two, just as God had commanded Noah.

The waters of the flood came on the earth. All the fountains of the great deep burst open, and the floodgates of the sky were opened. The rain came down on the earth for forty days and forty nights. The waters became deeper and lifted up the ark until it floated high above the earth.

The waters rose more than twenty feet above the mountains and covered them. All living creatures perished, including all mankind. Only Noah was left, as well as those who were with him in the ark. The waters overwhelmed the earth for one hundred fifty days.

God remembered Noah. So God caused a wind to pass over the earth, and the waters subsided. The waters kept receding from the earth. The ark came to rest on the mountains of Ararat.

Noah sent out a raven, and it kept flying back and forth, until the waters were dried up from the earth. Then he sent out a dove to see if the waters had receded, but the dove found no place to rest its foot, and it returned to him in the ark. Noah waited another seven days. Then he sent the dove out of the ark again. The dove came back to him at evening, and there in its mouth was an olive leaf. So Noah knew that the waters had receded from the earth. He waited another seven days and sent the dove out again. This time it did not return to him anymore.

Noah saw that the surface of the ground was dry. God spoke to Noah. He said, "Go out of the ark." Noah went out with his sons, his wife, and his sons' wives along with him. Every animal went out of the ship, species by species.

Noah built an altar to the LORD and offered burnt offerings on the altar. The LORD smelled the pleasant aroma. The LORD said in his heart, "I will never again curse the soil anymore because of man. Neither will I ever again strike every living thing, as I have done. While the earth remains, seedtime and harvest, cold and heat, summer and winter, and day and night shall not cease."

God blessed Noah and his sons and said to them, "Be fruitful and multiply and fill the earth. Every living, moving thing will be food for you. I have given everything to you, just as I gave you the green plants. But whoever sheds man's blood, by man his blood shall be shed, for God made man in his own image."

God said to Noah and to his sons, who were with him, "Listen, I will now establish my covenant with you and with your descendants after you: Never again will all living creatures be cut off by the waters of a flood. Neither will there ever again be a flood to destroy the earth. I have set my rainbow in the cloud, and it will be the sign of a covenant between me and the earth. Whenever I bring a cloud over the earth and the rainbow is seen in the cloud, I will remember my covenant and the waters will never again become a flood to destroy all flesh."

Lord God, thank you for not destroying us as our sins deserve, but instead lifting us above destruction, by faith in your Son, Jesus. Use your Word to keep us in the faith and make us ready for his return at the end of the world. Amen.

6. THE TOWER OF BABEL (GENESIS 9, 11)

Even after the judgment of the flood, the human race persists in sinful rebellion, but God shatters their pride and forces them to scatter by confusing their languages.

The sons of Noah who went out from the ark were Shem, Ham, and Japheth. These three were the sons of Noah, and from these, people spread out over the whole earth.

The whole earth had one language and a single vocabulary. As people traveled in the east, they found a plain in the land of Shinar, and they settled there. They said to one another, "Come, let's make bricks and bake them thoroughly." They used mud brick instead of stone for building material, and they used tar for mortar. They said, "Come, let's build a city for ourselves and a tower whose top reaches to the sky, and let's make a name for ourselves, so that we will not be scattered abroad over the face of the whole earth."

The Lord came down to see the city and the tower that the people were building. The Lord said, "If this is the first thing they are doing as one people, who all have one language, then nothing that they intend to do will be too difficult for them. Come, let's go down there and confuse their language, so that they cannot understand one another's speech."

So the Lord scattered them from there over the face of the whole earth, and they stopped building the city. It was named Babel, because there the Lord confused the language of the whole earth. From there the Lord scattered them over the face of the whole earth.

Lord God, we confess that at times we do things to serve and glorify ourselves. Forgive our sins, scatter our pride, and make us to live in godly peace and harmony with others. Thank you for bringing the gospel of our Savior Jesus to us in our English language, and we pray that you would bring it to people of every language, uniting them by faith to us and to you. Amen.

7. THE TRIALS OF JOB (JOB 1-2)

God allows believing Job to suffer, but preserves his faith.

There was a man in the land of Uz whose name was Job. This man was blameless and upright, a man who feared God and turned away from evil. Seven sons and three daughters were born to him. His possessions included seven thousand sheep, three thousand camels, five hundred yoke of oxen, and five hundred female donkeys. He also had a very large retinue of servants. This man was the greatest of all the men of the East.

There came a day when the sons of God came to present themselves before the LORD, and Satan also came. The LORD said to Satan, "Have you considered my servant Job? There is no one like him on the earth, a man who is blameless and upright, who fears God and turns away from evil."

Satan answered the LORD, "Is it without cause that Job fears God? You have blessed the work of his hands. But just stretch out your hand and strike everything that is his, and he will certainly curse you to your face!"

So the LORD said to Satan, "Very well, then. Everything that he has is in your hand. But you may not stretch out your hand against the man himself." So Satan left the presence of the LORD.

One day a messenger came to Job and said, "The oxen and the donkeys—the Sabeans swooped down and took them away. They put the servants to death, and I am the only one who has escaped to tell you!"

While he was still speaking, another servant came and said, "The fire of God fell from the sky and burned up the flocks and the servants and consumed them, and I am the only one who has escaped to tell you!"

While he was still speaking, another servant came and said, "The Chaldeans plundered the camels and took them away. They put the servants to death, and I am the only one who has escaped to tell you!"

While he was still speaking, another servant came and said, "Your sons and daughters were in the house of their oldest brother. Suddenly a powerful wind struck the house, and it collapsed on the young people, and they died, and I am the only one who has escaped to tell you!"

Then Job stood up, tore his robe, and shaved his head. He fell to the ground and worshipped. Then he said, "Naked I came from my mother's womb, and naked I will return. The LORD gave and the LORD has taken away. May the name of the LORD be blessed."

In all this, Job did not sin or blame God.

Another day arrived when the sons of God came to present themselves before the LORD, and Satan also came.

Then the LORD said to Satan, "Have you considered my servant Job? There is no one like him on the earth, a man who is blameless and upright, who fears God and turns away from evil. And he still maintains his integrity, even though you incited me against him to destroy him for no reason."

Satan answered the LORD, "A man will give all he has for his life. But stretch out your hand and strike his bones and flesh, and he will certainly curse you to your face!"

The LORD said to Satan, "Very well, then, he is in your hand, but preserve his life."

Satan then went out from the presence of the LORD. He struck Job with very painful sores from the sole of his foot to the top of his head. Job took a piece of broken pottery to scrape himself as he was sitting among the ashes.

Then his wife said to him, "Are you still maintaining your integrity? Curse God and die!"

But he said to her, "If we accept the good that comes from God, shouldn't we also accept the bad?" In all this, Job did not sin in what he said.

Three friends of Job, Eliphaz, Bildad, and Zophar, went to sympathize with Job and to comfort him. They sat on the ground with him for seven days and seven nights, but no one spoke a word to him because they saw that his suffering was very great.

Lord God, be our comfort and our strength in times of trouble. Remind us of all the blessings we have received from you, and assure us that Satan cannot really harm us as we are kept safe by our Savior Jesus. Amen.

8. JOB WRESTLES WITH HIS TRIALS (FROM JOB 3-4, 6, 8-9, 11-13, 15-16, 18-23, 25-27, 32-36, 38, 42)

Job assumes he is suffering unfairly because he did nothing wrong. Job's friends assume that he is suffering justly because he must have done something wrong. God shows that he owes no answer and often gives no answer as to why he in his wisdom allows suffering.

Finally, Job said, "May the day of my birth perish!"

Eliphaz responded, "Don't your blameless ways give you reason to hope? Who has ever perished if he was innocent?"

Job responded, "If God would crush me, I would still have this comfort: Even as I writhe in relentless pain, I have not denied the words of the Holy One. My righteousness is still intact."

Bildad responded, "How long will you say such things? Does God pervert justice? God does not reject a blameless man."

Job responded, "If someone wants to argue with God, he could not refute one charge out of a thousand. Even if I am in the right, I cannot answer him. I can only plead to my judge for grace. It makes no difference—blameless or wicked, he brings them all to the same end."

Zophar responded, "Can this man's bold talk be justified? You say, 'I am pure.' I wish God would speak up. Then you would know that God has even forgotten some of your guilt!"

Job responded, "I want to speak to the Almighty. All you do is plaster over problems with lies. Such useless healers, all of you! Please, listen. I have laid out my case. I know that I am innocent."

Eliphaz responded, "Your guilt instructs your mouth. Were you the first man to be born? What do you understand that we do not?"

Job responded, "I have heard many things just like these. I could speak just like you, if your lives were in the condition that my life is. But I would build you up. Surely, he has worn me out! His anger has torn me. When I was at ease, he shattered me."

Bildad responded, "Come to your senses! The wicked is torn away from safety. Nothing that belonged to him remains in his tent. Certainly this is the dwelling place for an evil man."

Job responded, "How long will you torment my soul? I cry out, 'Injustice,' but I get no answer. I call for help, but there is no justice. Oh how I wish that my words were engraved in rock forever: I know that my Redeemer lives, and that at the end of time he will stand over the dust. Then, even after my skin has been destroyed, nevertheless, in my own flesh I will see God. I myself will see him."

Zophar responded, "Don't you know this? The wicked will perish forever. This is God's sentence on the evil man."

Job responded, "How often is the lamp of the wicked extinguished? One person dies completely secure and at ease. Another person dies filled with bitterness. Both of them lie down together in the dust. I know your schemes to harm me. There is nothing left from your answers but fraud!"

Eliphaz responded, "Isn't your wickedness great? Isn't your guilt endless? Be reconciled with God. Then good will come to you."

Job responded, "My feet have followed his footsteps closely."

Bildad responded, "How can a man be righteous with God?"

Job responded, "God has deprived me of justice. May I be cursed if I ever admit you are right. I will never deny my integrity."

These three men gave up trying to answer Job, because he was righteous in his own eyes.

So Elihu burned with anger against Job because Job had justified himself rather than God. Elihu said, "God is greater than a man. Why do you bring charges against him just because he does not answer all of a man's questions? God never does anything wicked. Do you really think it is right when you say, 'My righteousness is greater than God's'? God is exalted far above our comprehension."

Then the LORD responded to Job out of a violent storm, "Who is this who spreads darkness over my plans with his ignorant words? Where were you when I laid the foundation of the earth? Who locked up the sea behind doors? Have you ever set a time for the sun to rise?"

Job responded to the LORD, "I know that you can do all things. No purpose of yours can be thwarted. I have made statements about things I did not understand. I repent in dust and ashes."

Then the LORD restored Job's fortunes. The LORD gave Job twice as much of everything as he had before. He had seven sons and three daughters. After this, Job lived one hundred forty years.

Lord God, when we face suffering and troubles we do not know how to handle, be with us and comfort us with the fact that you are in control and you know what is best. Cheer us with the knowledge that Jesus, our Redeemer, lives, and that thanks to his saving work we will see him face to face one day and be with him forever. Amen.

9. THE CALL OF ABRAM (GENESIS 12)

Out of all the families of the world, God chooses Abram to be the forefather of his special people and the ancestor of the promised Savior of all people.

Now the LORD said to Abram, "Get out of your country and away from your relatives and from your father's house and go to the land that I will show you. I will make you a great nation. I will bless you and make your name great. You will be a blessing. I will bless those who bless you, and I will curse anyone who dishonors you. All of the families of the earth will be blessed in you."

So Abram went, as the LORD had told him. Abram was seventy-five years old when he departed from Haran. Abram took Sarai his wife, Lot his brother's son, and all the possessions they had accumulated and the people that they had acquired in Haran, and they set out to travel to the land of Canaan. Eventually they arrived in the land of Canaan. The Canaanites were in the land at that time. The LORD appeared to Abram and said, "I will give this land to your descendants."

Lord God, you have eternally blessed people from all around the world through Abram's descendant, our Savior Jesus. Wherever we go in life, be with us and bless us, and give us one day the promised land of heaven. Amen.

10. ABRAM AND LOT (GENESIS 13-14)

Even in a foreign land, God richly blesses Abram, and through him blesses others.

Abram was very wealthy in livestock, in silver, and in gold. Lot, who went with Abram, also had flocks, herds, and tents. The land was not able to support them if they lived close together, because their possessions were so great that they could not live together. There was conflict between the herdsmen of Abram's livestock and the herdsmen of Lot's livestock. (The Canaanites and the Perizzites lived in the land at that time.)

Abram said to Lot, "Please, because we are close relatives, let there be no conflict between me and you and between my herdsmen and your herdsmen. Doesn't the whole land lie before you? Please separate yourself from me. If you go to the left, then I will go to the right. Or if you go to the right, then I will go to the left."

Lot looked up and saw the whole region around the Jordan River. It was well watered everywhere. So Lot chose the region around the Jordan for himself. Lot headed out toward the east, and they separated from each other. Abram lived in the land of Canaan, and Lot lived among the cities of the region around the Jordan and moved his tent close to Sodom. Now the men of Sodom were extremely wicked sinners against the LORD.

After Lot was separated from him, the LORD said to Abram, "Now, lift up your eyes, and look around from the place where you are. Look north and south, east and west, because all the land that you see, I will give to you and to your descendants permanently. I will make your descendants like the dust of the earth, so that if a man could count the dust of the earth, then your descendants could also be counted."

In those days Kedorlaomer and the kings who were with him came. The king of Sodom and the king of Gomorrah went out and lined up for battle in the Valley of Siddim against Kedorlaomer. Now the Valley of Siddim was full of tar pits. When the kings of Sodom and Gomorrah fled, they fell there. Those who survived fled to the hills. The raiders took all the possessions of Sodom and Gomorrah and then they went on their way. Because he had been living in Sodom, they took also Lot, the son of Abram's brother, and his possessions.

One person escaped and came and told Abram. When Abram heard that his relative was taken captive, he led out all his trained men who were born in his house, three hundred eighteen of them, and pursued them as far as Dan. He struck them and pursued them to Hobah, north of Damascus. He brought back all the possessions. He also brought back his relative Lot, and his possessions, and the women also, and the rest of the people.

After Abram's return from the defeat of Kedorlaomer and the kings who were with him, Melchizedek king of Salem brought out bread and wine. He was a priest of God Most High. He blessed Abram and said, "Blessed be Abram by God Most High, Creator of heaven and earth, and blessed be God Most High, who has delivered your enemies into your hand."

Abram gave him a tenth of everything.

The king of Sodom said to Abram, "Give me the people and take the goods for yourself."

Abram said to the king of Sodom, "So that you cannot say, 'I have made Abram rich,' I will take nothing."

Lord God, you have given us more gifts than we could ever begin to thank you for. But most of all we thank you for the gift of your Son, our high priest who sacrificed himself to restore our relationship with you, and our great king who brought us eternal peace. Amen.

11. GOD PROMISES ABRAHAM AN HEIR (GENESIS 15-17)

God gives Abram a promise, a covenant, a righteous status, and a new name.

After these events the word of the LORD came to Abram in a vision. He said, "Do not be afraid, Abram. I am your shield, your very great reward."

Abram said, "LORD God, what can you give me, since I remain childless, and the one who will inherit my estate is Eliezer of Damascus, a servant born in my house?"

Just then, the word of the LORD came to him. God said, "This man will not be your heir, but instead one who will come out of your own body will be your heir." The LORD then brought him outside and said, "Now look toward the sky and count the stars, if you are able to count them. This is what your descendants will be like." Abram believed in the LORD, and the LORD credited it to him as righteousness. He said to him, "I am the LORD, who brought you out of Ur of the Chaldeans to give you this land as a possession."

He said, "LORD God, how will I know that I will possess it?"

The LORD said to him, "Bring me a heifer, a goat, a ram, a turtledove, and a young pigeon." Abram gathered all of these, divided them in half, and laid the two halves across from each other, but he did not divide the birds in two.

The LORD said to Abram, "Know this! Your descendants will live as aliens in a land that is not theirs, and they will serve its people, who will afflict them for four hundred years. But I will surely judge the nation that they will serve. Afterward your descendants will come out with great wealth. In the fourth generation your descendants will come here again." Then when the sun had gone down and it was dark, suddenly a smoking oven and a flaming torch passed between the pieces. On that day the LORD made a covenant with Abram. He said, "To your descendants I have given this land."

Now Sarai, Abram's wife, bore no children for him. She had a servant girl, an Egyptian, whose name was Hagar. Sarai said to Abram, "See now, the LORD has prevented me from bearing children. It may be that I can build up a family through her." Sarai, Abram's wife, took her servant girl and gave her to Abram her husband to be his wife. Hagar gave birth to a son for Abram. Abram named his son, whom Hagar bore, Ishmael. Abram was eighty-six years old when Hagar bore Ishmael for him.

When Abram was ninety-nine years old, the LORD appeared to Abram and said to him, "As for me, you will be the father of many nations. Your name will not be Abram anymore, but your name will be Abraham, for I have made you the father of a large group of nations. I will be your God and the God of your descendants after you. I will give the land where you are living as an alien, all the land of Canaan, to you and to your descendants after you as a permanent possession. I will be their God."

God said to Abraham, "As for you, you must keep my covenant, you and your descendants after you throughout their generations. This is my covenant, which you shall keep, a covenant between me and you and your descendants after you: Every male among you shall be circumcised. It will be a sign of the covenant between me and you."

God said to Abraham, "As for Sarai your wife, you shall not call her Sarai anymore, but her name will be Sarah. I will bless her and even give you a son by her."

Then Abraham fell on his face and laughed and said in his heart, "Will a child be born to someone who is one hundred years old? Will Sarah, who is ninety years old, give birth?"

But God said, "Sarah, your wife, will bear a son for you. You shall name him Isaac. I will establish my covenant with him as an everlasting covenant for his descendants after him. As for Ishmael, I will make him fruitful and will multiply him very greatly. But my covenant I will establish with Isaac, whom Sarah will bear for you at this set time next year."

When he finished talking with him, God went up from Abraham. Both Abraham and Ishmael were circumcised.

Lord God, you have kept your covenant to send us
our Savior Jesus, through whom we are righteous in
your sight by faith and are forever blessed. Keep us
in that baptismal grace all the days of our lives. Amen.

12. THE LORD APPEARS TO ABRAHAM (GENESIS 18)

The Lord and two angels come to tell Abraham two pieces of important news, and Abraham responds with persistent prayer.

The LORD appeared to Abraham by the oaks of Mamre, as he was sitting by the door to his tent during the heat of the day. Abraham looked up, and he saw three men standing in front of him. When he saw them, he ran from the tent door to meet them, and he bowed down to the ground. He said, "My lord, if I have now found favor in your sight, please do not pass your servant by. Let me get some bread so that you can refresh yourselves."

They said, "Yes, do as you have said."

Abraham hurried into the tent to Sarah and said, "Quickly prepare twenty quarts of fine flour, knead it, and make some loaves of bread."

Abraham ran to the herd, brought a good, tender calf, and gave it to the servant. He hurried to prepare it. He took cheese curds, milk, and the calf that he had prepared and set it before them. He stood beside them under the tree while they ate.

They asked him, "Where is Sarah, your wife?"

He said, "She is over there in the tent."

One of the men said, "I will certainly return to you when this season comes around next year. Then Sarah your wife will have a son."

Sarah was listening to this from the tent door, which was behind him. Now Abraham and Sarah were old, well into old age. Sarah was past the age for childbearing. Sarah laughed to herself, saying, "After I am worn out, will I have pleasure, since my lord is also old?"

The Lord said to Abraham, "Why did Sarah laugh and say, 'Will I really give birth to a child though I am old?' Is anything impossible for the Lord? At the set time next year I will return to you, and Sarah will have a son."

Then Sarah denied it and said, "I did not laugh," because she was afraid.

The Lord said, "Yes, you did laugh."

The men got up from there and looked down toward Sodom. Abraham went with them to see them on their way. The Lord said, "Because the outcry against Sodom and Gomorrah is great, and because their sin is very flagrant, I will go down now and see if what they have done is as bad as the outcry that has come to me. If not, I will know."

The two men turned from there and went toward Sodom, but Abraham remained standing before the Lord. Abraham approached him and said, "Will you really sweep away the righteous along with the wicked? What if there are fifty righteous people in the city? You would never do such a thing, killing the righteous along with the wicked, treating the righteous the same as the wicked. The Judge of all the earth should do right, shouldn't he?"

The Lord said, "If I find fifty righteous people within the city of Sodom, then I will spare the entire place for their sake."

Abraham answered, "See now, I who am but dust and ashes have taken it on myself to speak to my Lord. What if there are five fewer than fifty righteous? Will you destroy the entire city if the number is five short?"

He said, "I will not destroy it if I find forty-five there."

He spoke to him yet again and said, "What if only forty are found there?"

He said, "I will not do it for the sake of the forty."

He said, "Please, do not be angry, my Lord, but I will speak again. What if thirty are found there?"

He said, "I will not do it, if I find thirty there."

He said, "See now, I have taken it upon myself to speak to my Lord. What if there are twenty found there?"

He said, "I will not destroy it for the sake of the twenty."

He said, "Please, do not be angry, my Lord, but I will speak just once more. What if ten are found there?"

He said, "I will not destroy it for the sake of the ten."

As soon as he had finished speaking with Abraham, the LORD went on his way, and Abraham returned to his place.

Lord God, you have made many promises to us, promises to provide, to forgive, to grant eternal life. Help us to cling to those promises firmly, and to turn to you in prayer boldly, persistently, and confidently for Jesus' sake. Amen.

13. SODOM AND GOMORRAH (GENESIS 19)

God destroys the wicked cities but answers Abraham's prayer by delivering his believing people from the destruction.

The two angels came to Sodom at evening. Lot, who was sitting in the gatehouse of Sodom, saw them and got up to meet them. He bowed down with his face to the ground, and he said, "See now, my lords, please turn aside into your servant's house and spend the night. Wash your feet, and you can get up early and go on your way."

They said, "No, we will spend the night in the street."

But he kept urging them, so they came with him and entered his house. But before they lay down, the men of Sodom surrounded the house. They called to Lot and said to him, "Where are the men who came to you tonight? Bring them out to us."

Lot went out to them and shut the door behind him. He said, "Please, my brothers, do not act so wickedly. See now, I have two daughters. Please let me bring them out to you, and you may do to them whatever seems good to you. Only do not do anything to these men, because they have come under the protection of my roof."

They said, "Get out of our way!" They also said, "This fellow came to live here as an alien, and now he appoints himself as a judge. Now we will treat you worse than them!" They kept pushing Lot back and were ready to break down the door. But the men inside reached out and grabbed Lot and pulled him into the house with them and shut the door. They struck the men who were pressing against the door of the house with blindness so that they wore themselves out trying to find the door.

The men said to Lot, "Do you have anyone else here? Sons-in-law, your sons, your daughters, whoever you have in the city, get them out of this place, for we are going to destroy this place, because the outcry against it has grown great before the LORD, so the LORD has sent us to destroy it."

So Lot went out and spoke to his sons-in-law, who were pledged to his daughters in marriage. He said, "Get up! Get out of this place, for the LORD is going to destroy the city." But to his sons-in-law he seemed to be joking.

When the dawn came, the angels urged Lot, "Get going! Take your wife and your two daughters who are here, so that you will not be swept away by the guilt of the city." But Lot was taking too much time, so the men grabbed his hand, his wife's hand, and the hands of his two daughters, because of the LORD's compassion for him. They led him out and placed him outside of the city. Then when they had taken them out, one of them said, "Run for your life! Don't look behind you, and don't stay anywhere in the plain. Escape to the mountains, so that you are not swept away!"

Lot said to them, "Oh no, my lord. See now, your servant has found favor in your sight, and you have shown me great mercy by saving my life. I cannot flee to the mountains, or this disaster will stick with me, and I will die. Look, this city is close enough to flee to, and it is a little one. Please let me flee there."

The man said to him, "Very well. Hurry, flee there, because I cannot do anything until you get there."

Then the LORD rained on Sodom and Gomorrah sulfur and fire out of the sky from the LORD. He overthrew those cities, as well as all the plain, all the inhabitants of the cities, and whatever grew in the soil.

But Lot's wife, who was behind him, looked back, and she became a pillar of salt.

Abraham got up early in the morning and went to the place where he had stood before the LORD. He looked down toward Sodom and Gomorrah and all the land of the plain. As he looked, he saw that the smoke from the land was going up like the smoke from a kiln.

And so when God destroyed the cities of the plain, God remembered Abraham and brought Lot out through the middle of the devastation, when he overthrew the cities where Lot had lived.

Lord God, in this world we are surrounded by sin and evil.
Keep us safe from the influence of the world around us
until you rescue us from it when your Son returns. Amen.

14. ABRAHAM AND ISAAC (GENESIS 21-22)

God gives Abraham the son for whom he had waited so long, and then teaches Abraham that his faith and love are still first toward the God who promised, not toward this promised son.

The LORD visited Sarah as he had said, and the LORD did for Sarah as he had promised. Sarah conceived and gave birth to a son for Abraham in his old age, at the set time which God had announced to him. Abraham named the son who was born to him—the son whom Sarah had borne to him—Isaac.

Some time later God tested Abraham. He called to him, "Abraham!"

Abraham answered, "I am here."

God said, "Now take your son, your only son, whom you love, Isaac, and go to the land of Moriah. Offer him there as a burnt offering on one of the mountains there, the one to which I direct you."

Abraham got up early in the morning, saddled his donkey, and took two of his young men with him, along with Isaac his son. Abraham split the wood for the burnt offering. Then he set out to go to the place that God had told him about. On the third day Abraham looked up and saw the place in the distance.

Abraham said to his young men, "Stay here with the donkey. The boy and I will go on over there. We will worship, and then we will come back to you." Abraham took the wood for the burnt offering and loaded it on Isaac his son. He took the firepot and the knife in his hand. The two of them went on together.

Isaac spoke to Abraham his father and said, "My father?"

He said, "I am here, my son."

He said, "Here are the fire and the wood, but where is the lamb for a burnt offering?"

Abraham said, "God himself will provide the lamb for a burnt offering, my son." So the two of them went on together. They came to the place that God had told him about. Abraham built the altar there. He arranged the wood, tied up Isaac his son, and laid him on the altar on top of the wood. Abraham stretched out his hand and took the knife to slaughter his son.

The Angel of the LORD called to him from heaven, "Abraham, Abraham!"

Abraham said, "I am here."

He said, "Do not lay your hand on the boy. Do not do anything to him. For now I know that you fear God, because you have not withheld your son, your only son, from me."

Abraham looked around and saw that behind him there was a ram caught in the thicket by its horns. Abraham went and took the ram and offered it up as a burnt offering instead of his son. Abraham called the name of that place "The LORD Will Provide." So it is said to this day, "On the mountain of the LORD it will be provided."

The Angel of the LORD called to Abraham a second time from heaven and said, "I have sworn by myself, declares the LORD, because you have done this thing and have not withheld your son, your only son, I will bless you greatly, and I will multiply your descendants greatly, like the stars of the sky and like the sand on the seashore. Your descendants will take possession of the city gates of their enemies. In your seed all the nations of the earth will be blessed, because you have obeyed my voice."

Lord God, claim our hearts and minds for yourself,
and let no one else rule there beside you.
Place our trust solely in you, who did not spare
your Son but sacrificed him for us. Amen.

15. ISAAC AND REBEKAH (GENESIS 23-25)

Abraham's son Isaac grows up and God provides him a wife.

Sarah died. Abraham buried Sarah his wife in the cave in the field at Machpelah in the land of Canaan. The field and the cave were deeded to Abraham by the descendants of Heth as his property to be used as a burial site.

Abraham was very old, well into old age. Abraham said to his servant, "Go to my country and to my relatives and acquire a wife for my son Isaac."

The servant took ten of his master's camels and went to Mesopotamia. He made the camels kneel down by the well outside the city. He said, "O LORD, please give me success this day, and show kindness to my master Abraham. Here I am, standing by the spring of water, and the daughters of the men of the city are coming out to draw water. Let this be the test: The young lady to whom I say, 'Please let down your water jar, so that I may drink,' will say, 'Drink, and I will also give your camels a drink.' She will be the one you have chosen for your servant Isaac."

Before he had even finished speaking, out came Rebekah with her water jar on her shoulder. She was the daughter of Bethuel, who was the son of Milcah, the wife of Nahor, Abraham's brother. The young lady was very beautiful. She went down to the spring, filled her water jar, and came up. The servant ran to meet her and said, "Please give me a drink."

She said, "Drink, my lord." She quickly let down her water jar into her hands and gave him a drink. When she was done giving him a drink, she said, "I will also draw water for your camels, until they have finished drinking." She hurried and emptied her water jar into the trough, ran to the well again to draw more water, and drew water for all his camels.

When the camels were finished drinking, the man asked, "Whose daughter are you?"

She said to him, "I am the daughter of Bethuel, the son of Milcah, whom she bore to Nahor."

The man bowed his head and worshipped the LORD. He said, "Blessed be the LORD, who has guided me to the house of my master's relatives."

The young lady ran and told her mother's household about these things. Rebekah had a brother whose name was Laban. Laban ran out to the spring to meet the man. Laban said, "Why are you standing outside when I have prepared the house and a place for the camels?"

The man came to the house and unloaded the camels. He said, "I am Abraham's servant. My master said, 'Go to my father's house and to my relatives and acquire a wife for my son.' The LORD, the God of my master Abraham, led me in the right way to find the daughter of my master's brother as a wife for his son."

Then Laban and Bethuel answered, "This matter has been determined by the LORD. Take her and go, and let her become the wife of your master's son, as the LORD has spoken."

So, when Abraham's servant heard their words, he bowed down to the ground before the LORD. The servant got up in the morning, and he said, "Send me on my way to my master."

Her brother and her mother said, "Let the young lady stay with us a few days, at least ten. After that she can go."

He said to them, "Do not hold me back, since the LORD has granted my journey success. Send me on my way so that I can go to my master."

They said, "We will call the young lady and ask her." They called Rebekah and asked her, "Do you want to go with this man?"

She said, "I do."

So they sent all of them on their way—their sister Rebekah with her nurse, Abraham's servant and his men.

In the evening Isaac had gone out into the field to meditate. He looked up and saw that there were camels coming. Rebekah also looked up, and when she saw Isaac, she jumped down from the camel. She took her veil and covered herself. Isaac took her as his wife. He loved her, and Isaac stopped mourning his mother's death.

Abraham lived a hundred and seventy-five years. Then Abraham died. His sons Isaac and Ishmael buried him in the Cave of Machpelah.

Lord God, all our blessings and all our successes come from you. Keep us from ever forgetting that your hand is helping and upholding us. Support us also by the companionship and influence of other believers, and use us to support them. Amen.

16. JACOB AND ESAU (GENESIS 25, 27)

Isaac and Rebekah's children deal with serious sibling rivalry.

Rebekah conceived. The children fought with each other inside her. She said, "What is this?"

The LORD said to her, "Two nations are in your womb. The elder will serve the younger."

When it was time for her to give birth, it was true: There were twins in her womb. The first came out red all over, like a hairy garment. They named him Esau. After that, his brother came out, with his hand grabbing Esau's heel. So he was named Jacob.

The boys grew up. Esau was a skillful hunter, an outdoorsman. Jacob was a quiet man, who stayed home among the tents. Now Isaac loved Esau more, because he ate Esau's wild game. Rebekah loved Jacob.

Once Jacob was cooking stew, and Esau came in from the field, and he was starving. Esau said to Jacob, "Come on, let me eat some of that red stew because I am starving."

Jacob said, "First, sell me your right as the firstborn."

Esau said, "Look, I am about to die. What good is the birthright to me?"

Jacob said, "Swear to me first."

So he swore to him and sold his birthright to Jacob.

When Isaac was old and his eyes were so dim that he could hardly see, he called Esau his older son and said to him, "Get some wild game for me. Make me tasty food, so that I may eat and I may bless you with all my soul before I die."

After Esau went to the open country to hunt for game, Rebekah spoke to Jacob her son and said, "Listen, I heard your father speak to Esau your brother and tell him, 'Bring me some wild game and make tasty food for me, that I may eat and give you a blessing from the LORD before my death.' I will make tasty food for your father. You will bring it to your father, so that he can eat it and bless you before his death."

Jacob said to his mother Rebekah, "But Esau my brother is a hairy man, and my skin is smooth. What if my father touches me?" Rebekah took the clothing of Esau, her older son, and put it on Jacob, her younger son. She put the skins of young goats on his hands and forearms and on the smooth part of his neck. She put tasty food that she had prepared into the hand of her son Jacob.

He came to his father and said, "I am Esau your firstborn. I have done what you asked me to do. Please get up, and eat some of my wild game, so that you may bless me with all your soul."

Isaac said to Jacob, "Please come near, so that I may feel you, my son, whether you are really my son Esau or not."

Jacob went close to Isaac his father, who felt him and said, "The voice is the voice of Jacob, but the hands are the hands of Esau." So he blessed him and said, "Let peoples serve you, and nations bow down to you. Be lord over your brothers."

As soon as Jacob had gone out, Esau his brother came in from his hunting. He said to his father, "Let my father get up and eat his son's wild game, so that you may bless me with all your soul."

Isaac his father said to him, "Who are you?"

He said, "I am your son, your firstborn, Esau."

Isaac trembled violently and said, "Then who was it that hunted wild game and brought it to me? I ate all of it before you came, and I have blessed him. And, yes, he will be blessed."

When Esau heard the words of his father, he let out a very loud and bitter cry and said to his father, "Bless me—me too, my father."

He said, "Your brother came deceitfully and has taken away your blessing."

Esau said, "Isn't he rightly named Jacob? For he has tripped me up these two times. He took away my birthright. And look, now he has taken away my blessing." He also asked, "Haven't you reserved a blessing for me?"

Isaac answered Esau, "I have made him your lord. So what can I do for you, my son?"

Lord God, we praise you that before the creation of the world you chose us to be your people, not because of anything we were or would be, but because of your grace to us in Jesus. Help us to live lives worthy of this calling we have received, showing love to everyone, and following your plan for our lives. Amen.

17. JACOB FLEES FROM HIS BROTHER (GENESIS 27-28)

Even when Jacob is on the run, God is with Jacob.

Esau hated Jacob. Esau said in his heart, "The days of mourning for my father are at hand. Then I will kill my brother Jacob."

The words of Esau, her older son, were told to Rebekah. She sent and called Jacob, her younger son, and said to him, "Listen, your brother Esau is planning to kill you. Flee to Laban, my brother."

Rebekah said to Isaac, "If Jacob takes a wife from the daughters of the land, what good will my life do me?"

So Isaac called Jacob, blessed him, and commanded him, "Go to the house of Bethuel, your mother's father. Take a wife from there from the daughters of Laban, your mother's brother. May God Almighty bless you, and make you fruitful, and multiply you, so that you may become a community of peoples. May he give you and your descendants along with you the blessing he gave to Abraham, so that you may inherit the land where you have been living as an alien, the land God gave to Abraham." So Isaac sent Jacob away.

Jacob set out from Beersheba and traveled toward Haran. He came to a certain place and decided to spend the night there, because the sun had set. He took one of the stones from that place, put it under his head, and lay down to sleep in that place. He had a dream in which he saw a stairway set up on the earth with its top reaching to heaven. There were angels of God ascending and descending on it. There at the top stood the LORD, who said, "I am the LORD, the God of your father Abraham and the God of Isaac. The land on which you are lying, I give to you and to your descendants. Your descendants will be like the dust of the earth, and you will spread abroad to the west, and to the east, and to the north, and to the south. In you and in your seed all the families of the earth will be blessed. Now, I am with you and will watch over you wherever you go, and I will bring you back again into this land. Indeed, I will not leave you, until I have done what I have promised to you."

Jacob woke up from his sleep, and he said, "Certainly the LORD is in this place, and I was not aware of it." He was afraid and he said, "How awe-inspiring is this place! This is nothing other than the house of God, and this is the gate to heaven."

Jacob got up early in the morning. He took the stone that he had put under his head and set it up as a sacred memorial stone and poured oil on top of it. He named that place Bethel. (Before this, the name of the city had been Luz.) Jacob took a vow, "If God will be with me to keep me safe on this journey I am making, and if he gives me food to eat and clothing to put on, and I come back to my father's house in safety, the LORD will be my God, and this stone that I have set up as a memorial stone will be God's house, and I will certainly give you a tenth of everything that you give me."

Lord God, reassure us with your promises that you are always with us, taking care of us. When we feel as though you are distant, remind us that your Son Jesus, as God and man, has connected us to you forever. Amen.

18. JACOB'S FAMILY (GENESIS 29-30)

Even when Laban and Jacob do not follow God's will for marriage, God blesses Jacob, and his family grows.

Jacob continued on his journey. He looked around and noticed a well in the field, and he saw three flocks of sheep lying there beside it. Rachel arrived with her father's sheep because she took care of them. When Jacob saw Rachel the daughter of Laban, his mother's brother, Jacob went up and watered the flock of Laban. Jacob kissed Rachel and wept loudly. Jacob told Rachel that he was her father's relative and that he was Rebekah's son. She ran and told her father, Laban.

Laban had two daughters. The name of the older one was Leah, and the name of the younger was Rachel. Leah had attractive eyes, but Rachel had a beautiful face and figure. Jacob loved Rachel. He said, "I will serve you seven years for Rachel, your younger daughter."

Laban said, "It is better for me to give her to you than to give her to another man. Stay with me."

Jacob served seven years for Rachel. They seemed to him like a few days, because of the love he had for her.

Jacob said to Laban, "Give me my wife, for my time of service is finished."

Laban gathered together all the local people and made a feast. When evening had arrived, he took Leah and brought her to Jacob, and Jacob went to her. When morning came, Jacob realized it was Leah. So Jacob said to Laban, "What is this you have done to me? Didn't I serve you for Rachel? Why have you deceived me?"

Laban said, "That is not the way we do it here. We do not give the younger before the firstborn. Fulfill the marriage week for this one, and we will give you the other one too—for seven more years of service."

So that is what Jacob did. When he fulfilled the marriage week, Laban gave him Rachel as his wife. Jacob loved Rachel more than Leah. He served Laban seven more years.

The Lord saw that Leah was not loved, and he allowed her to conceive, but Rachel had no children. Leah gave birth to a son and named him Reuben. She again gave birth to a son and named him Simeon. She again gave birth to a son. He was named Levi. She again gave birth to a son. She named him Judah.

When Rachel saw that she was bearing no children for Jacob, Rachel was jealous of her sister. So she gave her servant girl Bilhah to Jacob. Bilhah gave birth to a son for Jacob. Rachel named him Dan. Bilhah bore Jacob a second son. Rachel named him Naphtali.

Leah took her servant girl Zilpah and gave her to Jacob. Zilpah bore Jacob a son. Leah named him Gad. Zilpah bore a second son for Jacob. Leah named him Asher.

Leah bore Jacob a fifth son. She named him Issachar. Leah bore a sixth son to Jacob. She named him Zebulun. Afterward, she gave birth to a daughter and named her Dinah.

God remembered Rachel, and God listened to her and opened her womb. She bore a son, and she named him Joseph.

Lord God, we thank you for your gifts to us in marriage and family. May we and all your people follow your good designs for marriage and family. Amen.

19. STRIFE BETWEEN JACOB AND LABAN (GENESIS 30-31)

Richly blessed by God, Jacob leaves Laban to return home.

Jacob said to Laban, "Send me away, that I may go home to my own place in my own country."

Laban said to him, "Stay here, for the LORD has blessed me because of you. Set your wages for me, and I will pay them."

Jacob said, "If you will do this thing for me, I will continue to take your flock to pasture and watch over it: I will pass through all your flocks today and take all the speckled and spotted sheep and goats. These will be my wages."

Laban said, "Very well. We will do what you have said." But that day Laban removed all the goats that were streaked and spotted and all the dark sheep, and handed them over to his sons.

Jacob put branches that he had peeled into the gutters of the watering troughs where the flocks came to drink, so the flocks would see them. The flocks produced streaked, speckled, and spotted animals. Whenever the stronger animals in the flock were in heat, Jacob laid the branches in the gutters where the flocks could see them, so that they would conceive while looking at the branches. But when the weak animals in the flock were in heat, he did not put the branches in. So the weaker animals were Laban's, and the stronger were Jacob's. The man became much wealthier and had large flocks.

The LORD said to Jacob, "Return to the land of your fathers and to your relatives, and I will be with you." Then Jacob set out to go to Isaac his father in the land of Canaan.

Now when Laban had gone off to shear his sheep, Rachel stole her father's household gods.

Jacob deceived Laban by not telling him that he was running away. On the third day Laban was told that Jacob had fled. He pursued him. But God came to Laban in a dream during the night and said to him, "Be careful that you do not say anything to Jacob either good or bad."

Laban caught up with Jacob. Laban said to Jacob, "What have you done? Why have you deceived me? Why did you flee secretly and steal from me? Why didn't you tell me, so that I could have sent you away with a celebration? Why didn't you allow me to kiss my sons and my daughters? But even if you were so eager to leave, why have you stolen my gods?"

Jacob answered Laban, "I was afraid, because I thought that you might take your daughters away from me by force. But anyone with whom you find your gods shall not live." (Jacob did not know that Rachel had stolen the household gods.)

So Laban went into Jacob's tent, into Leah's tent, and into the tent of the two female servants, but he did not find the gods. He entered Rachel's tent. Rachel had taken the household gods and put them into her camel's saddle, and she was sitting on them. Laban searched, but he did not find the gods.

Jacob became angry and argued with Laban. Jacob responded to Laban, "What is my crime? Now that you have rummaged through all my belongings, what have you found there that came from your house? I served you fourteen years for your two daughters and six years for a share of your flock, and you have changed my wages ten times. Unless the God of my father, the God of Abraham and the God revered by Isaac, had been with me, you certainly would have now sent me away empty-handed."

Laban answered Jacob, "These daughters are my daughters. Let us make a covenant."

So they collected stones and piled them up. They ate there beside the pile of stones. Laban said, "May this pile be a witness that I will not cross over beyond this pile to you, and that you will not cross over beyond this pile and this memorial stone to harm me. May the God of Abraham and the God of Nahor, the God of their father, judge between us." They ate bread and stayed all night in the hill country. Early in the morning Laban departed and returned to his place.

Lord God, you have blessed us with so many good things.
Help us to realize that all good things come from you,
our only God. Help us to see that the greatest
of your blessings to us is the forgiveness
we have in your Son. Amen.

20. JACOB'S REUNION WITH ESAU (GENESIS 32-33, 35)

Jacob wrestles with God and reconciles with Esau.

Jacob went on his way. Jacob sent messengers ahead of him to Esau, his brother. He gave them a command. "Tell my lord, Esau, 'This is what your servant Jacob says: I have lived as an alien with Laban until very recently. I have cattle, donkeys, flocks, male servants, and female servants. I have sent this message to inform my lord, so that I may find favor in your sight.'"

The messengers returned to Jacob and reported, "We came to your brother Esau. Now he is coming to meet you, and he has four hundred men with him."

So Jacob was terrified and very distressed. He divided the people who were with him, as well as the flocks, herds, and camels, into two camps.

He said, "If Esau comes to one camp and strikes it, then the other camp will escape."

Jacob spent that night there and selected a gift for Esau his brother from the possessions he had with him. He handed them over to his servants and said, "Cross over in front of me, and keep some space between each herd and the next one. When Esau meets you and asks, 'Whose herds are these?' then you shall say, 'They belong to your servant Jacob. It is a gift sent to you, my lord Esau.' I will win his favor with the gift that I have sent ahead of me, and after that I will see his face, and perhaps he will accept me."

So the gift was sent over ahead of him, but he himself spent that night in the camp. He got up that night and took his two wives, his two maids, and his eleven sons, and crossed over the ford of the Jabbok. He took them and sent them across the stream, and he also sent his possessions across.

Jacob was left alone, and he wrestled with a man there until daybreak. When the man saw that he could not defeat him, he touched the socket of his thigh, and the socket of Jacob's thigh was dislocated as he wrestled. The man said, "Let me go. It's daybreak."

Jacob said, "I will not let you go, unless you bless me."

Then he said to him, "What is your name?"

He said, "Jacob."

Then he said, "Your name will no longer be Jacob, but Israel, because you have fought with God and with men, and you have won."

Jacob asked him, "Please tell me your name."

He said, "Why do you ask what my name is?" Then he blessed him there.

Jacob named the place Peniel, because he said, "I have seen God face to face, and my life has been spared." The sun rose as he crossed over at Peniel, and he was limping, because God touched the socket of Jacob's thigh on the tendon of the hip.

Jacob looked up, and there was Esau coming with four hundred men. Esau ran to meet him, embraced him, hugged him around the neck, and kissed him. They both wept. Esau said, "What did you mean by this whole camp that I met?"

Jacob said, "To gain favor in the sight of my lord. Please accept the gift from my hand, because when I saw your face, it was like seeing the face of God, now that you have accepted me." He urged him, and he accepted it.

Esau set out that day on his way back to Seir. Jacob traveled in the land of Canaan. As they were coming close to Ephrath, Rachel went into labor.

She was experiencing hard labor, and when she was in hard labor, the midwife said to her, "Don't be afraid, for now you will have another son."

Then as she was dying, she named her son Benoni, but his father named him Benjamin. So Rachel died and was buried on the way to Ephrath (that is, Bethlehem). Jacob set up a memorial stone on her grave. It is the marker for Rachel's tomb to this day. Israel traveled on.

Jacob came to his father Isaac at Mamre near Kiriath Arba (which is Hebron), where Abraham and Isaac had resided as aliens. The days of Isaac's life were one hundred eighty years. Isaac breathed his last and died. He was gathered to his people. He had lived a long, full life. Esau and Jacob, his sons, buried him.

Lord God, make us bold and persistent in prayer,
and make us kind and forgiving and at peace
with other people. Show us yourself in your Word.
Show us our Savior Jesus, until we see you
face to face in heaven. Amen.

21. JOSEPH AND HIS BROTHERS (GENESIS 37)

Joseph's jealous brothers sell him into slavery.

When Joseph was seventeen years old, he was tending the flock with his brothers. Joseph brought a bad report about them to their father. Now Israel loved Joseph more than all his other sons, because he was the son born in his old age, and he made him a special robe. His brothers saw that their father loved him more than all his brothers, so they hated him.

Once Joseph had a dream, and he told it to his brothers. "Please listen to this dream that I have dreamed: There we were, binding sheaves in the field, and suddenly my sheaf rose up and stood upright. Then your sheaves gathered around and bowed down to my sheaf."

His brothers said to him, "So will you really reign over us?" They hated him all the more because of his dreams.

Then he had another dream and told it to his brothers. He said, "Listen, I had another dream. This is what I saw: The sun and the moon and eleven stars bowed down to me." He told it to his father and to his brothers.

His father rebuked him and said to him, "Will I and your mother and your brothers really come and bow down to the ground in front of you?" His brothers were jealous of him, but his father kept what he had said in mind.

His brothers went to pasture their father's flock in Shechem. Israel said to Joseph, "Aren't your brothers pasturing the flock? Please go and see whether everything is going well with your brothers and with the flock. Then bring me word again." So Joseph went after his brothers and found them at Dothan.

They saw him in the distance, and before he came near to them, they conspired to kill him. They said to each other, "Look, here comes this master of dreams. Come on, let's kill him and throw him into one of the cisterns, and we will say, 'A wild animal has devoured him.' Then we will see what will become of his dreams."

Reuben heard this and said, "Let's not take his life. Throw him into this cistern in the wilderness, but do not lay a hand on him." He said this so that he could rescue him out of their hands and restore him to his father.

And so when Joseph came to his brothers, they stripped him of his special robe. Then they threw him into the cistern.

They sat down to eat bread, and they looked up and saw a caravan of Ishmaelites going to Egypt. Judah said to his brothers, "What profit is there in killing our brother and concealing his blood? Come on, let's sell him to the Ishmaelites." His brothers listened to him. The brothers pulled Joseph up out of the cistern and sold Joseph to the Ishmaelites for twenty pieces of silver. They brought Joseph to Egypt.

When Reuben returned to the cistern, he saw that Joseph was not in the cistern, so he tore his clothing. He returned to his brothers and said, "The boy is no longer here, and as for me, where will I go now?"

Then they took Joseph's robe, killed a goat, and dipped the robe in the goat's blood. They took the special robe, and they brought it to their father and said, "We have found this. Examine it and see whether it is your son's robe or not."

He recognized it and said, "It is my son's robe. A wild animal has devoured him. Without a doubt Joseph has been torn to pieces." Jacob tore his clothing, put sackcloth around his waist, and mourned for his son for many days. All his sons and all his daughters rose up to comfort him, but he refused to be comforted. He said, "No, I will mourn for my son until I go down to the grave." So his father wept for him.

Lord God, protect your people from both pride
and jealousy. Give your people unity and peace.
Forgive our sins for the sake of your Son, Jesus. Amen.

22. JOSEPH IN EGYPT (GENESIS 39-40)

Joseph faces ups and downs while in Egypt.

When Joseph was brought down to Egypt, Potiphar, the captain of the guard, bought Joseph from the Ishmaelites. The LORD was with Joseph, and he became successful. The LORD blessed the Egyptian's household for Joseph's sake, so he left Joseph in charge of everything that he had. He did not concern himself with anything except the food he ate.

Joseph was well built and handsome. His master's wife had her eye on Joseph, and she said, "Come, lie down with me."

But he refused and said to his master's wife, "Look, my master has put me in charge of everything that he has. How then could I do such a great evil and sin against God?"

She kept speaking to Joseph day after day, but he would not listen to her. He would not even be with her. But one day when he went into the house to do his work, none of the men of the household were there inside the house. She caught him by his garment and said, "Come, lie down with me!" He left behind his garment in her hand and ran outside.

She kept his garment beside her until his master came home. This is what she told him, "The Hebrew servant, whom you have brought to us, came to me to put me to shame and said to me, 'Let me lie down with you.' And look, when I screamed and cried out, he left behind his garment with me and ran outside." As soon as his master heard the words that his wife spoke to him, he became very angry. Joseph's master took him and put him into the prison.

But the LORD was with Joseph. The warden of the prison made Joseph responsible for all the prisoners in the prison.

Sometime after this, the cupbearer and the baker of the king of Egypt committed an offense against the king. He put them in the prison where Joseph was confined. While they were confined in the prison, the cupbearer and the baker of the king of Egypt each had a dream during the same night. Each man's dream had its own meaning. Joseph came to them in the morning, looked at them, and saw that they were troubled. He asked, "Why do you look so troubled today?"

They said to him, "We each had a dream, but there is no one who can interpret it."

Joseph said to them, "Interpretations belong to God, don't they? Please tell me the dreams."

The chief cupbearer told Joseph his dream. "In my dream, there was a vine in front of me, and the vine had three branches. As I watched, it produced ripe grapes. I took the grapes, pressed them into Pharaoh's cup, and handed the cup to Pharaoh."

Joseph said to him, "This is its interpretation: The three branches are three days. Within three days, Pharaoh will lift up your head and restore you to your office. You will place Pharaoh's cup into his hand, the way you used to do when you were his cupbearer. But remember me when everything is going well for you. Mention me to Pharaoh, and bring me out of this jail, because I also have done nothing here to deserve to be put into the dungeon."

When the chief baker saw that the interpretation was favorable, he said to Joseph, "I also had a dream. I saw three baskets of bread on my head. In the top basket there were all kinds of baked goods for Pharaoh, but the birds ate them out of the basket on my head."

Joseph answered, "This is its interpretation: The three baskets are three days. Within three days, Pharaoh will lift up your head from upon you and will hang you on a tree, and the birds will eat your flesh off of you."

And so it was that on the third day, which was Pharaoh's birthday, Pharaoh had a feast prepared for all his officials, and he lifted up the head of the chief cupbearer and the head of the chief baker among his officials. He restored the chief cupbearer to his position again, and he again placed the cup into Pharaoh's hand. But he hanged the chief baker, just as Joseph had explained to them. Nevertheless, the chief cupbearer did not remember Joseph, but forgot him.

Lord God, as we face ups and downs, keep us steady, trusting in your promise that you are taking care of us. Give us the strength to stand up against temptation and serve you, whatever the situation, whatever the cost. Amen.

23. JOSEPH AND PHARAOH (GENESIS 41)

God brings Joseph from the prison to the palace.

At the end of two full years Pharaoh also had a dream. In the dream he was standing beside the river. Seven beautiful, fat cows came up out of the river. Then seven ugly, thin cows came up out of the river. The ugly, thin cows ate up the seven beautiful, fat cows. Then Pharaoh woke up.

Pharaoh fell asleep again and dreamed a second time. He saw seven healthy, good heads of grain come up on one stalk. Right after that, seven thin heads of grain sprang up. The thin heads of grain swallowed up the seven healthy, full heads. Pharaoh woke up and realized that it was a dream.

The next morning he was very troubled, so he sent for all of Egypt's magicians and wise men. Pharaoh told them his dreams, but there was no one who could interpret them for Pharaoh.

Then the chief cupbearer said to Pharaoh, "In custody in the house of the captain of the guard was a young man, a Hebrew. He interpreted our dreams for us. It turned out exactly as he interpreted them for us. Pharaoh restored me to my office but hanged the chief baker." Then Pharaoh sent for Joseph, and they brought him quickly out of the dungeon.

Pharaoh said to Joseph, "I had a dream, and there is no one who can interpret it. I have heard it said about you, that when you hear a dream, you can interpret it."

Joseph answered Pharaoh, "It is not in my power. God will give Pharaoh an answer to give him peace of mind."

Pharaoh told the dream.

Joseph said to Pharaoh, "The seven good cattle are seven years, and the seven good heads of grain are seven years. The seven thin, ugly cattle that came up after them are seven years, and also the seven empty heads of grain. God has shown Pharaoh what he is about to do. Look, seven years of great abundance are coming throughout the whole land of Egypt. Seven years of famine will come up after them.

"Let Pharaoh, therefore, look for a man who is wise and discerning, and set him over the land of Egypt. When Pharaoh does this, let him appoint overseers over the land to collect one fifth of the produce of the land of Egypt during the seven years of abundance. The food will be a reserve for the land against the seven years of famine that will take place in the land of Egypt so that the land does not perish because of the famine."

The plan seemed good to Pharaoh and to all his officials. Pharaoh said to his officials, "Can we find anyone else like this man, a man who has the spirit of God?"

Pharaoh said to Joseph, "Because God has shown you all of this, there is no one as discerning and wise as you are. You shall be in charge of my house, and all my people will submit to your word." Pharaoh appointed him over the whole land of Egypt. Pharaoh gave Joseph Asenath as a wife.

Joseph traveled throughout the whole land of Egypt. During the seven years of abundance the earth produced plentiful harvests. He collected all the food during the seven good years in the land of Egypt. Joseph stored up a huge amount of grain, like the sand of the sea. Finally he stopped keeping track, because it was too much to measure.

Two sons were born to Joseph before the first year of famine arrived. Joseph named the firstborn Manasseh. He named the second son Ephraim.

So the seven years of abundance in the land of Egypt came to an end. The seven years of famine began, just as Joseph had said. Joseph opened all the storehouses and sold grain to the Egyptians. The whole world came to Joseph in Egypt to buy grain, because the famine was severe all over the whole world.

Lord God, you alone know the future. You alone
are in control. Take care of us and bless us,
as you have promised to do. Bring us
to our eternal home for Jesus' sake. Amen.

24. JOSEPH'S BROTHERS COME TO EGYPT (GENESIS 42-43)

Joseph's brothers meet their long-lost brother, but don't know it yet.

Jacob said to his sons, "Listen, I have heard that there is grain in Egypt. Go down there and buy some for us there, so that we may live and not die." So ten of Joseph's brothers went down to buy grain from Egypt. But Jacob did not send Joseph's brother Benjamin along with his other brothers, because he said, "Something bad might happen to him."

Joseph was the one who sold grain to all the people of the land. Joseph's brothers came and bowed down to him with their faces to the ground. Joseph saw his brothers and recognized them, but he acted like a stranger toward them and spoke harshly to them. He asked them, "Where did you come from?"

They said, "From the land of Canaan to buy food."

Joseph recognized his brothers, but they did not recognize him. Joseph remembered the dreams that he had dreamed about them and said to them, "You are spies!"

They said to him, "No, my lord, we, your servants, are twelve brothers. At the present time the youngest remains with our father, and one is no more."

Joseph said to them, "If you are honest men, let one of your brothers be confined in the jail, but the rest of you go and deliver grain to your houses to relieve the famine. Bring your youngest brother to me so that your words may be verified, and you will not die." So they did as he said.

They said to one another, "We are certainly guilty concerning our brother, because we saw the misery of his soul when he begged us, but we would not listen. Therefore this misery has come upon us."

Reuben answered them, "Didn't I tell you, 'Do not sin against the boy'? But you would not listen. So now payment for his blood is being required from us."

They did not know that Joseph understood them, because an interpreter was being used between them.

Joseph seized Simeon from among them and tied him up before their very eyes. Then Joseph gave a command to fill their containers with grain, to return each man's money into his sack, and to give them food for the journey.

They came to Jacob their father in the land of Canaan and told him everything that had happened to them. Then as they emptied their sacks, they were surprised to see that each man's pouch of money was in his sack. When they and their father saw their pouch of money, they were afraid.

Jacob said to them, "You have deprived me of my children! Joseph is no more. Simeon is no more. And now you want to take Benjamin away. My son shall not go down with you."

The famine in the land was severe, so when they had eaten all the grain that they had brought from Egypt, their father said to them, "Go back and buy a little more food for us."

Judah said to him, "If you send our brother with us, we will go down and buy food for you, but if you do not send him, we will not go down, because the man said to us, 'You shall not see my face unless your brother is with you.' Send the boy with me. I will serve as a guarantee for him. You can hold me accountable for him."

Israel said to them, "If it must be so, then take your brother. Get going and return to the man."

Lord God, we thank you for the food that you give us to eat. May we always recognize that you are the one who feeds us and preserves our life, and may we always recognize that you are the one who eternally saved our life through the life and death of your Son, Jesus Christ. Amen.

25. JOSEPH'S BROTHERS COME TO EGYPT A SECOND TIME (GENESIS 43-45)

Joseph tests his brothers and then reveals himself to him.

The men took double the amount of silver with them. They also took Benjamin. They went down to Egypt and stood before Joseph. Joseph said to the manager of his house, "Bring the men into the house. The men will dine with me at noon."

The brothers were afraid. They said, "We are being brought in so that he may seize us as slaves."

They approached the manager of Joseph's house and said, "Please, my lord, we really did come down the first time to buy food. When we opened our bags, to our surprise each man's silver was in his bag. We have brought it back with us. We have also brought down with us additional money to buy food."

He said, "There is no problem. Your God has given you treasure in your bags. I received your money." He brought Simeon out to them.

When Joseph came home, he asked them, "Is your father well? Is he still alive?"

They said, "Our father is well. He is still alive."

Joseph looked up and saw Benjamin. He asked, "Is this your youngest brother?" Joseph hurried out, because he was overcome by his emotions over his brother. He went into his room and wept there. Then he washed his face and came out.

The brothers were seated in front of him. They were lined up in order, starting with the firstborn down to the youngest, and the men expressed their amazement to each other. Benjamin's portion was five times as much as any of theirs.

Joseph commanded the manager of his house, "Fill the men's bags with food. Put each man's money into his bag. Put my silver cup into the bag of the youngest." The manager did exactly what Joseph told him to do.

In the morning the men were sent on their way. When they had left the city, Joseph said to his manager, "Pursue those men. Ask them, 'Why have you repaid evil for good? Isn't this the cup that my lord drinks from?'" The steward caught up to them and spoke those words to them.

They replied to him, "Your servants would never do such a thing! That money, which we found in our bags—we brought it back to you. Why then would we steal silver or gold out of your lord's house? If your cup is found with any of your servants, let him die, and we also will be my lord's slaves."

He said, "If it is found with anyone, he will be my slave, and the rest of you will be blameless."

Then each man quickly opened his bag. The cup was found in Benjamin's bag. Then they tore their clothing and returned to the city.

When Judah and his brothers came to Joseph's house, they fell to the ground before him. Judah said, "God has exposed the guilt of your servants. We are my lord's slaves."

Joseph said, "The man in whose hand the cup was found will be my slave, but as for the rest of you, go up in peace to your father."

Then Judah approached him and said, "Please let your servant stay as a slave to my lord instead of the boy, and let the boy go up with his brothers. For how can I go up to my father if the boy is not with me? How could I stand to see the evil that will come on my father?"

Joseph was unable to control himself. He wept out loud. Joseph said to his brothers, "I am Joseph!" His brothers could not answer him, because they were terrified.

Joseph said to his brothers, "I am Joseph, your brother, whom you sold into Egypt. Now do not be upset or angry with yourselves for selling me to this place, since God sent me ahead of you to preserve life. For two years now the famine has been in the land, and there are still five more years in which there will be neither plowing nor harvest. God sent me ahead of you to keep you alive by a great act of deliverance. So it was not you who sent me here, but God. Hurry, go up to my father and tell him God has made me lord of all Egypt. You shall live in the land of Goshen."

Lord God, we have treated others badly, including those closest to us. Grant us forgiveness in Jesus, and help us show that forgiveness to others as well. Give us repentant hearts which turn from sin to you. Amen.

26. ISRAEL COMES TO EGYPT (GENESIS 45-50)

God brings the Israelites to live in Egypt and provides for them there.

Joseph sent his brothers. They went up from Egypt and came to Jacob their father in the land of Canaan. They told Jacob every word that Joseph had said to them. Jacob brought all his offspring with him into Egypt. The total number of the souls in the house of Jacob who came into Egypt was seventy.

They arrived in the land of Goshen. Joseph went to meet Israel his father in Goshen. He approached him, hugged him, and wept on his shoulder for a long time. Israel said to Joseph, "Now I am ready to die, since I have seen you face to face and you are still alive."

Israel lived in the land of Egypt, in the land of Goshen, and they acquired possessions for themselves there. They were fruitful and multiplied greatly. Jacob lived in the land of Egypt for seventeen years. So the days of Jacob, the years of his life, were one hundred forty-seven years. The time drew near that Israel must die, so he called his son Joseph and said to him, "Please do not bury me in Egypt, but when I sleep with my fathers, you are to carry me out of Egypt and bury me in their burial place."

He said, "I will do as you have said."

When Jacob finished instructing his sons, he gathered up his feet into the bed, breathed his last breath, and was gathered to his people. When the days of mourning for Jacob were past, Joseph went up to bury his father, and all the officials of Pharaoh went up with him. His sons carried him to the land of Canaan and buried him in the cave in the field at Machpelah, which Abraham had purchased along with the field. After he had buried his father, Joseph returned to Egypt—he and his brothers, and all who had gone up with him to bury his father.

When Joseph's brothers saw that their father was dead, they said, "It may be that Joseph will hate us and will pay us back in full for all of the evil that we did to him."

Joseph said to them, "Do not be afraid, for am I in the place of God? You meant evil against me, but God meant it for good, to bring this to pass and to keep many people alive, as it is this day. Do not be afraid. I will nourish you and your little ones." He comforted them and spoke to them in a kind way.

Joseph lived one hundred ten years. Joseph said to his brothers, "I am dying, but God will surely visit you and bring you up out of this land to the land that he swore to Abraham, to Isaac, and to Jacob." Joseph made the descendants of Israel swear an oath. He said, "God will surely visit you. Then you shall carry my bones up from here." So Joseph died and they embalmed him, and he was put in a coffin in Egypt.

Lord God, you work all things out for our good. Be with us and take care of us as we live now in a world that we are not a part of, and graciously take us one day to the promised land prepared for us by Jesus. Amen.

PART 2

FROM SLAVERY TO THE PROMISED LAND (EXODUS TO JOSHUA)

When the Israelites came to Egypt, they enjoyed great respect and power through their connection to Joseph, but things did not stay that good for them. Eventually, when a new dynasty felt threatened by their numbers, they were enslaved and oppressed. But God then sent Moses to the Israelites to deliver his people, marked with the blood of a lamb, from their slavery in Egypt. This delivery gives us a picture of Christ, the Lamb of God, who delivers his people from their slavery in sin. These Israelites showed time and again that they did not deserve God's mercy, but still God brought them to the land he had promised them, again giving us a picture of Christ bringing his people into their eternal home.

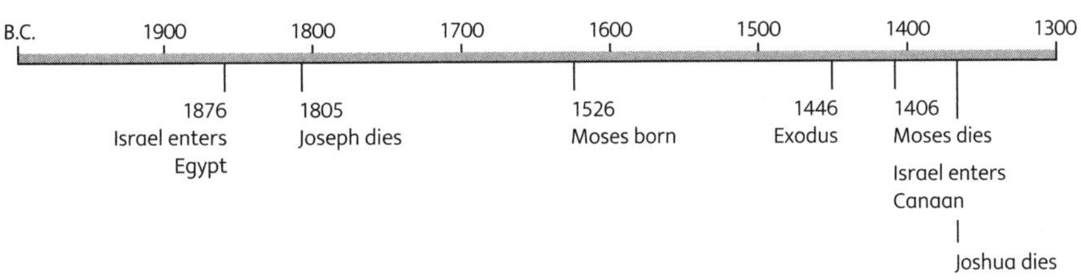

Mediterranean Sea
CANAAN
Jericho
Mt Nebo
Salt Sea
Rameses
GOSHEN
Sukkoth
Kadesh Barnea
DESERT OF ZIN
EDOM
DESERT OF SHUR
DESERT OF PARAN
EGYPT
Marah
Elim
SINAI
DESERT OF SIN
Red Sea
Dophkah
DESERT OF SINAI
MIDIAN
Rephidim
Mt Sinai
Red Sea
Red Sea
N
W
E
S
Israelite route

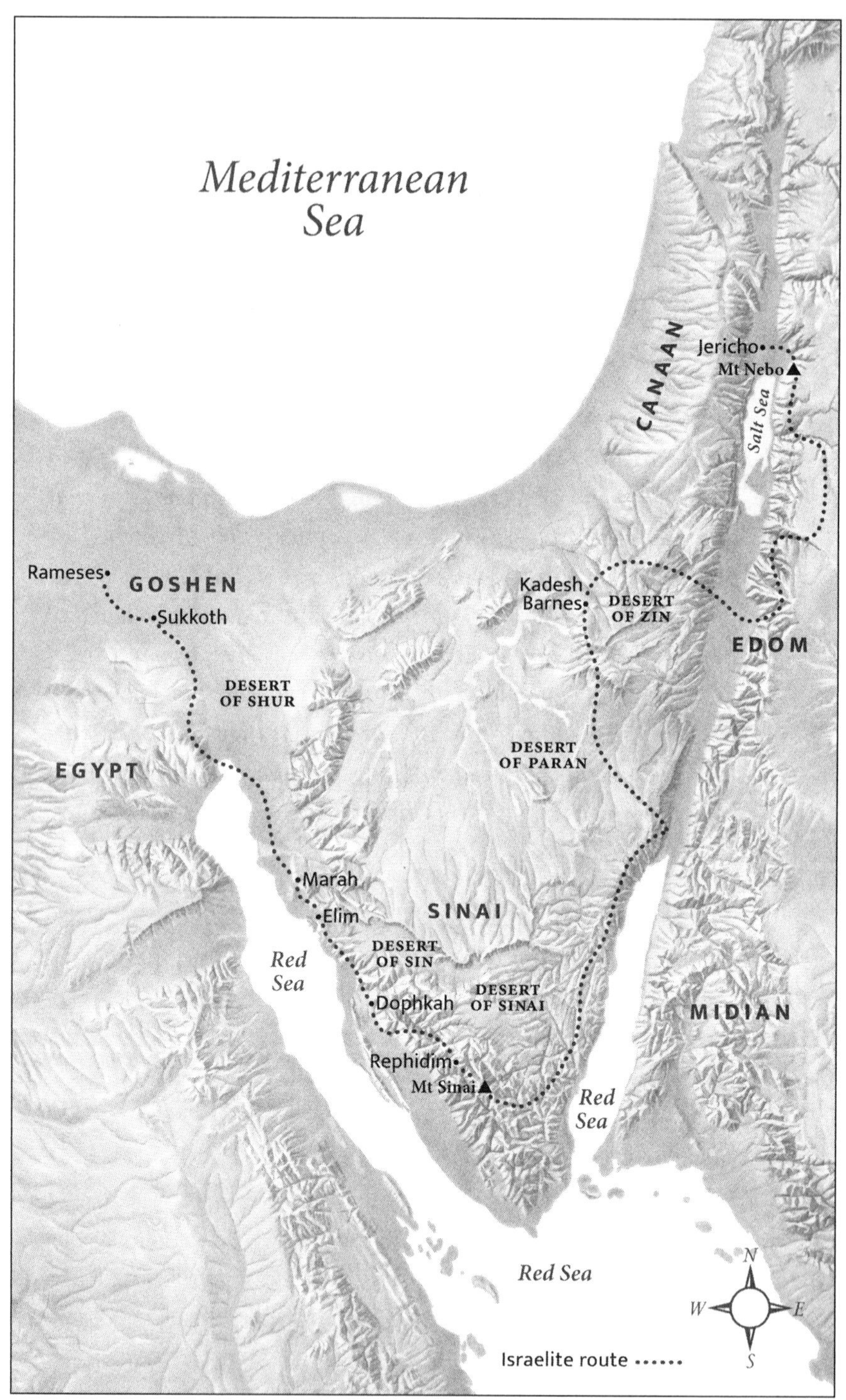

THE EXODUS

27. THE EARLY LIFE OF MOSES (EXODUS 1-2)

Four hundred years later, Israel's descendants, now a very large people, are slaves in Egypt, but God raises up Moses to be a deliverer. This deliverer, however, is not ready to deliver them quite yet.

The Israelites became very numerous. So the land was filled with them. Then a new king arose over Egypt, who did not know Joseph. He said to his people, "Look, the Israelites are more numerous and more powerful than we are. Let's come up with a wise plan to prevent them from increasing in number. Otherwise, if war breaks out, they would join with our enemies and fight against us." So the Egyptians placed taskmasters over them to oppress them with forced labor. But the more the Egyptians oppressed the Israelites, the more they increased in number. The Egyptians were filled with dread because of them. So the Egyptians oppressed the Israelites by forcing them to work very hard. The Egyptians made the Israelites' lives bitter with hard work, with brick and mortar, and with all kinds of work in the fields.

The king of Egypt also spoke to the Hebrew midwives. He said, "If the baby is a son, you are to kill him, but if it is a daughter, let her live." The midwives, however, feared God, so they did not do what the king of Egypt told them to do, but they let the boys live. So God treated the midwives well. Because the midwives feared God, he gave them families.

Pharaoh, however, commanded all his people, "Every son who is born you shall throw into the Nile, but every daughter you shall let live."

Now a man from the house of Levi went and took a Levite woman as a wife. The woman became pregnant and bore a son. When she saw that he was a special child, she hid him for three months. When she was no longer able to hide him, she got a papyrus basket, put the child into it, and placed it in the reeds along the bank of the Nile. His sister stood at a distance to see what would happen to him.

Pharaoh's daughter came down to bathe in the Nile. Pharaoh's daughter saw the basket among the reeds and sent her servant girl to get it. She opened it and saw the boy, and he was crying. She felt sorry for him and said, "This is one of the Hebrew boys."

Then his sister said to Pharaoh's daughter, "Should I go and call a wet nurse from the Hebrew women to nurse the child for you?"

Pharaoh's daughter said to her, "Yes, go."

So the young woman went and called the child's mother to come. Pharaoh's daughter said to her, "Take this child and nurse him for me, and I will pay you for doing it."

So the woman took the child and nursed him. When the child grew up, she brought him to Pharaoh's daughter, and he became her son. She named him Moses.

When Moses had grown up, he went out to his own people and observed their forced labor. He saw an Egyptian striking a Hebrew, one of his own people. After he looked this way and that, and he saw that no one was there, he struck down the Egyptian and hid him in the sand.

The next day when he went out, he came upon two Hebrew men who were fighting. He said to the one in the wrong, "Why were you striking your fellow Hebrew?"

The man said, "Who made you a ruler and a judge over us? Are you planning to kill me just as you killed the Egyptian?"

Moses was afraid and thought, "What I have done has definitely become known." When Pharaoh heard what Moses had done, he sought to kill Moses. Moses, however, fled from Pharaoh's presence and went to live in the land of Midian. There he sat down by a well.

Now a priest of Midian had seven daughters. They came and started drawing water. They filled the troughs to water their father's flock, but some shepherds came and drove them away. Moses, however, stood up and helped them. He then watered their flock. When the daughters came to their father, Reuel said, "Invite him to have something to eat."

Moses agreed to stay with the man. The man gave his daughter Zipporah to Moses as a wife.

Lord God, just as the Israelites were slaves under the power of Pharaoh, we were born as slaves under the power of sin. But you have raised up your Son, Jesus, to be our deliverer from sin and all its consequences. Give us the strength to always serve you and never return to serving sin, even when those around us encourage or command us to. Amen.

28. THE CALL OF MOSES (EXODUS 3-4)

Forty years after Moses had fled from Egypt, God appears to Moses and calls him to go and deliver Israel from the slavery of Egypt.

Moses was shepherding the flock of his father-in-law. He came to Horeb, the mountain of God. The Angel of the Lord appeared to him in blazing fire from within a bush. Moses saw that the bush was on fire, but the bush was not burning up. So he said, "I will go over and look at this amazing sight—to find out why the bush is not burning up."

When the LORD saw that Moses had gone over to take a look, God called to him from the middle of the bush and said, "Moses! Moses!"

Moses said, "I am here."

The LORD said, "Do not come any closer. Take your sandals off your feet, for the place where you are standing is holy ground." He then said, "I am the God of your fathers, the God of Abraham, the God of Isaac, and the God of Jacob. I have certainly seen the misery of my people in Egypt, and I have heard their cry for help because of their slave drivers. So I have come down to deliver them from the hand of the Egyptians and to bring them up out of that land to a good and spacious land, to a land flowing with milk and honey, to the place of the Canaanites. I will send you to Pharaoh to bring my people, the Israelites, out of Egypt."

But Moses said to God, "Who am I, that I should bring the Israelites out of Egypt?"

So he said, "I will certainly be with you."

But Moses said to God, "If I go to the Israelites and say to them, 'The God of your fathers has sent me to you,' and they ask me, 'What is his name?' what should I say to them?"

So God replied to Moses, "I AM WHO I AM. Say to the Israelites: 'I AM has sent me to you. The LORD, the God of your fathers—the God of Abraham, the God of Isaac, and the God of Jacob—has sent me to you.' This is my name forever. They will listen to your voice. Then you will go to the king of Egypt and say to him, 'Let us go.' But the king of Egypt will not allow you to go. So I will reach out my hand and strike Egypt with all my wonders. Afterward he will let you go."

But Moses responded, "What if they do not believe me?"

So the LORD said to him, "What is that in your hand?"

He said, "A staff."

He said, "Throw it on the ground." Moses threw it on the ground, and it became a snake, so he ran away from it.

The LORD said to Moses, "Stretch out your hand and take it by the tail." He stretched out his hand and took hold of it, and it became a staff in his hand.

The LORD also said to him, "Put your hand inside your cloak." So he put his hand inside his cloak, and when he took it out, his hand was leprous, as white as snow.

Then the Lord said, "Put your hand back inside your cloak." So he put his hand inside his cloak again, and when he took it out of his cloak, it was restored like the rest of his flesh.

The Lord said, "If they do not believe these two signs or listen to your voice, take some water from the Nile and pour it on the dry land. The water will become blood."

But Moses said to the Lord, "My mouth and tongue are slow and clumsy."

So the Lord said to him, "Who made a mouth for people? Is it not I, the Lord? Now go, and I will be with your mouth, and I will teach you what you will speak."

But he said, "Please, Lord, send someone else."

Then the Lord's anger burned against Moses, and the Lord said, "What about Aaron, your brother? I know that he can speak well. He will speak to the people for you. You will also take this staff in your hand, the one with which you will perform the signs." So Moses set out to return to the land of Egypt. Moses took the staff of God in his hand.

Lord God, your love for us is eternal, and you never change. Through your Word reassure us that you are always upholding us and at work in your world. May we never doubt your power and either act as if things depend on us or make excuses to keep us from doing what you have called us to do. Instead, keep us firmly trusting in you and your promise of the salvation you have prepared for us in Jesus. Amen.

29. THE FIRST NINE PLAGUES (EXODUS 5, 7-10)

God shows his almighty power for his people and against his enemies.

Moses and Aaron then went and gathered together every elder of the people of Israel. Aaron spoke all the words which the Lord had spoken to Moses and performed the signs in the sight of the people. The people believed.

Pharaoh said, "I certainly will not let Israel go." Pharaoh commanded the people's taskmasters, "Do not give the people straw for making bricks anymore. Let them go and gather their own straw. But require them to make the same number of bricks as they made before. Do not reduce it." So the people scattered all over the land of Egypt to gather stubble for straw.

The LORD said to Moses, "Now you will see what I will do to Pharaoh."

Moses and Aaron went to Pharaoh. Aaron threw down his staff in front of Pharaoh and his officials, and it became a snake. But then magicians of Egypt did the same thing by their occult practices. However, Aaron's staff swallowed up their staffs. But Pharaoh's heart was hard, and he did not listen to them, just as the LORD had said.

Aaron lifted up the staff and struck the water that was in the Nile. All the water in the Nile was turned to blood. But the magicians of Egypt did the same thing by their occult practices. So Pharaoh's heart was hard, and he did not listen to them, just as the LORD had told them.

Aaron stretched out his hand over the waters of Egypt. Frogs came up and covered the land of Egypt. But the magicians did the same thing by their occult practices. Pharaoh made his heart unyielding and did not listen to them, just as the LORD had said.

Aaron stretched out his hand with his staff and struck the dust of the ground. There were lice on the people and animals. The magicians tried to produce lice by their occult practices, but they could not. The magicians said to Pharaoh, "This is the finger of God." Pharaoh's heart was hard, and he did not listen to them, just as the LORD had said.

Then the LORD said, "I will send swarms of flies." So that is what the LORD did. Throughout Egypt, the land was ruined because of the swarms of flies. Pharaoh made his heart unyielding this time also, and he did not let the people go.

Then the LORD said, "The hand of the LORD will bring a very severe disease on your livestock." So the next day all the livestock of the Egyptians died. But Pharaoh's heart was unyielding, and he did not let the people go.

Moses took soot and tossed it toward the sky, and festering boils broke out on people and animals. But the LORD hardened Pharaoh's heart, and he did not listen to them, just as the LORD had said.

Then the LORD sent thunder and hail. The hail, with lightning flashing through it, was very severe. Throughout the entire land, the hail struck everything that was in the field, both people and animals. Pharaoh's heart was hard, and he did not let the Israelites go, just as the LORD had said.

Then Moses stretched out his staff over the land of Egypt, and the LORD brought locusts over the entire land of Egypt. They ate every plant of the land and all the fruit of the trees. But the LORD made Pharaoh's heart hard, and he did not let the Israelites go.

Then Moses stretched out his hand toward the sky, and there was a thick darkness in the entire land of Egypt for three days. No one could see anyone else, and for three days none of them moved from where they were. But the LORD hardened Pharaoh's heart, and he would not let them go.

Lord God, you rule over all creation.
Use your almighty power to keep us safe
from everything that would harm us. Amen.

30. THE PASSOVER (EXODUS 11-12)

God brings a tenth plague on Egypt and rescues his people from death by the blood of a lamb, instituting the Passover.

Then the LORD said to Moses, "I will bring one more plague on Pharaoh and on Egypt. After that, he will let you go."

So Moses said, "This is what the LORD says: About midnight I will go throughout Egypt, and every firstborn in the land of Egypt will die. But among all the Israelites, not a dog will bark at a person or animal, so that you may know that the LORD makes a distinction between Egypt and Israel."

The LORD told Moses and Aaron, "Tell the entire Israelite community that on the tenth day of this month, they are to take a lamb for themselves, one lamb per household. Your lamb must be unblemished, a year-old male. You are to keep it until the fourteenth day of this month. Then slaughter the lambs at sunset. Take some of the blood and put it on the two doorposts and the lintel of the houses where they eat the lamb. That night they shall eat the meat that has been roasted over a fire, along with unleavened bread. They shall eat it with bitter herbs. Whatever remains until the morning, you shall burn in the fire. Eat it with your cloak tucked into your belt ready for travel, your sandals on your feet, and your staff in your hand. Eat it in haste. It is the LORD's Passover.

"For on that night I will pass through the land of Egypt. I will strike down every firstborn in the land of Egypt. The blood will be a sign for you on the houses where you are. When I see the blood, I will pass over you. There will be no plague among you to destroy you, when I strike down the land of Egypt.

"This day shall be a memorial for you, and you are to celebrate it as a festival to the LORD. Throughout your generations you must celebrate it as a permanent regulation. You shall observe the Festival of Unleavened Bread, because on this very day I brought your divisions out from the land of Egypt. You shall observe this day throughout your generations as a permanent regulation. No yeast is to be found in your houses for seven days. You shall not eat anything leavened.

"You shall observe these instructions as a perpetual regulation for you and your descendants. When you enter the land that the LORD will give you just as he said he would, you shall observe this ceremony. So when your children ask you, 'What does this ceremony mean to you?' you will say, 'It is the sacrifice of the Passover to the LORD, who passed over the houses of the Israelites in Egypt. When he struck the Egyptians, he spared our houses.'"

The Israelites went and did all this. They did just as the LORD had commanded Moses and Aaron.

At midnight the LORD struck down all the firstborn in the land of Egypt, from the firstborn of Pharaoh, who sat on his throne, to the firstborn of the prisoner who was in the dungeon, even all the firstborn of the livestock. There was a loud outcry in Egypt, for there was not a house where there was not someone dead. Pharaoh summoned Moses and Aaron that night and said, "Get up, get away from my people!"

The Israelites set out from Rameses to Sukkoth, about six hundred thousand men on foot, besides their families. A mixed group of non-Israelites also went up along with them, as well as a large amount of livestock, both flocks and herds. The Israelites baked the dough which they had brought out of Egypt into unleavened loaves. The LORD brought the Israelites out of the land of Egypt.

Lord God, our great deliverer, you have powerfully rescued us from the slavery of sin through Christ, our Passover lamb, sacrificed for us. Keep us always in faith, covered by his blood, and deliver us from death through him. Amen.

31. CROSSING THE RED SEA (EXODUS 13-15)

God brings his people out of their slavery in Egypt through water.

When Pharaoh let the people go, God led the people toward the Red Sea. (Moses also took the bones of Joseph with him.) The LORD went in front of them in a pillar of cloud by day to lead them on their way and in a pillar of fire by night to give them light.

Pharaoh had a change of heart concerning the people. So Pharaoh prepared his chariot and took his troops with him. He also took all the chariots of Egypt with officers over all of them. The LORD hardened the heart of Pharaoh so that he pursued the Israelites. His army caught up with them where they were camping by the sea.

The Israelites were terrified and said to Moses, "Was it because there were no graves in Egypt that you took us to die in the wilderness? What have you done to us by bringing us out of Egypt? It would have been better for us to serve the Egyptians than to die in the wilderness."

Moses said to the people, "Do not be afraid. Stand firm, and see the salvation from the LORD, which he will perform for you today. For the Egyptians you see today, you will never see again. The LORD will fight for you. You must wait quietly."

The LORD said to Moses, "Lift up your staff, stretch out your hand over the sea, and divide the sea so that the Israelites can go through the middle of the sea on dry ground."

Then the Angel of God, who was going in front of the Israelite forces, moved and went behind them. The pillar of cloud moved from in front of them and stood behind them. It went between the Egyptian forces and the Israelite forces. The cloud was dark on one side, but it lit up the night on the other. Neither group approached the other all night long.

Then Moses stretched out his hand over the sea, and all night long the LORD drove the sea back with a strong east wind and turned the sea into dry land. The waters were divided. The Israelites went into the middle of the sea on dry ground. The waters were like a wall for them on their right and on their left. The Egyptians pursued them, and all of Pharaoh's horses, his chariots, and his charioteers went after them into the middle of the sea.

Then the LORD said to Moses, "Stretch out your hand over the sea, and the waters will come back over the Egyptians, over their chariots and their charioteers." So Moses stretched out his hand over the sea, and at daybreak the sea returned to its normal place. While the Egyptians were fleeing from it, the LORD threw the Egyptians into the middle of the sea. The waters came back and covered the chariots and the charioteers, the entire army of Pharaoh that went into the sea after the Israelites. Not even one of them survived.

But the Israelites went through the middle of the sea on dry land, and the waters were like a wall for them on their right and on their left. On that day the LORD saved Israel from the hand of the Egyptians, and Israel saw the Egyptians dead on the seashore. Then Moses and the Israelites sang, "I will sing to the LORD, for he is highly exalted. The horse and its rider he has thrown into the sea. The LORD is my strength and song. He has become my salvation."

Lord God, in the waters of baptism you have brought us from slavery to freedom, from death to life. Drown our sinful nature in us each day by bringing us back to you in repentance, and keep us trusting in Jesus all the days of our life. Amen.

32. GOD PROVIDES FOOD AND WATER IN THE WILDERNESS (EXODUS 15-17)

Even as they grumble against him, God takes care of his people on their way to the Promised Land.

Then Moses led Israel on from the Red Sea. They traveled for three days in the wilderness but found no water. When they came to Marah, they were not able to drink the waters, because they were bitter. The people grumbled against Moses. Then Moses cried out to the LORD, and the LORD showed him some wood. Moses threw it into the water, and the water became fit to drink.

Then they came to Elim where there were twelve springs of water and seventy palm trees.

The entire Israelite community set out from Elim and came to the Wilderness of Sin. The entire Israelite community grumbled against Moses and Aaron in the wilderness. The Israelites said to them, "If only we had died by the LORD's hand in the land of Egypt, when we sat around pots of meat and ate as much food as we wanted, but now you have brought us out into this wilderness to have this whole community die of hunger."

Then the LORD said to Moses, "I will rain down bread from heaven for you. I have heard the grumbling of the Israelites. Say to them, 'At evening you will eat meat, and in the morning you will eat bread until you are full. Then you will know that I am the LORD your God.' "

So in the evening quail came and covered the camp, and in the morning there were thin flakes on the surface of the wilderness, thin as frost on the ground. When the Israelites saw it, they said to one another, "What is it?" because they did not know what it was.

Moses said to them, "This is the bread which the LORD has given to you as food." The house of Israel called it manna. It looked like white coriander seed, and it tasted like wafers made with honey.

The entire Israelite community set out. They camped at Rephidim, but there was no water for the people to drink. So the people quarreled with

Moses and said, "Why did you ever bring us up out of Egypt to let us, our children, and our livestock die of thirst?"

Moses cried out to the LORD, "What shall I do with these people? They are almost ready to stone me!"

The LORD said to Moses, "Go in front of the people. Take the staff with which you struck the Nile and strike the rock. Water will come out of it, and the people will drink." Moses did that in the sight of the elders of Israel.

Then the Amalekites came and fought against the Israelites at Rephidim. Moses said to Joshua, "Select some men for us, and go out and fight against the Amalekites. Tomorrow I will stand on the hilltop, and God's staff will be in my hand." So Joshua did just as Moses told him.

While Joshua was fighting against the Amalekites, Moses, Aaron, and Hur went up to the hilltop. Whenever Moses held up his hand, the Israelites would start winning, but whenever he lowered his hand, the Amalekites would start winning. When Moses' arms became tired, they took a stone and placed it under him, and he sat on it. Aaron and Hur held up his hands—one on one side, and one on the other side. In this way his hands were steady until sunset. So Joshua defeated the Amalekite army with the sword.

Lord God, you take care of all of our physical needs
in this life, far better than we ever appreciate.
You have also sent us your Son as our bread of life,
our manna from heaven. Feed us through your Word
to strengthen us in this life we have in him by faith,
and give our hearts contentment in him. Amen.

33. THE LAW IS GIVEN AT MOUNT SINAI (EXODUS 19-20, 31)

Having rescued Israel and made them his people, God gives the Israelites his Law, showing them how to live as his people.

The Israelites set out from Rephidim and came to the Wilderness of Sinai. Israel camped there in front of the mountain.

Moses went up to God, and the LORD called to him from the mountain, "This is what you are to say to the house of Jacob and to tell the people of Israel: 'You have seen what I did to the Egyptians and how I carried you on eagles' wings and brought you to myself. Now if you will carefully listen to my voice and keep my covenant, then you will be my special treasure out of all the nations, although the entire earth is mine. You will be my kingdom of priests and my holy nation.'"

Moses went and summoned the elders of the people, and he set before them all these words that the LORD had commanded him. All the people answered together, "Everything that the LORD has said, we will do."

The LORD said to Moses, "Go to the people. Consecrate them, for on the third day the LORD will come down on Mount Sinai in the sight of all the people."

On the third day, when morning came, there was thunder and lightning. A thick cloud was over the mountain, and there was a very loud blast of a ram's horn. All the people in the camp trembled. All of Mount Sinai was covered with smoke, because the LORD descended on it in fire. The whole mountain trembled violently. The LORD then called Moses to the top of the mountain, and Moses went up.

The LORD said to Moses, "Go down and warn the people not to break through to see the LORD. If they do, many of them will fall." So Moses went down to the people and told them.

Then God spoke all these words:

"I am the LORD your God, who brought you out from the land of Egypt, where you were slaves.

"You shall have no other gods beside me. For I the LORD your God am a jealous God. I follow up on the guilt of the fathers with their children, their grandchildren, and their great-grandchildren, if they also hate me. But I show mercy to thousands who love me and keep my commandments.

"You shall not misuse the name of the LORD your God.

"Remember the Sabbath day by setting it apart as holy. Six days you are to serve and do all your regular work, but the seventh day shall be a sabbath rest to the LORD your God.

"Honor your father and your mother so that you may spend many days on the land that the LORD your God is giving to you.

"You shall not commit murder.

"You shall not commit adultery.

"You shall not steal.

"You shall not give false testimony against your neighbor.

"You shall not covet your neighbor's house. You shall not covet your neighbor's wife, his male servant, his female servant, his ox, his donkey, or anything else that belongs to your neighbor."

All the people saw and heard the thunder and the lightning and the sound of the ram's horn and the mountain smoking. They trembled and stood far away. Then they said to Moses, "Speak with us yourself, and we will listen, but do not let God speak with us, or we will die."

Moses said to the people, "Do not be afraid, for God has come to test you, so that you may always fear him, so that you do not sin."

When the Lord had finished speaking with Moses on Mount Sinai, he gave him the two tablets of the Testimony, stone tablets, written with God's finger.

Lord God, we thank you for giving us your law, so that we know how to serve you. Empower us to live according to your will. But even more so, we thank you for giving us your gospel, which shows us that Jesus has kept the law perfectly for us, and has died to pay for all the many times we have broken your law. Amen.

34. THE GOLDEN CALF (EXODUS 32, 34)

The people of Israel fall into idolatry.

When the people saw that it took so long for Moses to come down from the mountain, the people gathered around Aaron and said to him, "Make a god for us, because this Moses—we do not know what has become of him."

Aaron said to them, "Pull off the gold earrings from your wives and sons and daughters and bring them to me."

All the people pulled off their gold earrings and brought them to Aaron. He shaped it with an engraving tool and made it into a calf cast out of metal. Then they said, "This is your god, which brought you up out of the land of Egypt."

Aaron built an altar in front of it and said, "Tomorrow shall be a festival to the Lord."

They got up early the next day and offered burnt offerings. Then the people sat down to eat and to drink and got up to celebrate wildly.

The Lord spoke to Moses: "Hurry down, because your people have quickly turned from the way which I commanded them. So now leave me alone, so that my anger can burn hot against them, so that I may consume them and make you into a great nation."

Moses begged the Lord his God and said, "O Lord, why does your anger burn against your people? Remember Abraham, Isaac, and Israel. You said to them, 'I will multiply your seed like the stars of the sky, and I will give all this land that I have spoken about to your seed, and they shall inherit it forever.'"

Then the LORD changed his mind about the disaster which he said he would inflict on his people.

Moses went down the mountain with the two tablets of the Testimony in his hand. As he saw the calf and the dancing, Moses' anger burned. So he threw the tablets out of his hands and broke them. He took the calf, burned it with fire, ground it to powder, and scattered it on the water. Then he made the people of Israel drink it.

Moses said to Aaron, "What did these people do to you, that you have brought such a great sin on them?"

Aaron said, "Do not let the anger of my lord burn. You know these people. They are set on evil, so they said to me, 'Make a god for us, because this Moses—we do not know what has become of him.' So I said to them, 'Whoever has any gold, pull it off.' So they gave it to me. I threw it into the fire and out came this calf."

Moses said, "Whoever is on the LORD's side, come to me!"

All the descendants of Levi gathered themselves together to Moses. He said to them, "Go back and forth throughout the camp and kill." The Levites did what Moses said, and that day about three thousand men fell.

The LORD said to Moses, "Cut out two stone tablets. On these tablets I will write the same words that were on the first tablets, which you broke."

Moses cut out two stone tablets. Moses went up Mount Sinai, and he carried the two stone tablets in his hand. The LORD came down in the cloud and proclaimed the name of the LORD: "The LORD, the LORD, the compassionate and gracious God, slow to anger, and overflowing with mercy and truth, maintaining mercy for thousands, forgiving guilt and rebellion and sin. He will by no means clear the guilty. He calls their children and their children's children to account for the guilt of the fathers, even to the third and the fourth generation."

Moses wrote on the tablets the Ten Commandments.

When Moses came down from Mount Sinai with the two tablets of the Testimony in his hand, Moses did not realize that his face was shining because he had been speaking with the LORD. All the people of Israel were amazed that his face was shining, so they were afraid to come close to him. Moses gave them all of the commands that the LORD had spoken to him on Mount Sinai. When Moses was finished speaking with them, he put a veil over his face.

Lord God, you are our only God. Forgive us
for all the times that we have feared, loved, or trusted

anything else above you. Thank you for Jesus,
our only Way, Truth, and Life. Amen.

35. THE DWELLING (EXODUS 35-40)

God has the people construct a special dwelling for him, so that he will dwell among his people.

Moses spoke to the people of Israel. He told them what the LORD commanded: "Gather a special offering for the LORD. Whoever has a willing heart, let him bring the LORD's offering. Let every skilled craftsman among you come and make everything that the LORD has commanded: the Dwelling, the ark, the atonement seat, all its vessels and accessories, the altar and the holy garments for Aaron the priest." The LORD called Bezalel. He filled him with the Spirit of God, with the ability to create designs and to work in gold, silver, and bronze.

Then the people of Israel brought a voluntary offering to the LORD. Every man and woman whose heart was willing contributed to all the work which the LORD had commanded Moses to do. The people were restrained from bringing more, because the material they had brought was sufficient to complete all the work, with some left over.

All the skilled craftsmen among the workers made the dwelling out of curtains. They made a veil of blue, purple, and scarlet material, decorated with cherubim. They made a screen for the entry to the tent.

Bezalel made the ark of acacia wood. He overlaid it with pure gold. He made an atonement seat of pure gold. He made two cherubim of hammered gold for the two ends of the atonement seat, one cherub for one end and one cherub for the other.

He made a table of acacia wood, and overlaid it with pure gold. He made a lampstand of pure gold. He made seven lamps for it. He made the altar for incense. He overlaid it with pure gold.

He made the altar for burnt offerings from acacia wood. It was square. He overlaid the altar with bronze. He made a large bronze basin. He made the courtyard. All the stakes for the courtyard were bronze.

They made the holy garments for Aaron, just as the LORD had commanded Moses. He made the special vest from gold and from blue, purple, and scarlet material and fine woven linen. They took two onyx stones and mounted them in gold settings and engraved on them the names of the sons of Israel, like the engraving on signet seals. They mounted them on the shoulder straps of the vest. Bezalel made a folded pouch. They mounted on it four rows of precious stones. The pouch was kept right next to the woven sash of the vest. The robe that was to be worn under the vest was the work of a weaver. It was all blue. They made a medallion of pure gold to serve as a crest and engraved on it: Holy to the LORD. They put it on a blue cord to fasten it to the turban.

In this way all the work on the Dwelling was finished. The people of Israel did everything exactly as the LORD had commanded Moses. Then the Glory of the LORD filled the tent. Moses was not able to enter, because the cloud stayed over it, and the Glory of the LORD filled the tent. Throughout all their journeys, whenever the cloud was taken up from over the tent, the people of Israel would move forward. But if the cloud was not taken up, then they would not travel until the day when it was taken up. For in the sight of the whole house of Israel, the cloud of the LORD was above the tent by day, and there was fire in the cloud by night, throughout all their journeys.

Lord God, you have sent your Son to dwell among us, to sacrifice himself for us, and to cover our sins against your law with his own blood. Through your Word continue to send your Holy Spirit to dwell in our hearts through faith, and move our hearts to serve you freely and cheerfully with the possessions you have given us. Amen.

36. THE GREAT DAY OF ATONEMENT (LEVITICUS 16)

God sets a special day on which the sin of the people would be removed.

The LORD said to Moses, "Tell your brother Aaron that he must not enter into the Holy Place at any time he chooses by going inside the veil which is in front of the atonement seat that is on the ark. This is so that he will not die, for I appear in the cloud over the atonement seat.

"This is how Aaron shall enter the Holy Place: with a bull for a sin offering and a ram for a whole burnt offering. He is to wear a sacred linen tunic. He must wash his body with water and then put the garments on. From the congregation of the people of Israel he shall also receive two male goats for a sin offering and one ram for a whole burnt offering.

"Aaron shall present the bull for his own sin offering, to make atonement for himself and for his household.

"He shall take the two male goats and stand them before the LORD at the entrance to the Tent of Meeting. Aaron is to cast lots for the two goats, one lot marked 'for the LORD' and the other lot marked 'for the scapegoat.' Aaron shall bring forward the goat that received the lot 'for the LORD,' to prepare it as a sin offering, but the goat that received the lot marked 'for the scapegoat' is to be kept alive, to make atonement upon it in order to send it off into the wilderness as the scapegoat.

"After Aaron has presented the bull for his sin offering to make atonement for himself and for his household, he shall slaughter the bull for his sin offering. He is to put incense on the fire before the LORD so that the cloud from the incense covers the atonement seat that is over the Testimony, so he will not die. He is to take some of the blood of the bull and sprinkle it with his finger upon the surface of the atonement seat seven times.

"He shall then slaughter the goat for the sin offering of the people. He is to bring its blood inside the veil and sprinkle it on the atonement seat. He shall make atonement for the sanctuary to cleanse it from the uncleanness of the Israelites and from their rebellions and all their sins. In this way he shall make atonement for himself and his household, as well as for the entire assembly of Israel.

"When he has finished making atonement to cleanse the sanctuary, he shall present the live goat. Then Aaron shall lay his two hands on the head of the live goat and confess over it all the guilt of the people of Israel and all their rebellions and all their sins. He is to put them on the head of the goat and send it away into the wilderness. The goat will carry all their guilt on itself to a remote, desolate place.

"Then Aaron shall take off the special linen garments, bathe in water in a holy place, and put on his regular garments. Then he shall offer the burnt offering for himself and the burnt offering for the people to make atonement for himself and for the people.

"This shall be a permanent regulation for you: In the seventh month, on the tenth day of the month, you shall humble yourselves, and you shall not do any kind of work. For on this day atonement will be made on your behalf to cleanse you. You will become clean from all your sins in the presence of the LORD. The priest who is anointed and ordained to serve as priest in his father's place shall make atonement on behalf of the priests and all the people of the assembly. This shall be a permanent regulation for you to make atonement for the people of Israel from all their sins once a year."

So Aaron did as the LORD had commanded Moses.

Lord God, in one day your Son has atoned for all
of our sin by the sacrifice of himself, and he

has removed our sins forever from us. Cause us to live as holy and clean people, purified by his blood. Amen.

37. THE SCOUTS' REPORT (NUMBERS 10, 13-14)

God shows the people the land he promised them, but they are unwilling to enter and must wait forty years.

The cloud lifted up above the Dwelling of the Testimony. The Israelites set out on their journey from the Wilderness of Sinai. The cloud settled in the Wilderness of Paran. For the first time, they set out according to the command of the LORD through Moses.

The LORD spoke to Moses: "Send men to scout the land of Canaan, which I myself am giving to the Israelites, one man from each tribe."

Moses sent them to scout the land of Canaan and said to them, "See what the land is like."

The scouts came to the Valley of Eshcol, and there they cut down a branch with one cluster of grapes. They carried it on a pole between two men. At the end of forty days, they returned from scouting the land.

They brought back a report to them and to the entire community. They showed them some of the fruit of the land. They reported to him and said, "We went to the land where you sent us. It really does flow with milk and honey, and here is its fruit. However, the people who live in the land are strong, and the cities are fortified and very large. We are not able to go up against the people, because they are stronger than we are."

Joshua and Caleb, two of those who had scouted the land, spoke to the entire Israelite community, "The land that we explored and scouted is a very good land. If the LORD is pleased with us, he will bring us into this land and give it to us, a land that is flowing with milk and honey. Do not fear the people of the land, for the LORD is with us."

The entire community threatened to stone them to death.

The LORD said, "Tomorrow you are to turn back and set out into the wilderness along the route to the Red Sea. Every one of you twenty years old and up who have grumbled against me, I swear that none of you will go into the land where I promised to settle you, except for Caleb and Joshua. But your children I will bring in, and they will experience the land which you have rejected. But as for you, your corpses will fall in this wilderness. Your children will be shepherds in the wilderness for forty years. You will bear the consequences of your guilt for forty years, based on the number of days that you scouted the land, forty days, one year for every day."

Those men who brought the wicked, negative report about the land died by the plague before the LORD. Of those men who had gone to scout the land, only Joshua and Caleb remained alive.

The people got up early in the morning and said, "We are ready. We will go up to the place which the LORD spoke about. We admit we have sinned."

Moses said, "Why are you going against the LORD's command? This will not succeed. Do not go up, because the LORD is not among you. You will be struck down before your enemies."

But they dared to go up to the heights of the hill country. The Ark of the Covenant of the LORD and Moses did not leave the camp. Then the Amalekites and the Canaanites came down, attacked them, and beat them down them all the way to Hormah.

Lord God, free us from all fear of the world around us,
and focus our attention solely on your sure promise
to us that we have an eternal home awaiting us
through Jesus our Savior. Amen.

38. KORAH'S REBELLION (NUMBERS 16-17)

Some of the people challenge Moses and Aaron, but God makes clear who it is he has chosen as his representatives.

Now Korah joined with Dathan and Abiram. They gathered two hundred fifty well-known Israelites and they rose up against Moses. They assembled together against Moses and Aaron and said to them, "The entire community is holy, every one of them, and the LORD is among them! Why do you lift yourselves up above the LORD's assembly?"

Moses said to Korah and his followers, "The LORD will reveal which of you are his and which of you are holy, and he will have that person come near to him. Take censers, put fire in them, and place incense on them in the presence of the LORD tomorrow. The man whom the LORD chooses will be set aside as holy."

They each took their own censers, put fire in them, placed incense on them, and stood at the entrance to the Tent of Meeting with Moses and Aaron. Korah assembled the entire community opposite Moses and Aaron.

The LORD spoke to Moses: "Tell the assembly, 'Move away from the dwelling of Korah, Dathan, and Abiram!'" So Moses told the assembly, "Move back from the tents of these wicked men, or you will be swept away because of all their sins!" So from every side, they moved away from the dwelling of Korah, Dathan, and Abiram.

Moses said, "This is how you will know that the LORD has sent me to do all these things and that all this was not just my idea. If these men die a death like everyone else, then the LORD has not sent me. But if the ground opens its mouth and swallows them up, you will know that these men have treated the LORD with contempt."

As soon as he finished speaking all these words, the ground beneath them split open. The earth opened its mouth and swallowed up everyone who was with Korah. The earth closed up over them, and they disappeared from the midst of the assembly. Fire went out from the LORD and consumed the two hundred fifty men who offered the incense.

The LORD spoke to Moses: "Speak to the Israelites, and collect staffs from them, one from all their tribal chiefs, twelve staffs in all. Write each man's name on his staff. Write Aaron's name on the staff of Levi. You are to place them in the Tent of Meeting before the Testimony. The staff of the man whom I will choose will sprout."

So Moses spoke to the Israelites, and each one of their tribal chiefs gave him a staff, twelve staffs in all. Aaron's staff was among their staffs. Moses placed the staffs before the LORD in the Tent of the Testimony.

On the next day Moses went into the Tent of the Testimony and discovered that Aaron's staff had sprouted, budded, blossomed, and produced almonds. Moses brought out all the staffs from the LORD's presence to all the Israelites. They looked, and each man took his staff.

The LORD said to Moses, "Put Aaron's staff back in front of the Testimony to be kept as a sign against the rebellious. In this way you will put an end to their grumblings against me, so that they do not die." That is what Moses did. He did just as the LORD commanded him.

Lord God, thank you for the pastors and teachers who bring me your Word. Bless the work that they do. Amen.

39. MORE GRUMBLING IN THE WILDERNESS (NUMBERS 20-21)

The sin of the people of Israel deserves death, but God still brings healing and life.

The people of Israel, the entire community, came to the Wilderness of Zin, and the people stayed at Kadesh.

There was no water for the community, so they assembled together against Moses and Aaron. The people quarreled with Moses and said, "If only we had perished when our brothers perished before the LORD! Why have you brought the LORD's assembly into this wilderness for us and our livestock to die here? Why have you taken us up out of Egypt to bring us into this horrible place? There is no water to drink!"

Moses and Aaron went from the presence of the assembly to the entrance to the Tent of Meeting. They fell facedown. The Glory of the LORD appeared to them. The LORD spoke to Moses: "Take the staff and assemble the community. You and Aaron, speak to the rock before their eyes, and it will pour out its water. You will bring water for them from the rock and provide water for the community and their livestock."

Moses took the staff from the LORD's presence just as the LORD commanded him. Moses and Aaron gathered the assembly together before the rock, and he said to them, "Listen now, you rebels! Must we bring water out of this rock for you?" Moses lifted up his hand and struck the rock with his staff two times, and a great amount of water gushed out. The congregation and their livestock drank.

Then the LORD said to Moses and Aaron, "Because you did not trust me enough to honor me as holy in the eyes of the Israelites, therefore you will not bring this assembly into this land which I have given to them."

They set out along the road to the Red Sea to go around the land of Edom, but the people became very impatient along the way. The people spoke against God and against Moses, "Why have you brought us up out of Egypt to die in the wilderness? Look, there is no food! There is no water! And we are disgusted by this worthless food!"

The LORD sent venomous snakes among the people, and the snakes bit the people. As a result many people from Israel died. The people went to Moses and said, "We have sinned, because we have spoken against the LORD and against you. Pray to the LORD to take the snakes away from us." So Moses prayed on behalf of the people.

The LORD said to Moses, "Make a venomous snake and put it on a pole. If anyone who is bitten looks at it, he will live." Moses made a bronze snake and put it on the pole. If a snake had bitten anyone, if that person looked at the bronze snake, he lived.

Lord God, our complaining, our greed, our ungratefulness, and our sin deserve death, but you have lifted up your Son on the cross as our healing and our life. When our conscience troubles us, keep our eyes fixed firmly on him. Forgive us our sins for the sake of him who was made sin for us, and on the Last Day raise us to eternal life as you have promised. Amen.

40. BALAAM (NUMBERS 22-24)

God's enemies fail in their attempts to curse God's people because God is blessing them. Instead of cursing Israel, Balaam blesses them with a promise of a savior who is coming.

The Israelites set out and camped on the Plains of Moab. Moab was afraid of the people, because they were so numerous. Balak, king of Moab, sent messengers to summon Balaam. He said, "Please curse this people for me." Balaam went with the officials of Moab.

But God's anger burned because Balaam was going with them. So the Angel of the LORD stood in the road to oppose him. Balaam was riding on his donkey. The donkey saw the Angel of the LORD with his drawn sword. So the donkey turned off the road. Balaam struck the donkey to make it turn back to the road. Then the Angel of the LORD stood in a narrow path between vineyards with walls on both sides. The donkey saw the Angel of the LORD and pressed against the wall and squeezed Balaam's foot against the wall. Balaam struck the donkey again. Then the Angel of the LORD went ahead and stood in a narrow place where there was no room to turn. The donkey saw the Angel of the LORD and lay down under Balaam. Balaam's anger burned, and he struck the donkey with his staff.

The LORD opened the mouth of the donkey, which said to Balaam, "What have I done to you that you have struck me these three times?"

Then the LORD opened Balaam's eyes, and he saw the Angel of the LORD standing in the road with his drawn sword. The Angel of the LORD said to him, "Why have you struck your donkey? I have come out to oppose you, because your way is reckless. The donkey saw me and turned away from me these three times. If it had not, I would have surely killed you by now."

Balaam said to the Angel of the LORD, "I have sinned, for I didn't know that you stood in the road to confront me."

The Angel of the LORD said to Balaam, "Go with the men, but you will speak only the words that I speak to you." So Balaam went with Balak's officials.

When Balak heard that Balaam had come, he went out to meet him. Balaam said to Balak, "Look, I have come to you now. But I will speak only the words that God puts in my mouth."

The LORD put a message into Balaam's mouth. Balaam said: "How can I curse someone God has not cursed? Look! A people that dwells apart, that does not consider itself to be one of the nations. Who can count the dust of Jacob?"

Balak said to Balaam, "I brought you to curse my enemies, but you have just blessed them."

Balaam answered, "Don't I have to speak whatever the LORD puts in my mouth?"

Balak said to Balaam, "Please curse them for me."

The LORD met with Balaam and put a message in his mouth. Balaam said: "God is not a man, that he should lie, nor a son of man, that he changes his mind. Does he say something, and then not carry it out? Does he speak, and then not bring it about? Look, I have received a command to bless. He has blessed, and I cannot change that. No disaster is in sight for Israel. The LORD his God is with him."

Then Balak said to Balaam, "Do not curse them at all! Do not bless them at all!"

But Balaam answered Balak, "Didn't I say to you that I must do everything the LORD says?"

Balak said to Balaam, "Come on, curse them for me."

When Balaam lifted up his eyes and saw Israel dwelling according to their tribes, the Spirit of God was upon him. He said: "How beautiful are your tents, O Jacob, and your dwelling places, O Israel! The one who blesses you is blessed. The one who curses you is cursed."

Balak's anger burned against Balaam, and he said, "I summoned you to curse my enemies, but look, all you have done is bless them these three times. Now get out of here!"

Balaam said to Balak, "I can't go against the command of the LORD. Pay attention now—I will tell you what this people will do to your people in days to come. I see him, but not now. I behold him, but not near. A star will come out of Jacob. A scepter will rise up out of Israel. It will smash Moab."

Balaam got up and left to return to his place.

Lord God, you have blessed us with a forgiveness
and an eternal life which no one can take away.
Protect us always and keep us in the faith
by your powerful, unchanging Word. Amen.

41. MOSES' FAREWELL SERMON (DEUTERONOMY 1, 6-7, 18, 31-32, 34)

Moses dies right before Israel enters the Promised Land, but he leaves them important reminders.

These are the words that Moses spoke to all Israel in the area beyond the Jordan, in the wilderness in the fortieth year: "Fear the LORD your God by keeping all his statutes and his commandments all the days of your life, and so that your days may be long.

"Listen, O Israel, and be conscientious about doing those things, so it may go well for you and so you may increase greatly in a land flowing with milk and honey, just as the LORD, the God of your fathers, promised you. Hear, O Israel! The LORD is our God. The LORD is one! Love the LORD your God with all your heart and with all your soul and with all your might. These words that I am commanding you today are to be on your heart. Teach them diligently to your children, and speak about them when you sit in your house and when you walk on the road, when you lie down and when you get up. Tie them as a sign on your wrists, and they will serve as symbols on your forehead. Write them on the doorposts of your house and on your gates.

"Do not go after other gods from among the gods of the peoples around you. If you do, the LORD your God will destroy you from the face of the earth. For you are a people that is holy to the LORD your God, because the LORD your God has chosen you to belong to him as a people that is his treasured possession, chosen from all the peoples that are on the face of the earth. The LORD has chosen you, not because you were more numerous than all the peoples. Actually you were the fewest of all the peoples. But because of the LORD's love for you and because he was keeping the oath that he swore to your fathers, that is why the LORD brought you out by a strong hand and redeemed you from the house of slavery, from the hand of Pharaoh king of Egypt.

"The LORD your God will raise up for you a prophet like me from among you, from your brother Israelites. Listen to him.

"The LORD has said to me, 'You will not cross over this Jordan.' The LORD your God himself will cross over before you. He will destroy those nations before you, and you will take possession of their land. Joshua is the one who will cross over before you, as the LORD promised. Be strong and courageous. Do not be afraid and do not be terrified before them, because the LORD your God is going with you. He will not abandon you and he will not forsake you."

Then Moses spoke the words of this song: "God is the Rock! Perfect is his work. He is a faithful God. He does no wrong. Righteous and upright is he."

On this same day the LORD spoke to Moses: "Go up to Mount Nebo and view the land of Canaan that I am giving to the people of Israel as a possession, and die on the mountain, because you broke faith with me at the waters of Meribah Kadesh. You may view the land from a distance, but you will not go into the land that I am giving to the people of Israel."

Moses went up to Mount Nebo and the LORD showed him the whole land. Moses, the servant of the LORD, died there in the land of Moab as the LORD had said. The LORD buried him, but no one knows his burial place to this day. Moses was one hundred twenty years old at his death. His eyes had not grown dim, and his vigor had not declined. Now Joshua was filled with the spirit of wisdom, so the people of Israel listened to him.

Never again has a prophet risen in Israel like Moses, who knew the LORD face to face. No other prophet ever displayed all of the mighty power and the great, awesome deeds that Moses did in the sight of all Israel.

Lord God, in your holy Word you have shown us
the Promised Land of heaven which you have prepared
for us. Make us strong and courageous as we face
the dangers around us until you bring us there.
Keep yourself always in front of your eyes and
keep your Word always on our heart. Amen.

42. APPROACHING JERICHO (JOSHUA 1-3)

Under Joshua's leadership, Israel begins to enter the Promised Land.

The LORD said to Joshua son of Nun, the attendant of Moses, "Moses my servant is dead. So prepare to go into the land that I am about to give to the people of Israel. Be careful to act according to the entire Law which my servant Moses commanded for you. Do not turn from it to the right or to the left, so that you may succeed wherever you go. Be strong and courageous. Do not be terrified and do not be overwhelmed, because the LORD your God is with you wherever you go."

Joshua son of Nun secretly sent two men to be spies. He said, "Go and look over the land and Jericho." So they set out and came to the house of a woman who was a prostitute. Her name was Rahab. They settled in to spend the night there.

It was reported to the king of Jericho: "Some men from the people of Israel came here tonight to spy on the land." So the king of Jericho sent messengers to Rahab. They said, "Bring out the men who came to you, because they have come to spy on the whole land."

Now the woman had taken the two men and hidden both of them. So she said, "Yes, the men did come to me, but I did not know where they were from. When the gate was about to be shut at dark, the men left. I do not know where the men went." But she had actually taken them up to the roof and concealed them. Then the men of Jericho went to pursue them.

Before the men lay down, Rahab came up to them on the roof. She said to the men, "I know that the LORD has given you the land. All the inhabitants of the land are melting in fear before you. Indeed, we have heard that the LORD dried up the waters of the Red Sea in front of you when you came out of Egypt. The LORD your God is God in the heavens above and on the earth below. So now, please swear to me by the LORD that since I have shown kindness to you, you in turn will show kindness to my father's house. Give me a trustworthy sign that you will deliver our lives from death."

The men said to her, "If you do not reveal what we are doing, when the LORD gives us the land, we will show mercy and faithfulness to you."

She let them down through the window with a rope, since her house was built into the city wall.

The men said to her, "Tie this bright red cord in the window through which you let us down, and gather your entire household into your house. Anyone who goes outside the doors of your house, his blood will be on his own head. Anyone who is with you in the house, his blood will be on our heads if a hand is laid on him. If you tell what we are doing, we will be free from the oath that you made us swear."

She said, "Just as your words say, so be it!" Then she sent them out, and they went away. She tied the bright red cord in the window.

Then the two men came to Joshua son of Nun. They reported to him everything that had happened to them. They said to Joshua, "The LORD has without doubt given the entire land into our hands. What's more, all the inhabitants of the land are melting in fear before us."

The LORD said to Joshua, "Today I will begin to exalt you in the eyes of all Israel so that they will know that just as I was with Moses, so I will be with you."

So the people set out from their tents to cross the Jordan, and the priests carrying the Ark of the Covenant went ahead of the people. As soon as the priests carrying the ark came to the Jordan, and as soon as their feet dipped into the edge of the water, the waters flowing down from upstream came to a standstill. So the people crossed the Jordan. The priests carrying the Ark of the Covenant of the LORD stood on dry ground in the middle of the Jordan while all Israel was crossing over on dry ground, until the entire nation had finished crossing the Jordan.

Lord God, you forgive and save all who believe in you,
regardless of who they are or where they are from
or what they have done. Thank you for making us
your people by faith, and bring the news of
your salvation to all people. Amen.

43. THE FALL OF JERICHO (JOSHUA 5-6)

God gives his people the victory over Jericho completely by his own power.

When Joshua was at Jericho, he looked up and saw a man was standing right there in front of him with a drawn sword. Joshua went to him and said, "Are you one of us or one of our enemies?"

The man said, "Neither! I have now come as the commander of the army of the LORD." Joshua fell with his face to the ground and worshipped. Then he said to him, "What does my Lord have to say to his servant?"

The commander of the army of the LORD said to Joshua, "Take your sandals off your feet, because the place where you are standing is holy." So Joshua did so.

The LORD said to Joshua, "See, I have given Jericho and its king into your hands even though they are strong warriors. March around the city one time. Do this for six days. On the seventh day you shall march around the city seven times with the priests blowing the ram's horns. When there is a long blast on the special horn of jubilee, all the people shall shout with a loud war cry. Then the wall of the city will collapse on itself."

So Joshua said to the people, "March around the city. The armed contingent shall march in front of the Ark of the LORD." The armed contingent was marching in front of the priests. Joshua had given the order, "Do not let a word go out of your mouth until the day I say to you, 'Shout!' Then you shall shout!" So he had the Ark of the LORD go around the city one time. Then they came back to the camp and spent the night there. They did this for six days.

Then on the seventh day, they marched around the city seven times, following the directions they had been given. It was only on the seventh day that they marched around the city seven times. Then on the seventh time, the priests blew the ram's horns, and Joshua said to the people, "Shout, because the LORD has given you the city! The city will be devoted to destruction. Only Rahab the prostitute will live—she along with all who are with her in the house—because she hid the agents whom we sent. Keep away from the things devoted to destruction, or you will make yourselves and the camp of Israel subject to destruction."

The priests blew the ram's horns. When the people heard the sound of the ram's horns, they shouted with a loud war cry. Then the wall collapsed on itself. So they captured the city. Then they applied the decree of destruction by the sword to everything that was in the city.

To the two men who had spied on the land Joshua said, "Go to the house of the prostitute and bring out the woman and everyone who belongs to her, just as you swore to her." So the young men who had acted as spies went and brought out Rahab and all her family members, and they settled them outside the camp of Israel.

But the city and everything in it they burned with fire.

Lord God, defeat your enemies and drive out all who would harm your people. Protect us from everyone that threatens us, and fulfill your promise to bring us safely home to you. Amen.

44. ACHAN'S SIN (JOSHUA 7-8)

When they do not follow God, Israel falters.

Achan took some of the devoted things, and the anger of the LORD burned against the people of Israel.

Joshua sent men from Jericho to Ai. He said to them, "Go up and spy on the land." So the men went up and spied on Ai.

They returned to Joshua and told him, "All the people do not need to go up. Let about two or three thousand men go up, and they can defeat Ai." So about three thousand men from among the people went up there, but they fled from the men of Ai. The men of Ai struck dead about thirty-six of them. So the hearts of the people melted and turned to water.

Then Joshua tore his clothes and fell down with his face to the ground in front of the Ark of the LORD. The LORD said to Joshua: "Why are you falling on your face? Israel has sinned! They have taken some of the devoted things. They have stolen! That is why the people of Israel are not able to stand before their enemies. I will not continue to be with you unless you destroy the devoted things from among you. The man who is caught with the devoted things is to be burned with fire—he and all that belongs to him."

Joshua had Israel come forward tribe by tribe. Achan was identified.

Joshua said to Achan, "Tell me what you did. Do not conceal it from me."

Achan answered Joshua, "It is true. I am the one who has sinned against the LORD, the God of Israel, and this is what I did: Among the plunder I saw an expensive robe, two hundred shekels of silver, and one wedge of gold. I coveted them and I took them. Now they are hidden in the ground inside my tent."

So Joshua sent agents. They ran to the tent, and there it was! They took them from the middle of the tent and brought them to Joshua and to all the people of Israel, where they poured them out before the LORD.

Then Joshua took Achan and the silver, the garment, and the wedge of gold, as well as everything that belonged to him. All Israel, led by Joshua, brought them up to the Valley of Achor.

Joshua said, "Why have you brought disaster on us? The LORD will bring disaster on you this day!"

Then all Israel stoned Achan to death. They also burned him with fire.

The LORD said to Joshua, "Do not be afraid. Do not be overwhelmed. Take with you the whole military force and go up to Ai. I have given Ai into your hand. You shall do to Ai and to its king just as you did to Jericho and to its king, but its plunder and its livestock you may take as spoils of war for yourselves. Point toward Ai with the javelin that is in your hand, because I will give Ai into your hand."

So Joshua reached out toward the city with the javelin. The ambush force quickly went into the city, took it, and quickly set it on fire. They struck the men of Ai until there was no one left, no survivor, no escapee. Joshua did not lower his hand that held the javelin until he had completely destroyed all the inhabitants of Ai. But the livestock and the plunder from that city the Israelites took as spoils of war for themselves, according to the word of the LORD that he had commanded Joshua.

Lord God, we have disobeyed your commands.
We have been greedy and loved possessions more
than you. Forgive our sins for Jesus's sake, and give us
hearts which love you above all things, using what
you have given us to serve you. Amen.

45. JOSHUA'S FAREWELL SERMON (JOSHUA 21, 23-24)

After the capture of Jericho and Ai Joshua led Israel in two great campaigns to the south and to the north. During these campaigns Israel defeats thirty-one kings and takes possession of the whole land, which is divided among the twelve tribes of Israel.

Israel takes possession of all the land under Joshua, and Joshua leaves them final instructions.

The LORD gave to Israel all of the land that he had sworn to give to their fathers. They took possession of it and they lived in it. The LORD gave them rest all around, according to all that he had sworn to their fathers. Not one person out of all their enemies had withstood them. The LORD had given all their enemies into their hands. Not one promise out of all the good promises that the LORD had promised to the house of Israel failed. They all came true!

When Joshua had grown old and advanced in years, Joshua summoned all Israel and said to them: "You yourselves have seen everything that the LORD your God has done for you. Yes, the LORD your God was fighting for you! See now, I have allotted to your tribes an inheritance. It extends from the Jordan to the Mediterranean Sea in the west. Hold fast to the LORD your God, just as you have been doing to this day.

"See now, I am about to go the way of all the earth, and you know with all your heart and with all your soul that not one promise out of all the good promises that the LORD your God promised you has failed. All of them have come true for you. Not one promise from him has failed. Now, therefore, fear the LORD and serve him wholeheartedly and faithfully. But if you see no benefit in serving the LORD, then choose for yourselves today whomever you will serve. But as for me and my household—we will serve the LORD!"

The people responded by saying, "We too will serve the LORD, because he is our God!"

Then Joshua dismissed the people, each one to his own inheritance.

After these events Joshua, the servant of the LORD, died at the age of one hundred ten years. They buried him in the territory of his inheritance, in Timnath Serah. Israel served the LORD all the days of Joshua and all the days of the elders who outlived Joshua and who had experienced every deed that the LORD had done for Israel.

Lord God, you have given us an eternal home in heaven.
Make our households ones which serve the Lord, listening
to and clinging to your Word and your promises. Amen.

ISRAEL DIVIDED AMONG THE TWELVE TRIBES

PART 3

THE JUDGES
(JUDGES AND 1 SAMUEL)

Even though God had kept his promise to give his people the land of Canaan, the people did not remain faithful to God. Time and time again they went after other gods. Time and time again their idolatry led to disaster as other nations oppressed them. Time and time again they turned back to God for help. Time and time again God sent them a judge, a deliverer, to rescue them. While these judges are very flawed people themselves, they give us little pictures of God's great deliverer, Jesus, sent to rescue his people from the oppression caused by their sin.

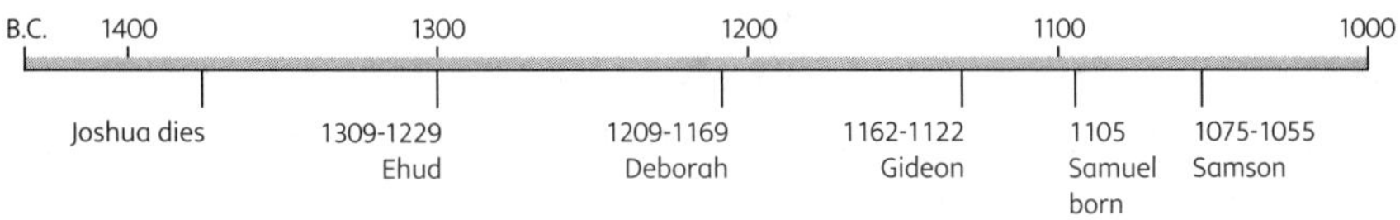

46. JUDGE EHUD (JUDGES 2-3)

After Joshua's death, Israel falls into apostasy. Then in repentance they call on the Lord. Then the Lord delivers them. Then they serve him for a while. Then, unfortunately, the cycle repeats and they fall back into apostasy.

After that whole generation had been gathered to their fathers, another generation arose after them, who did not know the LORD or the deeds that he had done for Israel. The people of Israel committed evil in the eyes of the LORD. They served the Baals, and they abandoned the LORD, the God of their fathers, who had brought them out of the land of Egypt. They went after other gods from among the gods of the peoples who were around them.

So the anger of the LORD burned against Israel, and he delivered them into the hand of raiders, who plundered them. He sold them into the hand of their enemies around them, and they were not able to stand up in the face of their enemies. Whenever the men of Israel went out, the hand of the LORD was against them to bring disaster on them, just as the LORD had said to them and just as the LORD had sworn to them. So they were greatly distressed.

Nevertheless, the LORD raised up judges, who saved them from the hand of those who plundered them, but they did not listen even to the judges! Instead, they prostituted themselves to other gods and bowed down to them. They quickly turned from the way in which their fathers, who had obeyed the commands of the LORD, had once walked. This generation did not act the same way their fathers had acted.

Whenever the LORD raised up a judge for them, the LORD was with that judge and saved them from their enemies during all the days of that judge, because the LORD had compassion when he heard their groaning under their tormenters and oppressors.

But then, after the death of the judge, Israel would turn back and become more corrupt than their fathers by going after other gods, by serving them, and by worshipping them. They refused to let go of their practices and their shameless ways.

So the LORD gave Eglon king of Moab power over Israel because they had committed evil in the eyes of the LORD.

Eglon attacked Israel and took possession of the City of Palms. So the people of Israel served Eglon king of Moab for eighteen years.

The people of Israel called out to the LORD, and the LORD raised up a deliverer for them. The deliverer was Ehud, who was left-handed.

The Israelites sent him with a tribute payment for Eglon king of Moab. Ehud made a double-edged sword for himself, about eighteen inches long, and he strapped it under his clothing on his right thigh.

Ehud presented the tribute payment to Eglon king of Moab, who was a very fat man. After Ehud had presented the tribute payment, he told the king, "I have a secret for you, O king!"

The king said, "Silence, everyone," so all his attendants left the room.

Ehud approached Eglon as Eglon was sitting in the cool upper chamber, all alone. Ehud said, "I have something from God for you." So Eglon stood up from the throne. Ehud reached out his left hand and took the sword that was on his right thigh and drove it into Eglon's belly. As the hilt went in after the blade, Eglon's fat closed behind the blade. Ehud did not draw the sword out from Eglon's belly. Ehud then went out, shut the doors behind him, and locked them. Then off he went!

When Eglon's servants came back, they were surprised to see that the doors of the upper chamber were locked. They said, "He must be using the toilet." They waited until the delay became embarrassing, but no one opened the doors. Finally they took the key and opened the door. And there he was. Their master was lying on the ground—dead!

While they delayed, Ehud had escaped to Seirah. When he arrived, the Israelites marched down from the hill country with Ehud leading the way. He said to them, "Follow me, because the Lord has given your enemies, the Moabites, into your hands." So they pursued and struck down about ten thousand men of Moab. Not one escaped. This is how Moab was humbled on that day under the hand of Israel, and the land was quiet for eighty years.

Lord God, when we turn our back on you and your Word and treat something else as if it were our god and somehow greater than you, bring us back to yourself. Deliver us from the oppression of sin which we bring on ourselves, and give us comfort and relief through the forgiveness we have in Jesus. Amen.

47. JUDGE DEBORAH (JUDGES 4-5)

God delivers his people through Deborah.

After Ehud died, once again the people of Israel committed evil in the eyes of the Lord. So the Lord sold them into the hand of Jabin king of Canaan. The commander of his army was Sisera. Again the people of Israel called out to the LORD, because Jabin had brutally oppressed the people of Israel for twenty years.

Deborah, a woman, a prophetess, was judging Israel at that time. The people of Israel would come to her for judgment.

She sent for Barak. She said to him, "The LORD, the God of Israel, has commanded, 'Go and march to Mount Tabor, and take with you ten thousand men. I will lure Sisera, commander of the army of Jabin, with his chariots and his horde, to you, and I will give him into your hand.' "

But Barak said to her, "If you go with me, I will go, but if you do not go with me, I will not go."

She answered, "All right. I will go with you, but because of the way you are going about it, the honor will not be yours. The LORD will sell Sisera into the hand of a woman." Then Deborah got up and went with Barak. Ten thousand men went up on foot, and Deborah also went up with him.

When Sisera was told that Barak had gone up to Mount Tabor, Sisera led out all his chariots (nine hundred iron chariots) and all the people who were with him to the stream Kishon.

Deborah said to Barak, "Get up! Today is the day that the LORD has given Sisera into your hands! Is not the LORD going ahead of you?" So Barak went down from Mount Tabor, and ten thousand men followed him.

The LORD threw Sisera, all his chariots, and all his troops into confusion with the sword of Barak. So Sisera got down from his chariot and fled on foot. Barak pursued the chariots and the troops. Sisera's whole army fell by the edge of the sword. Not a single man was left.

Sisera meanwhile fled on foot to the tent of Jael, the wife of Heber, because there was peace between Jabin and Heber. Jael came out to meet Sisera and said to him, "This way, my lord. Come here to me! Do not be afraid." So he went into her tent, and she hid him with a covering. She gave him some milk to drink.

He said to her, "Stand at the door of the tent, and if anyone comes and asks you, 'Is there anyone here?' say, 'No.' "

But then Jael took a tent stake, and gripping a hammer in her hand, she came to Sisera quietly and drove the stake through his temple, right through into the ground. Sisera had been fast asleep, exhausted—now he was dead!

When Barak arrived in pursuit of Sisera, Jael came out to meet him. She said to him, "Come in, and I will show you the man you are looking for." So he went with her, and there he was. Sisera was lying there dead, with the tent stake through his temple.

So on that day God subdued Jabin king of Canaan before the people of Israel, and the hand of the Israelites pressed harder and harder against Jabin king of Canaan, until they cut down Jabin king of Canaan.

Deborah and Barak sang this song: "Most blessed among women is Jael, the wife of Heber. She hammered Sisera. She shattered and pierced his temple. Thus may all your enemies perish, LORD. But those who love him will be like the sun coming forth in its strength."

Then the land was quiet for forty years.

Lord God, protect your people from all who would harm us. Give us the strength to boldly trust your promise that we have the eternal victory in your Son, Jesus. Amen.

48. JUDGE GIDEON (JUDGES 6-8)

God delivers his people through Gideon.

Again the people of Israel committed evil in the eyes of the LORD, and the LORD gave them into the hand of Midian for seven years. The hand of Midian was heavy upon Israel. Whenever Israel planted crops, Midian would ruin the crops. So Israel was laid low because of Midian, and the people of Israel cried out to the LORD.

Gideon was threshing wheat in the winepress, to hide it from the Midianites. The Angel of the LORD said to him, "The LORD is with you, mighty warrior. You will deliver Israel from the hand of Midian. Have I not sent you?"

Gideon said to God, "If you will save Israel by my hand as you have said, look here, I am placing a fleece of wool on the threshing floor. If dew is found only on the fleece, but all the ground around it is dry, then I will know that you will deliver Israel by my hand, as you have said." And that is exactly what happened! Gideon got up early in the morning and squeezed the fleece and wrung out dew from it—a bowlful of water!

But again Gideon said to God, "Please let me conduct just one more test with the fleece: This time let the fleece be dry, but on the ground all around let there be dew." That night God did that very thing! Only the fleece was dry, and there was dew on the ground all around.

Then Gideon and all the people who were with him set out. The Midianite camp was north of him.

The LORD said to Gideon, "There are too many people with you for me to give Midian into your hands. In that case, Israel would glorify itself at my expense and say, 'My own hand has delivered me.' So then, make an announcement for the people to hear, 'Whoever is trembling with fear, let him return.'" Twenty-two thousand people turned and left. Only ten thousand remained.

The LORD said to Gideon, "There are still too many people."

Gideon led the people down to the water, and the LORD said to Gideon, "Place everyone who laps water with his tongue, as a dog would lap, to one side. Place everyone who kneels down to drink on the other side." The number of those who lapped was three hundred men, while all the rest knelt down to drink water. The LORD said, "With the three hundred men who lapped I will deliver you, and I will give Midian into your hand. As for all the other people, let each man go back to his place."

The men who had been chosen took provisions in hand, along with their ram's horns, but Gideon sent every other Israelite man back to his own tent. He kept only the three hundred men. The camp of Midian lay below him in the valley.

That night the LORD said to Gideon, "Get up, go down against the Midianite camp, for I have given them into your hand."

Gideon said, "Get up, because the LORD has given the camp of Midian into your hand." He divided the three hundred men into three companies. He placed a ram's horn into the hand of each one of them, as well as empty jars with torches inside them. Then he said to them, "When I and all the men who are with me blow our ram's horns, the rest of you around the whole camp also blow your ram's horns and shout, 'For the LORD and for Gideon!'"

Gideon and the one hundred men with him went to the edge of the camp just after the Midianites had posted the guards. Gideon and his men blew their ram's horns and shattered the jars that were in their hands. All three companies blew their ram's horns and broke their jars. They held the torches in their left hands, and in their right hands they held the ram's horns that they were to blow. They shouted, "A sword for the LORD and for Gideon!" The whole Midianite camp started running, raised the alarm, and fled. The LORD turned the sword of each Midianite against the person next to him throughout the whole camp.

The Midianite army fled. Then all the men of Israel pursued Midian. In this way Midian was humbled before the people of Israel, and they did not raise their heads again. The land was quiet for forty years during the days of Gideon.

Lord God, it is not by our strength or might that we succeed, but by yours alone. Just as you alone have already won our victory over sin, be our sure defender and deliver us from all the evil in the world around us. Amen.

49. THE BIRTH OF JUDGE SAMSON (JUDGES 13-14)

God delivers his people through Samson.

The people of Israel again committed evil in the eyes of the LORD, so the LORD gave them into the hands of the Philistines for forty years.

Now there was a man whose name was Manoah. His wife was barren. The Angel of the LORD appeared and said to her, "Listen, you will become pregnant and give birth to a son. Do not drink wine and do not eat anything unclean. No razor is to touch his head, for the boy will be a Nazirite. He will deliver Israel from the Philistines."

Manoah said to the Angel of the LORD, "What is your name?"

The Angel of the LORD said to him, "Why do you ask about my name? It is wonderful."

Manoah said to his wife, "We will certainly die, because we have seen God."

But his wife said to him, "If the LORD wanted to kill us, he would not have let us hear this message."

The woman gave birth to a son, and she named him Samson. The boy grew, and the LORD blessed him. The Spirit of the LORD began to stir him.

Samson saw a young woman who was a Philistine. He told his father and his mother, "Get her for me as a wife."

But his father and mother said to him, "Is there not a suitable woman among all our people that you must go to take a wife from the uncircumcised Philistines?"

Samson insisted to his father, "No, get her for me—because, in my eyes, she is the right one."

His father and mother did not know that this was from the LORD, who was seeking an opportunity to confront the Philistines, who were ruling Israel at this time.

Samson went down to Timnah, and suddenly a young lion came roaring to meet him. At that moment the Spirit of the LORD powerfully rushed upon Samson, and he tore the young lion in two with his bare hands. But he did not tell his father or his mother what he had done. He went down and spoke to the woman.

After some days when he returned to take her as his wife, he turned aside to look at the carcass of the lion, and to his surprise there was a swarm of bees and honey in the carcass of the lion! So Samson scraped out some honey with his hands, and he ate it as he walked along.

Samson held a wedding feast there. The Philistines selected thirty young men to serve as attendants. Samson said to them, "Allow me to tell you a riddle. If you figure out the solution within the seven days of the feast, I will give you thirty linen garments. But if you are not able to tell me, you will give me thirty linen garments."

So they said to him, "Tell your riddle!"

Samson said to them, "Out of the eater comes something to eat. Out of the strong comes something sweet."

But they were not able to solve the riddle for three days.

Then, on the fourth day, they said to the Samson's wife, "Persuade your husband so that you can tell us the solution to the riddle, or we will set you on fire."

Samson's wife cried on his shoulder and said, "You certainly hate me and do not love me. You told a riddle to my people, but you have not explained it to me!"

Samson said to her, "Look! I have not told even my father and my mother, and I should tell you?" But she cried to him for the rest of the seven-day feast. Finally on the seventh day he told her, because she kept nagging him. Then she explained the riddle to the Philistine men.

So the men of the town said to Samson on the seventh day, just before the sun went down: "What is sweeter than honey, and what is stronger than a lion?"

But he said to them, "If you had not plowed with my heifer, you would not have solved my riddle."

Then the Spirit of the LORD rushed upon him, and he went down to Ashkelon and struck down thirty men from there. Then he took the clothing that he stripped off them and gave the clothing to the men who had solved the riddle. Meanwhile the Philistines gave Samson's wife to one of the men who had attended him.

Lord God, you have given us a special Savior,
one free from sin, one who is wonderful,
one who is God himself. May we find our strength
and our hope and our future in him. Amen.

50. THE DEATH OF JUDGE SAMSON (JUDGES 15–16)

God delivers his people through Samson, even as Samson dies.

Samson captured three hundred foxes, tied the foxes tail to tail, and fastened a torch between each pair of tails. He set fire to the torches and released the foxes into the standing grain of the Philistines. He burned up the grain, the vineyards, and the olive groves.

The Philistines came to meet him. But then the Spirit of the LORD rushed upon Samson. Samson found the fresh jawbone of a donkey. With it he struck down a thousand men.

Sometime after that, Samson fell in love with a woman whose name was Delilah. The Philistines approached her and said, "Persuade him to reveal where his great strength comes from. Each of us will give you eleven hundred pieces of silver."

So Delilah said to Samson, "Please tell me what the source of your great strength is."

Samson answered her, "If anyone ties me up with seven new bow-strings, I will be like any other man."

So the Philistines brought her seven new bowstrings, and she tied him up with them. She had men hiding in the room waiting to ambush Samson, and she said to him, "Philistines are upon you, Samson!" But he snapped the bowstrings as easily as thread.

Then Delilah said to Samson, "Look! You made a fool of me and told me lies. Now please tell me how you can be tied up."

Samson answered her, "Actually, if anyone ties me up with new ropes, I will be like any other man."

So Delilah took new ropes and tied him up with them. Then she said to him, "Philistines are upon you, Samson!" There were men hiding in the room waiting to ambush Samson, but he tore the ropes off his arms as if they were thread.

Delilah said to Samson, "So far you have made a fool of me and told me lies. Tell me how you may be tied up!"

So he said to her, "If you weave my hair, I will be as weak as any other man."

After she had waited for him to fall asleep, Delilah took the locks of his hair and wove them. She said to him, "Philistines are upon you, Samson!" But Samson woke up from his sleep and pulled out the pin.

She said to him, "How can you say, 'I love you,' when your heart is not with me? This makes three times you have made a fool of me." She nagged him until he was sick of it.

Finally he told her everything. He said, "A razor has never touched my head, because I have been a Nazirite. If I am ever shaved, my strength will desert me, and I will be like any other man."

When Delilah saw that he told her everything, she sent for the Philistines, saying, "Come back one more time."

The Philistines came up to her and brought the silver in their hands. Delilah let Samson fall asleep on her lap. Then she called for a man and shaved off the seven locks of his head. She said, "Philistines are upon you, Samson!" He awoke from his sleep, but he did not realize that the Lord had left him.

The Philistines seized him, gouged out his eyes, and restrained him with bronze shackles.

But the hair on his head began to grow after it had been shaved.

Meanwhile, the Philistines gathered to make a great sacrifice to their god Dagon and to celebrate. They said, "Our god has given our enemy Samson into our hands."

Samson served as their entertainment. They made Samson stand between the pillars. The building was full of Philistines. On the roof were about three thousand more men and women watching Samson.

Samson called out to the Lord. He said, "Lord God, give me strength, I pray, this one more time. Let me get revenge on the Philistines." Samson then grasped the two central pillars supporting the building. He leaned against them, one with his right hand and one with his left. Samson said, "Let me die with the Philistines." He pushed with all his strength, and the building fell upon all the people who were inside.

The Philistines he put to death when he died were more numerous than those he had put to death during his lifetime. He had served as judge of Israel for twenty years.

Lord God, your Son is our mighty Savior.
By his death he struck our enemies of sin and death
with a strong and fatal blow. Keep us faithful to him
as these enemies try to lure us into temptation. Amen.

51. RUTH BECOMES AN ANCESTOR OF JESUS (RUTH)

During the time of the judges a woman from another country becomes a believer in the true God and part of the family line of the Savior.

A famine occurred in the land. So a man left Bethlehem to stay in Moab. The man's name was Elimelek, his wife's name was Naomi, and the names of his sons were Mahlon and Kilion.

But Elimelek, Naomi's husband, died, so she was left with her two sons. They married Moabite wives, Orpah and Ruth. The sons also died. So the woman was left without her children and husband.

Naomi set out to return to Judah. Her daughters-in-law said to her, "We will return with you."

Naomi said, "Turn back. Why should you go with me?"

Then Orpah kissed her mother-in-law, but Ruth would not let her go.

Naomi said, "Look, your sister-in-law has returned to her people. Go back! Follow your sister-in-law."

But Ruth said, "Do not urge me to abandon you. Wherever you go, I will go. Your people will be my people, and your God will be my God. May the LORD punish me if anything but death separates me from you." So Naomi returned with Ruth the Moabite, her daughter-in-law. They entered Bethlehem.

Now Naomi had a relative, a wealthy man. His name was Boaz. Ruth went out and gleaned in the grain fields. It happened that she was in the field that belonged to Boaz. Boaz asked his servant, "Whose young woman is this?"

The servant answered, "She is the Moabite woman who returned with Naomi."

Then Boaz said to Ruth, "Do not go off to some other field."

Ruth said to Boaz, "Why have I found favor in your eyes, so that you acknowledge me even though I am a foreigner?"

Boaz replied to her, "I have been fully informed about all that you did for your mother-in-law and how you left behind your homeland and came to a people you did not know."

Boaz ordered his workers, "Pull out some stalks and drop them on purpose so she can glean them."

So Ruth gleaned in the field until evening. Naomi said to her, "Where did you glean today?"

She told her, "The man in whose field I worked today is Boaz."

Then Naomi said, "This man is related to us; he is one of our family's redeemers." So Ruth stuck close to Boaz's young women and gleaned.

Naomi said to her, "Boaz will be winnowing barley tonight. Go down to the threshing floor. When he lies down, go lie down there." So she went down to the threshing floor.

Boaz went to lie down at the edge of the grain pile. Then Ruth came up to him quietly and lay down there. In the middle of the night, the man turned over, and there was a woman lying on his legs!

He said, "Who are you?"

She said, "I am Ruth. Spread your robe over your servant, for you are a family redeemer."

Then he said, "May you be blessed by the LORD, my daughter! I will do everything you are asking. I am a family redeemer, but there is a redeemer who is closer than I am. Spend the night here. If in the morning he acts as a redeemer for you, good. But if he does not want to, then I will."

So she lay down at his feet until morning. Before it was light, Ruth came back to her mother-in-law.

Boaz went up to the city gate. Boaz said to the redeemer, "Naomi is putting up for sale the land that belongs to Elimelek. I thought I should call it to your attention. If you wish to redeem it, redeem it. But if you do not wish to, declare that to me."

The man said, "I will indeed redeem it."

Then Boaz said, "On the day that you acquire the field from the hand of Naomi, I will acquire from Ruth the Moabite the means to perpetuate the name of the deceased on his inheritance."

Then the redeemer said, "I am not able to redeem it for myself, or I would ruin my inheritance. Acquire it for yourself!"

Then Boaz acquired from Naomi everything that belonged to Elimelek. Boaz took Ruth, and she became his wife. The LORD enabled her to conceive, and she bore a son. Naomi took the boy and put him on her lap. They named him Obed. He became the father of Jesse, the father of David.

Lord God, we praise you for giving us your Son,
the perfect husband of your church, the Family Redeemer
who bought us back from sin, and the Savior of people
from every tribe and nation. Amen.

52. THE BIRTH OF SAMUEL (1 SAMUEL 1-2)

During the time of the judges God gives Hannah a child, Samuel, who would grow up to be the last judge of Israel.

There was a man whose name was Elkanah. He had two wives. The name of one was Hannah, and the name of the other was Peninnah. Peninnah had children, but Hannah had no children.

Every year this man went up from his city to worship and to sacrifice to the LORD of Armies at Shiloh. The two sons of Eli, Hophni and Phinehas, were serving there as priests of the LORD.

Year after year, when Hannah went up to the LORD's house, her rival taunted her, so Hannah would weep and would not eat. Her husband Elkanah said to her, "Hannah, why are you weeping? Why don't you eat? Why is your heart so sad? Am I not better to you than ten sons?"

Once, when Hannah got up after they had finished eating and drinking in Shiloh, Eli the priest was sitting on his chair by the doorpost of the LORD's temple. Hannah's spirit was very distressed, and as she prayed to the LORD, she sobbed and shed many tears. She made a vow and said, "O LORD of Armies, if you will give your servant a male child, then I will give him to the LORD all the days of his life, and no razor shall ever touch his head."

As she continued praying before the LORD, Eli was watching her mouth. Hannah was speaking silently from her heart. Although her lips were moving, her voice could not be heard. So Eli thought she was drunk, and he said to her, "How long are you going to be drunk? Get away from your wine!"

Hannah replied, "No, my lord, I am a woman with a very troubled spirit. I have not been drinking wine. I have poured out my soul to the LORD."

Then Eli answered, "Go in peace, and may the God of Israel give you what you have asked for." So the woman went on her way. She ate, and her face no longer looked sad.

The LORD remembered her. Hannah conceived and gave birth to a son. She named him Samuel.

When she had weaned him, she brought him to the house of the LORD in Shiloh. The boy was still young. They presented the child to Eli. She said, "Excuse me, my lord. I am the woman who stood here next to you, praying to the LORD. I prayed for this child, and the LORD has granted me what I asked for. So now I have also dedicated him to the LORD. As long as he lives he is dedicated to the LORD." So he worshipped the LORD there.

Hannah prayed and said, "My heart rejoices in the LORD! There is no one holy like the LORD. The LORD puts to death, and he makes alive. He brings down to the grave, and he raises up. The LORD makes some poor, and he makes others wealthy. He brings some low. He raises others up. The LORD will judge the ends of the earth. He will give strength to his king. He will raise up the horn of his anointed one."

Then Elkanah went home to Ramah, but the young boy served the LORD as an attendant to Eli the priest.

Lord God, you have raised up your lowly people
and exalted us high in Christ. Grant that all
Christian parents dedicate their children to you,
raising them in your Word. Amen.

53. THE CALL OF SAMUEL (1 SAMUEL 2-7)

God calls young Samuel to be a prophet and gives him a difficult message to share.

The sons of Eli were wicked scoundrels. Eli said to them, "Why do you do such things? I keep hearing from all these people about your evil actions." But they did not listen to their father.

Eli's eyes had begun to grow dim, so that he could not see. Once when Samuel was lying down in the LORD's temple, the LORD called Samuel. Samuel ran to Eli, and said, "I am here. You called me."

Eli said, "I did not call. Lie down again." So he went and lay down.

Then the LORD called once more, "Samuel!"

So Samuel got up and went to Eli and said, "I am here. You called me."

He answered, "I did not call. Lie down again."

Then the LORD called Samuel the third time. So he got up and went to Eli and said, "I am here. You called me."

Then Eli realized that the LORD was calling the boy. So Eli said to Samuel, "Go, lie down, and if he calls you, say, 'Speak, LORD, for your servant is listening.' "

So Samuel went and lay down again. The LORD called as he had the other times, "Samuel!"

Then Samuel said, "Speak, for your servant is listening."

The LORD said to Samuel, "Look, I am going to do something against Eli. I am going to judge his house forever because of their guilty behavior. This will happen because his sons brought a curse on themselves, and he did not restrain them."

Samuel was afraid to tell Eli about the vision. But Eli said, "What is the message that he has spoken to you? Please do not hide it from me." So Samuel told him everything and hid nothing from him.

Eli said, "He is the LORD. Let him do whatever is good in his eyes."

Samuel continued to grow, and the LORD was with him. The LORD let none of his words fall to the ground. So Samuel was confirmed as a prophet of the LORD.

In those days Israel went out to meet the Philistines for battle. The elders of Israel said, "Let us bring the Ark of the Covenant here so it may save us from our enemies."

So the people brought the Ark of the Covenant. The Philistines fought, and Israel was defeated. A very great slaughter took place. God's ark was taken, and the two sons of Eli died.

A man ran from the battlefield and told Eli, "Israel has fled from the Philistines, and there has also been a great slaughter among the people. Your two sons are dead, and God's ark has been captured." When he mentioned God's ark, Eli fell backwards off his seat, broke his neck, and died. He had judged Israel forty years.

After the Philistines had captured God's ark, they brought it into the house of Dagon and set it beside Dagon. When the people got up early the next day, there was Dagon—fallen facedown to the ground in front of the Ark of the LORD! So they took Dagon and set him in his place again. When they got up early the following morning, it had happened again! There was Dagon, fallen facedown in front of the Ark of the LORD. The head of Dagon and both of his hands were broken off and were lying on the threshold. Then the LORD's hand struck them with tumors. When the men saw what was taking place, they said, "The Ark of the God of Israel must not stay with us. Let it go back to its own place, so that it does not kill us and our people."

So they took two cows, hitched them to the cart, and put the Ark of the LORD on the cart. The cows headed straight along the highway to the border. The men of Kiriath Jearim came, took the Ark of the LORD, and the ark stayed in Kiriath Jearim for twenty years. The Philistines were subdued, and they no longer came into the territory of Israel all the days of Samuel.

Lord God, give us a heart which says, "Speak, Lord,
for your servant is listening," and which eagerly reads
your Word, believes everything you tell us there,
and shares that message with others. Amen.

PART 4

THE UNITED MONARCHY
(1 AND 2 SAMUEL, 1 KINGS)
(SELECTIONS FROM PSALMS, PROVERBS, SONG OF SOLOMON, AND ECCLESIASTES)

Three kings ruled over all of Israel. The first king, Saul, was rejected by God because he did not follow God. The second king, David, was a man after God's own heart, yet his sin too caused trouble for all Israel and for David's own family. The third king, David's son Solomon, was most wise, and yet his heart was led into idolatry. However, through these men, and at times in spite of these men, God was really the one ruling as king over his people. He took care of them and promised them a descendent of David and Solomon who would be the perfect eternal king for God's people.

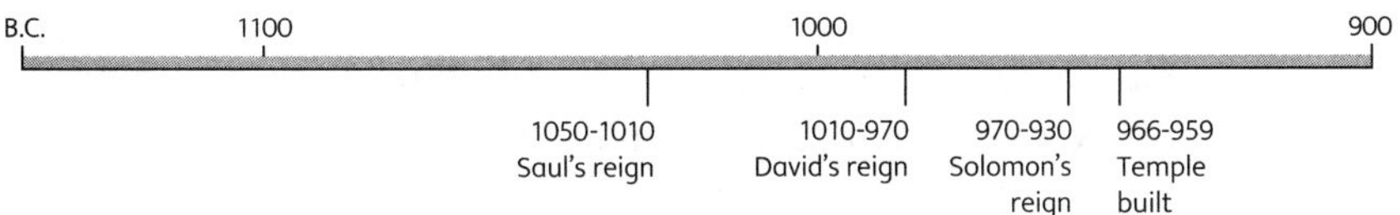

54. SAUL, THE FIRST KING OF ISRAEL (1 SAMUEL 8-11, 13)

Saul becomes the first king of Israel.

When Samuel was old, the elders of Israel said to him, "Appoint a king for us." But in Samuel's eyes their request was evil, so Samuel prayed to the LORD.

The LORD said to Samuel, "Listen to the people. It is not you they have rejected. I am the one they have rejected as king over them. Nevertheless, warn them strongly and show them what the king will do."

Samuel told the people: "This is what the king will do: He will take your sons, daughters, fields, vineyards, servants, and donkeys, and you will become his servants. In that day you will cry out because of your king whom you have chosen for yourselves, but the LORD will not answer you."

But the people refused to listen to Samuel. Instead they said, "No, we want a king, so that we also can be like all the nations, and our king can lead us out to fight our battles."

The LORD said to Samuel, "Appoint a king for them."

There was a man from the tribe of Benjamin whose name was Saul. The donkeys of Saul's father Kish were lost, so Kish said to Saul, "Go look for the donkeys." So Saul traveled through the land but did not find them.

When they had come to the land of Zuph, Saul said to the young man who was with him, "Let's go back."

But the young man said to him, "Wait! In this city there is a man of God. Maybe he can tell us which way we should go." So they went up to the city.

Just as they were coming into the city, there was Samuel coming toward them. When Samuel saw Saul, the LORD told him, "There, that is the man! He will exercise authority over my people."

Then Saul approached Samuel and said, "Please tell me where the seer's house is."

Samuel answered Saul, "I am the seer. You men are to eat with me today." So Saul ate with Samuel.

Samuel said to Saul, "Tell the young man to go on ahead of us." The young man went on ahead.

Then Samuel took a flask of oil, poured it on Saul's head, and said, "Hasn't the LORD anointed you to be ruler over his inheritance? When you leave me today, you will meet two men. They will tell you, 'The donkeys that you have been looking for have been found.' Go down to Gilgal. Wait until I come to you. I will let you know what to do."

As Saul was turning to leave, God gave him a changed heart.

Samuel called the people together at Mizpah. He said, "This is what the LORD, the God of Israel, says: 'I brought Israel up out of Egypt.' But you have rejected your God and have said to him, 'You must set a king over us.' Line up by tribes."

The tribe of Benjamin was chosen. Then the clan of the Matrites was chosen. Then Saul was chosen, but when they looked for him, he could not be found. They asked the LORD, "Has the man arrived here yet?"

The LORD answered, "He has hidden himself among the baggage."

So they ran and brought him from there. When he stood among the people, he was a head taller than any of the people. All the people shouted, "Long live the king!"

Nahash the Ammonite set up camp against Jabesh Gilead. Nahash said to them, "I will gouge out the right eye of every one of you in order to dishonor all Israel." When Saul heard those words, the Spirit of God rushed upon him. He took a yoke of oxen and cut them to pieces and sent the pieces throughout Israel in the hands of messengers who said, "This is what will be done to the oxen of anyone who does not turn out." The dread of the LORD fell on the people, and they turned out as one man. The men of Israel totaled three hundred and thirty thousand.

On the next day, Saul broke into the middle of the camp of the Ammonites and struck them down. Those who survived were so scattered that no two of them were left together.

So all the people went to Gilgal, and they made Saul king in the presence of the LORD there at Gilgal. Saul was thirty years old when he became king, and he reigned over Israel forty-two years.

Lord God, through your Word enable us to serve
and worship you alone as our true king.
Give our nation leaders who serve with selfless
and upright hearts for the good of our land. Amen.

55. SAUL'S REIGN TAKES A BAD TURN (1 SAMUEL 13-15)

Saul had started his reign following the Lord, but he does not continue to do so, and so God rejects him as king.

The Philistines assembled to fight against Israel with soldiers as numerous as the sand on the seashore. When the men of Israel saw that they were in trouble, the people hid in caves. Saul remained in Gilgal, and all the people with him were shaking with fear. He waited seven days, but Samuel did not come, and the people were starting to scatter. So Saul presented the burnt offering.

No sooner had he finished, than Samuel arrived. Samuel said, "What have you done?"

Saul said, "I saw that the people were scattering, so I forced myself to offer the burnt offering."

Samuel said to Saul, "You have not kept the command which the LORD your God gave to you. The LORD would have established your kingship forever. But now your kingship will not continue. The LORD has sought for himself a man after his own heart and appointed him to be ruler over his people."

Saul's son Jonathan said to the young man who carried his armor, "Let's go over to the Philistines' garrison."

So both of them showed themselves to the Philistines, and the Philistines said, "Come up to us."

So Jonathan climbed up on his hands and his feet, and his armor bearer followed him. Jonathan and his armor bearer killed about twenty men.

Panic spread throughout the entire Philistine army. The earth quaked, and there was a panic sent by God. Saul and all the troops who were with him assembled and joined the battle. There they saw the panicked Philistines striking each other with their swords. So the LORD saved Israel that day.

Samuel said to Saul, "This is what the LORD of Armies says: Go and strike Amalek. Devote everything they have to destruction. Kill men, women, oxen, sheep, camels, and donkeys."

So Saul summoned the troops and struck the Amalekites. He took Agag, the king of the Amalekites, alive, and he devoted all the people to destruction with the sword. But Saul spared Agag and the best of the sheep, cattle, and everything else that was good, because they were not willing to devote them to destruction.

Then the word of the LORD came to Samuel, "I regret that I have set up Saul to be king, for he has turned back from following me." Samuel cried to the LORD all night.

Samuel came to Saul. Samuel said, "What does this mean—this bleating of sheep in my ears and the lowing of cattle that I hear?"

Saul said, "The people spared the best of the sheep and the cattle to sacrifice to the LORD your God."

Then Samuel said to Saul, "Stop right there! Though you were insignificant, the LORD anointed you king over Israel. Then the LORD said,

'Go, and devote the Amalekites to destruction.' Why didn't you listen to the LORD?"

Saul said to Samuel, "But I have obeyed the LORD. I have captured Agag king of Amalek, and I have completely destroyed the Amalekites. But the people took some of the plunder to sacrifice to the LORD."

Samuel said, "Does the LORD take as much pleasure in burnt offerings and sacrifices as in obedience? Know this! To obey is better than sacrifice, and to pay attention is better than the fat of rams. Because you have rejected the word of the LORD, he has also rejected you as king. I will not return with you."

As Samuel turned to leave, Saul grabbed the edge of his robe, and it tore. Samuel said to him, "The LORD has torn the kingdom of Israel away from you today, and he has given it to a neighbor of yours who is better than you."

Then Samuel said, "Bring Agag here to me!" Agag came to him. Then Samuel cut Agag to pieces.

Then Samuel went to Ramah, and Saul went up to his house at Gibeah. Until the day of his death Samuel never again came to see Saul. Samuel did, however, mourn for Saul, but the LORD regretted that he had made Saul king over Israel.

Lord God, you have given us so many blessings in Jesus, seating us in the heavenly places in him. Keep us from ever turning from the faith and throwing all your good gifts away. Help us to trust in you and to follow your will throughout all our life. Amen.

56. DAVID ANOINTED KING (1 SAMUEL 16)

God selects David to be the new king and to begin a new dynasty.

The LORD said to Samuel, "How long will you mourn for Saul, since I have rejected him as king over Israel? Fill your horn with oil and go. I am sending you to Jesse of Bethlehem, for I see a king for myself among his sons. Take a heifer with you and say, 'I have come to sacrifice to the LORD.' Invite Jesse to the sacrifice. You are to anoint for me the person that I point out to you."

So Samuel did what the LORD had told him to do and went to Bethlehem. He consecrated Jesse and his sons and invited them to the sacrifice.

When they had come, he looked at Eliab and said, "Certainly this is the LORD's anointed."

But the LORD said to Samuel, "Do not look at his appearance, or at how tall he is, because I have rejected him. For the LORD does not look at things the way man does. For man looks at the outward appearance, but the LORD looks at the heart."

Then Jesse called Abinadab and had him pass in front of Samuel. But Samuel said, "The LORD has not chosen this one either."

Then Jesse had Shammah pass by. But Samuel said, "The LORD has not chosen this one either."

Jesse had seven of his sons pass before Samuel. Samuel said to Jesse, "The LORD has not chosen any of these. Is that all of the young men?"

Jesse said, "There still is the youngest, but he is tending the sheep."

Samuel said to Jesse, "Send for him."

He sent and brought him in. David was good-looking. The LORD said, "Get up! Anoint him, for this is the one."

So Samuel took the horn of oil and anointed him in the presence of his brothers. The Spirit of the LORD rushed on David with power from that day forward. After that Samuel set out and returned to Ramah.

The Spirit of the LORD departed from Saul, and an evil spirit from the LORD tormented him.

So Saul's servants said to him, "Please let your servants seek out a man who is skilled at playing the lyre. Then when the evil spirit from God is on you, he will play the lyre, and you will feel better."

So Saul said to his servants, "Find a man who can play well and bring him to me."

Then one of the young attendants replied, "I have seen a son of Jesse from Bethlehem who is a skillful player. He is a strong, brave man, fit for war. He shows good judgment in what he says and is a handsome man. And the LORD is with him."

So Saul sent messengers to Jesse and said, "Send me your son David." David came to Saul and stood before him. Saul loved him, and David became his armor bearer. Whenever the spirit from God came over Saul, David would take the lyre in his hand and play. So Saul would be soothed and feel better, and the evil spirit would depart from him.

Lord God, you do not look at things the way people look at them. You look at the heart. Give us hearts of faith, which trust in your Son as our only Savior. Give us hearts which love and serve you. As your people anointed with the Holy Spirit, always keep us safely within the kingdom of forgiveness, protection, and peace, the kingdom of David's son, our King Jesus. Amen.

57. DAVID AND GOLIATH (1 SAMUEL 17)

God's anointed champion saves his people from their enemy.

Now the Philistines gathered their troops for battle. Saul and the men of Israel also gathered together. The Philistines took up a position on one side of the valley, and the Israelites stationed themselves on the other side of the valley.

A challenger who represented the Philistines came out. He was named Goliath of Gath. He was nine feet, six inches tall. He had a bronze helmet and wore scaled body armor made of more than one hundred pounds of bronze. He would shout to the armies of Israel, "Choose a man to represent you. If he is able to kill me, we will be your servants. But if I kill him, you will become our servants." When Saul and all Israel heard those words, they were terrified.

Now the three oldest sons of Jesse had accompanied Saul to the battleground. Jesse said to David, "See how your brothers are doing."

David arrived at the camp just as Israel and the Philistines were lining up for battle. David saw Goliath coming up out of the ranks of the Philistines. He repeated his usual words, and David heard them. David spoke to the men near him. He asked, "Who is this Philistine who dares to defy the troops of the living God?"

Eliab, David's oldest brother, heard David. Eliab was very angry with David. He said, "Why have you come down? I know your pride."

David turned toward another person and asked the same thing again. The soldiers heard what David said. They reported it to Saul, and he sent for David.

David said to Saul, "Do not let anyone lose heart because of this Philistine! Your servant will go and fight him."

But Saul said, "You cannot go against this Philistine. You are just a boy, and he has been a warrior since he was a youth."

David said, "Your servant has been taking care of his father's sheep. When a lion or a bear took a lamb from the flock, I went after it, struck it, and rescued the lamb out of its mouth. Your servant struck both the lion and the bear. This Philistine will be like one of them, since he has defied the ranks of the living God. The LORD, who delivered me from the lion and the bear, will deliver me from this Philistine."

Saul said to David, "Go then!" Saul dressed David in his own gear. He put a bronze helmet and scaled body armor on him. David tried to walk around in them, since he had never trained with this kind of equipment before.

David said to Saul, "I cannot go in these, because I have never trained with them." So David took them off.

Then David picked five smooth stones out of the stream bed and put them into his bag. He took his sling in his hand and approached the Philistine.

When the Philistine got a good look at David, he despised him, because David was just a boy.

The Philistine said to David, "Am I a dog, that you come against me with sticks? I will give your flesh to the birds."

Then David said to the Philistine, "You come against me with a sword, but I come against you in the name of the LORD of Armies, the God of the ranks of Israel. Today the LORD will hand you over to me. I will strike you down and cut off your head. Today I will give the dead bodies of the army of the Philistines to the birds. Then all the earth will know that there is a God in Israel, and all those gathered here will know that the LORD does not save with sword and spear, for the battle belongs to the LORD, and he will deliver you into our hand."

The Philistine started advancing to attack David. David took a stone, slung it, and struck the Philistine on the forehead. The stone sank into his forehead, and he fell facedown to the ground. David ran, stood over the Philistine, took hold of his sword, drew it out of its sheath, and cut off his head with it.

When the Philistines saw that their champion was dead, they fled. The men of Israel pursued the Philistines all the way to Ekron.

Lord God, our enemies, sin, death, and the Devil,
are stronger than us, but you are stronger than they are.
Protect us with your mighty power, for you have
already given us the eternal victory through your
great champion, Jesus Christ, who by his death
has slain all your people's enemies. Amen.

58. PSALM 23

David, himself a shepherd, knows that the Lord is his shepherd and ours.

A psalm by David.

The Lord is my shepherd.
I lack nothing.
He causes me to lie down in green pastures.
He leads me beside quiet waters.
He restores my soul.
He guides me in paths of righteousness for his name's sake.
Even though I walk through the valley of the shadow of death,
I will fear no evil, for you are with me.
Your rod and your staff, they comfort me.
You set a table for me in the sight of my foes.
You drench my head with oil.
My cup is overflowing.
Surely goodness and mercy will pursue me all the days of my life,
and I will live in the house of the Lord forever.

Lord God, you have given us your Son,
our Good Shepherd, who laid down his life for us
and who picked it back up for us. As our shepherd,
take care of us and be with us as we walk through
the valley of the shadow of death. Defend us
with your Word until you bring us to live
in your house forever. Amen.

59. DAVID, JONATHAN, AND SAUL (1 SAMUEL 18-20)

As David's popularity grows, Saul tries to eliminate David, but Saul's son Jonathan shows friendship to David.

As David was returning from striking down the Philistine, women came out from all the cities of Israel and sang: "Saul has slain his thousands, and David his ten thousands."

Saul became furious, because he resented this saying. He said, "What more can be given to him but the kingship?" So Saul eyed David suspiciously from that day on.

On the next day, an evil spirit overcame Saul. David, lyre in hand, was playing as he did day by day. Saul, spear in hand, hurled the spear, because he thought, "I will pin David to the wall!" But David escaped from his presence twice.

Saul was afraid of David, because the LORD was with David, but he had departed from Saul. Saul sent David away from his court and made him a commander. David led the army out to battle and back again. When Saul saw that David was so successful, he was even more afraid of him. All Israel loved David.

Saul told his officials that they should kill David. But Saul's son Jonathan had great admiration for David. Jonathan told David, "My father Saul wants to kill you. So be careful."

David said to Jonathan, "Tomorrow I am expected to dine with the king, but let me go hide in the countryside. If your father misses me, say, 'David urged me to excuse him so that he could run to Bethlehem.' If he says, 'That is fine,' your servant will be at peace. But if it really displeases him, then you will know that he is planning evil."

Jonathan made a covenant with the house of David. Then Jonathan had David repeat the oath, for he loved him as he loved his own life.

Jonathan said to him, "On the day after tomorrow go by the stone named Ezel. I will shoot three arrows off to the side of it, as if I were shooting at a target. I will send the boy out and say, 'Go and find the arrows!' If I yell to the boy, 'The arrows are closer this way,' then you can come to me, because you are safe. But if I yell to the boy, 'The arrows are farther out,' then go on your way."

So David hid in the countryside. When the king sat down to eat his meal, David's place was empty.

Saul asked Jonathan, "Why didn't the son of Jesse come to the meal?"

Jonathan answered Saul, "David begged me for permission to go to Bethlehem."

Then Saul's anger burned against Jonathan, and he said to him, "I know that you have chosen the son of Jesse! Send for him and bring him to me, because he must surely die!"

Jonathan answered Saul, "Why? What has he done?"

Saul threw his spear at him to hit him. So Jonathan knew that his father was determined to put David to death.

In the morning Jonathan went out into the field at the time he had set with David. He took a young servant boy with him. He said to his boy,

"Run out and find the arrows that I shoot." As the boy ran, Jonathan shot an arrow beyond him. When the boy reached the area where Jonathan's arrow had landed, Jonathan yelled to the boy, "Isn't the arrow farther out from you?" As soon as the boy was gone, David got up from the south side of the mound. He fell down with his face to the ground and bowed three times. They kissed one another and wept together, but David wept the most. Jonathan said to David, "Go in peace, because we have both sworn in the LORD's name." David got up and left, and Jonathan went back into the city.

Lord God, thank you for the friends you have given us to be our companions and to comfort us as we go through life. Above all we thank you for the friend and savior we have in Jesus. Amen.

60. DAVID SPARES SAUL (1 SAMUEL 24, 26)

Saul tries to kill David, but David does not try to kill Saul.

Saul was told, "David is in the Wilderness of En Gedi." Then Saul took three thousand men and went to hunt for David.

Saul went into a cave to relieve himself. At that time David and his men were far back in the cave.

David's men said to him, "Look, this is the day the LORD told you about when he said, 'I will deliver your enemy into your hand.'" So David got up and cut off the edge of Saul's robe without being noticed.

Afterward, David had a guilty conscience, because he had cut off the edge of Saul's robe. He said to his men, "May I be cursed if I stretch out my hand against him, since he is the LORD's anointed." David restrained his men and did not allow them to attack Saul.

Saul left the cave and went on his way. David got up and followed him out of the cave and shouted to him, "My lord, why do you listen to the words of people who say, 'Watch out! David is seeking to harm you'? This very day you have seen with your own eyes how the LORD delivered you into my hand in the cave. Some urged me to kill you, but I spared you, because I said, 'I will not stretch out my hand against the LORD's anointed.' Take a good look at the piece of your robe that is here in my hand. Since I cut off the edge of your robe but did not kill you, you can be sure that I do not have any evil intent. I have not sinned against you, even though you keep hunting for me to take my life."

Saul broke down and wept. He said to David, "You are more righteous than I, for you have treated me well, but I have treated you badly. Now I know without a doubt that you will become king, and that the kingship over Israel will be established in your hand." Saul went back home, but David and his men went up to the stronghold.

The Ziphites came to Saul and said, "David is hiding at the Hill of Hakilah." So Saul set out and went down with three thousand men to search for David.

When David heard that Saul had come into the wilderness after him, he moved out and came to the place where Saul had set up camp. During the night David and Abishai went through the people in the camp, and they saw that Saul lay sleeping inside the defensive perimeter of the camp, with his spear stuck into the ground beside his head. Abner and the rest of the men were lying all around him.

Then Abishai said to David, "God has delivered your enemy into your hand today. Please let me strike him and pin him to the ground with my spear. One time, that's all I'll need. I won't need to strike him a second time."

But David said, "Do not destroy him, for who can stretch out his hand against the LORD's anointed and be guiltless? Take the spear that is beside his head and the jar of water, and we will go."

So David took the spear and the jar of water that were next to Saul's head, and they left. No one saw them. They were all sound asleep, because a deep sleep from the LORD had fallen on them.

Then David moved over across from the camp and stood on the top of the mountain some distance away. David shouted to Abner, "Abner, why haven't you kept watch over the king? For someone came into the camp to destroy the king. Look around! Where are the king's spear and the jar of water that was next to his head?"

Saul recognized David's voice and said, "Is this your voice, David?"

David said, "It is, my lord. Why does my lord pursue his servant? What have I done?"

Then Saul said, "I have sinned. I will not harm you anymore."

So David went on his way, and Saul returned to his own place.

Lord God, when others wrong us, we often get angry and even desire revenge. Give us hearts which forgive all wrongs done against us, just as you have forgiven us for Jesus' sake for all our wrongs done against you. Amen.

61. PSALM 1

This psalm, perhaps written by David, contrasts the good ways of the believer with the bad ways of the unbeliever.

How blessed is the man
who does not walk by the advice of the wicked.
He does not stand on the path with sinners,
and he does not sit in a meeting with mockers.
But his delight is in the teaching of the Lord,
and on his teaching he meditates day and night.
He is like a tree planted beside streams of water,
which yields its fruit in season, and its leaves do not wither.
Everything he does prospers.
Not so the wicked!
No, they are like chaff which the wind blows away.
Therefore the wicked will not stand in the judgment,
nor sinners in the assembly of the righteous.
Yes, the Lord approves of the way of the righteous,
but the way of the wicked will perish.

Lord God, your way is good and best. Thank you for making us your people by faith. Keep us on your path, keep us in your Word, keep us for yourself forever. Amen.

62. SAUL DIES AND DAVID BECOMES KING (1 SAMUEL 31; 2 SAMUEL 1-2, 5-6)

The dynasty of Saul comes to a tragic end, and the new dynasty of David begins.

The Philistines were fighting against Israel, and the men of Israel fled from the Philistines. The Philistines were closing in on Saul and his sons. They struck down Jonathan, Abinadab, and Malkishua, the sons of Saul. The attack directed at Saul was fierce. The archers targeted him and hit him, and he was seriously wounded.

Then Saul said to his armor bearer, "Draw your sword and run me through with it, so that these fellows cannot come and abuse me!"

But his armor bearer would not do it, because he was too afraid. So Saul took his own sword and fell on it. When his armor bearer saw that Saul was dead, he too fell on his sword. So Saul died together with his three sons, his armor bearer, and all his men, all on that same day.

After the death of Saul, a man from Saul's camp approached David. The man said, "Saul and Jonathan have died." David mourned Saul and Jonathan.

All the tribes of Israel came to David. They said, "Look, we are your flesh and blood. Day after day, even when Saul was king, you were the one leading Israel out to battle and back again. And you are the one to whom the LORD said, 'You will shepherd my people Israel. You will become leader over Israel.'" So all the elders of Israel anointed David king over Israel. David was thirty years old when he became king, and he ruled as king for forty years.

The king and his men went to Jerusalem against the Jebusites, who were living in the land. David captured the stronghold. David lived in the stronghold and called it the City of David. David built up all sides of the stronghold. David kept getting greater and greater, because the LORD, the God of Armies, was with him. David knew that the LORD had established him as king over Israel and had lifted up his kingdom for the sake of his people Israel.

The Philistines heard that David had been anointed king over Israel. So all the Philistines went up in search of David. David asked the LORD, "Shall I go up against the Philistines? Will you give them into my hand?"

The LORD said to David, "Go up, because I will certainly give the Philistines into your hand."

So David went to Baal Perazim and defeated them there. He said, "The LORD has broken through my enemies before me like a wall of water."

The Philistines came up again and spread out in the Valley of Rephaim. David inquired of the LORD, who said, "Do not go directly at them. Go around to their rear." So David did as the LORD commanded him. He struck the Philistines from Gibeon all the way to Gezer.

Then David and all the people who were with him set out to bring up the Ark of God. They transported the Ark of God on a new cart. David and all the house of Israel were celebrating before the LORD with all kinds of instruments. With rejoicing David went and brought up the Ark of God to the City of David. They brought the Ark of the LORD and set it in its place inside the tent that David had pitched for it, and David offered burnt offerings and fellowship offerings before the LORD.

Lord God, even in difficult times, remind us that
our times are in your hands, and keep us relying on you.
Bring us one day into your heavenly kingdom, where you
have a place prepared for us by our Savior Jesus. Amen.

63. THE LORD'S COVENANT WITH DAVID (2 SAMUEL 7)

God promises King David an eternal dynasty, culminating in the promised Savior.

The king said to Nathan the prophet, "Look, I live in a house of cedar, but the Ark of God sits under tent curtains."

That night the word of the LORD came to Nathan. He said, "Go and tell my servant David: Are you the one to build a house for me? I have not lived in a house from the day I brought the people of Israel up from Egypt until today. I have been moving around in the Tent and the Dwelling. Did I ever ask them, 'Why have you not built a house of cedar for me?'

"Also say this to my servant David: I took you from the pasture, from following sheep, to be ruler over my people Israel. I have been with you wherever you went. I have cut off all your enemies from before you. I will make your reputation great, like that of the great ones on the earth. I will set up a place for my people Israel. I will give you rest from all your enemies.

"The LORD also declares to you that the LORD himself will make a house for you. When your days are completed, I will raise up after you your seed, who will come from your own body. I will establish his kingdom. He will build a house for my name, and I will establish the throne of his kingdom forever. I will be his father, and he will be my son. When he sins, I will discipline him with a rod used by men and with blows of the sons of men. My faithful mercy will not depart from him as I removed it from Saul. Your house will stand firm, and your kingdom will endure forever before you. Your throne will be established forever."

Nathan told David all the words that had been revealed in this vision.

Then King David went and sat before the LORD and said. "Who am I, LORD God? And what is my house that you have brought me to this point? Yet this was a small thing in your eyes, LORD God. You have also spoken about the house of your servant for a long time into the future. What more can David say to you? Because of your word and according to the plan of your heart you have carried out this great thing in order to make your servant aware of it. LORD God, you are God. Your words are truth. You have promised this good thing to your servant. Now therefore, may it please you to bless the house of your servant, so that it will endure forever in your presence. For you, LORD God, have spoken. With your blessing the house of your servant will be blessed forever."

Lord God, nothing in this world lasts forever, but your Son's throne does. We praise you for the kingdom of forgiveness that King Jesus established for us by his cross. May he continue to rule in us through his Word and bring us one day into his kingdom of glory. Amen.

64. PSALM 110

David writes a psalm about the eternal priesthood and kingship of his descendent and Lord, Jesus.

By David. A psalm.

The decree of the LORD to my lord:
"Sit at my right hand until I make your enemies a footstool
under your feet."
The LORD will stretch out your strong scepter from Zion.
Rule in the midst of your enemies.
Your people will be willing on the day of your power.
In majesty of holiness, the dew of your youth will be yours.
The LORD has sworn and will not change his mind:
"You are a priest forever, in the manner of Melchizedek."
The Lord is at your right hand.
He will crush kings on the day of his wrath.
He will judge the nations.

Lord God, your Son, our Savior Jesus, is enthroned at your right hand. Accept us for the sake of his sacrifice and bless all your believing people through his powerful reign. Amen.

65. DAVID AND BATHSHEBA (2 SAMUEL 11-12)

David falls into sin, but is eventually restored to repentance.

Springtime arrived, the time when kings go out to war. David sent Joab out with his officers and with all Israel. But David stayed in Jerusalem.

One evening David was walking around on the roof of the palace. He saw a woman bathing. The woman was very good looking. David sent to inquire about the woman, and he was told, "Isn't this Bathsheba, the wife of Uriah the Hittite?"

David sent messengers and brought her. She came to him, and he lay down with her.

The woman became pregnant, so she told David, "I am pregnant."

David sent a message to Joab, "Send Uriah the Hittite to me." So Joab sent Uriah to David.

David asked how the war was going. Then David said to Uriah, "Go to your house."

But Uriah slept at the entrance to the palace with the servants. He did not go to his house.

David said to Uriah, "Why didn't you go to your house?"

Uriah said to David, "My master Joab and the servants of my master are camped on the bare ground in the open countryside. Should I go to my house to lie down with my wife?"

Then David got him drunk. But in the evening he slept where the servants were. He did not go to his house.

In the morning David wrote a letter to Joab, and he sent it in the hands of Uriah. In the letter he wrote, "Station Uriah opposite the fiercest fighting. Then withdraw so he will be struck down and die."

So Joab assigned Uriah to a place where he knew that the enemy's strongest warriors were. The men of the city came out and fought against Joab, and Uriah the Hittite died.

The wife of Uriah heard that her husband was dead, so she mourned for her husband. When her mourning was completed, David brought her to his house, and she became his wife. She gave birth to a son for him. But what David had done was evil in the eyes of the LORD.

So the LORD sent Nathan to David. He came and told him: "There were two men. One was rich and one poor. The rich man had a large number of flocks. The poor man did not own anything except one little ewe lamb that was like a daughter to him. When a traveler came to the rich man, the rich man was unwilling to take an animal from his flock. So he took the lamb from the poor man and prepared it for the man who had come to him."

David's anger flared up. He said to Nathan, "As the LORD lives, the man who has done this is as good as dead."

Nathan told David, "You are the man. This is what the LORD, the God of Israel, says: I anointed you king over Israel. I gave you the house of Israel. If this was too little, I would have added even more. Why have you despised the word of the LORD by doing evil in his eyes? You have struck down Uriah the Hittite with the sword. You have taken his wife as your own wife. So now the sword will not depart from your house forever."

David said to Nathan, "I have sinned against the LORD."

Nathan said to David, "The LORD has put away your sin. You will not die. Nevertheless, the child that is born to you shall surely die." Then Nathan went to his house.

The child became sick. David sought the LORD's mercy for the child. David fasted and spent the night lying on the ground. He would not eat food.

On the seventh day the child died. Then David got up from the ground and changed his clothes. He went to the house of the LORD and worshipped. He then asked for food and ate.

His servants said to him, "What are you doing? While the child was alive, you fasted and wept. But when the child died, you got up and ate food."

He said, "While the child was alive, I said, 'Who knows? Will the LORD be gracious to me and let my child live?' Now he has died. Am I able to return him to life again?"

David comforted Bathsheba. He went to her and she gave birth to a son. David called him Solomon.

Lord God, keep us from rebelling against you
and harboring sin in our hearts. Use your law
to show us our many sins, and then always comfort
our hearts with your wonderful gospel that
Jesus has taken our sin away. Amen.

66. PSALM 51

After his sin with Bathsheba, David expresses his sorrow over his sinfulness and his trust in God's forgiveness.

A psalm by David, when Nathan the prophet came to him
after he had gone to Bathsheba.

Be gracious to me, God, according to your mercy.
Blot out my acts of rebellion according to the greatness
of your compassion.
Scrub me clean from my guilt.
Purify me from my sin.
For I admit my rebellious acts.
My sin is always in front of me.
Against you, you only, have I sinned.
I have done this evil in your eyes.
So you are justified when you sentence me.
You are blameless when you judge.

Certainly, I was guilty when I was born.
I was sinful when my mother conceived me.
Remove my sin with hyssop, and I will be clean.
Wash me, and I will be whiter than snow.
Let me hear joy and gladness.
Let the bones you have crushed celebrate.
Hide your face from my sins.
Blot out all my guilty deeds.
Create in me a pure heart, O God.
Renew an unwavering spirit within me.
Do not cast me from your presence.
Do not take your Holy Spirit from me.
Restore to me the joy of your salvation.
Sustain me with a willing spirit.
I will teach rebels your ways,
and sinners will turn to you.
Deliver me from bloodshed, O God, the God who saves me.
My tongue will shout for joy about your righteousness.
Lord, open my lips,
and my mouth will declare your praise.
For you do not delight in sacrifice,
or I would give it.
You do not take pleasure in burnt offerings.
The sacrifices God wants are a broken spirit.
A broken and crushed heart, O God, you will not despise.

Lord God, I admit my sin. I have been guilty
my whole life. But you have washed me clean in Jesus.
Create in me a new heart which, moved
by your forgiveness, serves only you. Amen.

67. ABSALOM'S REBELLION (2 SAMUEL 13-19)

The consequence that Nathan had foretold concerning David's sin—that the sword would not depart from his family—comes true as David's son Absalom rebels against him.

David's son Absalom was handsome. There was not a blemish in him. When he shaved the hair on his head, the hair weighed five pounds.

Absalom would stand beside the gatehouse. Absalom would call out to every man who had a legal issue and say, "Your claims are valid, but there is no one from the king to listen to you. If only someone would make me judge. Then everyone who has a legal issue could come to me and I would give him justice." In this way Absalom stole the hearts of the men of Israel.

Absalom sent agents throughout all the tribes of Israel saying, "Absalom is king." Two hundred men from Jerusalem who had been invited went along with Absalom. Absalom summoned David's advisor, Ahithophel, to come. The conspiracy gained strength as more and more people were going over to Absalom.

A messenger came to David who said, "The hearts of the men of Israel are following Absalom."

So David said to his servants, "We must flee, or we will not escape." So the king set out with his entire household.

David went up along the ascent to the top of the Mount of Olives. David had been told, "Ahithophel is among the conspirators." So David said, "Please, LORD, make the advice of Ahithophel foolish."

David arrived at the summit. Hushai was there to meet him. David said to him, "Return to the city and say to Absalom, 'Let me be your servant, O King.' Then you will defeat the advice of Ahithophel for me." Hushai went to the city.

Absalom arrived at Jerusalem. Ahithophel was with him. When Hushai came to Absalom, Hushai said to Absalom, "Long live the king!"

Absalom said, "Why didn't you go with your friend?"

Hushai said, "No. The person whom all the men of Israel have chosen—this is the one I will be with."

Absalom said to Ahithophel, "Give us your advice. What should we do?"

Ahithophel said, "Let me pursue David tonight. I will come upon him when he is tired and weak. All the people with him will flee. Then I will strike down only the king." Ahithophel's plan seemed good to all the elders of Israel.

But Absalom said, "Call Hushai. Let us also hear what he has to say." So Hushai came to Absalom, and Absalom said to him, "This is what Ahithophel has said. Shall we do it?"

Hushai said to Absalom, "This time the advice Ahithophel has given is not good. You know your father and his men. They are fierce warriors. I advise you to gather all Israel and personally lead them into battle."

Absalom and all the men of Israel said, "The advice of Hushai is better than the advice of Ahithophel."

The LORD had arranged to defeat the good advice of Ahithophel, so that the LORD could bring disaster upon Absalom.

David organized the troops with him under the command of Joab, Abishai, and Ittai. The king gave orders: "Act gently with Absalom."

The troops went out to confront Israel. The battle took place in the forest. The men of Israel were defeated there by the followers of David. There was a great slaughter.

Absalom encountered the forces of David. As Absalom was riding on his mule, the mule went under a large terebinth tree, and Absalom's head caught in the terebinth. He was caught and the mule kept going.

A man noticed Absalom and told Joab. Joab took three spears and thrust them into the heart of Absalom and killed him.

Joab told a Cushite, "Go tell the king."

The Cushite arrived and said, "The LORD has delivered you from all who rose up against you."

The king asked the Cushite, "Is Absalom safe?"

The Cushite said, "May the enemies of my lord the king be like that young man."

The king wept and said, "My son Absalom! I wish I had died instead of you."

Joab came to the king and said, "You have put to shame all who today have saved your life. You have demonstrated clearly today that your followers are nothing to you. Go speak to the hearts of your servants. For if you do not go out, not a man will remain with you."

So the king took his seat by the gate. All the people came into the presence of the king. David turned the hearts of all the men of Judah as if they were one man.

Lord God, in arrogance we have many times rebelled against you and your commands, and we have brought the consequences of sin upon ourselves. Forgive us our sins, and do not treat us as our sins deserve. Spare us for the sake of our true eternal King, our Savior Jesus. Amen.

68. PSALM 22

David writes a psalm about the suffering and triumph of the coming Savior.

A psalm by David.

My God, my God, why have you forsaken me?
My groaning words do nothing to save me.

My God, I call out by day, but you do not answer.
I call out by night, but there is no relief for me.
I am a worm and not a man,
scorned by men and despised by the people.
All who see me mock me. They sneer.
They shake their heads.
They say, "Trust in the LORD."
"Let the LORD deliver him.
"Let him rescue him, if he delights in him."
Many bulls surround me.
Strong bulls from Bashan encircle me.
Enemies open their mouths wide against me,
like a lion which tears its prey and roars.
Like water I am poured out.
All my bones are pulled apart.
My heart has become like wax.
It has melted in the middle of my chest.
My strength is dried up like broken pottery,
and my tongue is stuck to the roof of my mouth.
You lay me in the dust of death.
For dogs have surrounded me.
A band of evil men has encircled me.
They have pierced my hands and my feet.
I can count all my bones.
They stare and gloat over me.
They divide my garments among them.
For my clothing they cast lots.
But you, O LORD, do not be distant.
O my Strength, come quickly to help me.
Deliver my life from the sword,
my only life from the power of the dog.
Save me from the mouth of the lion.
From the horns of the wild oxen answer me.
I will declare your name to my brothers.
In the middle of the congregation I will praise you.
You who fear the LORD, praise him!
All you descendants of Jacob, honor him!
Stand in awe of him, all you descendants of Israel!
For he has not despised nor detested the affliction of the afflicted.
He has not hidden his face from him,
but when he cried to him, he heard.

You are the source of my praise in the great congregation.
I will fulfill my vows in the presence of those who fear him.
The poor will eat and be satisfied.
Those who seek him will praise the LORD
—may he live in your hearts forever!
All the ends of the earth will remember and turn to the LORD,
and all the families of the nations will bow down before you.
For the kingdom belongs to the LORD,
and he rules over the nations.
All the rich of the earth will eat and bow down.
All who go down to the dust will kneel before him
—those who cannot keep themselves alive.
Descendants will serve him.
For generations people will be told about the Lord.
They will come and proclaim his righteousness to a people
yet to be born
—because he has done it.

Lord God, you sent your Son to suffer and be abandoned and to do it all for me. When I feel alone and rejected, comfort me with the glory that Jesus has won for me after this life. Amen.

69. SOLOMON'S WISDOM (1 KINGS 2-4)

David's dynasty continues as his son Solomon becomes king—a very wise one.

The day of David's death was approaching, so he gave the following commands to his son Solomon: "Be strong and act like a man! Fulfill your obligations to the LORD your God. Walk in his ways."

David rested with his fathers and was buried in the City of David. David was king over Israel for forty years.

Solomon was seated on the throne of his father David.

Solomon made a marriage alliance with Pharaoh king of Egypt. He married Pharaoh's daughter.

The LORD appeared to Solomon in Gibeon in a dream at night. God said, "Ask for whatever you want me to give you."

Solomon said, "You have shown great mercy and faithfulness to my father David. Now you have made your servant king in the place of my father David, but I am a little child. I do not know how to go out or come in. And your servant is among your people whom you have chosen, a great people, who cannot be counted or numbered because they are so many. Now give to your servant a perceptive heart to judge your people, to discern between good and evil."

In the eyes of the LORD Solomon's request was good. So God said to him, "Because you have asked for this, and you have not asked for a long life, nor have you asked for riches, nor have you asked for the life of your enemies, but you have asked for discernment, therefore I will act according your words. Yes, I will give you a wise and discerning heart, so that there has never been anyone like you before, nor will anyone like you rise up after you. In addition, I will give you what you have not asked for: such riches and glory so that there will not be anyone like you among the other kings throughout all your days. If you walk in my ways, I will give you a long life."

Then Solomon woke up and realized it was a dream.

Later, two prostitutes came and stood before the king.

One woman said, "This woman and I live in the same house. I gave birth. Three days after I gave birth, this woman also gave birth. One night this woman's son died because she lay on top of him. Then she got up in the middle of the night and took my son from beside me while I was sleeping. She laid him next to her, and her dead son she laid next to me. When I got up, my son was dead! But when I examined him closely in the morning, I saw it was not my son!"

But the other woman said, "No! The living child is really my son, and your son is the dead one!"

But the first one kept saying, "No! Your son is really the dead one, and my son is the living one!"

The king said "Bring me a sword. Cut the living child in two, and give half to this woman and half to that woman."

But the woman to whom the living child belonged said, "Give her the living child. Please don't kill him."

But the other woman said, "He will be neither mine nor yours. Cut him in two!"

The king answered, "Give the living child to the first woman, and do not kill him. She is his mother."

All Israel heard about the judgment which the king had rendered. They were filled with awe in his presence, because they saw that God's wisdom was in him to administer justice.

God gave Solomon wisdom and very great understanding and breadth of knowledge like sand on the seashore. He was wiser than any man. His name was known in all the surrounding nations. He spoke three thousand proverbs, and his songs numbered one thousand and five. He spoke about trees, animals, birds, reptiles, and fish. From all the earth people came to listen to his wisdom.

Lord God, through your Word give us discerning hearts
which know right from wrong, and give us the wisdom
to live in a way which is pleasing in your sight. Amen.

70. THE PROVERBS OF SOLOMON (PROVERBS 1, 3, 10-13, 15-16, 18-20, 22, 27, 29, 31)

Solomon wrote down many wise and practical sayings.

The proverbs of Solomon.

To learn wisdom and discipline, to understand sayings
that give insight.
A wise person should listen, and he will increase learning.
The fear of the LORD is the beginning of knowledge,
but stubborn fools despise wisdom and discipline.
Listen, my son, to your father's discipline,
and do not forsake your mother's teaching.
My son, if sinners lure you, do not go along with them.
Trust in the LORD with all your heart,
and do not rely on your own understanding.
In all your ways acknowledge him,
and he will make your paths straight.
Honor the LORD with your wealth,
with the firstfruits from your entire harvest.
Then your barns will be filled to capacity,
and your wine vats will overflow with fresh wine.
Do not reject the LORD's discipline, my son,
and do not despise his warning,
because the LORD warns the one he loves
as a father warns a son with whom he is pleased.
Hatred stirs up a quarrel, but love covers all sins.
Dishonest scales are disgusting to the LORD,
but an accurate weight wins his approval.

With his mouth the godless person destroys his neighbor,
but righteous people are rescued by knowledge.
Through the blessing of upright citizens, a city is raised up,
but by the mouth of the wicked, it is torn down.
A person who lacks sense despises his neighbor,
but an understanding person keeps silent.
A gossip goes around betraying secrets,
but a trustworthy spirit keeps a matter confidential.
Lying lips are disgusting to the LORD,
but those who act truthfully gain his favor.
A person who withholds his rod hates his son,
but one who loves him administers discipline promptly.
Better a little with the fear of the LORD than great wealth
with turmoil.
The LORD is far away from the wicked,
but he hears the prayer of the righteous.
All of a person's ways are pure in his own eyes,
but the LORD weighs motives.
Commit what you do to the LORD, and your plans will be established.
A person's heart plans his way,
but the LORD makes his steps secure.
Pride goes before destruction,
and a haughty spirit precedes a fall.
Better to share a humble spirit with the oppressed
than to share stolen goods with the haughty.
A fool's mouth is his destruction,
and his lips are a trap for his soul.
Before destruction a man's heart is proud,
but humility comes before honor.
Better to be a poor person who walks in his integrity
than one with perverse lips who is a fool.
Zeal without knowledge is certainly not good,
and a person who acts hastily sins.
A person who keeps a command preserves his life.
One who despises his ways will die.
Wine is a mocker, and beer is a brawler.
Whoever is intoxicated by them is not wise.
Many people claim to be loyal,
but who can find a trustworthy man?
Who can say, "I have purified my heart.
I am cleansed from my sinfulness"?

A good name is worth more than great wealth.
Respect is worth more than silver and gold.
Dedicate a child to the way he should go,
and even when he becomes old, he will not turn away from it.
Do not boast about tomorrow,
because you do not know what a day may produce.
Let someone else praise you, not your own mouth
—a stranger, not your own lips.
Have you seen a person who is hasty with his words?
There is more hope for a fool than for him.
Speak up for those who cannot speak.
Speak for the rights of all those who are defenseless.
Who can find a wife with strong character?
Her value is greater than that of gems.
Charm is deceptive, and beauty is vapor that vanishes,
but a woman who fears the LORD should be praised.

Lord God, fearing, loving, and trusting in you is where all wisdom is found. Through your Word teach us how to live lives which please you and which show our faith in Jesus. Amen.

71. SOLOMON'S TEMPLE (1 KINGS 6-8)

Solomon builds a temple for the LORD.

Solomon began to build the house for the LORD. The house was ninety feet long, thirty feet wide, and forty-five feet high. Only stones that had been finished at the quarry were used in the building. No hammer or chisel or any other iron tool was heard in the building. Solomon covered the house with cedar.

Thirty feet from the back wall of the building he built a wall of cedar boards from the floor to the ceiling. He built this wall inside the building to create an inner sanctuary, the Most Holy Place, as a place to set the Ark of the Covenant. The inner sanctuary was thirty feet long, thirty feet wide, and thirty feet high, and he overlaid it with pure gold. He also overlaid the cedar altar with gold.

For the inner sanctuary he made two cherubim of olive wood. Each one was fifteen feet high. He overlaid the cherubim with gold.

He built the inner courtyard with three courses of cut stone and one course of cedar beams.

Solomon made all the furnishings that were in the house of the LORD: the gold altar and the table for the Bread of the Presence, which was also gold. The lampstands were placed in front of the inner room of the sanctuary. They also were made of pure gold, as were the flowers, the lamps, the tongs, the basins, the snuffers, the sprinkling bowls, the small dishes, the fire pans, and the hinges, both for the doors of the inner sanctuary, that is, the Most Holy Place, and also for the doors of the front room. In this way all the work that King Solomon did for the house of the LORD was finished. Solomon brought the things which David his father had dedicated, the silver, the gold, and the vessels, and put them in the treasuries of the house of the LORD.

Then the priests brought the Ark of the Covenant of the LORD to its place in the Most Holy Place under the wings of the cherubim. When the priests came out from the Holy Place, the Glory of the LORD had filled the House of the LORD.

Then Solomon stood in front of the altar in the presence of the whole congregation of Israel and spread out his hands toward heaven. He said: "O LORD, God of Israel, there is no God like you. You have kept the word which you spoke to my father David.

"But will God really dwell on the earth? In truth, the heavens, even the highest heaven, cannot contain you. How much less this house which I have built! But turn your face toward the prayer of your servant and toward his plea for mercy. O LORD my God, listen to the cry and the prayer which your servant offers before you today.

"Let your eyes be open toward this house night and day, toward this place where you said, 'My Name will be there,' to hear the prayer which your servant offers toward this place. When you hear the plea for mercy of your servant and of your people Israel which they pray toward this place, then hear and forgive.

"Also for the foreigner who comes from a distant land because of your Name, hear and do everything for which the foreigner cries out to you, so that all the peoples of the earth may know your Name and fear you, just as your people Israel do, and because they know that your Name is proclaimed in this house which I have built."

When Solomon finished offering these prayers, he blessed the whole congregation of Israel with a loud voice: "Blessed be the LORD, who has given rest to his people Israel, just as he said he would. Not one word has failed from all his good words which he spoke through Moses his servant. May the LORD our God be with us, just as he was with our fathers. May he never leave us or abandon us. May he turn our hearts to him, to walk in all his ways."

Then the king and all Israel with him offered sacrifices and dedicated the House of the LORD. Then they went home, and their hearts were glad because of all the good which the LORD had done for his servant David and for his people Israel.

Lord God, dwell in us through your Word and make our hearts and minds your temple. Cast out all our sin, and purify us through the cleansing blood of your Son, who dwelled among us to make us your holy people. Amen.

72. SOLOMON'S GLORY AND HIS SIN (1 KINGS 10-11)

Despite his great wisdom, Solomon falls into great sin, and so the kingdom would be divided.

The Queen of Sheba heard about Solomon's fame, so she came to test him with hard questions. Solomon answered all her questions. There was nothing that he could not explain to her. It took her breath away. She said to the king, "The report I heard in my own country about your accomplishments and your wisdom is true. I did not believe the report until I came and saw it with my own eyes. The truth is, not even half of it was told to me! Your wisdom and wealth surpass the report which I heard. May the LORD your God be blessed, who was pleased to put you on the throne of Israel." She gave the king gold, spices, and precious stones. Then she and her servants returned to her country.

The weight of gold which came to Solomon in one year was six hundred sixty-six talents, not counting what he collected from merchants, traders, kings, and governors. All of Solomon's drinking vessels were gold. No silver was used, because it was considered of little value in Solomon's days, because Solomon's merchant fleet returned gold, silver, ivory, monkeys, and peacocks.

King Solomon was greater than all the kings of the earth in wealth and wisdom. The whole world sought an audience with Solomon to hear the wisdom which God put in his heart. They each brought gifts: articles of gold and silver, clothing, scents and spices, horses and mules, year after year. Solomon accumulated fourteen hundred chariots and twelve thousand charioteers.

But King Solomon loved many foreign women along with the daughter of Pharaoh. They came from the nations about which the LORD had said to the people of Israel, "You must not enter marriage with them or they will turn your hearts after other gods." Solomon clung to them in love. He had seven hundred wives and three hundred concubines. His wives turned his heart after other gods, so that his heart was not fully devoted to the LORD as the heart of his father David was. So the LORD was angry with Solomon because his heart had turned away from the LORD, the God of Israel. The LORD had given him the command not to follow other gods, but Solomon did not keep the LORD's command.

So the LORD said to Solomon, "Because you did not keep my covenant and my statutes which I commanded you, I will surely rip the kingdom out of your hands and give it to your servant. However, I will not do it in your lifetime because of your father David. I will rip it from your son's hand. But I will not rip away the whole kingdom. One tribe I will give to your son for the sake of my servant David."

Jeroboam son of Nebat was an Ephraimite. Jeroboam was Solomon's official, but he rebelled against the king. Solomon tried to kill Jeroboam, but Jeroboam fled to Egypt. He stayed in Egypt until Solomon died.

Lord God, keep us from relying on our own wisdom and strength, and keep us trusting solely in you. Keep away from us all bad influences which would lead us away from you. Keep us for yourself always. Amen.

73. SONG OF SONGS (SONGS OF SONGS)

Solomon, remembering his own failures when it comes to marriage, writes a song exalting marriage as God instituted it. In this poem, a woman and a man speak words of love to each other. Some friends of the woman also join in the conversation.

The Song of Songs, which is Solomon's.

The Man to the Woman: How beautiful you are, my darling!
How beautiful! Your eyes are doves.

The Woman to the Man: How beautiful you are, my lover!
How delightful!

The Woman to her Friends: He has brought me to the reception hall,
and his banner over me is love.
Daughters of Jerusalem, you must swear to me
that you will not awaken love until it so desires.

Listen! It's my lover! Look!
    Here he comes,
leaping on the mountains,
    bounding over the hills.

The Man to the Woman: Arise, come, my darling.
    My beautiful one, come.
Let me see how you look.
    Let me hear your voice,
because your voice is pleasant,
    and you are lovely to look at.

The Woman to her Friends: My lover is mine and I am his.
Daughters of Jerusalem, you must
    swear to me
that you will not awaken love until
    it so desires.

The Man to the Woman: Look at you. You are beautiful,
    my darling!
There is no flaw in you. Come with me,
    my bride.
You have stirred my heart.
How delightful it is to experience
    your love, my bride!
How much better is your love
    than wine,
and the fragrance of your perfume
    than any spice!

Friends to the Couple: Eat, friends! Drink! Be intoxicated
    with love!

The Woman to her Friends: My lover is radiant and ruddy,
outstanding among ten thousand.
He is completely desirable.
    This is my lover.
This is my friend, O daughters
    of Jerusalem.

The Man to the Woman: You are as beautiful, my darling,
    as Jerusalem.
My dove, my perfect one,
    is one-of-a-kind.
How beautiful you are and
    how pleasing,
O loved one, daughter of delights!

The Woman to her Friends: I belong to my lover, and his desire
is for me.
The Woman to the Man: Come, my lover, let us go to the fields.
Let us spend the night in the villages.
Let us go early to the vineyards.
Place me like a seal over your heart,
like a seal on your arm,
because love is as strong as death.
Its passion is as relentless as the grave.
Its flames are flames of fire,
a mighty blaze.
Many waters cannot quench such love.
Rivers cannot wash it away.
If a man were to offer all the wealth
of his house for love,
he would be utterly scorned.

Lord God, we thank you for the gift you have given us in marriage. Keep our thoughts pure and decent. Help all husbands and wives to love each other, following the perfect love of Jesus for us. Amen.

74. THE STRUGGLES OF ECCLESIASTES (ECCLESIASTES 1-3, 6, 7, 9, 11-12)

As an old man, Solomon considers how nothing in this life has any meaning apart from God.

The words of Ecclesiastes, David's son.

"Nothing but vapor," Ecclesiastes said. "Totally vapor. Everything is just vapor that vanishes."

What does anyone gain by all his hard work under the sun? Everything is tedious and tiresome. Whatever has been will be again. There is nothing new under the sun. No one remembers the people who came before us, and as for those who are coming—after they are gone, no one will remember them either.

I, Ecclesiastes, have been king over Israel. I have seen all the actions done under the sun, and, look, it is all nothing but vapor. It is all chasing the wind. I thought, "Look, I have accumulated more wisdom than anyone before me." I realized that this too is chasing the wind.

I thought, "Go ahead with pleasure." But that too is vapor. What good is it?

I undertook great projects. But when I turned my attention to everything that my hands had done—note this—it was all vapor, all chasing the wind. There was no benefit under the sun.

No one will remember the wise man or the fool for long. In days to come, all of them will already be forgotten. How does the wise man die? Just like the fool. Sure, there may be a man who has worked hard, but he must hand over whatever he accumulated by all his hard work to a man who has not worked hard for it. This too is vapor. It's so unfair! For what does a man gain through all his hard work?

There is nothing better than to find joy in work. This is from God's hand. For who can enjoy himself apart from him?

There is an appropriate time for every activity under heaven: a time to give birth and a time to die, a time to mourn and a time to dance, a time for war and a time for peace.

God has made everything beautiful in its time. Yes, he has also put eternity in their hearts, yet it is not possible for man to understand the work that God has done from beginning to end. Everything God does will last forever.

For who knows what is good for a man in life, in the few days of his life that vanishes like vapor, that passes like a shadow? Who will tell the man what will be after him, under the sun?

On a good day, enjoy the good, but on a bad day, consider carefully. God has made the one as well as the other, so no man can find out about anything that will come later.

During my days that vanish like vapor, I have seen it all. For instance, a righteous man perishes despite being righteous, while an evil man lives for a long time in spite of his evil. There is surely not a righteous man on earth who does good and does not sin. God made mankind upright, but they have gone off looking for many schemes. As it will be for the good, so it will be for the sinner.

Go ahead, eat your food with joy, and drink your wine with a happy heart, for God is already pleased with what you do. Enjoy life with the wife you love all the days of your life. Whatever your hand finds to do, do it with all your strength. I looked again and saw that under the sun the race is not won by the swift, nor the battle by the strong. Food is not given to the wise, nor is wealth given to those who have good judgment, nor is success given to those who have knowledge, because time and chance come upon all of them.

Certainly, no man knows his time. Even if a man lives many years, in all of them let him find joy, but let him keep in mind the days of darkness, for they will be many. Everything that is to come is vapor.

So remember your Creator in the days of your youth, before the dust goes back into the ground, as it was before, and the spirit goes back to God who gave it.

"Nothing but vapor," said Ecclesiastes, "It is all vapor."

This is the conclusion of the matter. Fear God and keep his commandments. For mankind, this is everything.

Yes, God will bring everything that is done into judgment, including everything that is hidden, whether good or evil.

Lord God, life without you is entirely meaningless
and nothing lasts. Give us hearts which focus on you
and fear, love, and trust in you above all things. Amen.

PART 5

THE DIVIDED MONARCHY

No longer would Israel be one single country. David's family continued to rule over the southern kingdom of Judah, but the northern kingdom of Israel became its own nation. That northern kingdom of Israel, by and large, rejected God, even while God was sending them prophets to call them back to him. As a result they were wiped out by the Assyrians, never to be seen again. The southern kingdom of Judah was not much better. They had some kings who led the people to follow the true God faithfully, but also some bad kings who led the people into idolatry. But always God was reaching out to the people through his prophets, calling the people back in repentance, and pointing them ahead to the coming Savior.

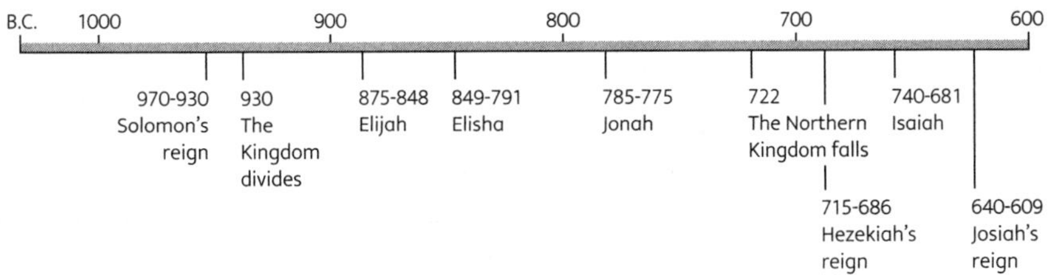

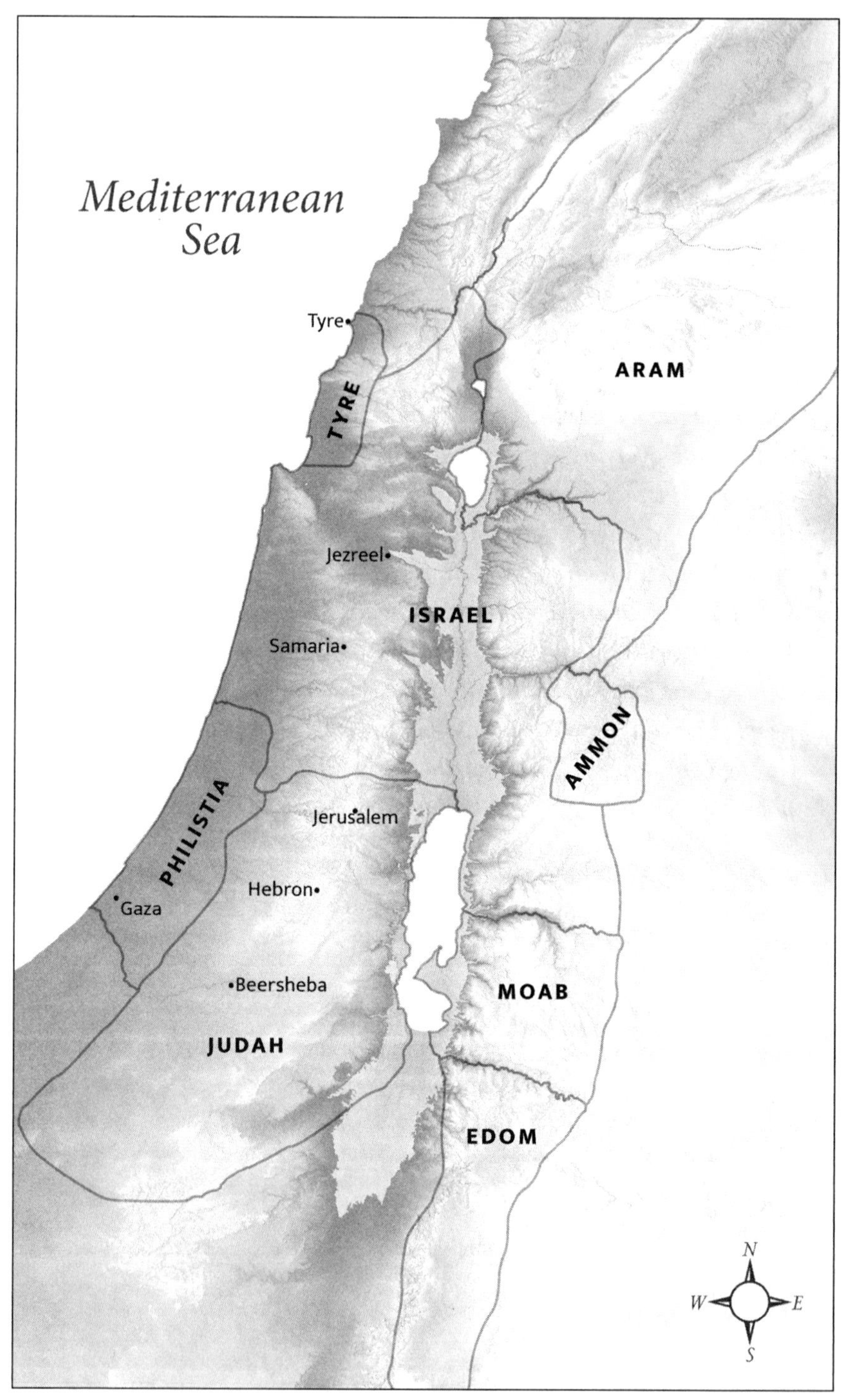

THE DIVIDED KINGDOM

75. ISRAEL DIVIDES INTO TWO KINGDOMS (1 KINGS 11-12)

As a consequence for Solomon's sins, the kingdom of Israel is divided into two parts. The northern kingdom of Israel immediately wanders from the Lord, but David's dynasty still rules over the southern kingdom of Judah.

Solomon was king over all Israel in Jerusalem for forty years. Solomon rested with his fathers and was buried in the City of David. His son Rehoboam became king in his place.

Then Jeroboam and the entire assembly of Israel came and said to Rehoboam, "Your father made our yoke heavy. Lighten the heavy yoke he laid on us, and we will serve you."

Then King Rehoboam consulted the elders who had served his father Solomon. He asked, "What answer do you advise me to give to these people?"

They said to him, "Become a servant to this people and answer them with kind words. Then they will be your servants for all time."

But he rejected the advice which the old men offered him. Instead he consulted the young men who had grown up with him. He said to them, "What answer do you advise that we should give to these people?"

The young men who had grown up with him said, "Tell them this: 'My little finger is thicker than my father's waist. My father imposed a heavy yoke on you. I will make your yoke heavier.' "

So the king answered the people harshly, because he had rejected the advice which the old men had offered. He spoke to them as the young men advised him: "My father made your yoke heavy, and I will add to your yoke."

This turn of events was from the Lord, in order to fulfill his word.

All Israel saw that the king had not listened to them. So the people answered the king: "What share do we have in David? No portion in the son of Jesse! To your tents, Israel! Now look after your own house, David!" So Israel went to their tents.

When all Israel heard that Jeroboam had returned, they made him king over all Israel. No tribe was left which followed the house of David, except the tribe of Judah alone.

Rehoboam assembled the whole house of Judah and the tribe of Benjamin to fight against the house of Israel and to restore the kingdom to Rehoboam.

The word of the God came to Shemaiah: "Say the following to Rehoboam: 'This is what the Lord says. Do not fight against your brothers, the people of Israel. Go home, every one of you, for this turn of events is from me.' "

So they listened to the word of the LORD, and they returned home, just as the LORD said.

But Jeroboam said in his heart, "If this people goes up to offer sacrifices in the House of the LORD in Jerusalem, then the hearts of the people will return to Rehoboam. Then they will kill me and return to Rehoboam."

The king made two golden calves and said to the people, "Going up to Jerusalem is too much trouble for you. Here are your gods, Israel, who brought you up from the land of Egypt!" He set up one in Bethel and the other one in Dan.

This sin took hold, and the people traveled as far as Dan to worship. Jeroboam also made shrines on the high places, and he appointed priests from all kinds of people, even though they were not Levites. Jeroboam instituted a festival in the eighth month, on the fifteenth day of the month, like the festival that is held in Judah. He offered sacrifices on the altar in Bethel, sacrificing to the calves he had made.

Lord God, make us, your servants, kind people
who answer people with loving words instead
of harsh words. Wherever we may go, do not allow us
to wander after other gods, but preserve us always
as a people belonging to you by faith
in our Savior Jesus. Amen.

76. ELIJAH AND THE DROUGHT (1 KINGS 16-17)

When a wicked king and queen rule over the northern kingdom of Israel, God sends the prophet Elijah to the nation to call them back to the right path.

Ahab became king over Israel. Ahab committed more evil in the eyes of the LORD than all those who had gone before him. He considered it a trivial thing to walk in the sins of Jeroboam. He married Jezebel daughter of Ethbaal, king of the Sidonians. He served Baal and bowed down to him. He erected an altar to Baal in Samaria.

Elijah said to Ahab, "As surely as the LORD lives, the God of Israel before whom I stand, there will be no dew or rain during the coming years, except at my word."

Then the word of the LORD came to him: "Leave this place. Hide yourself by the Kerith Ravine, east of the Jordan. You will drink from the stream, and I will command the ravens to provide for you there."

So Elijah went and lived in the Kerith Ravine, east of the Jordan. The ravens brought him bread and meat in the morning and in the evening, and he drank from the stream.

After some time the stream dried up because there had been no rain in the land. Then the word of the LORD came to him: "Get up! Go to Zarephath, which belongs to Sidon, and live there. I have commanded a woman there, a widow, to provide for you."

So he got up and went to Zarephath. There he saw a widow gathering sticks. He called to her, "Please bring me a piece of bread."

She said, "As surely as the LORD your God lives, I have no food except a handful of flour in a jar and a little oil in a pitcher. See, I am gathering a couple of sticks so that I can go and prepare it for myself and my son, so that we can eat it and then die."

Elijah said to her, "Do not be afraid. First make a small loaf of bread for me. Then go and make another for you and your son. For this is what the LORD, the God of Israel, says: The jar of flour will not run out and the pitcher of oil will not become empty until the day the LORD sends rain to water the surface of the ground."

So she went and did exactly as Elijah said. He and she and her household were able to eat for many days. The jar of flour did not run out, and the pitcher of oil did not become empty, just as the LORD had said through Elijah.

After these events, the son of the woman fell ill. The illness became worse until he stopped breathing.

Then she said to Elijah, "What is the issue between us, man of God? Have you come to remind me of my sins and to kill my son?"

He said to her, "Bring your son to me."

Then he stretched himself out on the boy three times, and he cried out to the LORD, "O LORD, my God, let this boy's soul return to his body!" The LORD listened to Elijah's voice, and the boy's soul returned to his body, and he came to life. Then Elijah took the boy and gave him to his mother.

Elijah said, "See, your son is alive!"

The woman said to Elijah, "Now I know that you are a man of God and that the word of the LORD in your mouth is true."

Lord God, in times of prosperity or in times of poverty,
be with us and provide for us. In times of sickness
and death, be with us and reassure us that you have
all power over death, and have destroyed death through

the resurrection of your Son. Raise us up on the Last Day to be with you forever, as you have promised to do. Amen.

77. ELIJAH AND THE PROPHETS OF BAAL (1 KINGS 18)

The Lord shows that he is the true and the only God.

After a long time, the word of the LORD came to Elijah. He said, "Go to Ahab, and I will send rain." So Elijah went to Ahab.

When Ahab saw Elijah, Ahab said to him, "Is that you, the one who brings trouble on Israel?"

Elijah said, "It is not I who have brought trouble on Israel, but rather you, because you abandoned the LORD's commandments and followed the Baals. But now gather all Israel before me on Mount Carmel, along with the four hundred fifty prophets of Baal." So Ahab sent word to all the people of Israel and assembled the prophets on Mount Carmel.

Then Elijah said to all the people, "How long will you stagger around on two crutches? If the LORD is God, follow him. If Baal is God, follow him." But the people did not answer him a single word.

Then Elijah said to the people, "I am the only one left of the LORD's prophets, but the prophets of Baal total four hundred fifty men. Let two bulls be provided for us. Let them choose one bull for themselves and cut it up and set it on the firewood. But they are not to light the fire. I will prepare the other bull and set it on the firewood, but I will not light the fire. Then you will call on the name of your gods, and I will call on the name of the LORD. The god who answers with fire, he is God."

All the people said, "This proposal is good."

Then Elijah said to the prophets of Baal, "You go first. Call on the name of your god. But do not light the fire."

So they took the bull and prepared it. Then they called on the name of Baal from morning until noon, "Baal! Answer us!" But there was not a sound. No one answered.

When noon came, Elijah mocked them: "Shout louder! He may be deep in thought or busy or on a journey. Perhaps he is asleep and will wake up!" So they cried out with a loud voice, and according to their practice they cut themselves until their blood flowed. They kept up a prophetic frenzy until the time of the evening sacrifice, but there was no sound. No one answered.

Then Elijah took twelve stones, one for each of the tribes of Israel. He built the stones into an altar in the name of the LORD. Around it he made a trench. He arranged the wood, cut up the bull, and put it on the wood.

Then he said, "Fill four jars with water and pour it on the sacrifice and on the wood." Then he said, "Do it again." So they did it again. Then he said, "Do it a third time." So they did it a third time. The water flowed all around the altar. It even filled the trench.

When the time of the evening sacrifice had arrived, Elijah the prophet stood up and said, "O LORD, the God of Abraham, Isaac, and Israel, let it be known this day that you are God in Israel and that I am your servant and that I have done all these things by your word. Answer me, LORD! Answer me so that this people will know that you, O LORD, are God and that you are turning their hearts back."

Fire from the LORD fell on the sacrifice and on the wood, the stones, and the dirt. It even licked up the water in the trench. When all the people saw this, they fell on their knees and said, "The LORD, he is God. The LORD, he is God!"

Elijah said to them, "Seize the prophets of Baal! Do not let a single one of them escape!" So they seized them, and Elijah slaughtered them.

Then Elijah said to Ahab, "Hitch up your chariot and go, so that the rain does not stop you."

Meanwhile, the skies darkened with clouds and wind, and there was a heavy rain. So Ahab got into his chariot and went to Jezre'el. But the hand of the LORD was on Elijah, and he ran ahead of Ahab until he came to Jezre'el.

Lord God, you are our only Lord. You are our only God. Remove all idols from our lives that we may serve you alone. May we look to your Son Jesus as our only Way, our only Truth, our only Life. Amen.

78. ELIJAH IN THE WILDERNESS (1 KINGS 19)

When Elijah is depressed and feeling alone, God reassures him.

Ahab told Jezebel everything that Elijah had done, including the fact that he had killed all their prophets with the sword. So Jezebel sent a messenger to say to Elijah, "May the gods punish me severely and even double it if by this time tomorrow I have not made your life like one of theirs."

Elijah ran for his life. He went a day's journey into the wilderness. There he sat down under a broom tree, where he prayed that he would die. He said, "I've had enough, LORD. Take my life." Then he lay down and went to sleep under the broom tree.

Suddenly an angel touched him and said, "Get up and eat."

Then he looked around, and near his head there was a loaf and a jar of water, so he ate and drank, and then he lay down again.

Then the angel of the LORD came back a second time and touched him and said, "Get up and eat, because the journey is too much for you."

So he got up and ate and drank. Then in the strength from that food he walked for forty days and forty nights to Horeb, the mountain of God. He came to a cave and spent the night there.

Then the word of the LORD suddenly came to him saying, "Why are you here, Elijah?"

He said, "I have been very zealous for the LORD, but the people of Israel have abandoned your covenant. They have torn down your altars and killed your prophets with the sword. I alone am left, and they are seeking to take my life."

Then the LORD said, "Go out and stand on the mountain, for the LORD is passing by." Then a great and powerful wind tore the mountains and shattered rocks before the LORD, but the LORD was not in the wind.

After the wind came an earthquake, but the LORD was not in the earthquake.

After the earthquake there was a fire, but the LORD was not in the fire.

After the fire there was a soft, whispering voice.

When Elijah heard it, he wrapped his face in his cloak, and he went out and stood at the entrance to the cave. Then a voice came to him and said, "Why are you here, Elijah?"

He said, "I have been very zealous for the LORD, but the people of Israel have abandoned your covenant. They have torn down your altars and killed your prophets with the sword. I alone am left, and they are seeking to take my life."

Then the LORD said to him, "Go back the way you came. You will anoint Jehu as king over Israel and Elisha as prophet in your place. I have preserved in Israel seven thousand whose knees have not bent to Baal and whose lips have not kissed him."

So Elijah went from there and found Elisha. Elisha was doing the plowing with twelve teams of oxen in front of him, and he himself was driving the twelfth team. Elijah crossed over to him and threw his cloak over him. Elisha took the team of oxen and slaughtered them. Using the equipment from the oxen as fuel, he cooked the meat and gave it to the people, and they ate. Then he got up and followed Elijah and served him.

Lord God, when we feel like nothing is going right,
use our fellow believers around us to encourage us,
and assure us that you are still at work, unseen,
through your gospel. Amen.

79. NABOTH'S VINEYARD (1 KINGS 21-22)

King Ahab continues in his evil ways and dies in battle.

Naboth had a vineyard next to the palace of Ahab. Ahab said to Naboth, "Give me your vineyard so I can use it as a vegetable garden, because it's beside my house, and I will give you a better vineyard in exchange. Or if you prefer, I will give you the purchase price in silver."

But Naboth said to Ahab, "May I be cursed by the LORD, if I were to give you the inheritance from my fathers."

Ahab went to his house sullen and angry because of what Naboth had said to him. Ahab lay down on his bed and turned his face away and did not eat anything.

Then his wife Jezebel came to him and said, "Why is your spirit so sullen, and why don't you eat?"

He told her, "I said to Naboth, 'Sell your vineyard to me,' but he said, 'I will not.'"

Then his wife Jezebel said to him, "I will give you the vineyard of Naboth."

Then Jezebel sent letters to the elders who were living in the city with Naboth. She wrote in the letters, "Seat Naboth at the head of the people. Seat two wicked men opposite him and have them testify, 'You cursed God and the king!' Then take him out and stone him to death."

The men of the city did exactly as Jezebel had commanded them. They seated Naboth at the head of the people. They brought two wicked men and seated them opposite him. The wicked men testified against Naboth before the people, "Naboth cursed God and the king!" So they took him outside the city and stoned him to death. Then they sent word to Jezebel.

When Jezebel heard that Naboth had been stoned to death, she said to Ahab, "Go and take possession of the vineyard of Naboth, which he refused to sell to you, because Naboth is dead." When Ahab heard that Naboth was dead, he went and took possession of the vineyard of Naboth.

Then the word of the LORD came to Elijah: "Go down to meet Ahab. Tell him: 'This is what the LORD says. Have you committed murder and seized this man's property?' Then say to him: 'This is what the LORD says. In the place where dogs licked Naboth's blood, dogs will lick your blood also.' "

Then Ahab said to Elijah, "Have you found me, my enemy?"

Elijah said, "You sold yourself to do evil in the eyes of the LORD, who says, 'I am bringing disaster against you. I will make your house like the house of Jeroboam, because you have provoked me to anger and caused Israel to sin. Dogs will eat Jezebel. The dead who belong to Ahab in the city the dogs will eat, and the dead in the country the birds of the air will eat.' "

Jehoshaphat king of Judah went down to visit the king of Israel. The king of Israel said to Jehoshaphat, "Will you come with me to wage war at Ramoth Gilead?"

Jehoshaphat said to the king of Israel, "I am like you. My people are like your people. My horses are like your horses."

Then the king of Israel and Jehoshaphat king of Judah went up to Ramoth Gilead.

The king of Israel said to Jehoshaphat, "I will disguise myself when I go into the battle, but you wear your robes." So the king of Israel disguised himself and went into battle.

The king of Aram had commanded his thirty-two chariot commanders, "Do not fight with anyone small or great, but only against the king of Israel."

When the chariot commanders saw Jehoshaphat, they said, "That is the king of Israel!" They turned to fight against him, and Jehoshaphat cried for help.

When the chariot commanders realized that he was not the king of Israel, they stopped pursuing him.

But a man shot an arrow at random and struck the king of Israel in the seam between two parts of his armor.

Ahab died in the evening, and the blood from his wound ran down on to the floor of the chariot. The king died, and they brought him to Samaria and buried the king in Samaria. They washed the chariot at the pool of Samaria, and dogs licked up his blood, in fulfillment of the word which the LORD had spoken.

Lord God, you have given us so many things. Make us
appreciative of all you have given us and keep us
from coveting the things you have given others.
Make our hearts content in the fact that you
have given us all eternal blessings in Jesus. Amen.

80. ELIJAH IS TAKEN TO HEAVEN (2 KINGS 2)

God takes Elijah to heaven without dying, and Elisha succeeds him as the Lord's prophet.

The LORD was about to take Elijah up to heaven in a whirlwind. Elijah was traveling with Elisha from Gilgal. Elijah said to Elisha, "Stay here, for the LORD has sent me to Bethel."

But Elisha said, "As surely as the LORD lives and as your soul lives, I will not leave you." So they went down to Bethel.

The sons of the prophets in Bethel came out to Elisha and said to him, "Do you know that today the LORD is taking your master away from you?"

Then he said, "Yes, I know. Be quiet."

Then Elijah said to him, "Elisha, stay here because the LORD has sent me to Jericho."

But he said, "As surely as the LORD lives and as your soul lives, I will not leave you." So they went to Jericho.

Then the sons of the prophets in Jericho approached Elisha and said to him, "Do you know that today the LORD is taking your master away from you?"

He said, "Yes, I know. Be quiet."

Then Elijah said to him, "Stay here because the LORD has sent me to the Jordan."

But he said, "As surely as the LORD lives and as you live, I will not leave you." So the two of them went on.

The two of them were standing at the Jordan. Elijah took his cloak, folded it together, and struck the water. The water divided to the right and to the left. Then the two of them crossed on dry land.

When they had crossed, Elijah said to Elisha, "What I can do for you before I am taken from you?"

Then Elisha said, "Let there be a double portion of your spirit on me."

He said, "You have asked a difficult thing. If you see me being taken from you, it will surely be yours."

Suddenly a chariot made of fire, and horses made of fire came and separated them. Elijah went up to heaven in a whirlwind. Elisha was watching and crying out, "My father! My father! Israel's chariot and its charioteers!" Then he did not see him anymore.

Then he picked up Elijah's cloak, which had fallen from him. He returned and stood at the edge of the Jordan. He took Elijah's cloak and struck the water. As soon as he struck the water, it divided to the right and to the left so that Elisha could cross.

When the sons of the prophets saw this, they said, "Elijah's spirit is resting on Elisha." They went to meet him and bowed down to the ground before him.

Then the men of the city said to Elisha, "Look, the water is bad, and the land deprives people of children."

So he said, "Bring me salt." So they brought it to him.

Then he went out to the spring and threw the salt in. He said, "This is what the LORD says: I have healed this water. No longer will death or loss of children come from it." So the water remained healed, according to the word which Elisha spoke.

He went up from there to Bethel. While he was going, young boys came and mocked him. They said, "Go up, baldy! Go up, baldy!"

So he turned around and cursed them in the name of the LORD. Then two bears came out from the woods, and they tore forty-two boys to pieces.

Lord God, you have all power over death. Give your messengers who proclaim your Word the strength and wisdom to speak it boldly. Make them your chariots and charioteers as you win victories with your gospel. Enable us to support and respect them, so that their labor among us is not a burden but a joy. Amen.

81. THE MIRACLES OF ELISHA (2 KINGS 4)

God performs many miracles through the prophet Elisha.

The wife of one of the sons of the prophets cried out to Elisha, "My husband is dead. The moneylender is coming to take my two sons as slaves."

Then Elisha said to her, "What shall I do for you? Tell me, what do you have in your house?"

She said, "Nothing at all except a jar of olive oil."

He told her, "Go and ask for jars from all your neighbors—empty jars. Don't ask for only a few. Then go inside and shut the door behind you and your sons. Then pour oil into all the jars. When each one is full, set it aside."

So they brought the jars, and she poured. When a jar was filled, she said to her son, "Bring me another jar."

But he said, "There aren't any more." Then the oil stopped.

The man of God said, "Go and sell the oil and pay your debt. Then you and your sons can live off what's left."

One day Elisha went to Shunem. A wealthy woman lived there, and she urged him to eat a meal with her. So whenever he passed by, he would stop there for a meal.

Then Elisha said to Gehazi, "What can be done for her?"

Then Gehazi said, "Well, she has no son, and her husband is old."

So he said to her, "At this time next year, you will be holding a son."

The woman conceived, and she gave birth to a son at that same time of the year, just as Elisha said to her.

The boy grew up. One day he said to his father, "My head! My head!"

His father said to his servant, "Carry him to his mother." So he picked him up and carried him to his mother, and the boy sat on her lap until noon. Then he died.

Then she went to the man of God and grasped his feet. Elisha came to the house. There was the boy—dead, lying on his bed. So he went in and he shut the door behind the two of them. Then he prayed to the LORD. He got up and lay down on top of the boy. The boy's flesh became warm. Then the boy sneezed seven times. Then the boy opened his eyes.

The woman came in and fell at Elisha's feet and bowed down to the ground. Then she picked up her son and went out.

Elisha returned to Gilgal. There was a famine in the land. He said to his servant, "Put the large cooking pot on the fire, and cook some stew."

One of the men went out to the field to gather herbs. He found a wild vine and picked some wild gourds from it. He cut them into pieces for the pot of stew. But they did not know what they were. They served it to the men to eat. While they were eating the stew, they cried out, "There is death in the pot, man of God!" And they could not eat it.

But he said, "Take some flour and throw it into the pot." Then he said, "Serve it to the people." They ate, and there was nothing harmful in the pot.

A man came and brought the man of God twenty loves of barley bread and some new grain in his sack. Elisha said, "Set it before the people so that they can eat."

His attendant said, "How can I set this before one hundred men?"

But he said, "Set it before the people so that they may eat, for this is what the LORD says: They will eat and have some left over." So he set it before them. They ate, and they had some left over, just as the LORD had said.

Lord God, your Son has all power in heaven and
on earth and he uses it to take care of us. Thank you
for defeating death for us, and raise us up
to life on the Last Day. Amen.

82. NA'AMAN IS HEALED OF LEPROSY (2 KINGS 5)

God uses ordinary water to cleanse Na'aman of his leprosy.

Na'aman, the commander of the king of Aram's army, was a great man in the opinion of his master. He was highly honored because the LORD had provided victory for Aram through him. Although he was a powerful warrior, he had leprosy.

Raiding parties had once gone out from Aram and brought back a young girl. She served Na'aman's wife. She said to her mistress, "I wish my master stood before the prophet who is in Samaria, because he would cure him of his leprosy."

So Na'aman went and told his master, "The servant girl from the land of Israel said this."

Then the king of Aram said, "Go there. I will send a letter to the king of Israel." So Na'aman went, and he took ten talents of silver and six thousand shekels of gold and ten sets of clothing. He brought the king of Israel the letter.

When the king of Israel read the letter, he tore his clothes and said, "Why is he sending a man to me for me to heal him from his leprosy?"

But when Elisha heard that the king of Israel had torn his clothes, he sent a message to the king: "Why have you torn your clothes? Let him come to me, and he will know that there is a prophet in Israel."

So Na'aman went and stopped in front of the door of Elisha's house. But Elisha sent a messenger to him to say, "Go and wash seven times in the Jordan. Then your flesh will be restored and you be clean."

But Na'aman was angry and he left, saying, "Look, I said to myself, 'He will surely come out and stand and call on the name of the LORD his God and wave his hand over the place, and I would be cured of the leprosy!' Aren't the rivers of Damascus better than all the waters of Israel? Couldn't I wash in them and be cleansed?" So he turned and went away in a burning rage.

But his servants approached and spoke to him. They said, "My father, if the prophet had told you to do some great thing, would you not do it? How much more when he says to you, 'Wash and be clean'?"

So he went down and dipped in the Jordan seven times, just as the man of God had said. Then his flesh was restored and he was clean.

Then he and his whole escort went back to the man of God. He stood in front of Elisha and said, "Now I know that there is no God in all the earth except in Israel. Accept a gift from your servant."

But he said, "As surely as the LORD lives, I will not take anything."

Then Na'aman said, "Let me be given as much dirt as two donkeys can carry, for your servant will never again burn incense or sacrifice to others gods, but only to the LORD. But let the LORD forgive your servant this one thing: When my master goes into the house of Rimmon to bow down there and he supports himself on my arm, then I too have to bow down in the house of Rimmon."

Elisha said to him, "Go in peace."

When Na'aman had gone some distance from him, Gehazi, the servant of Elisha, chased after Na'aman. When Na'aman saw him running after him, he got down from his chariot to meet him. Gehazi said, "My master sent me to say, 'Look, just now two men have come to me. Give them please a talent of silver and two sets of clothing.'"

Na'aman said, "Certainly! Take two talents!" Na'aman gave them to Gehazi. Gehazi hid them in the house.

Elisha said to him, "Where were you, Gehazi?"

Gehazi said, "Your servant didn't go anywhere."

Then Elisha said to him, "Is this the time to take silver or clothes? Na'aman's leprosy will cling to you and to your descendants forever." Then Gehazi went out from his presence, leprous like snow.

Lord God, thank you for washing us
clean of all our sins in baptism. Remind us
each day of your gift to us in baptism and
renew our hearts to live as your people. Amen.

83. MORE MIRACLES OF ELISHA (2 KINGS 6-7)

God performs even more miracles through the prophet Elisha.

The sons of the prophets said to Elisha, "Let us go to the Jordan, and let every one of us take a log from there so we can build a place there for us to live." So he went with them to the Jordan. But while one of them was cutting down a log, the ax fell into the water.

He cried out, "Oh no, my lord! It was borrowed!"

But the man of God cut off a piece of wood and threw it into the water, and the ax floated.

Then he said, "Pick it up." So he stretched out his hand and took it.

Now when the king of Aram was waging war against Israel, he would make plans with his officials, saying, "My camp will be at such and such a place."

But the man of God would send a message to the king of Israel, saying, "Be careful when you pass this place because the Arameans are going down there." So the king of Israel would send scouts to the place the man of God had pointed out.

The king of Aram was enraged because of this. He summoned his officials and said to them, "Who of us is for the king of Israel?"

One of his officials said, "No, Elisha tells the king of Israel the words which you speak in your bedroom."

Then he said, "Then I'll capture him." So he sent horses and chariots at night.

When the man of God's servant got up early and went out, there were soldiers, horses, and chariots surrounding the city. So his attendant said to Elisha, "What will we do?"

He answered, "Don't be afraid, for those who are with us are more than those who are with them."

Then Elisha prayed, "O Lord, open his eyes so that he may see." Then the LORD opened the servant's eyes, and he saw that the hills were full of horses and chariots of fire, all around Elisha.

When the Arameans came down, Elisha prayed to the LORD, "Strike these people with blindness." So he struck them with blindness, just as Elisha asked.

Then Elisha said to them, "This is not the road and this is not the city. Follow me and I will take you to the man you are looking for." So he brought them to Samaria. When they came into Samaria, then Elisha prayed, "O LORD, open their eyes so that they can see." Then the LORD opened their eyes, and they saw that they were right in the middle of Samaria.

When the king of Israel saw them, he said to Elisha, "Shall I strike them down?"

He said, "Do not strike them down. Set food and water before them so that they can eat and drink and then go back to their master." So he gave a great feast for them. Then he sent them on their way. The Aramean raiding parties did not come into the land of Israel anymore.

After these things, Ben Hadad king of Aram mustered his whole army and went up and laid siege to Samaria. There was a great famine in Samaria.

Elisha said, "This what the LORD says. At this time tomorrow at the gate of Samaria, twelve pounds of fine flour will sell for a shekel and twenty-four pounds of barley for a shekel."

Then the officer on whose arm the king was leaning answered, "Really! Could this happen?"

Elisha said, "You yourself will see it with your own eyes, but you will not eat any of it."

The LORD caused the Arameans to hear the sound of a great army. They said to each other, "Listen! The king of Israel has hired the Hittites and Egypt to come against us!" They left their tents, horses, and donkeys and fled for their lives.

Then the people went out and plundered the Aramean camp. So twelve pounds of fine flour sold for a shekel and twenty-four pounds of barley for a shekel, just as the LORD had said. The king appointed the officer on whose arm he leaned to be in charge of the gate. But the people trampled him and he died, just as the man of God had said.

Lord God, often we feel surrounded by our enemies,
the Devil, the world, and our own sinful flesh.
Comfort us with the knowledge that not only has your
Son defeated all our enemies by his death
and resurrection, but also you and your armies surround
and protect us from all that would harm us. Amen.

84. THE REIGN OF JEHU (2 KINGS 9-10, 13)

As God had told Elijah, Jezebel is killed and Jehu becomes king.

Then Elisha called one of the sons of the prophets and told him, "Take this flask of oil in your hand and go to Jehu son of Jehoshaphat. Take the flask of oil, pour it out on his head, and say, 'This is what the LORD says. I anoint you king over Israel.' "

So the servant of the prophet found Jehu and poured the oil on his head and said, "This is what the LORD, the God of Israel, says: I anoint you king over the LORD's people Israel. You will strike down the house of Ahab, and I will avenge the blood of all the servants of the LORD that was shed by Jezebel. The whole house of Ahab will perish. I will make the house of Ahab like the house of Jeroboam. The dogs will eat Jezebel on the plot of ground in Jezre'el, and no one will bury her.'"

Then they blew the ram's horn and said, "Jehu is king!"

Then Jehu mounted his chariot and went to Jezre'el. When Jezebel heard it, she put on eye make-up and arranged her hair. Then she looked down through a window. When Jehu came into the gate, she said, "Do you come in peace?"

He looked up to the window and said, "Who is with me?" Two or three eunuchs looked down to him. Then he said, "Throw her down!" So they threw her down, and her blood splattered the wall, and he and the horses rode over her. Then he went inside and ate and drank. Then Jehu said, "See to that cursed woman and bury her, because she was a king's daughter."

But when they went to bury her, they did not find her, except for her skull, her feet, and the palms of her hands. So they came back and told him. Then Jehu said, "This is the word of the LORD which he spoke through his servant Elijah: On the plot of ground of Jezre'el, the dogs will eat the flesh of Jezebel.'"

Then Jehu struck down all those who were left to Ahab. He wiped out Ahab completely, according to the word which the LORD had spoken to Elijah.

Then Jehu assembled all the people and said to them, "Ahab served Baal a little. Jehu will serve him a great deal. Gather all the prophets of Baal, all his servants, and all his priests! Let no one be missing because I am going to make a great sacrifice to Baal." But Jehu was acting deceptively in order to exterminate the servants of Baal.

All the servants of Baal came. They came into the temple of Baal so that the temple of Baal was filled from end to end. Then he said to the person in charge of the wardrobe, "Bring out garments for all the servants of Baal." So he brought out robes for them.

Then Jehu said to the servants of Baal, "Make a careful search, and see to it that there are no servants of the LORD with you—only servants of Baal."

Then they went in to make sacrifices. But Jehu had stationed eighty men outside. Jehu said to the guards and to the officers, "Go strike them down! Don't let anyone out!" So they struck them down with their swords. Then they tore down the temple of Baal. In this way Jehu exterminated Baal worship from Israel.

But Jehu was not careful to walk in the law of the Lord, the God of Israel, with all his heart. He did not turn from the sins which Jeroboam caused Israel to commit. Jehu was king over Israel twenty-eight years.

Then Elisha died, and they buried him.

Raiders from Moab were coming into the land. While a man was being buried, they suddenly saw the raiders, so they threw the man into the tomb of Elisha. When the man touched the bones of Elisha, he came to life, and he got up on his feet.

Lord God, nothing can stand in the way of you fulfilling your promises. So, as you have promised us, forgive our sins, and raise us up from the dead on the Last Day to live with you forever. Amen.

85. JOASH ESCAPES AND RULES AS KING (2 KINGS 8-9, 11-12)

David's family line, the line of the Savior, is nearly wiped out, but God delivers young Joash.

Ahaziah became king and ruled as king in Jerusalem. His mother's name was Athaliah, granddaughter of Omri, king of Israel. He walked in the way of the house of Ahab and did evil in the eyes of the Lord as the house of Ahab had done, because he was a son-in-law of the house of Ahab. So Jehu pursued him too and shot him in his chariot.

When Athaliah, the mother of Ahaziah, saw that her son was dead, she went into action and destroyed all the royal heirs. But Jehosheba, Ahaziah's sister, took Joash, the son of Ahaziah. She stole him away from among the king's sons, who were to be killed. She put him and his nurse in a bedroom. He was kept hidden from Athaliah so that he was not killed. He was kept hidden with her in the House of the Lord for six years while Athaliah was ruling over the land.

In the seventh year, Jehoiada the priest gave officers the spears and shields which belonged to King David and were in the House of the Lord. So the guards, each one with his weapons in his hand, stood around the king. Then Jehoiada brought out the king's son and set the crown on him. Then they proclaimed him king. They anointed him and clapped their hands and said, "Long live the king!"

When Athaliah heard the noise, she went to the House of the Lord. She looked, and there was the king standing beside the pillar, and the officers and the trumpeters were in front of the king, and all the people of the land were rejoicing. Then Athaliah tore her clothes and cried, "Treason! Treason!"

Then Jehoiada the priest commanded the officers, "Bring her out between the ranks! And anyone who follows her, kill them with the sword!" Because the priest had said, "She is not to be killed in the House of the LORD," they laid hands on her as she was going through the passageway where the horses enter the king's palace, and they killed her there.

Then Jehoiada made a covenant between the LORD and the king and the people that they would be the LORD's people. He also made a covenant between the king and the people. Then all the people of the land went to the temple of Baal and tore it down. Then they brought the king down from the House of the LORD. They entered the king's palace through the gate of the guards. Then he sat on the throne of the kings. All the people of the land rejoiced, and the city was quiet. Athaliah had been put to death with the sword in the king's palace.

Joash was seven years old when he became king. He was king in Jerusalem for forty years. Joash did what was right in the eyes of the LORD during the whole time that Jehoiada the priest instructed him.

Jehoash said to the priests, "All the silver from the sacred offerings which is brought into the House of the LORD—let the priests take it and repair whatever damage is found in the house."

Then they gave the silver which had been weighed out to those overseeing the work on the House of the LORD. They paid it out to the carpenters, the builders, the bricklayers, and the stonemasons, who used it to repair the damage to the House of the LORD and to meet all the expenses for repairing the house. They did not audit the men to whom they gave the silver to do the work, because they were working honestly.

Lord God, you protect your people and make good on your promise to save. Thank you for sending Jesus to save us from our sins, and bring about the day of his second coming where he will bring us out of the evil of this world. Amen.

86. THE PROPHET OBADIAH (OBADIAH)

God prophesies punishment for Edom, the descendants of Esau, for what they did to Israel. He also promises to bring deliverance for Jerusalem.

The vision of Obadiah. This is what the LORD God says about Edom.

We have heard news from the LORD, and an envoy has been sent among the nations: "Get up. Let us rise up against her in battle." Listen, I will make you insignificant among the nations. You will be completely despised. The pride of your heart has deceived you. Your dwelling is so high that you say in your heart, "Who can bring me down to the ground?" Even if you would soar as high as an eagle, and even if your nest is set among the stars, I will bring you down from there, declares the LORD.

Oh, how completely Esau will be ransacked! His hidden treasures will be searched out and looted! All your allies will push you back to your border. Those who were at peace with you will deceive you and overpower you.

Will I not destroy the wise men of Edom on that day, declares the LORD? Will I not take away those who have understanding from the mountain of Esau? Everyone from the mountain of Esau will be cut down by the massacre.

Because of the violence done to your brother Jacob, shame will cover you, and you will be cut off forever. When strangers carried away Jacob's wealth, and foreigners entered his gate, you were just like one of them. Do not look down on your brother on the day of his misfortune. Do not rejoice over the people of Judah on the day when they are destroyed. Do not speak proudly on the day of distress.

Yes, the Day of the LORD is near for all the nations! As you have done, it will be done to you. Your deeds will return upon your own head. It will be as though the Edomites never existed.

But on Mount Zion, there will be some who escape, and it will be holy. The house of Jacob will recapture its territory. The house of Jacob will be a fire, the house of Joseph a flame, but the house of Esau will be stubble. The Israelites set them on fire and consume them. There will not be any survivors for the house of Esau. Yes, the LORD has spoken. Saviors will go up on Mount Zion to judge the mountains of Esau, and the kingdom will belong to the LORD.

Lord God, the kingdom belongs to you.
Look with kindness on us as we suffer in this life.
Rescue us from our enemies and bring us to
the eternal life that our Savior Jesus won for us. Amen.

87. THE PROPHET JOEL (JOEL)

After Israel experiences God's judgment in a day of the Lord brought by a locust plague, God points them ahead to greater days of the Lord, including Pentecost and the Last Day.

The word of the LORD that came to Joel.

Listen, all of you who live in the land. Has anything like this ever happened? Tell it to your children, and let your children tell it to their children. What the grasshoppers have left, the locusts have eaten. The fields are devastated. The soil mourns. The grain is devastated. The wine has run dry. The olive oil runs out.

Put on sackcloth and lament. Set aside a day of fasting. Cry out to the LORD!

How terrible that day will be! Yes, the Day of the LORD is near. It will come like destruction from the Almighty. Hasn't the food been cut off right before our eyes? Happiness and celebration are cut off from the house of our God. To you, O LORD, I call.

Blow the ram's horn in Zion. Sound the alarm on my holy mountain. Tremble with fear, for the Day of the LORD is coming. It is close at hand—a day of darkness and gloom, a day of clouds and frightening darkness.

Like dawn spreading across the mountains a large and mighty people is coming. In front of them, the land is like the Garden of Eden. Behind them, it is a desolate wilderness. There is no escaping them. In front of them the earth quakes. The sky shudders. The sun and moon become dark, and the stars stop shining. The LORD shouts at the head of his army. His forces are very numerous. The Day of the LORD is great. It is terrifying. Who can endure it?

Even now, declares the LORD, return to me with all your heart, with fasting and weeping and grief. Tear your heart and not your clothing. Return to the LORD your God, for he is gracious and compassionate, slow to anger and abounding in mercy, and he relents from sending disaster. Who knows? He may turn and have pity and leave behind a blessing.

The LORD is zealous for his land, and he will take pity on his people. The LORD will respond to them: "I am sending you grain, new wine, and fresh oil, enough to satisfy you fully. Never again will I subject you to scorn among the nations. I will drive the invaders far from you."

Yes, the LORD has done great things. Do not be afraid, O earth. Celebrate and be glad. Yes, the LORD has done great things. You will have plenty to eat. You will eat until you are full, and you will praise the name of the LORD your God, who has worked wonders for you.

Never again will my people be put to shame! Then you will know that I am in the midst of Israel, that I am the LORD your God, and that there is no other. Never again will my people be put to shame!

After this, I will pour out my Spirit on all flesh. Your sons and your daughters will prophesy. Your old men will dream dreams. Your young men will see visions. Even on the servants, both male and female, I will pour out my Spirit in those days. I will show warning signs in the heavens and on the earth: blood and fire and pillars of smoke. The sun will be turned to darkness and the moon to blood, before the coming of the great and terrifying day of the LORD. And everyone who calls on the name of the LORD will be saved. So on Mount Zion and in Jerusalem there will be deliverance, as the LORD has promised, among the survivors whom the LORD calls.

Look! In those days and at that time, when I restore the fortunes of Judah and Jerusalem, I will gather all nations and enter into judgment against them for the sake of my possession, my people Israel, whom they scattered among the nations. Judah will be inhabited forever, and Jerusalem through all generations. I will pardon their bloodguilt. The LORD dwells in Zion!

Lord God, pour out your Holy Spirit on us through your Word, as we learn more and more of what you have done to save us. Strengthen our faith in your Son Jesus and equip all your people to proclaim his name as we await the great day of his return. Amen.

88. THE PROPHET JONAH (JONAH)

God teaches Jonah about his grace, both toward Jonah himself and toward the people of Nineveh.

The word of the LORD came to Jonah: "Go to Nineveh and preach against it."

But Jonah went down to Joppa and found a ship going to Tarshish. He boarded the ship to go with them, away from the presence of the LORD.

But the LORD hurled such a great storm on the sea that the ship was about to break apart. The sailors were afraid, and each one cried out to his gods.

Jonah had gone down into the hold of the ship. He was lying down and sleeping soundly. The captain approached him and said, "How can you be sleeping so soundly? Get up and call on your god! Maybe your god will treat us with favor so that we will not perish."

Then the sailors said to each other, "Let's cast lots so that we can find out whose fault it is that this disaster has come to us." So they cast lots, and the lot fell on Jonah.

So they said to him, "What have you done? What should we do to quiet the sea?"

He said, "Throw me into the sea. Then the sea will calm down for you, for this violent storm striking against you has come about because of me."

They cried out to the Lord and said, "Please, Lord, do not charge innocent blood against us, for you, Lord, have done as you pleased." So they picked Jonah up and threw him into the sea, and the sea stopped its raging. Then the men feared the Lord greatly.

The Lord provided a large fish to swallow Jonah, and Jonah was in the belly of the fish three days and three nights.

Then Jonah prayed to the Lord his God from the belly of the fish. He said: "You threw me into the depths, into the heart of the seas. But you brought my life up from the pit, O Lord, my God. Salvation belongs to the Lord!"

Then the Lord commanded the fish, and it vomited Jonah onto dry land.

Then the word of the Lord came to Jonah a second time: "Go to Nineveh and preach to it the message that I tell you."

So Jonah set out and went to Nineveh just as the word of the Lord had commanded. Jonah walked through the city for a day, and he called out, "Forty more days and Nineveh is going to be overthrown!"

The men of Nineveh believed God. They proclaimed a fast and put on sackcloth. The king of Nineveh issued a proclamation: "Let everyone call fervently to God. Let them turn from their evil way and from the violence that is in their hands. Who knows? God may turn and relent."

When God saw that they had turned from their evil way, God relented from the disaster which he said he would bring on them, and he did not carry it out.

But to Jonah all this seemed very bad, and he became very angry. He prayed to the Lord, "Lord, wasn't this exactly what I said when I was still in my own country? That is why I previously fled to Tarshish, because I knew that you are a gracious and merciful God, slow to anger and abounding in mercy, and you relent from sending disaster."

But the Lord replied, "Is it right for you to be angry?"

Jonah sat down east of the city, waiting to see what would happen. Then the Lord God provided a plant and made it grow up over Jonah to provide shade over his head. Jonah was very happy about the plant. But the next day God provided a worm, and it attacked the plant so that it withered. When the sun rose, God provided a scorching east wind. The sun beat down on Jonah's head so that he grew faint. He wanted to die.

But God said to Jonah, "Is it right for you to be angry about the plant?"

Jonah said, "I do have a right to be angry—angry enough to die!"

So the LORD said, "You have been concerned about this plant. You did not work for it or make it grow. So should I not be concerned for Nineveh, in which there are more than one hundred twenty thousand people?"

Lord God, you are everywhere. Watch over and protect us wherever we go. Give us the strength to carry out the tasks you have given us. Move us to reach out to those who do not know you, and use our words to bring them to you in repentance. Amen.

89. THE PROPHET AMOS (AMOS 1-2, 5, 8-9)

God promises to punish Israel for its cruelty and hypocrisy, but also promises to restore David's dynasty one day.

The words of Amos, who was among the sheep breeders from Tekoa. He saw a vision concerning Israel during the days of Uzziah king of Judah and during the days of Jeroboam king of Israel.

This is what the LORD says: Because of three sins of Israel, because of four, I will not hold back judgment. They sell the righteous for silver and the needy for a pair of sandals. They trample the heads of the poor and turn aside the claims of the oppressed. They stretch themselves out beside every altar on pieces of clothing they seized as collateral. In the temple of their gods they drink wine obtained through fines.

I was the one who destroyed the Amorites in front of them. I myself brought you up from the land of Egypt, and I led you in the wilderness for forty years, so that you would take possession of the land. I raised up some of your sons to be prophets. Israel has fallen, and she will not rise again. She is abandoned on her own soil. There is no one to lift her up. Seek the LORD and live, or he will rush upon the house of Joseph like fire. The fire will consume, and no one will extinguish it.

There are those who hate an arbitrator in the city gate. They despise anyone who speaks honestly. You trample on the poor and collect taxes on their grain. You have built houses of cut stones, but you will not live in them. You have planted choice vineyards, but you will not drink their wine. For I know that your rebellious deeds are many, and your sins are numerous, you who are enemies of a righteous man, you who take bribes.

Seek good and not evil, so that you may live, and then it will be like this for you: The LORD, the God of Armies, will be with you, as you claim. Hate evil and love good. Establish justice in the city gate. Perhaps the LORD, the God of Armies, will be gracious to the remnant of Joseph.

Woe to those who long for the Day of the LORD! What good will the Day of the LORD be for you? It will be darkness and not light.

I hate, I reject your festivals! Even if you offer up to me your whole burnt offerings and your grain offerings, I will not accept them. Get the noise of your songs away from me! I will not listen to the music of your harps. But let justice roll like the waters, and righteousness like an ever-flowing stream. You lifted up images of your star god, which you made for yourselves. So I will exile you beyond Damascus, says the LORD, whose name is the God of Armies. The LORD swears, "I will never forget any of their deeds!" I will turn your festivals into mourning and all of your songs into a lamentation. I will send a famine into the land—a famine of hearing the words of the LORD.

Look, the eyes of the LORD God are on the sinful kingdom, and I will destroy it from the face of the earth. But I will never completely destroy the house of Jacob, declares the LORD. Listen! I am giving a command, and among all the nations I will shake the house of Israel as the contents of a sieve are shaken, and not even one pebble will fall out to the ground. By a sword, all the sinners among my people will die, those who are saying, "Disaster will not overtake us. It will not confront us."

In that day I will raise up the fallen shelter of David. I will repair the broken parts of its walls, and I will raise up its ruins. I will rebuild it as in days of old, so that they will possess all the nations who are called by my name, declares the LORD, who is doing this.

Look, days are coming, declares the LORD, when I will restore the fortunes of my people Israel. They will rebuild the desolate cities and dwell in them. They will plant vineyards and drink their wine. They will make gardens and eat their fruit. I will plant them in their soil, and they will never again be uprooted from the soil that I have given to them, says the LORD your God.

Lord God, give us hearts which treat those
who are disadvantaged kindly and treat all people fairly,
as you have been more than kind and more than fair
in pouring out blessings of forgiveness and
life on us through Jesus. Amen.

90. THE PROPHET HOSEA (HOSEA 1-3, 14)

God prophesies that he will be a faithful husband to unfaithful Israel.

The word of the Lord that came to Hosea in the days of Uzziah, Jotham, Ahaz, and Hezekiah, the kings of Judah, and in the days of Jeroboam king of Israel.

The Lord said to Hosea, "Take for yourself an immoral wife, because the land has been committing flagrant immorality, turning away from the Lord."

So he went and took Gomer. She conceived and gave birth to a son for him. The Lord said to him, "Name him Jezre'el, because in a little while I will destroy the ruling power of Israel in the Valley of Jezre'el."

She conceived again and gave birth to a daughter. The Lord said to him, "Name her Lo Ruhamah, because I will no longer have compassion on the house of Israel. Indeed, I will certainly not forgive them. But I will have compassion on the house of Judah. I will save them by the Lord their God. I will not save them by bow, sword, battle, horses, or horsemen."

Gomer conceived and gave birth to a son. The Lord said, "Name him Lo Ammi, because you are not my people, and I will not be the Lord for you."

Nevertheless, the number of the people of Israel will be like the sand of the sea, which cannot be measured or counted. Then, in the place where they were told, "You are not my people," they will be told, "You are children of the living God." The people of Judah and the people of Israel will be gathered together.

Plead with your mother! Plead with her, because she is not my wife, and I am not her husband. Let her put away her adultery. I will have no compassion on her children. She who conceived them has acted shamefully. No one will deliver her from my hand. I will devastate her. I will punish her for the days with the Baals.

But watch! I am going to court her. I will bring her into the wilderness. I will speak tenderly to her. I will pledge you to myself in marriage forever. I will pledge you to myself in marriage—with righteousness, justice, mercy, and compassion. In faithfulness I will pledge you to myself in marriage, and you will know the Lord. I will have compassion for Lo Ruhamah, and I will tell Lo Ammi, "You are my people," and he will say, "You are my God!"

The Lord said to me, "Again show love to a woman who keeps committing adultery. Show love just as the Lord loves the people of Israel, even though they keep turning to other gods."

So I said to her, "You will stay with me. And I will also be for you."

So the people of Israel will live many days without king or prince. Afterward the people of Israel will return and seek the LORD their God and David their king. They will come trembling to the LORD and to his goodness in the latter days.

Israel, return to the LORD your God, for you have stumbled because of your guilt. Say to him, "Forgive all our guilt and receive us graciously."

I will cure them of their unfaithfulness. I will love them freely, for my anger has turned away from them. Who is wise? Let him understand these things. Who is discerning? Let him know them. For the ways of the LORD are right, and the righteous walk in them, but the rebellious stumble in them.

Lord God, we have been unfaithful toward you,
putting ourselves and other things first. We praise
you for your faithfulness to us, showing us
such forgiving love and keeping your promise
to send our Savior Jesus. Amen.

91. ISAIAH'S CALL AND VISION (ISAIAH 6)

God shows Isaiah a vision of his throne room and calls him to be a prophet.

In the year that King Uzziah died, I saw the LORD sitting on a throne, high and exalted, and the train of his robe filled the temple. Above him stood the seraphim. Each one had six wings. With two they covered their faces. With two they covered their feet. With two they flew. One called to another and said, "Holy, holy, holy, is the LORD of Armies! The whole earth is full of his glory!" The foundations of the thresholds shook at the voice of the one who called, and the temple was filled with smoke.

Then I said, "I am doomed! I am ruined, because I am a man with unclean lips, and I dwell among a people with unclean lips, and because my eyes have seen the King, the LORD of Armies!"

Then one of the seraphim flew to me, carrying a glowing coal in his hand which he had taken from the altar with tongs. He touched my mouth with the coal and said, "Look, this has touched your lips, so your guilt is taken away, and your sin is forgiven."

Then I heard the Lord's voice, saying, "Whom shall I send? Who will go for us?"

Then I said, "Here I am. Send me!"

He said: "Go! You are to tell this people, 'Keep listening, but you will never understand. Keep looking, but you will never get it.' "

Then I said, "Lord, how long?"

He answered, "Until the LORD has removed the people far away and the abandoned places within the land are many. Like a terebinth or an oak, whose stump remains when it is cut down, so the holy seed is its stump."

Lord God, you alone are holy, and you have made us
holy through the sacrifice of your Son Jesus for our sins.
Send us with this good news to others. Amen.

92. THE CHILD IMMANUEL (ISAIAH 7, 9)

God prophesies the special birth of a special Savior. Immanuel, God with us, will be born of a virgin.

When Ahaz, the son of Jotham, the son of Uzziah, was king of Judah, Rezin king of Aram and Pekah son of Remaliah, the king of Israel, marched up to Jerusalem to wage war against it, but they could not capture it. Ahaz and his people trembled as the trees of the forest tremble in the wind.

Then the LORD said to Isaiah, "Go tell Ahaz, 'Do not be afraid. Do not lose your courage even though Aram, Ephraim, and the son of Remaliah have plotted evil against you. Their plan shall not succeed. It shall not take place. Within sixty-five years Ephraim will be broken into pieces, so that it will no longer be a people. If you do not stand firm in faith, you will not stand at all.' "

The LORD spoke to Ahaz again. He said, "Ask for a sign from the LORD your God. Ask for it either in the depths below or in the heights above."

But Ahaz responded, "I will not ask. I will not test the LORD."

So Isaiah said, "Listen now, you house of David. Is it not enough for you to test the patience of men? Will you test the patience of my God as well? Therefore the Lord himself will give a sign for all of you. Look! The virgin will conceive and give birth to a son and name him Immanuel. He will eat curds and honey by the time he knows how to refuse evil and choose good, because even before the child knows how to refuse evil and choose good, the land whose two kings you dread will be forsaken. The LORD will bring on you, on your people, and on your father's house, days worse than any since the day that Ephraim broke away from Judah. The LORD will bring the king of Assyria."

Nevertheless, there will be no more gloom for the land that was in anguish. In former times, he humbled the land of Zebulun and the land of Naphtali, but in the latter time he will cause it to be glorious, along the way of the sea, beyond the Jordan, in Galilee of the Gentiles.

The people walking in darkness have seen a great light. For those living in the land of the shadow of death, the light has dawned. For to us a child is born. To us a son is given. The authority to rule will rest on his shoulders. He will be named: Wonderful Counselor, Mighty God, Everlasting Father, Prince of Peace. There will be no limit to his authority and no end to the peace he brings. He will rule on David's throne and over his kingdom, to establish it and to uphold it with justice and righteousness from now on, into eternity. The zeal of the LORD of Armies will accomplish this.

Lord God, thank you for sending your Son, to be born for us, to live for us, to die for us, to rise for us, and to rule all things for us. Amen.

93. THE BRANCH (ISAIAH 11-12)

God describes the peace that the Savior will bring.

A shoot will spring up from the stump of Jesse, and a Branch from his roots will bear fruit. The Spirit of the LORD will rest on him: the Spirit of wisdom and understanding, the Spirit of counsel and might, the Spirit of knowledge and the fear of the LORD. With righteousness he will judge the poor, and he will render fair decisions in favor of the oppressed on the earth. He will strike the earth with the rod of his mouth, and with the breath from his lips he will put the wicked to death. Righteousness will be the belt around his waist, and faithfulness the belt around his hips.

The wolf will dwell with the lamb, and the leopard will lie down with the young goat, the calf, the young lion, and the fattened calf together, and a little child will lead them. The cow and the bear will graze together, and their young ones will lie down together. The lion will eat straw like the cattle. The child will play near a cobra's hole, and the child will put his hand into a viper's den. They will not hurt or destroy anywhere on my holy mountain, for the earth will be full of the knowledge of the LORD, as the waters cover the sea.

This is what will take place on that day. The peoples will seek the Root of Jesse, who will be standing like a banner for the peoples, and his resting place will be glorious. On that day the Lord will reach out his hand for the second time to reclaim the remnant of this people. He will set up a banner for the nations, and he will assemble the outcasts of Israel, and gather together the scattered people of Judah, from the four corners of the earth.

In that day you will say: I will give thanks to you, LORD, for though you were angry with me, your anger has turned away, and you comfort me. Surely God is my salvation. I will trust him and will not be afraid, because the LORD is my strength and song, and he has become my salvation. Therefore with joy you will draw water from the wells of salvation.

In that day you will say: Give thanks to the LORD! Proclaim his name. Declare among the peoples what he has done. Proclaim that his name is exalted! Sing to the LORD, for he has done amazing things! Let this be known in all the earth! Shout aloud and sing for joy, daughter of Zion, for the Holy One of Israel is great among you!

Lord God, your Son has brought us peace, peace with you and peace in our now-forgiven conscience. Help us to live at peace with each other. Amen.

94. THE DESTRUCTION OF THE NORTHERN KINGDOM (2 KINGS 17)

God allows the Northern Kingdom to be destroyed by the Assyrians for its sins, and they are replaced in the land by the people who would be known as the Samaritans.

Hoshea became king over Israel in Samaria. He did evil in the eyes of the LORD, but not like the kings of Israel who came before him.

Shalmaneser king of Assyria went up against him, and Hoshea became his vassal and paid tribute to him. But the king of Assyria caught Hoshea in a conspiracy. He had sent messengers to So king of Egypt, and he did not send tribute to the king of Assyria as in previous years. Therefore the king of Assyria arrested him and confined him in prison.

Then the king of Assyria invaded the whole land. He went up against Samaria and laid siege to it for three years. In Hoshea's ninth year, the king of Assyria captured Samaria and exiled Israel to Assyria. He made them live in Halah and along the Habur River and in the cities of the Medes.

This happened because the people of Israel sinned against the LORD their God, who had brought them up from the land of Egypt. They feared other gods. They walked in the practices of the nations whom the LORD had driven out before the people of Israel and the practices which the kings of Israel had introduced. They built high places for themselves in all their cities. They did evil things, provoking the LORD to anger. They served filthy idols even though the LORD had said to them, "You must not do this."

The LORD had warned Israel and Judah through all his prophets and seers, saying, "Turn back from your evil ways and keep my commands." But they did not listen. They made their necks just as stiff as their fathers had, who did not trust in the LORD their God. So the LORD was furious with Israel, and he removed them from his presence. None was left—only the tribe of Judah.

Even Judah did not keep the commands of the LORD their God. They walked in the practices which Israel introduced. So the LORD rejected all the seed of Israel, and he afflicted them. He gave them into the hand of plunderers until he cast them out of his presence.

Israel went to Assyria, into exile from her homeland.

The king of Assyria brought people from Babylon, Kuthah, Avva, Hamath, and Sepharvaim, and he settled them in the cities of Samaria in the place of the people of Israel. They took possession of Samaria and lived in its cities. When they began to settle there, they did not fear the LORD, so the LORD sent lions among them. The lions were killing people, so they said to the king of Assyria, "Lions are killing people, because there aren't any people left who know the customs of the god of the land."

So the king of Assyria commanded, "Get one of the priests who was exiled from there. He will go and live there and teach the customs of the god of the land." So one of the priests who had been exiled from Samaria came and lived in Bethel. He was teaching them how they should fear the LORD.

But each nation was still making its own gods. They were fearing the LORD, and they were also serving their gods according to the custom of the nations from which they had been deported. There is no one who acts according to the commands which the LORD commanded Israel. Their children and their grandchildren did just as their fathers did.

Lord God, in our sinfulness we often make a mess of things, and in our sinfulness we deserve eternal destruction. Have mercy on us for the sake of our Savior Jesus and forgive us all our sins. Keep your Word and worship pure among us. Keep us from changing your teachings or from letting our own thoughts or the thoughts of others lead us at all away from you. Amen.

95. SENNACHERIB'S INVASION (2 KINGS 18-19)

God miraculously protects the Southern Kingdom from the Assyrians.

Hezekiah, son of Ahaz king of Judah, became king. He ruled for twenty-nine years in Jerusalem. He did what was right in the eyes of the LORD, like everything that his father David had done. He removed the high places. He trusted in the LORD, the God of Israel, and there was no one like him among the kings of Judah, before him or after him. The LORD was with him. Wherever he went, the LORD gave him success.

In King Hezekiah's fourteenth year, Sennacherib king of Assyria came up against all the fortified cities of Judah and seized them. The herald said, "Tell Hezekiah what the great king of Assyria, says: What are you relying on? You say that you have the power for war, but this is only words. So who are you trusting when you rebel against me? Make a bargain with the king of Assyria."

Then Eliakim said to the herald, "Please speak to your servants in Aramaic, for we understand it. But don't speak with us in Hebrew in the hearing of the people."

Then the herald said to them, "Is it only to you that my lord sent me to speak these words? Is it not also to the people?" The herald called out in a loud voice in Hebrew, "Listen to the words of the great king of Assyria: Don't let Hezekiah deceive you, because he can't save you from my hand. And don't let Hezekiah cause you to trust in the LORD by saying, 'The LORD will surely save us!' Make a peace treaty with me and come out to me, and each of you will eat from his own vine and drink from his own cistern."

But the people were silent because the king had commanded them not to answer. Then Eliakim went to Hezekiah and told him the words of the herald.

When King Hezekiah heard this, he tore his clothes and put on sackcloth. Then he went into the House of the LORD. He sent Eliakim and the elders of the priests to Isaiah.

Isaiah said to them, "Say this to your lord: This is what the LORD says: Do not be afraid of these words which you heard. He will return to his country, and I will make him fall by the sword in his own land."

Hezekiah prayed before the LORD: "O LORD God of Israel, you are seated above the cherubim. You alone are God over all the kingdoms of the earth. You made the heavens and the earth. Bend your ear, O LORD, and hear. Open your eyes, LORD, and see. Hear Sennacherib's words, which he sent to taunt the living God. Please save us from his hand, so that all the kingdoms of the earth will know that you, O LORD, are God, you alone."

Then Isaiah sent a message to Hezekiah, saying, "This is what the LORD, the God of Israel, says: I have heard what you have prayed to me about Sennacherib. This is the message which the LORD has spoken about the king of Assyria: He will not come into this city. By the same way he came he will go back. I will protect and save this city for my own sake and for the sake of my servant David."

That night, the angel of the LORD went out and struck down one hundred eighty-five thousand men in the camp of Assyria. When they woke up in the morning, there they were—all dead bodies! Then Sennacherib king of Assyria broke camp and returned and lived in Nineveh. One day when he was worshipping in the house of his god Nisrok, his sons killed him with the sword.

Lord God, assure us that our struggles and battles depend not on us, but on you. Fight for your people, preserve us in our earthly lives, and strengthen our trust in you. Amen.

96. HEZEKIAH'S ILLNESS (2 KINGS 20)

God spares King Hezekiah, but tells him that there will be difficult days ahead for his people.

In those days Hezekiah became sick. Isaiah came to him and said, "This is what the LORD says: Give instructions to your house because you are going to die. You will not recover."

Then Hezekiah prayed to the LORD, saying, "Please, O LORD, remember how I have walked before you in truth and with a whole heart and have done what is good in your eyes." Hezekiah wept bitterly.

Isaiah had not yet gone out from the middle courtyard when the word of the LORD came to him: "Go back and tell Hezekiah that this is what the LORD says: I have heard your prayer. I will certainly heal you. On the third day from now you will go up to the House of the LORD. I will add fifteen years to your life, and I will rescue you and this city from the hand of the king of Assyria. I will protect this city for my own sake and for the sake of my servant David."

Then Isaiah said, "Get a cake of figs." So they got it and put it on the infected sore, and Hezekiah recovered.

Then Hezekiah asked Isaiah, "What will be the sign that the LORD will heal me?"

Isaiah said, "Shall the shadow extend forward over ten more steps, or shall it move backwards ten steps?"

Hezekiah said, "It's easy for the shadow to get longer and cover ten more steps. Instead, have it go back ten steps."

Then the prophet Isaiah called out to the LORD, and he caused the shadow on the steps to go backwards ten steps.

At that time, Merodak Baladan son of Baladan, the king of Babylon, sent letters and a gift to Hezekiah because he heard that Hezekiah had been sick. Hezekiah heard the envoys and showed them all that was found in his treasuries. There was nothing which Hezekiah did not show them in his palace or in his whole kingdom.

Then Isaiah the prophet came to King Hezekiah and said, "What did these men say, and where did they come from?"

Hezekiah said, "From Babylon."

Then Isaiah asked, "What did they see in your palace?"

Hezekiah said, "They saw everything in my palace. There is nothing in my treasuries which they did not see."

Then Isaiah said to Hezekiah, "The days are coming when whatever is in your palace will be taken to Babylon. Not a thing will be left behind, says the LORD. And some of your descendants will be in the palace of the king of Babylon."

Then Hezekiah said to Isaiah, "The word of the LORD which you have spoken is good." He said, "Won't there be peace and security in my days?"

Lord God, our times are in your hands. Protect and preserve our lives, and have us always ready to be taken to our eternal home by faith in Jesus. Amen.

97. COMFORT, COMFORT MY PEOPLE (ISAIAH 40-41)

God prophesies through Isaiah that he would restore his people as he would come to them.

Comfort, comfort my people, says your God. Speak to the heart of Jerusalem and call out to her. Her warfare really is over. Her guilt is fully paid for. Yes, she has received from the LORD's hand double for all her sins.

A voice is calling out: "In the wilderness prepare the way for the LORD. In the wasteland make a level highway for our God. Every valley will be raised up, and every mountain and hill will be made low. The rugged ground will become level, and the rough places will become a plain. Then the glory of the LORD will be revealed, and all flesh together will see it. Yes, the mouth of the LORD has spoken."

A voice was saying, "Cry out!"

And I said, "What shall I cry out?"

All flesh is grass, and all its beauty is like a wildflower in the countryside. Grass withers, flowers fade, when the breath of the LORD blows on them. Yes, the people are grass. Grass withers, flowers fade, but the Word of our God endures forever.

Get up on a high mountain, O Zion, you herald of good news. Lift up your voice with strength, O Jerusalem, you herald of good news. Lift it up! Do not be afraid! Say to the cities of Judah, "Here is your God!" Look, God the LORD will come with strength, and his arm is ruling for him. Look, his reward is with him. The result of his work is in front of him. Like a shepherd he will care for his flock. With his arm he will gather the lambs. He will lift them up on his lap. He will gently lead the nursing mothers.

Do you not know? Have you not heard? The LORD is the eternal God. He is the Creator of the ends of the earth. He will not grow tired, and he will not become weary. No one can find a limit to his understanding. He is the one who gives strength to the weak, and he increases the strength of those who lack power. Young men grow tired and become weary. Even strong men stumble and fall. But those who wait for the LORD will receive new strength. They will lift up their wings and soar like eagles. They will run and not become weary. They will walk and not become tired.

Do not fear, for I am with you. Do not be overwhelmed, for I am your God. I will strengthen you. Yes, I will help you. I will uphold you with my righteous right hand.

Lord God, your Son has entered into our world to save us from all of our sins. Comfort us with the knowledge that through his work you have given us forgiveness that more than covers all our sins. Use this comforting truth to strengthen us and carry us through this life. Amen.

98. THE SUFFERING SERVANT (ISAIAH 52-53)

God prophesies through Isaiah that the promised Savior would suffer for the sins of the people but then he would live again.

Look, my servant will succeed. He will rise. He will be lifted up. He will be highly exalted. Just as many were appalled at him—his appearance was so disfigured that he did not look like a man, and his form was disfigured more than any other person—so he will sprinkle many nations, and kings will shut their mouths because of him.

He grew up like a tender shoot and like a root from dry ground. He had no attractiveness and no majesty. When we saw him, nothing about his appearance made us desire him. He was despised and rejected by men, a man who knew grief, who was well acquainted with suffering. Like someone whom people cannot bear to look at, he was despised, and we thought nothing of him.

Surely he was taking up our weaknesses, and he was carrying our sufferings. We thought it was because of God that he was stricken, smitten, and afflicted, but it was because of our rebellion that he was pierced. He was crushed for the guilt our sins deserved. The punishment that brought us peace was upon him, and by his wounds we are healed. We all have gone astray like sheep. Each of us has turned to his own way, but the LORD has charged all our guilt to him.

He was oppressed, and he was afflicted, yet he did not open his mouth. Like a lamb he was led to the slaughter, and like a sheep that is silent in front of its shearers, he did not open his mouth. He was taken away without a fair trial and without justice, and of his generation, who even cared? So, he was cut off from the land of the living. He was struck because of the rebellion of my people. They would have assigned him a grave with the wicked, but he was given a grave with the rich in his death, because he had done no violence, and no deceit was in his mouth.

Yet it was the LORD's will to crush him and allow him to suffer. Because you made his life a guilt offering, he will see offspring. He will prolong his days, and the LORD's gracious plan will succeed in his hand. After his soul experiences anguish, he will see the light of life. He will provide satisfaction. Through their knowledge of him, my just servant will justify the many, for he himself carried their guilt. Therefore I will give him an allotment among the great, and with the strong he will share plunder, because he poured out his life to death, and he let himself be counted with rebellious sinners. He himself carried the sin of many, and he intercedes for the rebels.

Lord God, we confess that it was for our sins that your Son suffered and died. Because he took our place, we are forgiven. When we feel guilty, remind us that he has taken all our guilt away. Amen.

99. THE PROPHET MICAH (MICAH 1-2, 4-5, 7)

God prophesies through Micah that an eternal ruler will come to restore God's people.

This is the word of the LORD that came to Micah in the days of Jotham, Ahaz, and Hezekiah, kings of Judah.

Listen, all you peoples! The LORD God will testify against you. He will come down and will trample the high places of the land because of the sins of the house of Israel.

Woe to those who plan wickedness while lying on their beds. By the morning light they carry it out. They covet fields and seize them. They covet houses and take them away. They deprive a person of his house, and a man of his inheritance.

Therefore this is what the LORD says: Look, I making plans for a disaster from which you cannot save your necks. You will not be able to hold your heads high, because it will be an evil time.

Should the house of Jacob say, "Would he really do these things?" Will my words fail to accomplish good things for people who walk uprightly? But lately my people have stood up like an enemy.

I will surely assemble all of you, Jacob. I will surely gather together the surviving remnant of Israel. I will establish them like a flock in its fold.

In the last days, the mountain of the House of the LORD will be established as the highest among the mountains. Many nations will come and say, "Come, let us go up to the Mountain of the LORD. He will teach us his ways that we may walk in his paths." The law will go out from Zion and the word of the LORD from Jerusalem. Nation will not raise the sword against nation. There will be no one to make them afraid, for the mouth of the LORD of Armies has spoken. For all the other peoples walk in the names of their gods, but we will walk in the name of the LORD our God forever and ever.

On that day, says the LORD, I will bring in the lame and gather the scattered, even those I have afflicted. I will establish the lame as survivors and the scattered as a powerful nation. The LORD will rule over them on Mount Zion from that time on and forever. The kingship will return to Jerusalem.

But you, Bethlehem Ephrathah, though you are small among the clans of Judah, from you will go out the one who will be the ruler for me in Israel. His goings forth are from the beginning, from the days of eternity. Therefore the LORD will give them up, until the time when the woman who is in labor bears a child. Then the remaining survivors from his brothers will return to the people of Israel. He will stand and shepherd with the strength of the LORD. They will dwell securely, for at that time he will be great to the ends of the earth. This one will be their peace.

I am miserable. The faithful have been carried off from the land. There is no one upright among mankind. A man's enemies are the members of his own household. But I will keep watching for the LORD. I will wait for God my Savior. My God will hear me.

Do not rejoice over me, my enemy. When I fall, I will rise. When I sit in the darkness, the LORD will be a light for me. Because I have sinned against him, I will bear the LORD's wrath, until he pleads my case and obtains a favorable verdict for me. He will bring me to the light. I will see his righteousness.

As I did in the days you came out from the land of Egypt, I will show you wonderful miracles. The nations will see and be ashamed. They will come trembling to the LORD our God, and they will be afraid in your presence.

Who is a God like you, who forgives guilt, and who passes over the rebellion of the survivors from his inheritance? He does not hold onto his anger forever. He delights in showing mercy. He will have compassion on us again. He will overcome our guilty deeds. You will throw all their sins into the depths of the sea. You will give truth to Jacob and mercy to Abraham, as you swore to our fathers from days of old.

Lord God, you have made us your people through your Son, our eternal King. May he rule over us forever and bring us mercy and peace. Amen.

100. KING MANASSEH (2 KINGS 20-21)

Good King Hezekiah is succeeded by bad King Manasseh.

Hezekiah rested with his fathers. Then his son Manasseh became king in his place.

Manasseh was twelve years old when he became king, and he reigned for fifty-five years in Jerusalem. He did evil in the eyes of the LORD, following the disgusting practices of the nations which the LORD had driven out before the people of Israel. He rebuilt the high places which his father Hezekiah had destroyed. He erected altars to Baal, just as Ahab king of Israel had done. Manasseh led them astray so that they did more evil than the nations whom the LORD exterminated before the children of Israel.

Then the LORD said through his prophets: "Because Manasseh king of Judah has engaged in these disgusting practices and caused Judah to sin with his filthy idols, I am bringing such disaster on Judah that the ears of all who hear of it will tingle. I will wipe away Jerusalem and give them into the hand of their enemies, because they have done what is evil in my eyes and have provoked me to anger."

Manasseh rested with his fathers, and his son Amon became king in his place. Amon ruled for two years. He did what was evil in the eyes of the LORD just as his father Manasseh had done. Amon's servants conspired against him, and they killed the king in his palace. Then the people of the land struck down all those who had conspired against King Amon, and they made his son Josiah king in his place.

Lord God, we thank you for those who taught us to know you as our God and to know your Son as our Savior. Keep us from ever turning away from this good instruction all the days of our life. Provide us with good rulers and protect us from evil rulers. Amen.

101. KING JOSIAH (2 KINGS 22-23)

After bad King Manasseh, God restores his Word and worship to his people through good King Josiah.

Josiah was eight years old when he became king, and he ruled for thirty-one years in Jerusalem. He did what was right in the eyes of the LORD. He walked in all the ways of his father David. He did not turn aside to the right or to the left.

In King Josiah's eighteenth year, the king sent Shaphan the secretary to the House of the LORD, saying, "Go up to Hilkiah the high priest and have him weigh out the entire amount of silver which has been brought to the House of the LORD. It is to be given to those who are working in the LORD's house to repair the damage in the temple."

Then Hilkiah said to Shaphan, "I have found the Book of the Law in the House of the LORD." Hilkiah gave the scroll to Shaphan and he read it.

Then Shaphan went to the king and reported: "Hilkiah the priest has given me a scroll." Then Shaphan read it in the presence of the king.

When the king heard the words of the Book of the Law he tore his clothes. Then the king summoned all the elders of Judah. The king went up to the House of the LORD, and every man of Judah and all the inhabitants of Jerusalem, the priests and the prophets and all the people from the least to the greatest, went with him. He read in their hearing all the words of the Book of the Covenant, which had been found in the House of the LORD.

Then the king stood before the pillar and made a covenant before the LORD to follow the LORD, to keep his commandments, his testimony, and his statutes with all his heart, and with all his soul to uphold the words of this covenant which were written in this book.

Then all the people affirmed this covenant.

The king commanded that they should remove from the temple of the LORD all the articles which had been made for Baal. He burned them outside. He removed the idolatrous priests who burned incense to Baal. Then he defiled the high places. On the altars he slaughtered all the priests of the high places who were present there. Then he went back to Jerusalem.

Then the king commanded all the people, "Observe the Passover to the LORD your God just as it is written in the Book of the Covenant." For they had not observed a Passover like this during the days of the judges or during the days of the kings. But in King Josiah's eighteenth year, this Passover to the LORD was observed in Jerusalem. Josiah destroyed the mediums and spiritists and all the detestable idols which were seen in the land of Judah, in order to comply with the words of the law, which were written in the book that Hilkiah the priest had found in the House of the LORD.

There was no king like him before him who turned to the LORD with all his heart and with all his soul and with all his strength, according to all the Law of Moses, and after him no one like him arose. But even so, the LORD did not turn from his great wrath which burned against Judah because of all the offenses with which Manasseh had provoked him. So the LORD said, "I will also remove Judah from my presence just as I removed Israel."

Pharaoh Neco, king of Egypt, went to the king of Assyria for war at the Euphrates River. King Josiah went to meet Neco in battle, but Neco killed King Josiah at Megiddo when he faced him. His servants transported his body from Megiddo to Jerusalem in a chariot, and they buried him in his own tomb.

Lord God, we praise you that you have brought the truth of your Word to us, and preserved it among us. Make us always glad to hear and learn it. Amen.

102. THE PROPHET NAHUM (NAHUM)

Through Nahum God prophesies judgment against Assyria and prosperity for Israel.

A threatening oracle against Nineveh. The book of the vision of Nahum.

The LORD is a jealous and avenging God. The LORD takes vengeance against his adversaries. The LORD is slow to anger, yet great in power. The LORD will certainly not let the guilty go unpunished. He marches out in the whirlwind and in the storm. Who can withstand his anger? Who can resist his fury? His rage is poured out like fire, and the rocks are torn down by him.

The LORD is good. He is a place of safety in the day of distress. He knows those who seek safety in him, but he will bring this place to a complete end by an overwhelming flood. He will drive his enemies into darkness.

No matter what you plot against the LORD, he will destroy your plot completely. Disaster will not need to strike them twice, because like fully dried stubble they will be consumed. The LORD has issued a decree against you: There will be no descendants to carry on your name. I will put an end to the idols in the temple of your gods. I will dig your grave because you are cursed.

Look! A herald is coming over the mountain to proclaim this good news: Peace! Celebrate your sacred festivals, Judah! Fulfill your sacred vows to praise God! For never again will wickedness overwhelm you. It has been completely destroyed. The LORD is about to restore the majesty of Jacob, as well as the majesty of Israel, even though their enemies have plundered them completely and have destroyed their vines.

Woe to the city of bloodshed! She is full of lies. She is filled with plunder. She is never without victims. Beware! I am against you, declares the LORD of Armies. The gates of your land will be wide open. The fire will consume you. The sword will cut you down. It will devour you as a swarm of grasshoppers would.

King of Assyria, your shepherds are drowsy! Your powerful men slumber! Your people are scattered on the mountains, and there are none left to gather together. There is no healing for your wound. Your injury is fatal! All who hear what has happened to you will clap their hands for joy, for no one ever escaped your endless cruelty!

Lord God, we thank you for the opportunity you give us
in our land to worship you and to read your Word.
We thank you even more for the spiritual blessings
you give us through that Word–freedom from sin,
from death, from fear–because of our Savior Jesus. Amen.

103. THE PROPHET ZEPHANIAH (ZEPHANIAH)

Through Zephaniah God prophesies judgment against all sin in the world and deliverance for his people everywhere.

This is the word of the LORD which came to Zephaniah in the days of Josiah, king of Judah.

I will completely sweep away everything from the face of the earth, declares the LORD. I will cut off mankind from the face of the earth.

I will stretch out my hand against Judah and all the inhabitants of Jerusalem. I will cut off every trace of Baal from this place. I will also cut off those who turn away from following the LORD.

Keep silent before the Lord God, for the great Day of the LORD is near. It is near and coming very quickly. Listen! That day is a day of wrath, a day of trouble and distress, a day of devastation and total destruction, a day of darkness and gloom, a day of clouds and thick darkness.

I will bring distress upon all people, so that they walk like blind men, because they have sinned against the LORD. That is why their blood will be poured out like dust. Their gold will not be able to deliver them on the day of the LORD's wrath. Instead, the whole earth will be consumed by the fire of his jealousy, because he will make an end—yes, a terrifying end of all who dwell on the earth.

Gather yourselves together, you shameless nation, before the decree takes effect, before the day of the LORD's anger comes upon you. Seek the LORD, all you humble people of the earth. Seek righteousness. Seek humility. Maybe then you will be sheltered in the day of the LORD's anger.

Woe to the filthy, foul city, the city of oppressors. She does not listen. She does not even trust the LORD or draw near to her God. They have committed violence against the law. The LORD in her midst is just. He does no wrong. Every morning he brings his justice to light. He does not fail. But those who are unjust are shameless.

I have cut off nations. Their cities are laid waste, with no one living there. I said, "Certainly you will fear me. You will accept correction so that your dwelling place will not be destroyed by everything I have threatened."

But they eagerly sinned in everything they did. So wait for me, declares the LORD, until the day that I rise up. For I am determined to gather the nations and to pour out my indignation upon them. All the earth will be consumed with the fire of my zeal.

I will purify the lips of the people so that they all call on the name of the LORD. From beyond the rivers of Cush, my worshippers, my scattered people, will bring offerings to me. In that day you will no longer bear the shame of your rebellions against me. Then I will remove the proud boasters from among you, and you will never again be arrogant on my holy hill. But I will leave among you the people who are humble and weak. They will seek refuge in the name of the LORD. The Israelites who remain will no longer act unjustly. They will not lie, and a deceitful tongue will not be found in their mouth. Instead, they will graze peacefully like sheep and lie down. No one will terrify them.

Sing out, Zion! Shout aloud, Israel! The LORD has removed the judgment against you. He has turned back your enemy. Israel's king, the LORD, is in your midst! You no longer need to fear disaster. The LORD your God is with you as a hero who will save you. He takes great delight in you. He will quiet you with his love. He will rejoice over you with singing.

At that time I will deal with those who mistreated you. I will rescue the lame and gather together the scattered. I will give them praise and honor in every land where they were put to shame. At that time I will bring you in. At that time will I gather you. I will give you a name and praise among all the peoples of the earth when I restore your fortunes before your eyes, declares the LORD.

Lord God, hasten your Son's return to end this world of sin. Rescue us from all the evil and take us, the people purified by faith in your Son, to live with you forever. Amen.

104. THE PROPHET HABAKKUK (HABAKKUK)

Habakkuk wonders why God allows so much evil, and God tells him that he will make it all right in time.

How long, LORD, must I cry for help, but you do not listen? I call out to you, "Violence!" but you do not save! Justice is never carried out. In fact, the wicked overwhelm the righteous so that justice is perverted.

Look at the nations and pay attention! Be completely dumbfounded, because I will do something in your lifetime that you will not believe, even though you are warned ahead of time. Watch, I am raising up the Chaldeans, that savage, reckless nation. They will sweep across the whole earth, seizing lands and homes that do not belong to them. They are frightening and terrifying.

LORD, you have made them your instrument of judgment. You whose eyes are too pure to tolerate evil, why do you put up with treacherous people? Why do you keep silent when the wicked swallow up those who are more righteous than they are?

I will stand at my watch post and station myself on the city wall. I will look to see what he will say to me, and what answer he will give to my complaint.

Then the LORD answered me. He said: Record the vision and write it plainly on tablets so that a herald may run with it. Indeed, the vision is waiting for the appointed time. It longs for fulfillment and will not prove false. If it seems slow in coming, wait for it, because it will certainly come.

Look, his soul is puffed up and is not righteous within him—but the righteous one will live by his faith.

Woe to the one who accumulates what is not his. How long will this last? Because you robbed many countries, all those who are left among the nations will rob you.

Be sure of this: The LORD of Armies has determined that the things that the peoples of the world labor for are only fuel for the fire, and that the nations tire themselves out with nothing to show for it. So the earth will be as filled with the knowledge of the glory of the LORD as the waters that cover the sea.

What benefit is provided by a carved idol? Why would the maker trust his own creation? He makes useless gods that cannot speak. Can that thing be your teacher? Although it is covered with gold and silver, there is no life in it at all. But the LORD is in his holy temple. Let the whole earth be silent before him.

This is the prayer of Habakkuk: O LORD, I have heard the report about you, and I stand in awe of your deeds, LORD. In the midst of our years revive those deeds. In your rage, remember to have mercy. God stands up and shakes the earth. He looks, and the nations jump in fright. The ancient mountains are shattered. The age-old hills are flattened. But he goes on forever. The sun and the moon stand still in their palace when your flying arrows flash, when your spear is bright as lightning. In fury you march through the earth. In anger you trample the nations. You march out to save your people, to deliver your anointed one. You strike the head of the wicked nation. When I hear about it, my stomach churns. My lips quiver as I wait for the day of disaster to come upon the people who attack us.

The tree may have no buds, the fields may yield no food, and there may be no cattle in the barns, but I will delight in the LORD and rejoice in God who saves me. The LORD God is my strength. He will give me feet like a deer and make me leap along the high hills.

Lord God, forgive our impatience when we so often have expected things to be fixed immediately. Help us to trust and wait on you to make all things eternally right for us in Jesus, when he returns to give us the salvation he already won for us. Amen.

PART 6

THE EXILE IN BABYLON

The southern kingdom of Judah should have learned their lesson from watching what happened to the northern kingdom of Israel, but they too turned from the Lord. God told them that they would be carried off into captivity for their sin, but he also promised to bring them back from captivity and resettle them in the Promised Land. And so God's people were taken away into captivity in Babylon and waited for the time God would bring them back. But even in a foreign land, God is God and God is with his people.

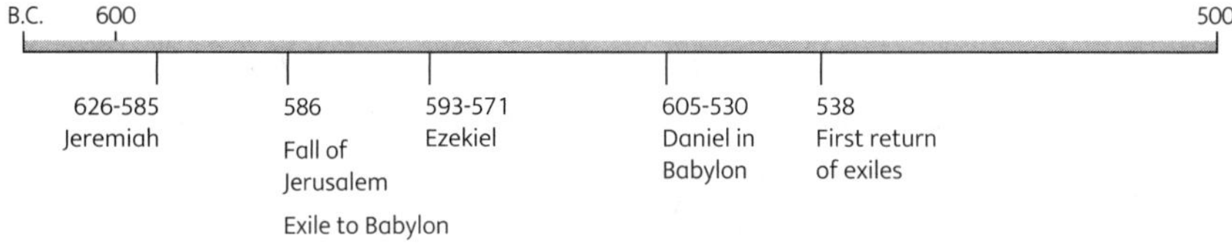

105. THE CALL OF JEREMIAH (JEREMIAH 1)

God calls Jeremiah to be his prophet.

The words of Jeremiah, who was one of the priests.

The word of the LORD came to him in the thirteenth year of the reign of Josiah and continued until the eleventh year of Zedekiah up to the time of the exile of Jerusalem.

The word of the LORD came to me: "Before I formed you in the womb, I knew you, and before you were born, I set you apart. I appointed you to be a prophet to the nations."

But I said, "Ah, LORD God! I really do not know how to speak! I am only a child!"

The LORD said to me, "Do not say, 'I am only a child.' You must go to everyone to whom I send you and say whatever I command you. Do not be afraid of them, because I am with you, and I will rescue you, declares the LORD."

Then the LORD stretched out his hand and touched my mouth. The LORD said to me: "There! I have now placed my words in your mouth. Look, today I appoint you over nations and kingdoms, to uproot and to tear down, to destroy and to overthrow, to build and to plant.

Again the word of the LORD came to me: "What do you see, Jeremiah?"

I answered, "I see a boiling pot tipped away from the north."

Then the LORD said to me: "Disaster will boil over from the north on everyone who lives in the land. Listen, I am summoning all the clans from the northern kingdoms, declares the LORD. They will come against all the cities of Judah. I will pronounce my judgments against Judah because of their wickedness. They have abandoned me. They have made burnt offerings to other gods, and they have bowed down to the work of their own hands.

"Now you, get ready. Rise up and tell them everything I am commanding you. Do not be frightened by them, or I will frighten you in their presence. Look, today I have made you like a fortified city, like an iron pillar, and like bronze walls, to take a stand against the whole land. Stand against the kings of Judah, its officials, its priests, and the people of the land. They will fight against you, but they will not overcome you, because I am with you to rescue you, declares the LORD."

Lord God, you chose us for yourself long before
we were born, and you have brought your Word to us.
Strengthen our faith in Jesus and equip us
to speak your Word to others. Amen.

106. THE LUMP OF CLAY AND THE JAR OF CLAY (JEREMIAH 18-19)

God has Jeremiah use clay to illustrate his judgment and his mercy.

This is the word that came to Jeremiah from the LORD: "Get up, and go down to the potter's house, and there I will reveal my words to you."

So I went down to the potter's house, and he was making something on the wheel. But the pot he was forming out of the clay was ruined. So the potter formed it into a different pot, whatever he saw fit to make.

Then the word of the LORD came to me: "House of Israel, can I not do with you as this potter does? See, like clay in the potter's hands, that is what you are in my hands, house of Israel. I may say that a nation is to be destroyed, but if that nation I spoke about repents of its evil, then I will relent and not bring the disaster I had planned to bring against it. I may say that a nation is to be built, but if they do what is evil in my sight by not listening to my voice, then I will not bring about the good I said I would do for them.

"Now therefore say this to the men of Judah and to those who live in Jerusalem. This is what the LORD says. Look! I am forming a disaster against you. I am devising a plan against you. Turn from your evil ways, each of you, and reform your ways and your actions.

"But they will say, 'It is hopeless! Each of us will always walk in the stubbornness of his own evil heart.'

"Therefore this is what the LORD says. Ask among the nations, 'Who has ever heard anything like this?' Israel has done a most terrible thing. My people have forgotten me. They burn incense to false gods. I will scatter them in front of their enemies like the east wind. I will show them my back and not my face on the day of their calamity."

Some people said, "Come on! Let's make plans against Jeremiah. Let's attack him with words and pay no attention to anything he says."

"This is what the LORD says: Go and buy a clay jar from a potter. Take along some of the elders of the people and some of the priests. Go out to the Valley of Ben Hinnom. Say this to them: 'This is what the LORD of Armies, the God of Israel, says: Watch out! I am going to bring a disaster on this place that will make the ears of all who hear about it ring, because they have forsaken me and have defiled this place. They have burned incense in it to other gods that neither they nor their fathers nor the kings of Judah ever knew. They have filled this place with the blood of the innocent. So the days are coming, declares the LORD, when people will no longer call this place Ben Hinnom, but the Valley of Slaughter.'

"Then break the jar in the sight of the men who are with you. Tell them this is what the LORD of Armies says: 'This is how I will break this people and this city, like a potter's jar that is so smashed that it cannot be made whole again.'"

Then Jeremiah stood in the courtyard of the House of the LORD and said to all the people: "This is what the LORD of Armies, the God of Israel, says. I will certainly bring on this city and on all its towns every disaster that I have proclaimed against it, because they have become stiff-necked, refusing to hear my words."

Lord God, we did not deserve any of what you did to save us from your sin, but we thank and praise you that you did send Jesus to take away our sins and you have through your Word given us the Holy Spirit to bring us to faith. Keep us from ever turning away from you and your Word. Amen.

107. THE RIGHTEOUS BRANCH, THE RETURN, AND THE NEW COVENANT (JEREMIAH 23, 29, 31)

God promises his people better leaders, better deliverances, and a better covenant than the ones they had had up until this point.

Woe to the shepherds who destroy and scatter the sheep of my pasture! declares the LORD. Therefore, this is what the LORD, the God of Israel, says about the shepherds who shepherd my people: You have scattered my flock. You have driven them away. You have not taken care of them, but I will certainly take care of you, because of the evil things you have done, declares the LORD.

I will gather what is left of my flock out of all the countries where I have driven them, and I will bring them back to their pastures. They will be fruitful and multiply. I will raise up shepherds over them who will shepherd them. They will no longer be afraid or terrified, nor will any be missing, declares the LORD.

Listen, the days are coming, declares the LORD, when I will raise up for David a righteous Branch, who will reign wisely as king and establish justice and righteousness on earth. In his days Judah will be saved and Israel will dwell securely. This is his name by which he will be called: The LORD Our Righteousness.

So, mark my words, the days are coming, declares the LORD, when it will no longer be said, "As surely as the LORD lives who brought the Israelites up out of Egypt," but, "as surely as the LORD lives who brought up the descendants of the house of Israel and led them out of a land in the north and from all the countries where I had driven them." Then they will dwell in their own land.

The LORD of Armies, the God of Israel, says this to all the exiles whom I have deported from Jerusalem to Babylon: After seventy years have passed in Babylon, I will come to you and fulfill my gracious word to bring you back to this place. For I know the plans I have for you, declares the LORD, plans to give you peace, not disaster, plans to give you hope and a future. Then you will call on me and come to pray to me, and I will listen to you. When you seek me, you will find me, when you will seek me with all your heart. I will let you find me, declares the LORD, and I will bring you back from your exile. I will gather you from all the nations and from all the places where I have sent you as exiles, declares the LORD. I will bring you back to the place from which I sent you into exile.

At that time, declares the LORD, I will be the God of all the families of Israel, and they will be my people. I have loved you with an everlasting love. I have drawn you with mercy. I will build you up again, and you will be built up, Israel.

Yes, the days are coming, declares the LORD, when I will make a new covenant with the house of Israel and with the house of Judah. It will not be like the covenant I made with their fathers when I led them out of the land of Egypt. They broke that covenant. But this is the covenant I will make with the house of Israel after those days, declares the LORD. I will put my law in their minds, and I will write it on their hearts. I will be their God, and they will be my people. They will all know me, from the least of them to the greatest, declares the LORD, for I will forgive their guilt, and I will remember their sins no more.

Lord God, your Son is our righteousness by which we stand before you. We thank you for this wonderful deliverance from sin that we have in him, and for the eternal covenant he has given us where all depends on your forgiveness and nothing depends on us. Carry out your plans to bless us eternally by faith in him. Amen.

108. DANIEL AND HIS FRIENDS IN BABYLON (DANIEL 1)

Some of the Israelites are deported to Babylon, but God is still with them even there in a foreign land.

In the third year of the reign of Jehoiakim king of Judah, Nebuchadnezzar king of Babylon came to Jerusalem and besieged it. The Lord gave Jehoiakim king of Judah into Nebuchadnezzar's hand, along with some of the vessels of the House of God, and he brought them to the land of Shinar, into the house of his god.

The king told the chief of his court officials to bring some young Israelite men from the royal family or from the nobility, young men who were good looking, who possessed knowledge, understanding, and learning, and who were capable of serving in the king's palace. The king assigned them daily rations from the special royal food and from the king's own wine. In this group of young men were the Judeans Daniel, Hananiah, Mishael, and Azariah. The chief of the officials gave them new names. He gave Daniel the name Belteshazzar, Hananiah the name Shadrak, Mishael the name Meshak, and Azariah the name Abednego.

Daniel made up his mind that he would not defile himself with the special food of the king or with the wine that he drank. So he sought permission from the chief official. The chief of the officials said to Daniel, "I am afraid of my lord the king, who assigned your food and your drink. Why should he see your faces looking less healthy than those of the other young men?"

Daniel said to the superintendent whom the chief of the officials had placed over Daniel, Hananiah, Mishael, and Azariah, "Please test your servants for ten days. Tell them to give us only vegetables, and we will eat them and drink water. Observe our appearance and the appearance of the young men who eat the special royal food. Then deal with your servants based on what you see." So he listened to what they said about this and tested them for ten days.

At the end of ten days, their appearance was noticeably better than that of the others. They were healthier than any of the young men who had been eating the special royal food. So the superintendent permanently took away the special royal food and the wine they were to drink and gave them only vegetables. As for these four young men, God gave them knowledge and insight into all kinds of literature, as well as wisdom. In addition, Daniel also understood every kind of vision and dream. None of the others were found to be comparable to Daniel, Hananiah, Mishael, and Azariah. So they served the king. In every matter concerning wisdom and understanding that the king sought from them, he found them ten times better than all the magicians in his entire kingdom.

Lord God, we live in a world which is not our home, surrounded by those who hate you. Be with us during this life and preserve us in the midst of those who would lead us away from you. Keep us strong in the faith until you bring us out of this world to be with you. Amen.

109. DANIEL INTERPRETS NEBUCHADNEZZAR'S DREAM (DANIEL 2)

God uses Daniel to interpret Nebuchadnezzar's dream that pictures the future rise and fall of nations (Babylon, Persia, Greece, Rome) and the coming Savior.

In the second year of the reign of Nebuchadnezzar, Nebuchadnezzar had a dream. His spirit was troubled, but he fell back to sleep again. The king gave orders to summon the magicians to relate the king's dream to him. So they came and stood before the king. The king said to them, "I had a dream, and my spirit was troubled because I did not understand the dream. If you do not tell me the dream and what it means, your body shall be cut to pieces, and your houses will be made into a pile of rubble. However, if you explain the dream and its meaning, you will receive gifts and honor from me."

They responded, "Let the king tell the dream to his servants, and we will explain its meaning."

The king answered, "You are buying time. You have conspired to give me a lying and cheating response. So, tell me the dream, and I will know that you are also able to explain its meaning to me."

The astrologers responded to the king, "There is no person on earth who is able to reveal what the king wants. No king has ever asked for a thing like this from any magician. No one can reveal it to the king except the gods."

Because of this the king became very angry. He gave orders to put the wise men of Babylon to death. The decree was issued that all the wise men were to be executed. So executioners looked for Daniel and his companions to execute them.

Daniel then entered the court. The king said to Daniel, "Are you able to make known to me the dream that I saw and its meaning?"

Daniel answered the king, "The mystery that the king is asking about, no magicians are able to explain to the king. However, there is a God in heaven who reveals mysteries, and he has made known to King Nebuchadnezzar what will happen in the latter days. This is your dream, the visions in your head while you were on your bed were this:

"You, Your Majesty, were looking, and there was a very great statue. Its head was fine gold, its chest and its arms were silver, its abdomen and its thighs were bronze, its shins were iron, and its feet were partly iron and partly fired clay. You continued to watch until a stone was cut, but not by human hands. It struck the statue on its feet and smashed them. Then all at once the iron, the clay, the bronze, the silver, and the gold were crushed and became like the chaff on the threshing floors of summer. The wind carried them away, and no trace of them could be found. However, the stone that struck the statue became a great mountain and filled the entire earth. This is the dream.

"So now we will interpret its meaning for Your Majesty. You, Your Majesty, are the king of kings to whom the God of Heaven has given a kingdom, power, strength, and glory. You are the head of gold. After you another kingdom will arise that will be inferior to yours. Then a third kingdom of bronze will arise. This kingdom will rule the entire earth. A fourth kingdom will be as strong as iron. It will smash all of these other kingdoms. Because you saw feet partly of potter's clay and partly of iron, part of the kingdom will be strong and part of it will be brittle.

"In the days of those kings, the God of Heaven will establish a kingdom that will never be destroyed. It will crush and put an end to all of these kingdoms, but it will stand forever, just as you saw that a stone was cut from the mountain, but not by human hands, and it crushed the iron, the bronze, the clay, the silver, and the gold. A great God has made known to Your Majesty what will happen after this. The dream is sure, and its interpretation is certain."

Then King Nebuchadnezzar fell facedown and paid homage to Daniel. He promoted Daniel to a high position and gave him many valuable gifts. He made him ruler over the entire province of Babylon and chief prefect over all the wise men of Babylon. When Daniel requested it, the king appointed Shadrak, Meshak, and Abednego over the administration of the province of Babylon. Daniel remained in the royal court.

Lord God, kingdoms rise and kingdoms fall,
but the kingdom of your Son stands forever. Help us
to look not to the kingdoms of this world but to him
and his kingdom of forgiveness and life. Amen.

110. THE FIERY FURNACE (DANIEL 3)

Nebuchadnezzar tries to force God's people into idolatry, but God delivers them when they refuse.

King Nebuchadnezzar made a golden statue. It was ninety feet tall and nine feet wide. He set it up in the plain of Dura in the province of Babylon. King Nebuchadnezzar sent word to all of the rulers of the provinces to come to the dedication of the statue. Then all of the rulers of the provinces assembled for the dedication of King Nebuchadnezzar's statue.

The herald called out loudly, "When you hear the sound of all kinds of musical instruments, you will fall down and worship the gold statue. Whoever does not fall down and worship will immediately be thrown into the blazing fiery furnace." Therefore, when all the peoples heard the sound of all kinds of musical instruments, all the peoples fell down and worshipped the golden statue.

Some Chaldeans approached the king and said, "Shadrak, Meshak, and Abednego do not pay attention to you, Your Majesty. They do not serve your gods, and they do not worship the gold statue that you set up."

In a furious rage Nebuchadnezzar said to bring Shadrak, Meshak, and Abednego. So these men were brought before the king. Nebuchadnezzar said to them, "Is it true, Shadrak, Meshak, and Abednego, that you do not serve my gods and that you do not worship the golden statue that I set up? Now, if you are ready, at the time when you hear the sound of all kinds of musical instruments, you must fall down and worship the statue I made. But if you do not worship, you will immediately be thrown into the blazing fiery furnace. What god will be able to save you from my hands?"

Shadrak, Meshak, and Abednego answered King Nebuchadnezzar, "We have no need to answer you about this matter. Since our God, whom we serve, does exist, he is able to save us from the blazing fiery furnace. So, he may save us from your hand, Your Majesty. But if he does not, you should know that we will not serve your gods, and we will not worship the golden statue that you set up."

Nebuchadnezzar was filled with rage. He said to heat the furnace seven times hotter than it was usually heated. He ordered some soldiers to bind Shadrak, Meshak, and Abednego in order to throw them into the blazing fiery furnace. So these men were bound in their clothing, and they were thrown into the middle of the blazing fiery furnace. Because the king's order was urgent and the furnace was extremely hot, those men who carried Shadrak, Meshak, and Abednego were killed by the intense heat of the fire. But these three men, Shadrak, Meshak, and Abednego, who had been tied up, fell into the blazing fiery furnace.

Then King Nebuchadnezzar was startled and immediately stood up. He said to his advisors, "Didn't we throw three men, who had been tied up, into the fire?"

They answered the king, "Certainly, Your Majesty."

He said, "Look! I see four men, who are untied and walking around in the middle of the fire, unharmed. What is more, the appearance of the fourth is like a son of the gods."

Then Nebuchadnezzar approached the door of the blazing fiery furnace. He said, "Shadrak, Meshak, and Abednego, servants of the Most High God, come out!" Then Shadrak, Meshak, and Abednego came out from the furnace. The royal advisors gathered together and looked at these men. Not a hair on their head was singed, their robes were not damaged, and the smell of fire had not stuck to them.

Nebuchadnezzar said, "Blessed be the God of Shadrak, Meshak, and Abednego, who sent his angel and saved his servants, who trusted in God and ignored the king's command. They gave up their bodies and did not worship any god except their God. So I order that every people that speaks any blasphemy against the God of Shadrak, Meshak, and Abednego shall be cut to pieces, and his house shall be turned into a pile of rubble, because there is no other god who is able to save like this."

Then the king promoted Shadrak, Meshak, and Abednego in the province of Babylon.

Lord God, make us bold confessors of your truth,
unwilling to depart from your Word or serve anything
besides you alone. Preserve us and protect us
through your Son, who rules over all. Amen.

111. THE SUFFERINGS OF JEREMIAH (JEREMIAH 32, 33, 36, 38)

Back in Jerusalem, Jeremiah continues to proclaim God's Word despite opposition.

In the tenth year of Zedekiah, the army of the king of Babylon was besieging Jerusalem. Jeremiah was confined in the courtyard of the guard. Zedekiah had confined him there.

Zedekiah had said, "Why do you prophesy that the Lord says that he will give this city into the hand of the king of Babylon? Why do you say that Zedekiah will not escape from the king of Babylon?"

Then the word of the Lord came to Jeremiah: "Listen to me. I am the Lord, the God who rules over all flesh. Is anything too difficult for me? Watch, I am going to hand over this city to Nebuchadnezzar king of Babylon. The Chaldeans who attack this city will set fire to it. For the people of Israel and the people of Judah have done nothing but evil in my sight.

"The days are coming, declares the Lord, when I will fulfill the good promises that I have spoken to the house of Israel. In those days I will cause a righteous Branch to grow up from David's line. He will establish justice and righteousness on earth. In those days Judah will be saved, and Jerusalem will dwell securely. David will never fail to have a man to sit on the throne. Neither will the priests fail to have a man to stand before me. If you could break my covenant with the day and the night, so that there would no longer be day or night at their appointed times, only then could my covenant with my servant David be broken, so that he would not have a son to reign on his throne. Only then could my covenant with the priests be broken. Just as the stars of the sky cannot be counted and the sand of the seashore cannot be measured, in the same way I will multiply the offspring of my servant David. I will restore them from captivity, and I will have mercy on them."

This word came to Jeremiah from the Lord: "Take a scroll and write on it all the words I have spoken to you." While Jeremiah dictated, Baruch wrote them on the scroll. Baruch brought the scroll to the king. Jehudi read it to the king. Whenever Jehudi had read three or four columns, the king would cut it off with a scribe's knife and throw it into the fire until the entire scroll was burned up in the fire.

The word of the Lord came to Jeremiah: "Take another scroll, and write all the words on it that were on the first scroll." Jeremiah took another scroll and gave it to Baruch, who wrote on it all the same words.

Jeremiah told the people, "This is what the Lord says: Whoever remains in this city will die, but whoever goes over to the Chaldeans will live. This city will surely be handed over to the king of Babylon."

Then the officials said to the king, "This man should be put to death. He is demoralizing all the people by saying these things to them."

King Zedekiah answered, "Very well. He is in your hands."

So they took Jeremiah and threw him into the cistern of Malkijah. Jeremiah sank down into the mud.

Ebed Melek, an official in the king's house, heard that they had put Jeremiah in the cistern. Ebed Melek said to the king, "My lord the king, everything that these men have done to Jeremiah the prophet is evil. They have thrown him into a cistern, where he is likely to die because of the famine."

Then the king gave orders to Ebed Melek: "Lift Jeremiah the prophet up out of the cistern before he dies."

So Ebed Melek lifted him up with ropes and pulled him out of the cistern.

King Zedekiah then sent for Jeremiah. He said to Jeremiah, "As surely as the LORD lives, I will not put you to death, and I will not hand you over to the men who seek your life."

Then Jeremiah said to Zedekiah, "If you surrender to the Babylonian king's officials, your life will be spared, and this city will not be burned. But if you will not surrender to the Babylonian king's officials, then this city will be handed over to the Chaldeans. They will burn it down, and you will not escape from their hands."

Jeremiah remained in the courtyard of the guard until the day Jerusalem was captured. He was still there when Jerusalem fell.

Lord God, when we unjustly suffer as your people, remind us that your Son is our justice and righteousness. Help us to cling to and proclaim your good news whatever the cost. Amen.

112. THE DESTRUCTION OF THE SOUTHERN KINGDOM (2 KINGS 24-25)

God allows the Southern Kingdom to be destroyed by the Babylonians for its sins.

Zedekiah ruled for eleven years. He did evil in the eyes of the LORD. Surely it was because of the LORD's wrath that all this fell upon Judah. Then Zedekiah rebelled against the king of Babylon.

Nebuchadnezzar king of Babylon and all his army came up against Jerusalem. He laid siege to it and built a rampart around it. Famine gripped the city, and the people of the land had no bread.

Then the city wall was breached, and all the soldiers fled. But the Chaldean army pursued the king. They caught him in the Arabah near Jericho. His whole army was scattered from him. So they seized the king. They brought him to the king of Babylon. They slaughtered Zedekiah's sons before his eyes, and then Zedekiah was blinded. They bound him with bronze shackles and took him to Babylon.

Nebuzaradan, captain of the guard of the king of Babylon, came to Jerusalem. He burned the LORD's house and the king's palace and all the houses of Jerusalem. He burned down every large building. The whole Chaldean army tore down the walls around Jerusalem. Nebuzaradan exiled the rest of the people who were left. But the captain of the guard left the poorest people of the land to tend the vineyards and farms.

The Chaldeans took all the utensils which Solomon had made for the House of the LORD.

So Judah went into exile from her country.

Lord God, often the hardships and troubles and shame
we face are very much our own fault. Remember
your mercy to us, and rescue us from our affliction,
through your Son, Jesus Christ. Amen.

113. THE LAMENTATIONS OF JEREMIAH (LAMENTATIONS 1-3, 5)

Jeremiah weeps over the destruction of Jerusalem, but there is still hope.

How lonely the city sits, which once was full of people!
She, who was great among the nations, is now a widow.
She, who was a princess among the provinces, now works as a slave.
At night she weeps bitterly. All her friends have betrayed her.
They are now her enemies.
Judah has gone into exile. She endures affliction and harsh labor.
She lives among the nations. She finds no rest. All her gates
 are deserted.
Her enemies prosper.
Because of her many acts of rebellion, the LORD has brought grief
 to her.
Her children have gone into captivity in the presence of the foe.
Jerusalem has sinned terribly, so she is unclean.
All who once honored her now despise her.
She can only sigh and turn away.
She did not consider the outcome of her sin.
Her collapse was astonishing.

There was no one to comfort her.
Look, LORD, at my affliction, for the enemy has done awful things.
Look, LORD, and see that I have become despised.
Look and see if there is any pain like my pain,
which the LORD caused me to suffer on the day of his burning anger.
From on high he sent fire into my bones and overpowered me.
He made me desolate. I was sick all day long.
The yoke of my sinful rebellion is fastened to my neck.
My sins are bound together by his hand. The LORD is righteous.
I am the one who rebelled against the word from his mouth.
People have heard that I am groaning. There is no one who comforts me.
All my enemies have heard about my misery,
and they rejoiced that you did this.
Yes, my groans are many, and my heart is sick.
How the Lord, in his anger, has covered the daughter of Zion with a dark cloud!
He threw down the beauty of Israel from heaven to earth.
He withdrew his right hand in the presence of the enemy.
On the tent of the daughter of Zion, he poured out his wrath like fire.
The Lord was like an enemy. He swallowed up Israel.
The Lord rejected his altar. He abandoned his holy place.
He delivered her walls and palaces into the hand of the enemy.
Her king and her officials are exiled among the nations.
There is no law. I am emotionally drained over the breaking of my people.
Nevertheless, I keep this in my heart. This is the reason I have hope:
By the mercies of the LORD we are not consumed,
for his compassions do not fail. They are new every morning.
Great is your faithfulness.
My soul says, "The LORD is my portion. Therefore, I will hope in him."
The LORD is good to those who wait for him, to the soul who seeks him.
It is good to hope quietly for the salvation of the LORD.
For the Lord will not push us away forever.
Even though he brings grief,
he will show compassion on the basis of his great mercy.
Certainly, it is not what his heart desires when he causes affliction,
when he brings grief to the children of men.
Remember, LORD, what happened to us.

Look and see our disgrace.
Our inheritance has been turned over to strangers, our houses
to foreigners.
We have become orphans without a father. Our mothers are widows.
Our pursuers are at our throat. We are exhausted. We are given
no rest.
The joy of our hearts has ceased. Our dancing has turned
into mourning.
The crown has fallen off our head. Woe to us, because we have sinned!
Our heart is sick over this.
You, LORD, remain forever. Your throne remains for generation
after generation.
Why do you forget us completely? Why do you abandon us
for so long?
LORD, turn us back to you, and we will return.
Renew our days like long ago, unless you have completely rejected us
and you will be angry at us without limit.

Lord God, we are saddened by our guilt and by the destruction our sin has caused. Remind us, though, that our situation is not hopeless, because you are compassionate, and have forgiven us through Jesus. Bless us for his sake. Amen.

114. EZEKIEL'S VISION OF THE FOUR CREATURES (EZEKIEL 1-3)

While Ezekiel is exiled in Babylon, God shows him a vision of his glory and commissions him to proclaim his Word.

When I was among the exiles by the Kebar Canal, the heavens were opened, and I saw visions of God.

As I watched, I noticed a windstorm coming from the north. There was a large cloud with fire flashing through it, and there was a bright light all around it.

I saw what looked like four living creatures. Each of them had a human appearance, but each one had four faces and four wings. Each one had a face like a man's face, a face like a lion, a face like an ox, also a face like an eagle. Their wings were stretched upward. Each of them had one pair of wings which touched the wings of each of the cherubs next to it, and another pair of wings which covered their bodies. The appearance of the living creatures was like red-hot coals, like the appearance of blazing torches. They looked like jagged bolts of lightning.

As I looked at the living creatures, I noticed one wheel on the ground beside each one of the living creatures. The appearance of the wheels and their design were like the sparkle of topaz and like a wheel within a wheel. They could go in any of the four directions, but the wheels did not turn from side to side when they moved. Their rims were high and intimidating and full of eyes all the way around. Whenever the living creatures moved, the wheels would move with them.

There was something above the heads of the living creatures like the dome of a vaulted ceiling. It looked like ice. It was spectacular. It stretched out above their heads. I heard the sound of their wings, like the sound of rushing water. It was like the voice of the Almighty when they moved—a sound of commotion, like the noise in an army camp.

Above the dome was something that appeared to be a sapphire that was shaped like a throne. Seated on that throne was a figure that looked like a man. I saw something like the gleam of glowing metal with fire in it and all around it. It extended upward from what appeared to be the man's waist. Below what appeared to be his waist, I saw what appeared to be fire, and a bright light surrounded him. The bright light that surrounded him looked like the rainbow that is in the clouds on a rainy day.

This was the appearance of the likeness of the Glory of the LORD. When I saw this, I fell on my face, and I heard a voice speaking. He said to me, "Son of man, stand up on your feet, and I will speak with you." The Spirit entered into me as he spoke to me and brought me up to my feet. Then I heard him speaking to me.

He said to me, "Son of man, I am sending you to the people of Israel, who have been disloyal to me. They and their fathers have rebelled against me to this very day. You are to tell them that this is what the LORD God says. Then, whether they listen or not, then they will know that a prophet has been among them."

Then I looked, and I saw a hand stretched out toward me, and in it there was a rolled-up scroll. Then he said to me, "Son of man, eat what you have received. Eat this scroll, and then go, speak to the house of Israel." I opened my mouth, and he fed me the scroll. It was sweet like honey.

The word of the LORD came to me and said, "Son of man, I have appointed you as a watchman for the house of Israel. When you hear a word from my mouth, you must give them a warning from me. When I announce to a wicked man, "You shall surely die," if you do not warn him, then that wicked man will die because of his guilt, and I will hold you responsible for his blood. But if you warn the wicked man, and he does not turn from his wickedness, he shall die because of his guilt, but you will have saved your own life. But if you warn that man not to sin, and he does not sin, he shall certainly live, and you will have saved your own life."

Lord God, all glory is yours. Give us hearts that listen to your Word and lips that speak it. Amen.

115. EZEKIEL'S VISION OF THE TEMPLE (EZEKIEL 8-11)

God shows Ezekiel a vision of his glory leaving the temple and the people being judged, but those who believe are rescued from the destruction and would be restored.

The hand of the LORD God fell upon me. I looked, and there I saw a figure that looked like a man. From what appeared to be his waist down, he looked like fire, and from his waist up, he had the appearance of a dazzling light, something like glowing metal. He reached out with what looked like a hand and seized me by a lock of hair. Then the Spirit lifted me up between earth and heaven and brought me to Jerusalem, while I was experiencing visions from God. He brought me to the gate into the inner courtyard of the Temple, where the idolatrous image which provokes jealousy was located. When I entered, I looked around, and what did I see! Filthy idols were engraved on the wall, all around. The elders of Israel were standing in front of the images, each with his censer in his hand, and the fragrance of the cloud of incense was ascending. Next I saw twenty-five men bowing down to the sun. Then he said to me, "Have you seen this? Is it too trivial for the house of Judah to commit the abominations they are committing here? Do they also have to fill the land with violence? But I also will act in wrath."

Then he called out with a loud voice, "Bring the supervisors of the city here, each one of them with his weapon of destruction in his hand." Then I noticed six men coming, each with a war club in his hand. There was also one man in the middle with a scribe's kit at his waist. They stood beside the bronze altar.

God called out to the man who had the scribe's kit. The LORD said to him, "Go through Jerusalem and put a cross on the foreheads of those who moan over the abominations being committed in her." To the others he said, "Follow him through the city and strike the people down. Do not show pity. Keep killing until you wipe them out completely. But do not go near anyone who has been marked with the cross." So they went and struck them down throughout the city.

Now the cherubim were standing on the south side of the temple. These were the living creatures that I had seen by the Kebar Canal. Then the Glory of the LORD moved out from the temple and took a position above the cherubim.

The Spirit of the LORD fell upon me and told me to say: "This is what the LORD says. You have killed many people in this city and filled its streets with the slain. But I will drive you out of it. I will bring the sword upon you, declares the LORD God. At the border of Israel I will judge you. Then you will know that I am the LORD, in whose statutes you have not walked."

Then the word of the LORD came to me: "Although I have scattered them among the lands, I will be a sanctuary for them for a little while in the lands to which they have gone. Therefore say, 'This is what the LORD God says. I will gather you from the peoples and assemble you from the lands where you have been scattered, and I will give you the land of Israel. When they arrive back there, they will remove from it all its abominations. I will give them one heart, and I will put a new spirit within you. I will remove the heart of stone from their body and give them a heart of flesh, so that they will walk in my statutes. They will be my people, and I will be their God.' "

Then the cherubim lifted up their wings. The Glory of the God of Israel was positioned above them. The Glory of the LORD went up from the city and stood on the mountain east of the city.

Lord God, it often feels as if you have abandoned your people, but you have claimed us for yourself in Christ's cross and in baptism. Be our sanctuary in this life and renew our hearts. Amen.

116. THE PROMISE OF A SHEPHERD (EZEKIEL 34)

God promises a better Shepherd than the ones the people have right now.

The word of the LORD came to me. "Son of man, prophesy against the shepherds of Israel. Say to those shepherds that this is what the LORD God says:

"Woe to you, shepherds of Israel, who have been shepherding for themselves. Aren't shepherds supposed to shepherd for the benefit of the sheep? You eat the fat. You wear the wool. You slaughter the fattened ones—but you do not shepherd the flock. You have not strengthened the weak. You have not healed the sick. You have not bound up the injured. You have not brought back the strays, and you have not searched for the lost. Instead you have abused them with force. So they scattered, because there was no shepherd, and they became food for all the wild animals. My sheep wandered over the face of the whole earth, with no one looking for them.

"Therefore, this is what the Lord God says. I am against the shepherds. Watch! I will remove my flock from their hand. I will rescue my flock from their mouths, so that they will no longer be food for them. Here I am. I myself will seek the welfare of my flock and carefully search for them. As a shepherd I will search for my flock and rescue them from all the places where they were scattered on a day of darkness. I will gather them from the countries and bring them to their own soil. I will shepherd them on the mountains of Israel. I will lead them into good pasture. I myself will shepherd my flock. I myself will let them lie down, declares the Lord God. I will seek the lost. I will bring back the strays. I will bind up the injured. I will strengthen the weak. I will destroy the fat and the strong, and I will shepherd them with justice.

"Then I will raise up over them one shepherd, and he will tend them. My servant David will tend them, and he will be their shepherd. I, the Lord, will be their God, and my servant David will be the prince among them. I, the Lord, have spoken. Then I will establish a covenant of peace with them, and I will rid the land of wild animals, so they may live securely in the wilderness and sleep in the forests.

"I will make them a blessing. I will send the rain showers down in their season. They will be showers of blessing. The trees in the field will yield their fruit, and the earth will yield its produce. They will be secure on their own land and know that I am the Lord, when I break the bars of their yoke and rescue them from the hand of those who enslaved them. No more will they be plundered by the nations, nor will wild animals devour them. They will live in security, with no one to make them afraid. They will no longer bear the scorn of the nations. They will know that I, the Lord their God, am with them, and that they, the house of Israel, are my people, declares the Lord God. You are my flock of sheep, the sheep of my pasture. You are my people, and I am your God, declares the Lord God."

Lord God, we thank you for Jesus, our Good Shepherd,
who laid his life down for us and took it back up
again for us. Give us shepherds, pastors and teachers,
who faithfully serve us with the good news of
our Good Shepherd. Amen.

117. THE VALLEY OF DRY BONES (EZEKIEL 37)

God shows Ezekiel his ability to give life to dead people and to a dead nation.

The hand of the LORD was upon me. He brought me out by the Spirit of the LORD and set me down in the middle of a valley which was full of bones. There were very many on the valley floor, and they were very dry.

He said to me, "Can these dry bones live?"

I answered, "LORD God, you know."

Then he said to me, "Prophesy to these bones and say to them, 'Dry bones, hear the word of the LORD: I am about to make breath enter you so that you will live. I will attach tendons to you. I will put flesh back on you. I will cover you with skin and put breath in you, and you will live. Then you will know that I am the LORD.' "

So I prophesied as I had been commanded, and as I was prophesying there was a noise, a rattling, as the bones came together, one bone connecting to another. As I watched, tendons were attached to them, then flesh grew over them, and skin covered them. Breath entered them, and they came back to life. They stood on their feet, a very, very large army.

Then he said to me, "These bones are the whole house of Israel. They are saying, 'Our bones are dried up. Our hope is lost. We have been completely cut off.' Therefore, prophesy and say to them that this is what the LORD God says: My people, I am going to open your graves and raise you up from your graves and bring you back to the soil of Israel. Then you will know that I am the LORD, when I open your graves and raise you up from your graves. I will put my Spirit in you, and you will live. I will settle you on your own land, and you will know that I, the LORD, have spoken, and I have done it, declares the LORD.

"My servant David will be king over them, and they will all have one shepherd. They will follow my ordinances and be conscientious about keeping my statutes. They will live on the land I gave my servant Jacob, where your fathers lived. They will live there permanently—they, their children, and their grandchildren—and my servant David will be their prince forever. I will make a covenant of peace with them. It will be an everlasting covenant with them. I will establish them, and I will multiply them and set my sanctuary in their midst forever. My Dwelling Place will be over them. I will be their God, and they will be my people. Then the nations will know that I, the LORD, make Israel holy when my holy place is in their midst forever."

Lord God, when things seem to not be going well
in this life, and when we are facing the end of this life,
comfort us with your amazing power to raise the dead.
Raise us up on the Last Day to enter the eternal life
Jesus has won for us, as you have promised to do. Amen.

118. THE GLORY OF THE LORD RETURNS (EZEKIEL 40, 43, 48)

God shows Ezekiel that his glory will return to his people.

In the fourteenth year after the city was struck down, the hand of the LORD came upon me. In visions of God, he brought me to the land of Israel and set me down on a very high mountain. There was a structure that resembled a city. When he brought me there, I saw a man, who said to me, "Son of man, pay attention to everything that I am about to show you. Report everything you see to the house of Israel."

I saw a temple. Suddenly the Glory of the God of Israel was coming from the east. The appearance of the vision that I saw was like the vision I saw when he came to destroy the city—visions like the vision I saw by the Kebar Canal—and I fell on my face. The Glory of the LORD entered and filled the temple.

Someone said to me: "This is the place of my throne, where I will dwell in the midst of the people of Israel forever. Describe the temple to the house of Israel. Let them measure its perfect pattern."

These are the outside boundaries of the city. The north side is four thousand five hundred cubits long. Three gates are located on the north: one gate of Reuben, one gate of Judah, and one gate of Levi. On the east side, which is four thousand five hundred cubits long, there are three gates: one gate of Joseph, one gate of Benjamin, and one gate of Dan. On the south side, which is four thousand five hundred cubits long, there are three gates: one gate of Simeon, one gate of Issachar, and one gate of Zebulun. On the west side, which is four thousand five hundred cubits long, their gates are three: one gate of Gad, one gate of Asher, and one gate of Naphtali. The perimeter of the city is eighteen thousand cubits, and the name of the city from that day on is "The LORD Is There."

Lord God, fulfill your promise and bring about
your Son's return. Bring all your people together
to the perfect home that he has prepared for us. Amen.

119. THE WRITING ON THE WALL (DANIEL 5)

The kingdom of Babylon falls and is replaced by the kingdom of the Medes and Persians.

King Belshazzar made a great feast for a thousand of his nobles. Belshazzar said to bring the gold and silver vessels that Nebuchadnezzar had taken from the temple in Jerusalem, so that the king and his nobles, his wives and his concubines could drink from them. Then they brought the gold vessels that they had taken from the temple in Jerusalem. So the king and his nobles, his wives and his concubines drank from them. They drank wine and praised gods of gold and silver, of bronze, iron, wood, and stone.

At that moment the fingers of a human hand appeared and wrote on the plaster of the wall of the king's palace. The king saw the hand that was writing. Then the king's cheerful appearance changed, his face grew pale, and his thoughts troubled him. His legs went limp, and his knees knocked together.

The king called out loudly to bring the diviners. The king said to the wise men of Babylon, "Whoever is able to read this writing and explain its meaning will be clothed in purple, with a gold chain around his neck, and he will rule as third highest in the kingdom."

Then all the king's wise men came in, but they were not able to read the writing or tell the king what it meant. Then King Belshazzar was really terrified. He grew even paler, and his nobles were perplexed.

The queen said, "There is a man in your kingdom in whom is a spirit of the holy gods. King Nebuchadnezzar appointed him chief of the magicians because an outstanding spirit and knowledge and insight in interpreting dreams and explaining riddles and solving knotty problems were found in this Daniel, whom the king named Belteshazzar. Now let Daniel be summoned, and he will explain the meaning of the writing."

Then Daniel was brought before the king. The king said to Daniel, "Those wise men who were brought before me to read this writing and to make its meaning known to me were not able to explain the meaning of the message. I have heard about you that you are able to explain meanings clearly and to solve knotty problems. Therefore, if you are able to read the writing and make its meaning known to me, you will be clothed in purple, with a gold chain around your neck, and you will rule as the third in the kingdom."

Then Daniel answered the king: "Keep your gifts for yourself! Nevertheless, I will read the writing to the king, and I will make its meaning known to him. The Most High God gave the kingdom, greatness, splendor, and glory to Nebuchadnezzar. But you, Belshazzar, lifted yourself against the Lord of Heaven. The vessels from his house were brought before you, and you and your nobles, your wives and your concubines drank wine from them. Then you praised gods of silver, gold, bronze, iron, wood, and stone, who do not see and do not hear and do not know. But you did not honor the God who holds your breath in his hand and who controls all your ways. So the hand was sent by him, and this writing was inscribed.

"Now this is the writing that was inscribed: MENE MENE TEKEL PARSIN.

"This is the meaning of the message: *Mene* means that God has counted up your kingdom and paid it out. *Tekel* means that you have been weighed in the scales, and you are too light. *Parsin* means that your kingdom has been broken in two and given to the Medes and the Persians."

Then Belshazzar spoke, and they dressed Daniel in purple, with a gold chain around his neck, and they made him the third highest ruler in the kingdom.

That very night, King Belshazzar the Chaldean was killed. Darius the Mede received the kingdom.

Lord God, teach us to number our days aright,
that we may gain a heart of wisdom. Give us humility
at all times. Whether you have in store for us a long life
or a short life on this earth, use your Word to keep us
always prepared to meet you and in the meantime
to serve you. Amen.

120. DANIEL IN THE LIONS' DEN (DANIEL 6)

Daniel trusts God, and God delivers him from danger.

It seemed like a good plan to Darius to appoint one hundred twenty satraps to rule throughout the kingdom. Above them there would be three supervisors. Daniel was one of them. Daniel distinguished himself above the supervisors and satraps, because there was an outstanding spirit in him. So the king intended to promote him so that he would be in charge of the entire kingdom.

Then the supervisors and satraps kept trying to find a basis for an accusation against Daniel. However, they were unable to come up with an accusation or any evidence of corruption, because he was trustworthy and no neglect of duty or evidence of corruption could be found against him. Then these men said, "We will not find any accusation to bring against this Daniel unless we find something against him concerning the law of his God."

So these supervisors and satraps came as a group to the king and said to him, "All the supervisors and satraps advise the king to establish and enforce a decree that prohibits anyone to pray a prayer to any god or person for thirty days except to you, Your Majesty. Anyone who does so will be thrown into the den of lions. Please establish the decree and sign a document that cannot be changed, according to the law of the Medes and the Persians that cannot be revoked." King Darius signed the written decree.

Now, when Daniel learned that the document had been signed, he went to his house. It had windows on its upper story that opened toward Jerusalem. Three times each day he would get on his knees and pray and offer praise before his God. He continued to do that just as he had been doing before this.

These men came as a group and found Daniel praying and seeking favor from his God. They then went to the king. "Daniel does not pay attention to you, Your Majesty, or to the decree that you signed. Three times each day he is praying his prayers."

When the king heard this report, he was determined to save Daniel. So until sunset he worked hard to rescue him. These men kept saying to the king, "It is the law of the Medes and the Persians that every decree that the king establishes cannot be changed."

Then the king gave the order, and Daniel was brought and thrown into the lions' den. The king said to Daniel, "May your God, whom you serve continually, rescue you." A stone was brought and placed over the mouth of the pit. The king sealed it with his signet ring so that nothing could be changed with regard to Daniel's situation. The king went to his palace. He spent the night without food, and no entertainment was brought before him. But he could not sleep.

At dawn the king arose as soon as it was light and hurried to the lions' den. In a fearful voice the king said to Daniel, "Daniel, servant of the living God, was your God, whom you serve continually, able to rescue you from the lions?"

Then Daniel spoke with the king. "Your Majesty, my God sent his angel and shut the mouth of the lions. They have not hurt me."

Then the king was very glad and said that Daniel should be brought up from the pit. So Daniel was brought up from the pit. He was unharmed because he trusted in his God. The king gave the order, and those men who maliciously accused Daniel were brought and thrown into the lions' den. They had not reached the bottom of the pit when the lions overpowered them and crushed all their bones.

Then King Darius wrote to all the peoples that dwell in the entire earth: "I give this command throughout my royal dominion: People should continually tremble and be afraid before the God of Daniel, because he is the living God, who endures forever. His kingdom will not be destroyed, and his dominion is eternal. He rescues and he saves. He works signs and wonders in heaven and on earth. So he saved Daniel from the power of the lions."

So this Daniel prospered during the reign of Darius.

Lord God, give your representatives in the government wise and upright hearts to govern us well. Spare us from all oppression from the government for our faith and from all commands which would tell us to sin against you. When we are ordered to do something wrong, give us the strength to disobey them and to serve and obey only you. Be with your people that we all may persevere in the faith. Amen.

PART 7

THE RETURN FROM EXILE

Just as God had promised, he rescued his people from their captivity in a foreign land. He did this in an even greater way when Jesus rescued his people from their captivity to sin. Things were nevertheless not always easy now that Israel was back in their promised land. God's people were still sinners, and they were still surrounded by enemies, but now enjoying their homeland once again, they looked forward to the Savior whom God promised would one day come to his people in that land.

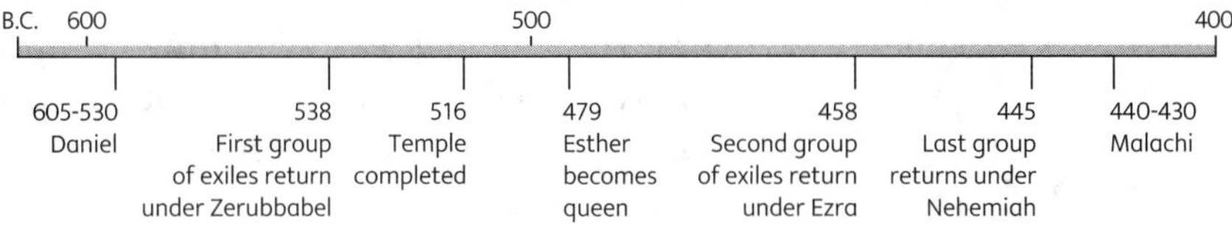

121. THE FIRST RETURN, UNDER ZERUBBABEL (EZRA 1-4)

As God had promised, the Israelites return from their captivity in Babylon to the land of Israel.

In the first year of Cyrus king of Persia, to fulfill the word of the LORD from the mouth of Jeremiah, the LORD stirred up the spirit of Cyrus king of Persia. Cyrus circulated a proclamation throughout his kingdom: "The LORD, the God of Heaven, has given all the kingdoms of the earth to me. He has appointed me to build a house for him in Jerusalem, which is in Judah. From all his people, whoever among you is willing is permitted to go up to Jerusalem in Judah. He may build the House of the LORD, the God of Israel. Any of the exiles, in any place where they are living, may receive support from the people of that place."

King Cyrus also brought out the vessels of the House of the LORD which Nebuchadnezzar had carried away from Jerusalem and put into the house of his gods. Sheshbazzar, the leader of Judah, brought them up with the exiles who went up to Jerusalem.

The people went up from captivity and return to Judah. The entire assembly together numbered 42,360.

Then Jeshua with his fellow priests, and Zerubbabel with his colleagues built the altar of the God of Israel in order to offer burnt offerings upon it. They offered burnt offerings to the LORD upon it.

In the second year after their arrival, Zerubbabel, Jeshua, and everyone who returned from the captivity began to work on the house for the LORD. The builders laid the foundation of the temple of the LORD, and the priests, dressed in their robes, stood by with trumpets, and the Levites, the descendants of Asaph, stood by with cymbals to praise the LORD as prescribed by David king of Israel. They sang antiphonally to praise and thank the LORD: "Truly, he is good, because his mercy toward Israel endures forever."

All the people shouted loud praise to the LORD at the laying of the foundation of the House of the LORD. However, when many of the older priests, Levites, and heads of the families, who had seen the first house, saw this house being founded, they wept loudly, although many raised their voices in a shout of joy. The people could not distinguish the sound of the joyful cry from the sound of the people weeping, because the people were shouting loudly, and the sound could be heard far away.

When the enemies of Judah heard that the exiles were building a temple for the LORD, they approached Zerubbabel and said, "Let us build with you, because, like you, we seek your God, and we have been sacrificing to him since the days Assyria brought us here."

Zerubbabel and Jeshua said to them, "It is not for you to join us in building a house for our God, because we ourselves will build for the Lord."

Then the people of the land kept discouraging the people of Judah and kept trying to make them too frightened to build. They kept bribing officials against them to try to frustrate their plans. In this way the work on the house of God in Jerusalem was stopped.

Lord God, we were held captive to sin, but you have brought us out of exile and made us to be your people. Make us your temple and dwell within us. Chase away the gloom of guilt and give us joy at your salvation. Amen.

122. THE PROPHET HAGGAI (HAGGAI)

Through Haggai God tells the people to consider the way they use their possessions, and he promises to bless the second temple more than the first.

In the second year of King Darius the word of the Lord came through Haggai the prophet to Zerubbabel, governor of Judah, and to Joshua, the high priest.

This is what the Lord of Armies says. This people has said, "It is not the right time for the House of the Lord to be built."

So the word of the Lord came through Haggai the prophet: "Is it time for you to live in your paneled houses while this house lies in ruins? Consider your ways carefully. You sow much seed but you harvest little. You eat but you are never satisfied. This is what the Lord of Armies says. Consider your ways carefully. Go up to the mountains, bring lumber down, and build the House. I will be pleased with it, and I will be glorified, says the Lord. You expected much, but look, there was little. Why? Because my house lies in ruins while each of you is busy with your own house. So it is because of you that the heavens have withheld the dew and the earth has withheld its produce. I called for a drought on everything which the soil produces, on people, on livestock, and on all the labor of your hands."

Then Zerubbabel and Joshua with all the surviving remnant of the people listened to the voice of the Lord their God and to the words of Haggai the prophet, because the Lord their God had sent him. So the people feared the Lord. Then Haggai, the Lord's messenger, spoke the Lord's message to the people: "I am with you, declares the Lord." The

LORD stirred up the spirit of Zerubbabel and the spirit of Joshua and the spirit of all the surviving remnant of the people, and they came and worked on the house for the LORD of Armies, their God, in the second year of King Darius.

The word of the LORD came through Haggai the prophet: "Speak to Zerubbabel and to Joshua and to the remnant of the people: Who is left among you who saw this house in its former glory? How does it look now? Doesn't it seem like nothing in your eyes?

"But now, be strong, Zerubbabel, declares the LORD. Be strong, Joshua! Be strong, all you people of the land, declares the LORD. Get to work, and I will be with you, declares the LORD of Armies. This is the promise I made to you when you left Egypt. My Spirit remains in your midst. Do not be afraid!

"Listen, this is what the LORD of Armies says. In a little while, I will shake all the nations, and the desired of all the nations will come, and I will fill this house with glory, says the LORD of Armies. The glory of this second house will be greater than that of the first one, for in this place I will provide peace."

The word of the LORD came to Haggai: "Speak to Zerubbabel. Say, 'I will shake the heavens and the earth. I will overthrow the thrones of kingdoms. I will destroy the strength of the kingdoms of the nations. On that day, declares the LORD of Armies, I will take you, Zerubbabel, my servant, and I will make you like a signet ring, for I have chosen you, declares the LORD of Armies."

Lord God, we often are selfish with the things
you have given us and do not use them to serve you.
Move us to carefully consider all of our ways.
We thank you for the great forgiveness and glory
and peace you have brought us, your believing people,
by sending our Savior Jesus. Amen.

123. THE TEMPLE IS REBUILT (EZRA 5-6)

The Israelites listen to God and rebuild his temple.

The prophets Haggai and Zechariah prophesied to the Judeans. Zerubbabel and Jeshua began to build the house of the God.

Tattenai governor of Trans-Euphrates said to them, "Who gave you an order to construct this building and to finish this project?"

However, the eye of their God was on the Judean elders, and the officials did not make them stop until the report could go to Darius, and they could respond on the basis of a document concerning this matter.

King Darius issued a decree: "A scroll was located in Ecbatana, and this was written on it:

"'Memorandum: In the first year of King Cyrus, King Cyrus issued a decree regarding the house of God in Jerusalem. That house is to be rebuilt. The cost will be paid by the house of the king. Also the gold and silver vessels of the house of God, which Nebuchadnezzar took from the temple that is in Jerusalem and brought to Babylon, are to be returned, and each vessel is to be taken to the temple that is in Jerusalem.'

"Tattenai governor of Trans-Euphrates, leave the work on that house of God alone. Let the Judeans rebuild that house of God on its site. Furthermore, the complete cost will be paid to these men from the royal treasury, out of the taxes of the trans-Euphrates area, so that the builders will not have to stop.

"May the God who caused his name to dwell there overthrow any king or people who take action in order to destroy that house of God that is in Jerusalem.

"I, Darius, have issued a decree. Let it be carried out exactly."

Then Tattenai did exactly this. So the Judeans continued to build and prosper throughout the prophetic ministry of Haggai and Zechariah. They finished building the temple by the decree of the God of Israel and by the decree of Cyrus, Darius, and King Artaxerxes of Persia.

The Israelites dedicated this house of God with joy. For the dedication of this house of God, they offered bulls, rams, lambs, as well as goats.

The exiles celebrated the Passover. The Israelites who had returned from the exile ate the Passover lambs, together with every person who had separated himself from the impurity of the nations of the land in order to join them, in order to seek the Lord, the God of Israel. For seven days they celebrated the Festival of Unleavened Bread with joy, because the Lord had made them joyful.

Lord God, thank you for giving us a place
where we can go to learn about you and your Son.
Move us to joyfully go there to hear your Word and
sing your praises. Amen.

124. PSALM 118

God's people thank him for the eternal mercy found in the coming Savior.

Give thanks to the LORD, for he is good,
for his mercy endures forever.
Under pressure I cried to the LORD
The LORD answered me.
He set me in a wide open space.
The LORD is with me.
I will not be afraid.
What can people do to me?
The LORD is my helper,
so I will look in triumph on my enemies.
It is better to take refuge in the LORD
than to trust in people.
It is better to take refuge in the LORD
than to trust in human benefactors.
All the nations surrounded me,
but in the name of the LORD I cut them off.
My strength and song is the LORD,
and he has become salvation for me.
Loud shouts of victory are heard in the tents of the righteous:
"The right hand of the LORD has done a mighty deed!"
I will not die. No, I will live,
and I will proclaim the works of the LORD.
The LORD has chastened me severely,
but he has not handed me over to death.
Open for me the gates of righteousness.
I will enter them. I will give thanks to the LORD.
This is the gate to the LORD.
The righteous enter it.
I will give you thanks,
for you answered me,
and you have become salvation for me.
The stone the builders rejected has become the cornerstone.
This is from the LORD.
It is marvelous in our eyes.
This is the day the LORD has made.
Let us rejoice and be glad in it.

O LORD, please save us now.
O LORD, grant us success.
Blessed is he who comes in the name of the LORD.
We bless you from the house of the LORD.
The LORD is God,
and he makes light shine on us.
You are my God, and I will give you thanks.
You are my God, and I will exalt you.
Give thanks to the LORD, for he is good,
for his mercy endures forever.

Lord God, we thank you for your goodness and mercy to us. Your risen Son is the rock on which we are built. He is our salvation from sin. He is our life from death. May we thank and praise you forever. Amen.

125. ZECHARIAH'S VISIONS (ZECHARIAH 1-3, 6)

God shows Zechariah visions of his blessings to come on Israel.

In the second year of Darius, the word of the LORD came to the prophet Zechariah.

The LORD was very angry with your forefathers. Therefore, now you are to tell this people that this is what the LORD of Armies says to them: Return to me, declares the LORD of Armies, and I will return to you.

Then they returned and said, "Because of our ways and our deeds, the LORD of Armies has done to us just as he planned to do to us."

I saw a vision at night. The angel said to me, "This is what the LORD of Armies says: I am very zealous for Jerusalem and for Zion. I have turned to Jerusalem with compassionate feelings. My house will be built in Jerusalem, declares the LORD of Armies, and the measuring line will be stretched out over Jerusalem. Once again my towns will overflow with prosperity. Once again the LORD will console Zion. Once again he will choose Jerusalem."

Then I looked up, and I saw a man there with a measuring line in his hand. I asked him, "Where are you going?"

He answered me, "To measure Jerusalem."

Another angel came and said, "Jerusalem will be inhabited as a city without walls because of the large number of people and livestock in it. For I myself will be a wall of fire around it, declares the LORD, and I will be the glory within it. Attention, Zion! Escape, you who dwell with the daughter of Babylon. For this is what the LORD of Armies says. For the sake of his glory he sent me to the nations that plundered you, because whoever touches you touches the apple of his eye. Yes, I myself will swing my hand over them, and they will become plunder for their own slaves. Sing loudly and rejoice, daughter of Zion. Yes, look! I am coming, and I will dwell among you, declares the LORD. Many nations will be joined to the LORD on that day, and they will become my people. I will dwell among you. Then the LORD will take possession of Judah as his special portion of the holy soil, and he will again choose Jerusalem. Keep silent before the LORD, all flesh, because he has roused himself from his holy dwelling."

Then he showed me Joshua, the high priest, standing before the Angel of the LORD, and Satan was standing at his right hand to accuse him.

The LORD said to Satan, "The LORD rebuke you, Satan! The LORD, who has chosen Jerusalem, rebuke you! Isn't this man a burning stick plucked from a fire?"

Now Joshua was clothed in filthy clothing and standing in front of the angel. Then the Angel of the LORD spoke to those who were standing in front of him: "Remove his filthy clothing."

Then he said to Joshua, "See, I have taken your guilt away from you, so that I may clothe you in a special robe."

I said, "Let them place a clean turban on his head." So they placed a clean turban on his head and got him dressed.

Then the Angel of the LORD spoke solemnly to Joshua: "Look! I am going to bring my servant, the Branch, and I will remove the guilt of this land in a single day. On that day, declares the LORD of Armies, each one of you will invite his neighbor to join him under his vine and under his fig tree."

The word of the LORD came to me: "Take silver and gold and make a crown, and place it on the head of Joshua, the high priest. Tell him that this is what the LORD of Armies says: 'There is a man whose name is the Branch, because he will branch out from his place and build the temple of the LORD. He is the one who will build the temple of the LORD. He will be clothed with majesty, and he will sit and rule on his throne. He will be a priest on his throne, and there will be peaceful relations between the two offices.'"

Lord God, your Son Jesus is our priest who
has taken away all of our sin and our king who rules
over us and brings us prosperity and peace.
May he protect us and defend us
from every attack and accusation of the Devil. Amen.

126. ZECHARIAH'S PROPHECIES (ZECHARIAH 9, 12-14)

Through Zechariah God prophesies about Palm Sunday, Good Friday, and Judgment Day.

Rejoice greatly, Daughter of Zion! Shout, Daughter of Jerusalem! Look! Your King is coming to you. He is righteous and brings salvation. He is humble and is riding on a donkey, on a colt, the foal of a donkey. He will proclaim peace to the nations. His kingdom will extend to the ends of the earth. Because of the blood of my covenant with you, I will release your prisoners from the waterless pit.

On that day I will make Jerusalem a heavy stone for all the peoples. All who lift it will be seriously injured, and all the nations of the earth will be gathered together against it. The LORD will save the tents of Judah. The LORD will protect the inhabitants of Jerusalem. Anyone among them who is feeble will be like David on that day, and the house of David will be like God, like the Angel of the LORD, before them. On that day I will set out to destroy all the nations that come against Jerusalem.

I will pour out on the house of David and on the inhabitants of Jerusalem the Spirit of grace, who pleads for mercy. Then they will look at me, the one they have pierced. They will mourn for him as one mourns for an only child. They will grieve bitterly for him, as one grieves over his firstborn.

On that day a fountain will be opened for the house of David and for the inhabitants of Jerusalem, for sin and for uncleanness. I will cut off the names of the idols from the land, and they will no longer be remembered. I will also remove the prophets and the impure spirit from the land.

Awake, O sword, against my shepherd, declares the LORD of Armies. Strike the shepherd, and the sheep will be scattered, and I will turn my hand against the little ones. Two thirds will be cut off and perish, but one third will be left. I will put that third into the fire, and I will refine them as silver is refined, and I will test them as gold is tested. They will call on my name, and I will answer them. I will say, "This is my people." And they will say, "The LORD is my God."

Listen! A day is coming for the LORD when the plunder taken from you will be divided in your presence. I will gather all the nations to battle against Jerusalem. Then the LORD will go out and fight against those nations. On that day his feet will stand on the Mount of Olives. The LORD my God will come, and all the holy ones will come with him. On that day there will be no light. The light sources will freeze over. It will be a unique day—known to the LORD—neither day nor night. But at evening time there will be light.

On that day living water will flow out from Jerusalem, half of it toward the eastern sea and half of it toward the western sea. It will continue to flow in summer and in winter. The LORD will be King over all the earth. On that day the LORD will be the one, and his name will be the one.

The whole land will be changed into a plain. Jerusalem will be elevated and remain in her place. It will be inhabited, and it will no longer be devoted to destruction. Jerusalem will dwell in security.

This will be the plague with which the LORD will strike all the peoples who have waged war against Jerusalem: Their flesh, their eyes, and their tongues will rot. Every survivor who is left from all the nations will go up year after year to worship the King, the LORD of Armies. But if any of the families of the earth do not go up to Jerusalem to worship the King, the LORD of Armies, no rain will fall on them.

In that day this will be inscribed on the bells of the horses: "HOLY TO THE LORD." The cooking pots will be like the sprinkling bowls in front of the altar. Every pot in Judah will be holy to the LORD of Armies, and all who sacrifice will cook in them.

Lord God, your Son is our humble but conquering king.
We look to him, the one pierced for us, for our salvation.
Bring his return on the Last Day where we will
clearly see his rule over all. Amen.

127. HAMAN'S PLOT (ESTHER 1-5)

The people of Israel who are still in Persia face a deadly threat.

King Xerxes gave a banquet. He commanded the eunuchs to bring before him Queen Vashti in order to show the people her beauty. Queen Vashti refused to come. The king was infuriated. So the king spoke to his advisors. He asked, "What should be done with Queen Vashti?"

Memucan said, "Give her status as queen to a different person, one better than she is."

The advice seemed good to the king, so the king did as Memucan had said.

The attendants to the king said, "Gather all the good-looking, young virgins to the harem. The young woman who pleases the king should be queen instead of Vashti." The king agreed and implemented the plan.

At Susa there was a Jew named Mordecai. Mordecai had raised his cousin Esther because she had no father or mother. She was shapely and good-looking.

Esther was taken to the king's palace. Esther had not revealed her nationality because Mordecai had told her not to. Every young woman received a turn to go to King Xerxes. When her turn came, the king loved Esther more than he loved all the other women. He placed the crown on her head and made her queen instead of Vashti.

When Mordecai was sitting in the king's gatehouse, two of the king's eunuchs plotted to kill King Xerxes. When Mordecai learned about this, he told Queen Esther. She passed the report along to the king, crediting Mordecai by name. The charges were found to be true, and both of them were hanged. This incident was recorded in the record book.

After these events King Xerxes honored Haman. All the servants of the king were bowing down in Haman's presence, but Mordecai did not bow down. When Haman saw that Mordecai was not bowing down in his presence, Haman was enraged. Because the king's servants had made Haman aware of Mordecai's nationality, Haman sought to destroy all the Jews throughout the whole kingdom.

Haman said to King Xerxes, "There is a group of people scattered among your kingdom. They do not keep the laws of the king. It is not good for the king to allow them to get away with this. If the king agrees, a directive should be written to destroy them."

The king said to Haman, "Do with them whatever seems good to you."

Letters were sent to all the provinces to kill all the Jews on the thirteenth day of the twelfth month. The decree was proclaimed to all the peoples in every province so that they could be ready for that day.

When Mordecai became aware of everything that had happened, he sent Hathak to take this message to Esther: "If you keep silent, deliverance for the Jews will spring up from somewhere. Who knows whether you have become queen for a time like this!"

Esther responded to Mordecai, "I will go to the king, contrary to the law. And if I perish, I perish!"

Esther stood in the inner court of the king's palace. The king was sitting on the throne in the reception hall, opposite the entrance.

When the king saw Queen Esther standing in the court, the king held out to Esther the golden scepter. Esther approached and touched the scepter.

The king said to her, "What concerns you, Queen Esther?"

Esther said, "If it is agreeable to the king, the king and Haman should come today to a banquet that I have made."

So the king and Haman came to the banquet that Esther had prepared.

While the king was drinking wine, he said to Esther, "What is your request?"

Esther answered, "If it pleases the king, let the king and Haman come to a banquet, which I will make for them tomorrow."

Haman went out that day full of joy. But when Haman saw Mordecai at the king's gate, and Mordecai did not stand before him, Haman was filled with rage. Haman went to his house and called together his friends and his wife Zeresh. Haman reviewed for them how the king had elevated him. Haman said, "But none of this means anything to me whenever I see Mordecai the Jew."

Zeresh his wife and all his friends said to him, "Make a gallows seventy-five feet high. In the morning tell the king that Mordecai should be hanged on it." In Haman's opinion this was good advice, so he had the gallows made.

Lord God, preserve us as we live as your people
in a land that is not our own. Help us to faithfully
use our resources, abilities, and positions to make
the most of the times and opportunities you
have given us to serve you. Amen.

128. ESTHER SAVES THE JEWS (ESTHER 6-10)

God saves his people through what looks like a string of coincidences.

That night the king could not sleep, so he ordered that the chronicles of his reign be brought to him. These accounts were read to the king. They found the account about the incident when Mordecai had reported the king's two eunuchs who had tried to assassinate King Xerxes.

The king said, "What honor has been given to Mordecai for this?"

The servants said, "Nothing has been done for him."

Just then Haman had come to the outer court of the king's palace to speak to the king about hanging Mordecai.

When Haman came in, the king said to him, "What should be done to honor the man with whom the king is pleased?"

Haman said in his heart, "Who could there be that the king would be more pleased to honor than me?"

Haman said to the king, "The man whom the king is pleased to honor should be clothed with garments, given a horse, and crowned with a crown. Let him ride on the horse in the public square of the city. Walking in front of him, they will proclaim, "This is what is done for the man whom the king is pleased to honor."

The king said to Haman, "Do this for Mordecai the Jew. Do not leave out a thing from whatever you have said."

Haman took the clothing and the horse, clothed Mordecai, had him ride through the public square of the city, and proclaimed before him, "This is what is done for the man whom the king is pleased to honor."

Haman hurried to his home, mourning, with his head covered. The king's eunuchs arrived and rushed Haman to the banquet that Esther had prepared.

So the king and Haman went to the feast with Queen Esther. When they were again drinking wine, the king said to Esther, "What is your request, Queen Esther?"

Queen Esther responded, "My King, if I have found favor in your eyes, I am asking that my life be spared, and I am seeking the lives of my people, because I and my people have been sold to be killed."

King Xerxes said to Queen Esther, "Who is this person who has the audacity to do this?"

Esther said, "This hateful enemy is this evil Haman!" Haman was terrified.

The king rose angrily from the place and went to the palace garden. But Haman stayed to beg for his life from Queen Esther, because he saw the king had evil plans for him.

Just as the king was returning to the hall, Haman was falling onto the couch on which Esther was lying. The king said, "Will he even assault the queen when I am in the building?"

One of the eunuchs present with the king said, "You know, there is a gallows seventy-five feet high standing by the house of Haman, which he made for Mordecai, the person who spoke up for the benefit of the king."

The king said, "Hang him on it."

So they hanged Haman on the gallows which he had prepared for Mordecai.

The king took off his signet ring that he had taken from Haman and gave it to Mordecai.

Esther spoke to the king. She fell at his feet and said, "If I have found favor, a decree should be written to nullify the letters for the plot of Haman."

The king gave the Jews in every city the right to gather together to defend their own lives and to kill any people that might attack them. In all the provinces, a law proclaimed to all the peoples that on the thirteenth day of the twelfth month the Jews would be ready to avenge themselves on their enemies.

In every province and in every city which the message of the king reached, his edict brought gladness and joy to the Jews. There was a feast and a holiday. Many of the peoples of the land declared themselves Jews because the fear of the Jews had fallen upon them.

On the day on which the enemies of the Jews hoped to obtain power over them, the situation was reversed so that the Jews would gain power over those who hated them. The Jews struck all their enemies with the sword, slaughtering and destroying them.

The king promoted Mordecai the Jew: second in command to King Xerxes.

Lord God, you work through all events, big and small, to
bring about what is best for us. Give us a faith
which trusts you even when things look bleak,
even when we cannot understand what you are doing.
Remind us that all things will work out
for our good in Christ Jesus. Amen.

129. THE SECOND RETURN, UNDER EZRA (EZRA 7-10)

God brings more of his people back from captivity, and they again follow God's Word.

During the reign of King Artaxerxes of Persia, Ezra came up from Babylon. He was a scribe skilled in the Law of Moses. The king granted him his entire request, because the hand of the Lord his God was upon him. Some of the Israelites went up to Jerusalem.

The hand of our God was upon us, and he delivered us from the hand of enemies and from ambushes on the way. We arrived in Jerusalem.

The leaders approached me and said, "The people of Israel have not separated themselves from the peoples of the lands, who live according to their detestable practices. They have taken wives from their daughters for themselves and for their sons. They have thereby mixed the holy seed with the peoples of the lands!"

When I heard about this situation, I tore my clothing and my robe, and I pulled out some of the hair on my head and my beard. I got down on my knees and stretched out my hands to the Lord my God. I said, "My God, I am ashamed to lift my face to you, because our guilt is so great that it reaches to the heavens. From the days of our ancestors until today, we have been extremely guilty.

"Now, for a short time, mercy has been shown to us from the LORD, in order to leave us a remnant that has escaped and to give us a stake in his Holy Place, so that our God may give us a little relief in our slavery. However, even in our slavery our God has not abandoned us but has extended favor to us before the kings of Persia to raise up the house of our God and to restore its ruins, and to give us a protective wall in Judah and in Jerusalem.

"Now, what can we say after this, our God? For we have forsaken your commandments. You, God, punished us less than we deserved and gave us a remnant that has escaped like this. Should we break your commandments again by intermarrying with the peoples who commit these detestable practices?

"LORD, God of Israel, it is because you are righteous that we are left with a remnant today. Here we are before you in our guilt, but no one can stand before you because of this."

Now as Ezra prayed and confessed, weeping and throwing himself down in front of the house of God, a very large crowd from Israel gathered to him, including men, women, and children. The people also wept bitterly.

Then Shekaniah responded to Ezra, "We have been unfaithful to our God and have married foreign wives from the peoples of the land. However, now there is hope for Israel in this matter. So now let us make a covenant with our God to send away all our wives and the children born to them. Let it be done according to the law. We are with you."

Then Ezra got up and required all Israel to take an oath that they would deal with this matter. So they took an oath. Then a proclamation was made throughout Judah for all the exiles to gather in Jerusalem. Anyone who would not come within three days would forfeit all his property, and he would be banished from the community of the exiles. So all the men of Judah gathered in Jerusalem within three days. Ezra said to them, "You have been unfaithful and have married foreign wives, thereby adding to the guilt of Israel. So now, give praise to the LORD, the God of your fathers, and do his will—separate yourselves from the peoples of the land and from your foreign wives."

The entire assembly answered in a loud voice, "It is so! We must do as you have said."

So the exiles acted according to this decision.

Lord God, your Word is a lamp to our feet and a light for our pathway. Fix our eyes and hearts on your Word and use it to increase our faith and direct our lives. Amen.

130. THE THIRD RETURN, UNDER NEHEMIAH (NEHEMIAH 1-2, 4, 6)

God brings even more of his people back from captivity, and Nehemiah leads them in rebuilding Jerusalem's walls.

The words of Nehemiah:

I was in Susa. Hanani came to me with men from Judah. I asked them about the remnant of the Jews who had survived the captivity and had escaped from it, and about Jerusalem.

They said to me, "The survivors from the captivity who are there in the province are in great misery and shame. The wall of Jerusalem is broken down, and its gates have been burned."

When I heard about these things, I sat down and wept. I mourned for days, fasting and praying before the God of Heaven.

I was cupbearer to the King. In the twentieth year of King Artaxerxes, wine was being served to the king, and I took the wine and gave it to the king. I had never been sad in his presence, so the king said to me, "Why do you look sad?"

I said to the king, "The place of my ancestors' tombs lies in ruins and its gates have been consumed by fire."

Then the king said to me, "What do you want?"

So I prayed to the God of Heaven, and I said to the king, "If it seems good to the king, then send me to Judah, to the city where my ancestors' tombs are, and let me rebuild it." The king was pleased to send me.

So I arrived at Jerusalem. I began inspecting the walls of Jerusalem, which had been breached, and its gates, which had been consumed by fire. The officials did not know where I had gone and what I was doing. I had not yet told the people. So I said to them, "Come, let's rebuild the wall of Jerusalem, and we will no longer be disgraced."

They said, "Let's rebuild!"

When Sanballat the Horonite, Tobiah the Ammonite official, and Geshem the Arab heard about it, they ridiculed us and held us in contempt. They said, "What are you doing? Are you rebelling against the king?"

I responded, "The God of Heaven will make us successful. We, his servants, will rise up and rebuild."

So we built the wall, and the entire wall was completed, up to half its height, because the people were determined to do it.

Now when Sanballat, Tobiah, the Arabs, the Ammonites, and the Ashdodites heard that the repair of Jerusalem's walls had progressed, it infuriated them. So all of them conspired to come to attack Jerusalem. However, we prayed to our God, and we posted a guard over the builders day and night. Half of the young men were doing the work, and half of them were holding shields, spears, and bows and wearing armor. As they built, the builders were armed. So we continued to work with half of the people holding spears, from the crack of dawn until the stars came out.

The wall was finished in fifty-two days. As all our enemies heard about it, all the nations that were around us became afraid and lost their confidence. They knew that this work had been accomplished by our God.

Lord God, come to the aid of your people throughout the world as they face hardship and persecution.
Use us to help our neighbor with our words and actions and to build up your church with your Word.
Keep us from forgetting that you are the one who does all good things. Amen.

131. EZRA READS THE LAW (NEHEMIAH 8)

God's people hear God's Word.

All the people gathered together at the public square. They told Ezra the scribe to bring the Book of the Law of Moses, which the LORD had commanded Israel. So on the first day of the seventh month, Ezra the priest brought the Law before the congregation. From dawn until midday in front of the public square, he read from the scroll. All the people listened attentively to the Book of the Law.

Ezra stood on a wooden platform made for the occasion. All the people could see Ezra. As he opened the scroll, all the people stood. Then Ezra blessed the LORD, the great God, and all the people answered, "Amen! Amen!" while they lifted up their hands and then knelt and bowed down with their faces to the ground.

Jeshua and the rest of the Levites helped the people understand the Law, while the people remained standing in their places. So they read from the Book of the Law of God clearly and interpreted it, and the people understood what was read.

Then Nehemiah the governor, Ezra the priest and scribe, and the Levites said to all the people, "Today is holy to the LORD your God. Do not mourn or cry!" because all the people were crying as they heard the words of the Law.

Nehemiah said to them, "Go, eat rich food and drink sweet drinks and send portions to those who have nothing prepared, because today is holy to our Lord. Do not grieve, because the joy of the LORD is your strength."

Then the Levites silenced all the people, saying, "Hush! Today is holy. Do not grieve."

All the people went to eat and drink and to send portions to others and to celebrate with great joy, because they understood the words that had been made known to them.

On the second day, they found written in the Law that the Israelites should dwell in temporary shelters during the festival of the seventh month. So the people went out and made shelters for themselves. The entire congregation that had returned from the captivity made shelters and stayed in the shelters. From the days of Joshua until that day, the Israelites had not celebrated in this way, because there was very great joy. Ezra also read from the Book of the Law of God every day, from the first day to the last day of the festival. They celebrated a festival for seven days, and on the eighth day they held an assembly according to the ordinance.

Lord God, keep us steadfast in your Word and
open our heart to read it each day. Through your Word
about your Son, give us the joy of sins forgiven.
May this always be our strength in life. Amen.

132. PSALM 119 (PSALM 119)

This psalm celebrates the wonderful gift God has given us in his Word.

How I love your laws!
I meditate on them all day long.
Your commandment makes me wiser than my enemies,
because it is always with me.
I have more wisdom than all my teachers,
because your testimonies are my meditation.
I have more understanding than the elders,

because I guard your precepts.
I have kept my feet off every evil path
in order to keep your words.
I have not turned from your judgments,
because you yourself have instructed me.
How sweet are your sayings to my taste,
sweeter than honey to my mouth!
From your precepts I gain understanding,
therefore I hate every false path.
Your words are a lamp for my feet
and a light for my pathway.
I have sworn and affirmed,
that I will keep your righteous judgments.
I have suffered much.
LORD, give me life according to your words.
LORD, please accept the willing praise from my mouth
and teach me your judgments.
I take my life in my hands constantly,
but I will not forget your law.
The wicked have set a snare for me,
but I have not wandered from your precepts.
I have inherited your testimonies forever.
Yes, they are the joy of my heart.
I turn my heart to do your statutes
forever, right to the end.

Lord God, we thank you for giving us your Word,
in which you show us our sinfulness but also our Savior.
Continue to bless us as we read your Word.
Strengthen our faith and grow our love through it. Amen.

133. MALACHI, THE LAST OLD TESTAMENT PROPHET (MALACHI)

God through Malachi shows his people's hypocrisy, but then promises to send a messenger (John the Baptist) followed by another messenger (Jesus) who would bring righteousness and healing.

The word of the LORD to Israel through Malachi.
I have loved you, says the LORD.
But you say, "How have you loved us?"

Was not Esau Jacob's brother? declares the LORD. I loved Jacob, but I hated Esau. I turned Esau's mountains into a desolate place.

You despise my name by bringing defiled food to my altar.

But you say, "How have we defiled you?"

You defile me when you bring a blind animal as a sacrifice. When you bring something lame and sick, isn't that evil? Try bringing that to your governor. Would he be pleased with you? I am not pleased with an offering from your hand.

Yes, from the rising of the sun to the place where it sets, my name will be great among the nations! In every place a pure offering will be presented to my name, because my name is great among the nations, says the LORD of Armies.

Why do we violate our vows to each other, polluting the covenant of our fathers? Judah has acted unfaithfully. Judah is married to the daughter of a foreign god. May the LORD cut off from the tents of Jacob any man who does this, even if he brings an offering to the LORD of Armies!

This is the second thing you do: You cover the LORD's altar with tears, with weeping and crying, because there is no longer any favorable response to your offering. So you ask, "Why is this happening?" This is why—because the LORD is a witness in the case between you and the wife you married when you were young, because you have betrayed her—though she was your partner, the wife with whom you made a covenant! So guard yourselves in your spirit, and do not act unfaithfully against the wife you married when you were young. He hates divorce! That is what the LORD says.

You have made the LORD weary with your words.

You say, "How have we made him weary?"

Whenever you say that anyone who does evil is good in the LORD's eyes or that the LORD takes pleasure in evildoers. Or whenever you say, "Where is the God of justice?"

Look! I am sending my messenger! He will prepare the way before me. Then suddenly the Lord, whom you are seeking, will come to his temple! The Messenger of the Covenant, in whom you delight, will surely come, says the LORD of Armies.

But who can endure the day when he comes? Who will remain standing when he appears? For he will be like a refiner's fire, like launderers bleach! He will purify the sons of Levi and refine them like gold and like silver. They will belong to the LORD and bring him an offering in righteousness. Judah and Jerusalem's offerings will be pleasing to the LORD as they were in the days of old.

Certainly I, the LORD, do not change. That is why you, sons of Jacob, have not come to an end. Since the days of your fathers, you have turned aside from my statutes and have not kept them. Return to me, and I will return to you, says the LORD of Armies.

You say, "In what way should we return?"

Will a man rob God? You are robbing me!

You say, "How have we robbed you?"

In regard to the tithe and the special offering. Bring the complete tithe to the storehouse so that there may be food in my house. Just test me in this, says the LORD of Armies. See whether I do not open for you the windows of heaven and pour down blessing on you, until there is more than enough.

Look! The day is coming, burning like a blast furnace. All the arrogant and every evildoer will be stubble. But for you who fear my name, the sun of righteousness will rise, and there will be healing in its wings. You will go out and jump around like calves from the stall. You will trample the wicked.

Remember the law of my servant Moses, which I commanded to him at Horeb to serve as statutes over all Israel.

Look! I am going to send Elijah the prophet to you before the great and fearful day of the LORD comes! He will turn the hearts of fathers to their children and the hearts of children to their fathers. Otherwise, I will come and strike the land with complete destruction.

Lord God, we confess that we have not kept
your commandments in our thoughts, words, and
actions. But you have restored our hearts in repentance
and purified them in your Son. As we rejoice in
his first coming, we long for his second coming.
Keep us for yourself until that day. Amen.

THE NEW TESTAMENT

PART 1

THE EARLY LIFE OF CHRIST (THE FOUR GOSPELS)

For about four hundred years after God's words through his prophet Malachi, God did not give his people any new messages. They continued to wait for that promised Savior as well as for the messenger God said he would send to prepare his way. While the Jewish people waited, many changes took place in the world they lived in. The Persian Empire was defeated by Alexander the Great, the leader of the Greeks. When a later Greek king defiled the temple and tried to force the Jewish people to worship idols, they rebelled and reclaimed their land. The Jewish celebration Hanukkah celebrates their rededication of the temple. Unfortunately, the Jewish people, when they finally ruled themselves again, descended into civil war, and the new world empire, Rome, intervened and took control. They set up an Edomite named Herod as the local leader in Israel. It is against this backdrop and into this world that God fulfills his promise and sends the Savior that God's people had been waiting for centuries: Jesus. Jesus, both God and man, would be a very different kind of king than the people were used to. But as one who rescues us from sin by his life and death, he is the exact kind of king we all need.

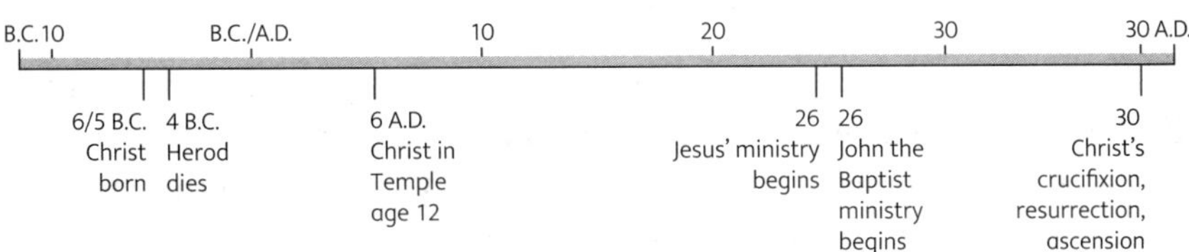

134. INTRODUCTION TO THE NEW TESTAMENT (JOHN 1)

Jesus, the Word of God, the same one through whom the world was created, is the one who became man to save the world.

In the beginning was the Word, and the Word was with God, and the Word was God. He was with God in the beginning. Through him everything was made, and without him not one thing was made that has been made. In him was life, and the life was the light of mankind. The light is shining in the darkness, and the darkness has not overcome it.

There was a man, sent from God, whose name was John. He came as an eyewitness to testify about the light so that everyone would believe through him. He was not the light, but he came to testify about the light.

The real light that shines on everyone was coming into the world. He was in the world, and the world was made through him, yet the world did not recognize him. He came to what was his own, yet his own people did not receive him. But to all who did receive him, to those who believe in his name, he gave the right to become children of God. They were born, not of blood, or of the desire of the flesh, or of a husband's will, but born of God.

The Word became flesh and dwelled among us. We have seen his glory, the glory he has as the only-begotten from the Father, full of grace and truth. For out of his fullness we have all received grace upon grace. For the law was given through Moses; grace and truth came through Jesus Christ. No one has ever seen God. The only-begotten Son, who is close to the Father's side, has made him known.

Lord God, you created all things through Christ,
and it is only through him that we know you.
We thank you for his becoming a human being
just like us to take our place. Teach us more
about him as we read your Word. Amen.

135. THE BIRTH OF JOHN THE BAPTIST ANNOUNCED (LUKE 1)

God sends an angel to announce the birth of the forerunner of the Savior, but Zechariah does not believe it.

In the days of Herod, king of Judea, there was a certain priest named Zechariah. His wife was from the daughters of Aaron, and her name was Elizabeth. They were both righteous before God, walking blamelessly in all the commandments and righteous decrees of the Lord. They did not have a child because Elizabeth was unable to bear children, and they were both well along in years. On one occasion, while Zechariah was serving as priest before God and his division was on duty, he was chosen by lot to go into the temple of the Lord and burn incense. The whole crowd of people were praying outside the temple during the hour of the incense offering.

An angel of the Lord appeared to him, standing on the right side of the altar of incense. When Zechariah saw him, he was startled and overcome by fear. But the angel said to him, "Do not be afraid, Zechariah, because your prayer has been heard. Your wife Elizabeth will bear a son for you, and you are to name him John. You will have joy and gladness, and many will rejoice at his birth, because he will be great in the sight of the Lord. He is never to drink wine or beer. He will be filled with the Holy Spirit, even from his mother's womb. He will turn many of the sons of Israel back to the Lord their God. He will go before him in the spirit and power of Elijah, to turn the hearts of the fathers to the children, and to turn the disobedient to the wisdom of the righteous, to prepare a people who are ready for the Lord."

Zechariah said to the angel, "How can I be sure of this, because I am an old man, and my wife is well along in years?"

The angel answered him, "I am Gabriel. I stand in the presence of God and was sent to speak to you in order to tell you this good news. Now listen, you will be silent and unable to speak until the day when these things happen, because you did not believe my words, which will be fulfilled at the proper time."

Meanwhile, the people were waiting for Zechariah and wondering what was taking him so long in the temple. When he did come out, he was unable to speak to them. Then they realized that he had seen a vision in the temple. He kept making signs to them and remained unable to speak.

When the days of his priestly service were completed, he went back to his home.

After those days his wife Elizabeth conceived. She kept herself in seclusion for five months, saying, "The Lord has done this for me in the days when he looked with favor on me and took away my disgrace among the people."

Lord God, your promises are always certain and
your words are always true. Give us hearts which eagerly
believe everything you have to say and which
do not give in to doubt. Amen.

136. THE BIRTH OF JESUS ANNOUNCED (LUKE 1)

God sends an angel to announce to Mary the birth of the Savior of the world. Unlike Zechariah, Mary responds with faith and joy.

In the sixth month, the angel Gabriel was sent from God to a town of Galilee named Nazareth, to a virgin pledged in marriage to a man whose name was Joseph, of the house of David. The virgin's name was Mary. The angel went to her and said, "Greetings, you who are highly favored! The Lord is with you. Blessed are you among women."

But she was greatly troubled by the statement and was wondering what kind of greeting this could be. The angel said to her, "Do not be afraid, Mary, because you have found favor with God. Listen, you will conceive and give birth to a son, and you are to name him Jesus. He will be great and will be called the Son of the Most High. The Lord God will give him the throne of his father David. He will reign over the house of Jacob forever, and his kingdom will never end."

Mary said to the angel, "How will this be, since I am a virgin?"

The angel answered her, "The Holy Spirit will come upon you, and the power of the Most High will overshadow you. So the holy one to be born will be called the Son of God. Listen, Elizabeth, your relative, has also conceived a son in her old age even though she was called barren, and this is her sixth month. For nothing will be impossible for God."

Then Mary said, "See, I am the Lord's servant. May it happen to me as you have said." Then the angel left her.

In those days Mary hurried to Judah. She entered the home of Zechariah and greeted Elizabeth. Just as Elizabeth heard Mary's greeting, the baby leaped in her womb, and Elizabeth was filled with the Holy Spirit. She called out with a loud voice and said, "Blessed are you among women, and blessed is the fruit of your womb! But why am I so favored that the mother of my Lord should come to me? In fact, just now, as soon as the sound of your greeting reached my ears, the baby in my womb leaped for joy! Blessed is she who believed, because the promises spoken to her from the Lord will be fulfilled!"

Then Mary said, "My soul proclaims the greatness of the Lord, and my spirit has rejoiced in God my Savior, because he has looked with favor on the humble state of his servant. Surely, from now on all generations will call me blessed, because the Mighty One has done great things for me, and holy is his name. His mercy is for those who fear him from generation to generation. He has shown strength with his arm. He has scattered those who were proud in the thoughts of their hearts. He has brought down rulers from their thrones. He has lifted up the lowly. He has filled the hungry with good things, but the rich he has sent away empty. He has come to the aid of his servant Israel, remembering his mercy, as he spoke to our fathers, to Abraham and his offspring forever."

Mary stayed with Elizabeth about three months and then returned to her home.

Lord God, nothing is impossible with you. We thank
and praise you that you have done what seems impossible
to us—sending your Son to be born of a virgin,
sending your Son to be born as a human being,
sending your Son to be our Savior. Scatter our pride
and give us humble hearts which see our sin.
Lift us up in the forgiveness of your Son Jesus. Amen.

137. THE BIRTH OF JOHN THE BAPTIST (LUKE 1)

The forerunner of the Savior is born.

When the time came for Elizabeth to have her baby, she gave birth to a son. Her neighbors and relatives heard that the Lord had shown her great mercy, and they were rejoicing with her. On the eighth day they came to circumcise the child. They wanted to call him Zechariah after the name of the father. But his mother answered, "No. He will be called John."

They said to her, "There is no one among your relatives who is called by this name." They made signs to his father, to see what he wanted to name him.

He asked for a writing tablet and wrote, "His name is John." And they were all amazed.

Immediately Zechariah's mouth was opened, his tongue was loosed, and he began to speak, praising God. Fear came on all who lived around them. In the entire hill country of Judea people were talking about all these things. And everyone who heard this took it to heart, saying, "What then will this child be?" Clearly, the hand of the Lord was with him.

His father Zechariah was filled with the Holy Spirit and prophesied: "Blessed is the Lord, the God of Israel, because he has visited us and prepared redemption for his people. He has raised up a horn of salvation for us in the house of his servant David, just as he said long ago through the mouth of his holy prophets. He raised up salvation from our enemies and from the hand of all who hate us, in order to show mercy to our fathers by remembering his holy covenant, the oath which he swore to Abraham our father, to grant deliverance to us from the hand of our enemies, so that we are able to serve him without fear, in holiness and righteousness before him all our days. And you, child, will be called a prophet of the Most High, because you will go before the Lord to prepare his ways, to give his people the knowledge of salvation by the forgiveness of their sins, because of God's tender mercies, by which the Rising Sun from on high will visit us, to shine on those who sit in darkness and in the shadow of death, to guide our feet into the way of peace."

The child continued to grow and became strong in spirit. He lived in the wilderness until the day of his public appearance to Israel.

Lord God, all praise to you who have kept your promises and sent us your salvation. Now that you have set us free from guilt and punishment and fear, enable us to serve you in holiness and righteousness all our days. Amen.

138. THE BIRTH OF JESUS (LUKE 2)

Christ the Savior is born.

In those days a decree went out from Caesar Augustus that all the world should be registered. This was the first census taken while Quirinius was governing Syria. And everyone went to register, each to his own town. And Joseph also went up from Galilee, out of the town of Nazareth, into Judea, to the town of David, which is called Bethlehem, because he was from the house and family line of David. He went to be registered with Mary, his wife, who was pledged to him in marriage and was expecting a child.

And so it was that while they were there, the time came for her to give birth. And she gave birth to her firstborn son, wrapped him in swaddling cloths, and laid him in a manger, because there was no room for them in the inn.

There were in the same country shepherds staying out in the fields, keeping watch over their flock at night. An angel of the Lord appeared to them, and the glory of the Lord shone around them, and they were terrified! But the angel said to them, "Do not be afraid. For behold, I bring you good news of great joy, which will be for all people: Today in the town of David, a Savior was born for you. He is Christ the Lord. And this will be a sign for you: You will find a baby wrapped in swaddling cloths and lying in a manger." Suddenly, there was with the angel a multitude from the heavenly army, praising God and saying, "Glory to God in the highest, and on earth peace, good will toward mankind."

When the angels went away from them into heaven, the shepherds said to one another, "Now let's go to Bethlehem and see this thing that has happened, which the Lord has made known to us." So they hurried off and found Mary and Joseph, and the baby, who was lying in the manger. When they had seen him, they told others the message they had been told about this child. And all who heard it were amazed by what the shepherds said to them. But Mary treasured up all these things, pondering them in her heart. And the shepherds returned, glorifying and praising God for all the things that they had heard and seen, which were just as they had been told.

After eight days passed, when the child was circumcised, he was named Jesus, the name given by the angel before he was conceived in the womb.

Lord God, you gave us the greatest present in
your Son, who was born in humble circumstances
to be our substitute and Savior. May we treasure
these events like Mary, pondering them in our hearts,
and may we always praise you and tell this good news
to others as the shepherds did. Amen.

139. SIMEON AND ANNA (LUKE 2)

The infant Jesus is brought to the temple, and there God speaks about him through prophets.

When the time came for their purification according to the law of Moses, they brought him up to Jerusalem to present him to the Lord and to offer a sacrifice according to what was said in the law of the Lord, "A pair of turtledoves or two young pigeons."

Now there was a man in Jerusalem whose name was Simeon. This man was righteous and devout, waiting for the comfort of Israel, and the Holy Spirit was on him. It had been revealed to him by the Holy Spirit that he would not see death before he had seen the Lord's Christ. Moved by the Spirit he went into the temple courts. When the parents brought in the child Jesus, Simeon took him into his arms and praised God. He said, "Lord, you now dismiss your servant in peace, according to your word, because my eyes have seen your salvation, which you have prepared before the face of all people, a light for revelation to the Gentiles, and the glory of your people Israel."

Joseph and the child's mother were amazed at the things that were spoken about him. Then Simeon blessed them and said to Mary his mother, "Listen carefully, this child is appointed for the falling and rising of many in Israel, and a sword will pierce your own soul too."

Anna, a prophetess, was there. She was very old. She had lived with her husband for seven years after her marriage, and then she was a widow of eighty-four years. She did not leave the temple complex, since she was worshipping with fasting and prayers night and day. Standing nearby at that very hour, she gave thanks to the Lord. She kept speaking about the child to all who were waiting for the redemption of Jerusalem.

Lord God, just like your servant Simeon we have seen
your promised Savior Jesus in your Word and
in your sacraments. Thank you for giving
our hearts peace as we wait for you
to take us to be with you. Amen.

140. THE WISE MEN (MATTHEW 2)

Wise Men come from a distant land to worship Jesus, because Jesus is a Savior for all people.

Wise Men from the east came to Jerusalem. They asked, "Where is he who has been born King of the Jews? We saw his star when it rose and have come to worship him." When King Herod heard this, he was alarmed, and all Jerusalem with him. He gathered together all the people's chief priests and experts in the law. He asked them where the Christ was to be born. They said to him, "In Bethlehem of Judea, because this was written through the prophet: 'You, Bethlehem, in the land of Judah, are certainly not least among the rulers of Judah: because out of you will come a ruler, who will shepherd my people Israel.' "

Then Herod secretly summoned the Wise Men and found out from them exactly when the star had appeared. He sent them to Bethlehem and said, "Go and search carefully for the child. When you find him, report to me, so that I may also go and worship him."

After listening to the king, they went on their way. Then the star they had seen when it rose went ahead of them, until it stood still over the place where the child was. When they saw the star, they rejoiced with overwhelming joy. After they went into the house and saw the child with Mary, his mother, they bowed down and worshipped him. Then they opened their treasures and offered him gifts: gold, frankincense, and myrrh. Since they had been warned in a dream not to return to Herod, they went back to their own country by another route.

After the Wise Men were gone, an angel of the Lord suddenly appeared to Joseph in a dream. He said, "Get up, take the child and his mother, and flee to Egypt. Stay there until I tell you, because Herod will search for the child in order to kill him."

Joseph got up, took the child and his mother during the night, and left for Egypt. He stayed there until the death of Herod. This happened to fulfill what was spoken by the Lord through the prophet: "Out of Egypt I called my son."

When Herod realized that he had been outwitted by the Wise Men, he was furious. He issued orders to kill all the boys in Bethlehem two years old and under, in keeping with the exact time he had learned from the Wise Men. Then what was spoken through Jeremiah the prophet was fulfilled: "Rachel weeping for her children, and she refused to be comforted, because they are no more."

After Herod died, an angel of the Lord suddenly appeared in a dream to Joseph in Egypt. The angel said, "Get up, take the child and his mother, and go to the land of Israel, for those who were trying to kill the child are dead."

Joseph got up, took the child and his mother, and went to the land of Israel. But when he heard that Archelaus, Herod's son, had succeeded his father as ruler in Judea, he was afraid to go there. He went to the region of Galilee. When he arrived there, he settled in a city called Nazareth. So what was spoken through the prophets was fulfilled: "He will be called a Nazarene."

Lord God, you have brought us to our King not
by the light of a star but by the light of your Word.
For this we thank and praise you. Lead us to worship
you by giving our treasures to you as joyful offerings.
As you kept your Son safe from harm so that
at the right time he would save us,
protect us from every danger which
threatens us, until it is the time
you have chosen to save us from
this evil world to be with him and you. Amen.

141. THE BOY JESUS IN THE TEMPLE (LUKE 2)

As Jesus grows up, he is devoted to his Father and to his Father's Word.

The child grew and became strong. He was filled with wisdom, and God's favor was on him.

Every year his parents traveled to Jerusalem for the Passover Festival. When he was twelve years old, they went up according to the custom of the Festival. When the days had ended, as they were returning, the boy Jesus stayed behind in Jerusalem. His parents did not know it. Since they thought he was in their group, they went a day's journey. Then they began to look for him among their relatives and friends. When they did not find him, they returned to Jerusalem, searching for him.

After three days they found him in the temple courts, sitting among the teachers, listening to them and asking them questions. And all who heard him were amazed at his understanding and his answers. When his parents saw him, they were astonished. His mother said to him, "Son, why have you treated us this way? See, your father and I have been anxiously looking for you."

He said to them, "Why were you looking for me? Did you not know that I must be taking care of my Father's business?" They did not understand what he was telling them.

He went down with them and came to Nazareth. He was always obedient to them. And his mother treasured up all these things in her heart. Jesus grew in wisdom and stature, and in favor with God and with people.

Lord God, we confess that we are not as diligent
as we should be when it comes to hearing your Word.
We thank and praise you that Jesus, your Son and
our brother, faithfully devoted himself to your Word
for us and has died to take away all our sin.
Make us, your forgiven people, faithful hearers
of your Word. Amen.

PART 2

CHRIST'S PUBLIC MINISTRY

We know very little about Jesus' life before he was thirty. Much of it probably looked very ordinary. But we know that Jesus came to live our life for us, perfectly, without any sin. After being anointed as the Christ by John the Baptist, Jesus carried out his work more publicly, showing the people who he was by his miracles and his teachings. Some of what he did made people love him. Some of what he did made people hate him. But all of it reveals to us that he is not just a great teacher, not just a great miracle worker, but he is the Son of God who came to save us from our sins.

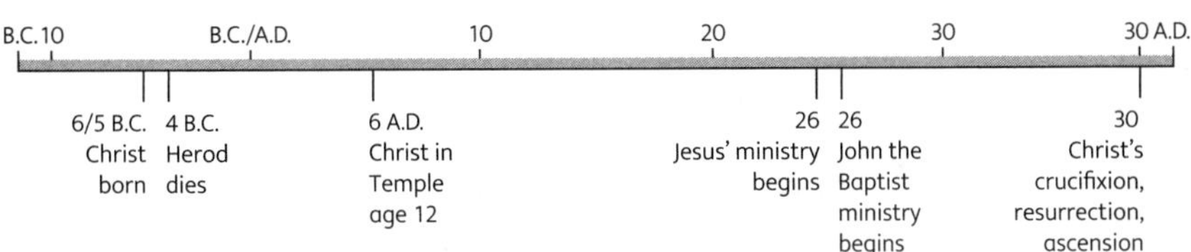

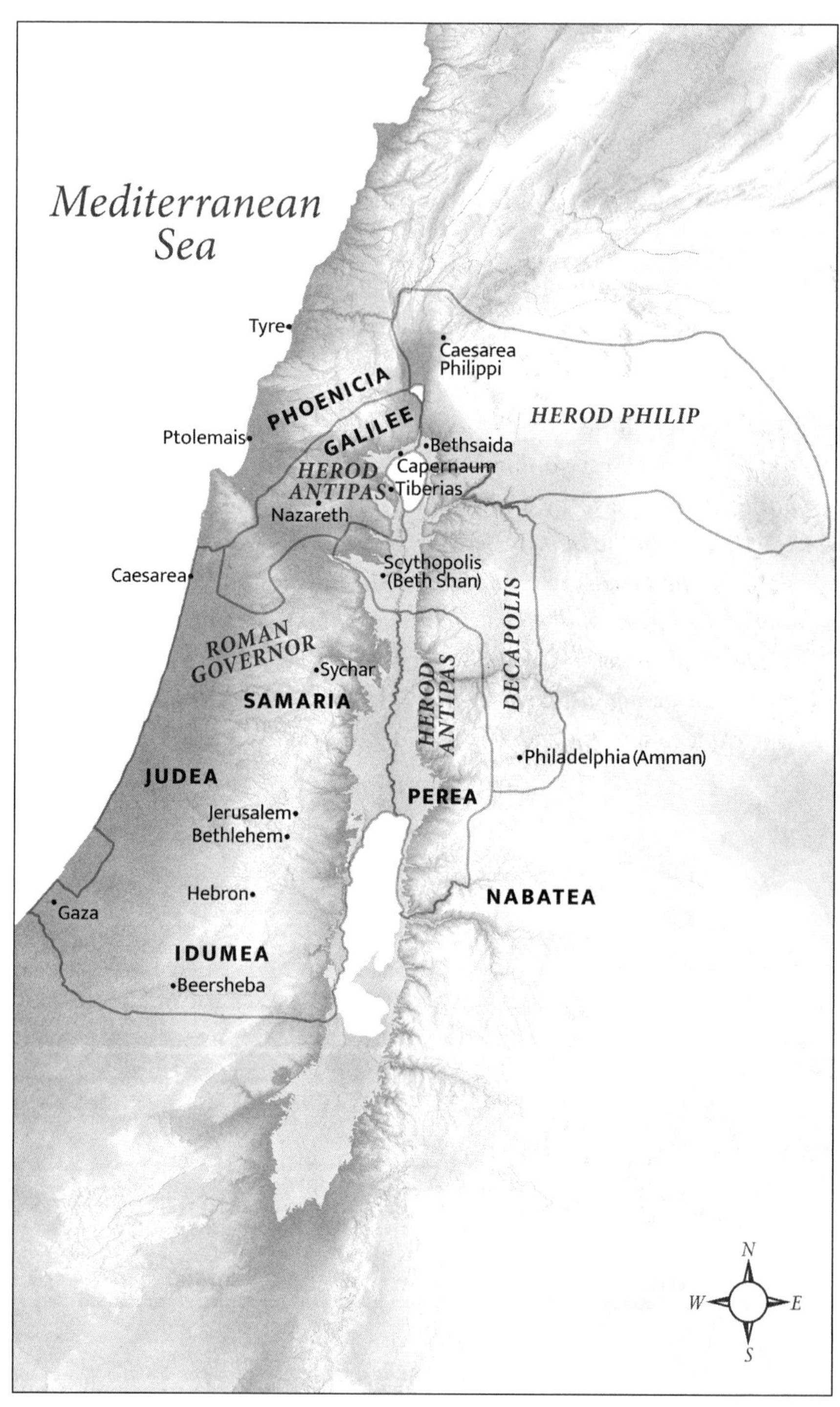

PALESTINE AT THE TIME OF JESUS

142. JOHN THE BAPTIST PREPARES THE WAY (LUKE 3)

John the Baptist baptizes people and points them to the Savior who would be coming soon.

In the fifteenth year of the reign of Tiberius, the word of God came to John, the son of Zechariah, in the wilderness. He went into the whole region around the Jordan, preaching a baptism of repentance for the forgiveness of sins. Just as it is written in the book of the words of Isaiah the prophet: "A voice of one calling in the wilderness, 'Prepare the way of the Lord! Make his paths straight.' And everyone will see the salvation of God."

John kept saying to the crowds who came out to be baptized by him, "Produce fruits in keeping with repentance. Do not even think of saying to yourselves, 'We have Abraham as our father,' because I tell you that God is able to raise up children for Abraham from these stones. Even now the ax is ready to strike the root of the trees. So every tree that does not produce good fruit is going to be cut down and thrown into the fire."

The crowds began to ask him, "What should we do then?"

He answered them, "Whoever has two shirts should share with the person who has none, and whoever has food should do the same."

Tax collectors also came to be baptized. They said, "Teacher, what should we do?"

To them he said, "Collect no more than what you were authorized to."

Soldiers were also asking him, "And what should we do?"

He told them, "Do not extort money from anyone by force or false accusation. Be satisfied with your wages."

The people were all wondering whether John could be the Christ. John answered them all, "I baptize you with water. But someone mightier than I is coming. I am not worthy to untie the strap of his sandals. He will baptize you with the Holy Spirit and fire. His winnowing shovel is in his hand, and he will thoroughly clean out his threshing floor. He will gather the wheat into his barn, but he will burn up the chaff with unquenchable fire."

Then with many other words, he appealed to them and was preaching good news to the people.

Lord God, you have claimed us as your own and washed away all our sins in baptism. Remind us of our baptism each day and bring our hearts back to it in daily repentance. Amen.

143. THE BAPTISM AND TEMPTATION OF JESUS (MATTHEW 3-4)

Jesus, coming to live for us a human life just like ours, except perfectly, is baptized and tempted.

Then Jesus came from Galilee to be baptized by John at the Jordan. But John tried to stop him, saying, "I need to be baptized by you, and yet you come to me?"

But Jesus answered him, "Let it be so now, because it is proper for us to fulfill all righteousness." Then John let him. After Jesus was baptized, he immediately went up out of the water. Suddenly, the heavens were opened for him! He saw the Spirit of God, descending like a dove and landing on him, and a voice out of the heavens said, "This is my Son, whom I love. I am well pleased with him."

Then Jesus was led by the Spirit into the wilderness to be tempted by the Devil. After he had fasted forty days and forty nights, he was hungry.

The Tempter came and said to him, "If you are the Son of God, command these stones to become bread."

But Jesus answered, "It is written: 'Man shall not live by bread alone, but by every word that comes out of the mouth of God.'"

Then the Devil took him into the holy city. He placed him on the pinnacle of the temple, and he said to him, "If you are the Son of God, throw yourself down. For it is written: 'He will command his angels concerning you. And they will lift you up in their hands, so that you will not strike your foot against a stone.'"

Jesus said to him, "Again, it is written: 'You shall not test the Lord your God.'"

Again the Devil took him to a very high mountain and showed him all the kingdoms of the world and their glory. He said to him, "I will give you all of these things, if you will bow down and worship me."

Then Jesus said to him, "Go away, Satan! For it is written, 'Worship the Lord your God, and serve him only.'"

Then the Devil left him, and just then angels came and served him.

Lord God, you have declared yourself to be our Father
as you adopted us as your children through baptism.
Remind us that your baptismal promises to us are
always good. As you have poured out your Holy Spirit
on us in baptism, continue to pour him out on us

through your Word that we may live as your children
and overcome the Devil's temptations using your Word,
knowing that by his perfect life and innocent death
Jesus has already defeated the Devil for us. Amen.

144. JOHN THE BAPTIST POINTS TO JESUS (JOHN 1)

John the Baptist directs his followers to follow Jesus, the Lamb of God.

This is the testimony John gave when the Jews from Jerusalem sent priests and Levites to ask him, "Who are you?"

He confessed and did not deny. He confessed, "I am not the Christ."

And they asked him, "Who are you then? Are you Elijah?"

He said, "I am not."

"Are you the Prophet?"

"No," he answered.

Then they asked him, "Who are you? Tell us so we can give an answer to those who sent us. What do you say about yourself?"

He said, "I am the voice of one crying out in the wilderness, 'Make straight the way of the Lord,' just as Isaiah the prophet said."

They had been sent from the Pharisees. So they asked John, "Why then do you baptize, if you are not the Christ, or Elijah, or the Prophet?"

"I baptize with water," John answered. "Among you stands one you do not know. He is the one coming after me, whose sandal strap I am not worthy to untie."

These things happened in Bethany beyond the Jordan, where John was baptizing.

The next day, John saw Jesus coming toward him and said, "Look! The Lamb of God, who takes away the sin of the world! This is the one I was talking about when I said, 'The one coming after me outranks me because he existed before me.' I myself did not know who he was, but I came baptizing with water so that he would be revealed to Israel."

John also testified, "I saw the Spirit descend like a dove from heaven and remain on him. I myself did not recognize him, but the one who sent me to baptize with water said to me, 'The one on whom you see the Spirit descend and remain, he is the one who will baptize with the Holy Spirit.' I saw this myself and have testified that this is the Son of God."

The next day, John was standing there again with two of his disciples. When John saw Jesus passing by, he said, "Look! The Lamb of God!" The two disciples heard him say this, and they followed Jesus. They stayed with him that day.

Andrew, Simon Peter's brother, was one of the two who heard John and followed Jesus. The first thing Andrew did was to find his own brother Simon and say to him, "We have found the Messiah!" (which is translated "the Christ"). He brought him to Jesus.

Looking at him, Jesus said, "You are Simon, son of Jonah. You will be called Cephas" (which means "Peter").

The next day, Jesus wanted to leave for Galilee. He found Philip and said to him, "Follow me."

Philip found Nathanael and told him, "We have found the one Moses wrote about in the Law, and about whom the prophets also wrote—Jesus of Nazareth, the son of Joseph."

Nathanael said to him, "Nazareth! Can anything good come from there?"

"Come and see!" Philip told him.

Jesus saw Nathanael coming toward him and said about him, "Truly, here is an Israelite in whom there is no deceit."

Nathanael asked him, "How do you know me?"

Jesus answered, "Before Philip called you, while you were under the fig tree, I saw you."

Nathanael answered him, "Rabbi, you are the Son of God! You are the King of Israel!"

Jesus replied, "You believe because I told you that I saw you under the fig tree. You will see greater things than that!" Then he added, "Amen, Amen, I tell you: You will see heaven opened and the angels of God ascending and descending on the Son of Man."

Lord God, we thank you for your Son, the Lamb of God, who has taken away the sin of the world, and for showing him to us through your Word. Lead us to share the good news about him with everyone we know. Amen.

145. JESUS CHANGES WATER INTO WINE AND CLEANSES THE TEMPLE (JOHN 2)

Jesus performs his first miracle and defends his Father's house.

Three days later, there was a wedding in Cana of Galilee. Jesus' mother was there. Jesus and his disciples were also invited to the wedding.

When the wine was gone, Jesus' mother said to him, "They have no wine."

Jesus said to her, "Woman, what does that have to do with you and me? My time has not come yet."

His mother said to the servants, "Do whatever he tells you."

Six stone water jars were standing there, each holding twenty or thirty gallons. Jesus told them, "Fill the jars with water." So they filled them to the brim. Then he said to them, "Now draw some out and take it to the head waiter." And they did.

When the master of the banquet tasted the water that had now become wine, he did not know where it came from (though the servants who had drawn the water knew). The master of the banquet called the bridegroom and said to him, "Everyone serves the good wine first, and when the guests have had plenty to drink, then the cheaper wine. You saved the good wine until now!"

This, the beginning of his miraculous signs, Jesus performed in Cana of Galilee. He revealed his glory, and his disciples believed in him.

The Jewish Passover was near, so Jesus went up to Jerusalem.

In the temple courts he found people selling cattle, sheep, and doves, and money changers sitting at tables. He made a whip of cords and drove everyone out of the temple courts, along with the sheep and oxen. He scattered the coins of the money changers and overturned their tables. To those selling doves he said, "Get these things out of here! Stop turning my Father's house into a place of business!"

His disciples remembered that it was written, "Zeal for your house will consume me."

So the Jews responded, "What sign are you going to show us to prove you can do these things?"

Jesus answered them, "Destroy this temple, and in three days I will raise it up again."

The Jews said, "It took forty-six years to build this temple! And you are going to raise it in three days?" But Jesus was speaking about the temple of his body. When Jesus was raised from the dead, his disciples remembered that he had said this. Then they believed the Scripture and what Jesus had said.

Lord God, all that is good, all joy and gladness that we have in our lives, comes from you. Lead us to realize that you are the source of all our blessings, and to thank you for all your gifts to us, especially the gift of eternal joy and salvation found in your Son Jesus. Let nothing ever distract us as we hear and learn about him in your Word. Keep us from ever putting anything in this life above the truths you teach us in your Word. Amen.

146. NICODEMUS COMES TO JESUS (JOHN 3)

Jesus shows a curious Pharisee the importance of being baptized and of faith in him.

There was a man of the Pharisees named Nicodemus, a member of the Jewish ruling council. He came to Jesus at night and said to him, "Rabbi, we know that you are a teacher who has come from God, for no one can do these miraculous signs you are doing unless God is with him."

Jesus replied, "Amen, Amen, I tell you: Unless someone is born from above, he cannot see the kingdom of God."

Nicodemus said to him, "How can a man be born when he is old? He cannot enter a second time into his mother's womb and be born, can he?"

Jesus answered, "Amen, Amen, I tell you: Unless someone is born of water and the Spirit, he cannot enter the kingdom of God! Whatever is born of the flesh is flesh. Whatever is born of the Spirit is spirit. Do not be surprised when I tell you that you must be born from above."

"How can these things be?" asked Nicodemus.

"You are the teacher of Israel," Jesus answered, "and you do not know these things? If I have told you earthly things and you do not believe, how will you believe if I tell you heavenly things? No one has ascended into heaven, except the one who descended from heaven, the Son of Man, who is in heaven. Just as Moses lifted up the snake in the wilderness, so the Son of Man must be lifted up, so that everyone who believes in him shall not perish but have eternal life.

"For God so loved the world that he gave his only-begotten Son, that whoever believes in him shall not perish, but have eternal life. For God did not send his Son into the world to condemn the world, but to save the world through him. The one who believes in him is not condemned, but the one who does not believe is condemned already, because he has not believed in the name of the only-begotten Son of God."

Lord God, we thank and praise you that you have given us new birth through baptism.

Keep us always looking to your Son in faith
that we may live with you forever. Amen.

147. THE SAMARITAN WOMAN (JOHN 4)

Jesus reaches out to people regardless of their gender, their ethnicity, their religious background, or the sins of their past.

Jesus left Judea and went back again to Galilee. He had to go through Samaria. So he came to a town in Samaria called Sychar, near Jacob's well. Jesus, being tired from the journey, sat down by the well.

A woman from Samaria came to draw water. Jesus said to her, "Give me a drink." (His disciples had gone into town to buy food.)

The Samaritan woman said to him, "How is it that you, a Jew, ask for a drink from me, a Samaritan woman?" (For Jews do not associate with Samaritans.)

Jesus answered her, "If you knew the gift of God and who it is that is saying to you, 'Give me a drink,' you would have asked him, and he would have given you living water."

"Sir," she said, "you don't even have a bucket, and the well is deep. So where do you get this living water? You are not greater than our father Jacob, are you? He gave us this well and drank from it himself, as did his sons and his animals."

Jesus answered her, "Everyone who drinks this water will be thirsty again, but whoever drinks the water I will give him will never be thirsty ever again. Rather, the water I will give him will become in him a spring of water, bubbling up to eternal life."

"Sir, give me this water," the woman said to him, "so I won't get thirsty and have to keep coming here to draw water."

Jesus told her, "Go, call your husband, and come back here."

"I have no husband," the woman answered.

Jesus said to her, "You are right when you say, 'I have no husband.' In fact, you have had five husbands, and the man you have now is not your husband. What you have said is true."

"Sir," the woman replied, "I see that you are a prophet. Our fathers worshipped on this mountain, but you Jews insist that the place where we must worship is in Jerusalem."

Jesus said to her, "Believe me, woman, a time is coming when you will not worship the Father on this mountain or in Jerusalem. You Samaritans worship what you do not know. We worship what we do know, because salvation is from the Jews. But a time is coming and now is here when the real worshippers will worship the Father in spirit and in truth, for those are the kind of worshippers the Father seeks. God is spirit, and those who worship him must worship in spirit and in truth."

The woman said to him, "I know that Messiah is coming. When he comes, he will explain everything to us."

Jesus said to her, "I, the one speaking to you, am he."

Just then his disciples returned and were surprised that he was talking to a woman. Yet no one asked, "Why are you talking to her?"

Then the woman left her water jar and went back into town. She said to the people, "Come, see the man who told me everything I ever did. Could this be the Christ?" They left the town and came to him. Many Samaritans from that town believed in him because of the woman's testimony: "He told me everything I ever did."

So when the Samaritans came to him, they asked him to stay with them. And he stayed there two days. Many more believed because of his message. They told the woman, "We no longer believe because of what you said. Now we have heard for ourselves. And we know that this really is the Savior of the world."

Lord God, all people are important to you. Comfort us
with the truth that you love even sinners like us, and
give us a love which reaches out to all others too. Amen.

148. JESUS IS REJECTED IN HIS HOMETOWN, NAZARETH (LUKE 4)

Jesus' hometown is impressed by his preaching and miracles, but cannot accept that their hometown boy is the Savior.

News about him spread through all the surrounding area. He was teaching in their synagogues and being honored by everyone.

He went to Nazareth, where he had been brought up. As was his custom, he went into the synagogue on the Sabbath day and stood up to read. The scroll of the prophet Isaiah was handed to him. He unrolled the scroll and found the place where it was written: "The Spirit of the Lord is on me, because he anointed me to preach good news to the poor. He has sent me to proclaim freedom to the captives and recovery of sight to the blind, to set free those who are oppressed, and to proclaim the year of the Lord's favor."

He rolled up the scroll, gave it back to the attendant, and sat down. The eyes of everyone in the synagogue were fastened on him. He began to tell them, "Today, this Scripture is fulfilled in your hearing."

They all were impressed by the words of grace that came from his mouth. And they kept saying, "Isn't this Joseph's son?"

He told them, "Certainly you will quote this proverb to me, 'Physician, heal yourself!' Do here in your hometown everything we heard you did in Capernaum.' Amen I tell you: No prophet is accepted in his hometown. There were many widows in Israel in the days of Elijah, when a great famine came over all the land. Elijah was not sent to any of them, but to a widow of Zarephath, in Sidon. And there were many lepers in Israel in the time of Elisha the prophet, yet not one of them was healed except Naaman the Syrian."

All those who were in the synagogue were filled with rage when they heard these things. They got up and drove him out of the town. They led him to the brow of the hill on which their town was built, in order to throw him off the cliff. But he passed through the middle of them and went on his way. He went down to Capernaum, a town of Galilee.

Lord God, your Son became a human being just like us
so that he could take our place. We thank you that
you have taught us to know him for as long as we have.
Keep familiarity with our Savior and his Word
from ever bringing us to contempt or boredom
towards him. Keep us joyful and trusting
toward him all our lives. Amen.

149. JESUS CALLS HIS FIRST DISCIPLES (LUKE 5)

These men already believe in Jesus, but now they are called to follow him full-time.

One time, while the crowd was pressing in on Jesus and listening to the word of God, he was standing by the Lake of Gennesaret. He saw two boats there along the lakeshore. (The fishermen had left them and were washing their nets.) Jesus got into one of the boats, which belonged to Simon, and asked him to put out a little from the shore. He sat down and began teaching the crowds from the boat.

When he had finished speaking, he said to Simon, "Put out into the deep water, and let down your nets for a catch."

Simon answered him, "Master, we worked hard all through the night and caught nothing. But at your word I will let down the nets."

When they had done this, they caught a great number of fish, and their nets were about to tear apart. They signaled their partners in the other boat to come and help them. They came and filled both boats, so that they began to sink. When Simon Peter saw this, he fell down at Jesus' knees, saying, "Go away from me, because I am a sinful man, Lord." For Peter and all those with him were amazed at the number of fish they had caught, and so were James and John, the sons of Zebedee, who were partners with Simon.

Jesus said to Simon, "Have no fear. From now on you will be catching people."

After they brought their boats to the shore, they left everything and followed him.

Lord God, we thank you that you have made us Jesus' disciples. Help us to follow him in all aspects of our lives. Bless our proclamation of your Word and use it to catch more disciples for yourself. Amen.

150. JESUS HEALS A PARALYZED MAN (LUKE 5)

Jesus shows his authority to both forgive sins and heal earthly ailments.

On one of the days while Jesus was teaching, Pharisees and teachers of the law were sitting there who had come from every village of Galilee and Judea and from Jerusalem. The power of the Lord was with him to heal. Just then, men who were carrying a paralyzed man on a stretcher tried to bring him in and lay him in front of Jesus. Since they did not find a way to bring him in because of the crowd, they went up on the roof and lowered him down through the tiles on his stretcher into the middle of the crowd, right in front of Jesus. When he saw their faith, he said, "Man, your sins have been forgiven."

The experts in the law and the Pharisees began to think to themselves, "Who is this fellow who speaks blasphemies? Who can forgive sins except God alone?"

But Jesus knew their thoughts and answered them, "Why are you thinking this in your hearts? Which is easier: to say, 'Your sins have been forgiven,' or to say, 'Get up and walk'? But so that you may know that the

Son of Man has authority on earth to forgive sins . . ." He said to the paralyzed man, "I tell you, get up, take your stretcher, and go home."

Immediately, he stood up in front of them, picked up what he had been lying on, and went home glorifying God. They were all astonished and glorified God. They were also filled with reverence and said, "We have seen wonderful things today."

Lord God, we thank you for the forgiveness
we have in your Son. As you have healed our souls,
give health to our bodies also. Amen.

151. THE CALLING OF MATTHEW AND THE OTHER APOSTLES (MATTHEW 9-10)

Of the disciples whom he called, Jesus designates twelve of them as the apostles.

As Jesus went on from there, he saw a man named Matthew sitting in the tax collector's booth. He said to him, "Follow me." Matthew got up and followed him.

As Jesus was reclining at the table in Matthew's house, many tax collectors and sinners were actually there too, eating with Jesus and his disciples. When the Pharisees saw this, they said to his disciples, "Why does your teacher eat with tax collectors and sinners?"

When Jesus heard this, he said to them, "The healthy do not need a physician, but the sick do. I did not come to call the righteous, but sinners."

These are the names of the twelve apostles: first, Simon (who is called Peter) and his brother Andrew; James the son of Zebedee and his brother John; Philip and Bartholomew; Thomas and Matthew the tax collector; James the son of Alphaeus, and Thaddaeus; Simon the Zealot and Judas Iscariot, who betrayed him.

Lord God, we thank you for the apostles
who witnessed your Son's resurrection,
proclaimed that good news throughout the world,
and by your Spirit wrote that truth down for us to read.
Bless us as we read that Word. Amen.

152. THE SERMON ON THE MOUNT, PART 1 (MATTHEW 5-6)

In his most famous sermon, Jesus is not teaching his disciples how to be saved, but how to live in light of the fact they are saved.

When Jesus saw the crowds, he went up onto a mountain. When he sat down, his disciples came to him. He said: "Blessed are the poor in spirit, because theirs is the kingdom of heaven. Blessed are those who mourn, because they will be comforted. Blessed are the gentle, because they will inherit the earth. Blessed are those who are persecuted because of righteousness, because theirs is the kingdom of heaven.

"You are the salt of the earth, but if salt has lost its flavor, how will it become salty again? Then it is no good for anything except to be thrown out and trampled on by people.

"You are the light of the world. A city located on a hill cannot be hidden. People do not light a lamp and put it under a basket. No, they put it on a stand, and it gives light to all who are in the house. In the same way let your light shine in people's presence, so that they may see your good works and glorify your Father who is in heaven.

"Do not think that I came to destroy the Law or the Prophets. I did not come to destroy them but to fulfill them. Amen I tell you: Until heaven and earth pass away, not even the smallest letter, or even part of a letter, will in any way pass away from the Law until everything is fulfilled. So whoever breaks one of the least of these commandments and teaches others to do the same will be called least in the kingdom of heaven. But whoever practices and teaches them will be called great in the kingdom of heaven. Indeed I tell you that unless your righteousness surpasses that of the Pharisees and experts in the law, you will never enter the kingdom of heaven.

"You have heard that it was said, 'You shall not murder,' and but I tell you that everyone who is angry with his brother without a cause will be subject to judgment. You have heard that it was said, 'You shall not commit adultery,' but I tell you that everyone who looks at a woman with lust has already committed adultery with her in his heart. If your eye causes you to fall into sin, pluck it out and throw it away from you. It is better for you to lose one part of your body than for your whole body to be thrown into hell. Again you have heard that it was said, 'Do not break your oaths,' but I tell you, do not swear at all. Instead, let your statement be, 'Yes, yes,' or 'No, no.' Whatever goes beyond these is from the Evil One.

"You have heard that it was said, 'An eye for an eye, and a tooth for a tooth.' But I tell you, do not resist an evildoer. If someone strikes you on your right cheek, turn to him the other also. Give to the one who asks you, and do not turn away from the one who wants to borrow from you.

"You have heard that it was said, 'Love your neighbor and hate your enemy.' But I tell you, love your enemies and pray for those who persecute you. Your Father in heaven makes his sun to rise on the evil and the good and sends rain on the righteous and the unrighteous. So then, be perfect, as your heavenly Father is perfect.

"Do not do your righteous works in front of people, so that they will notice. Instead, when you perform acts of mercy, do not let your left hand know what your right hand is doing. Then your acts of mercy will be in secret, and your Father who sees what is done in secret will reward you."

Lord God, often we arrogantly like to lower the standards of your law in our mind, so that we can feel good about ourselves, but we admit that your law demands perfection in every way and we have fallen far short of it. Forgive us all our sins for the sake of Jesus, who perfectly fulfilled all the law in our place, bringing us your eternal blessing. Amen.

153. THE SERMON ON THE MOUNT, PART 2 (MATTHEW 6-7)

Jesus' most famous sermon continues, as he teaches his disciples about prayer and priorities.

"Whenever you pray, do not be like the hypocrites. They love to be seen by people. But whenever you pray, go into your private room. And your Father, who sees what others cannot see, will reward you.

"And when you pray, do not babble like the heathen, since they think that they will be heard because of their many words. Do not be like them, because your Father knows what you need before you ask him. Therefore pray like this: 'Our Father in heaven, hallowed be your name. Your kingdom come. Your will be done on earth as it is in heaven. Give us today our daily bread. Forgive us our debts, as we also forgive our debtors. Lead us not into temptation, but deliver us from evil.'

"Do not store up treasures for yourselves on earth, where moth and rust destroy, and where thieves break in and steal. Store up treasures for yourselves in heaven. Because where your treasure is, there your heart will be also. No one can serve two masters. You cannot serve both God and mammon.

"Do not worry about what you will eat or drink or about what you will wear. Is not life more than food and the body more than clothing? Look at the birds of the air. They do not sow or reap or gather into barns, and yet your heavenly Father feeds them. Are you not worth much more than they?

"Which of you can add a single moment to his lifespan by worrying? Why do you worry about clothing? Consider how the lilies of the field grow. They do not labor or spin, but I tell you that not even Solomon in all his glory was dressed like one of these. If that is how God clothes the grass of the field, which is alive today and tomorrow is thrown into the furnace, will he not clothe you even more, you of little faith?

"So do not worry, saying, 'What will we eat?' or 'What will we drink?' or 'What will we wear?' Certainly your heavenly Father knows that you need all these things. But seek first the kingdom of God and his righteousness, and all these things will be given to you as well.

"Stop judging, so that you will not be judged. For with whatever standard you judge, you will be judged. Why do you focus on the speck in your brother's eye, but do not consider the beam in your own eye? Hypocrite! First remove the beam from your own eye, and then you will see clearly to remove the speck from your brother's eye.

"Keep asking, and it will be given to you. Keep seeking, and you will find. Keep knocking, and it will be opened for you. For everyone who asks receives, and everyone who seeks finds, and to the one who knocks, it will be opened. Who among you, if his son asks him for bread, would give him a stone? If you know how to give good gifts to your children, even though you are evil, how much more will your Father in heaven give good gifts to those who ask him!

"So do for others whatever you want people to do for you, because this is the Law and the Prophets.

"Enter through the narrow gate, for wide is the gate that leads to destruction, and many are those who enter through it. How narrow is the gate that leads to life, and there are few who find it.

"Watch out for false prophets. They come to you in sheep's clothing, but inwardly they are ravenous wolves. By their fruit you will recognize them. Every good tree produces good fruit, but a bad tree produces bad fruit. So then, by their fruit you will recognize them.

"Everyone who hears these words of mine and does them will be like a wise man who built his house on bedrock. The rain came down, the rivers rose, and the winds blew and beat against that house. But it did not fall, because it was founded on bedrock. Everyone who hears these words of mine but does not do them will be like a foolish man who built his house on sand. The rain came down, the rivers rose, and the winds blew and beat against that house, and it fell."

Lord God, ground us firmly on your Son, our Rock,
so that we may stand against all the world's storms.
Keep us prayerful and watchful so that no false teacher
ever leads us from your truth, and remind us
of your promises to provide for us so that
we never give in to worry. Amen.

154. THE CENTURION'S SERVANT AND THE YOUNG MAN OF NAIN (LUKE 7)

Jesus shows his power over illness and death.

After Jesus had finished saying all these things to the people who were listening, he went into Capernaum. A centurion's servant, who was valuable to him, was sick and about to die. When the centurion heard about Jesus, he sent some elders of the Jews to him, asking him to come and heal his servant. When they came to Jesus, they begged him earnestly, saying, "He is worthy of having you do this for him, because he loves our nation, and he built our synagogue for us."

Jesus went with them. When he was not far from the house, the centurion sent friends to tell Jesus, "Lord, do not trouble yourself, because I do not deserve to have you come under my roof. That is why I did not consider myself worthy to come to you. But say the word, and my servant will be healed. For I am also a man placed under authority, having soldiers under me. I say to this one, 'Go!' and he goes; and to another one, 'Come!' and he comes; and to my servant, 'Do this,' and he does it."

When Jesus heard these things, he was amazed at him. He turned to the crowd that was following him and said, "I tell you, I have not found such great faith, not even in Israel."

And when the men who had been sent returned to the house, they found the servant well.

Soon afterward Jesus went on his way to a town called Nain, and his disciples and a large crowd were traveling with him. As he was approaching the town gate, there was a dead man being carried out, the only son of his mother. She was a widow. A considerable crowd from the town was with her. When the Lord saw her, he had compassion on her and said to her, "Do not cry." He went up to the open coffin, touched it, and the pallbearers stopped. He said, "Young man, I say to you, get up!" The dead man sat up and began to speak, and Jesus gave him to his mother.

Fear gripped all of them, and they glorified God, saying, "A great prophet has arisen among us" and "God has visited his people!" This was reported about him in all of Judea and in all the surrounding countryside.

Lord God, your Son has power over life and death.
Give us good health in this life, and on the Last Day
raise us to new life to live with you forever. Amen.

155. A QUESTION FROM JOHN THE BAPTIST (MATTHEW 11)

John the Baptist sends a question to Jesus, who confirms that he is the promised Savior.

While John was in prison, he heard about the things Christ was doing. He sent two of his disciples to ask him, "Are you the Coming One or should we wait for someone else?"

Jesus answered them, "Go, report to John what you hear and see: The blind receive sight, the lame walk, those who have leprosy are cured, the deaf hear, the dead are raised, and the gospel is preached to the poor. Blessed is the one who does not take offense at me."

As these two were leaving, Jesus began to talk to the crowds about John. "What did you go out into the wilderness to see? A prophet? Yes, I tell you! And he is much more than a prophet. This is the one about whom it is written, 'Look, I am sending my messenger ahead of you, who will prepare your way before you.' Among those born of women there has not appeared anyone greater than John the Baptist. Yet whoever is least in the kingdom of heaven is greater than he."

At that time, Jesus continued, "I praise you, Father, Lord of heaven and earth, that you have hidden these things from clever and learned people and have revealed them to little children. Yes, Father, because this was pleasing to you. Everything has been entrusted to me by my Father. No one knows the Son except the Father, and no one knows the Father except the Son and anyone to whom the Son wants to reveal him.

"Come to me all you who are weary and burdened, and I will give you rest. Take my yoke upon you and learn from me, because I am gentle and humble in heart, and you will find rest for your souls. For my yoke is easy and my burden is light."

Lord God, comfort us in all our doubts with the sure hope of forgiveness and life in your Son Jesus. Thank you for revealing him to us through your Word and for bringing us to faith in him. Give our souls the rest that comes from sins forgiven. Amen.

156. JESUS IS ANOINTED BY A SINFUL WOMAN (LUKE 7)

Jesus shows how great his forgiveness is and how it leads to great appreciation.

One of the Pharisees asked Jesus to eat with him. Jesus entered the Pharisee's house and reclined at the table. A sinful woman from that town learned that he was reclining in the Pharisee's house. She brought an alabaster jar of perfume, stood behind him near his feet weeping, and began to wet his feet with her tears. Then she began to wipe them with her hair while also kissing his feet and anointing them with the perfume. When the Pharisee who had invited him saw this, he said to himself, "If this man were a prophet, he would realize who is touching him and what kind of woman she is, because she is a sinner."

Jesus answered him, "Simon, a certain moneylender had two debtors. The one owed five hundred denarii, and the other fifty. When they could not pay, he forgave them both. So, which of them will love him more?"

Simon answered, "I suppose the one who had the larger debt forgiven."

Then he told him, "You have judged correctly." Turning toward the woman, he said to Simon, "Do you see this woman? I entered your house, but you did not give me water for my feet. Yet she has wet my feet with her tears and wiped them with her hair. You did not give me a kiss, but she, from the time I entered, has not stopped kissing my feet. You did not anoint my head with oil, but she has anointed my feet with perfume. Therefore I tell you, her many sins have been forgiven; that is why she loved so much. But the one who is forgiven little loves little." Then Jesus said to her, "Your sins have been forgiven."

Those reclining at the table with him began to say among themselves, "Who is this who even forgives sins?"

He said to the woman, "Your faith has saved you. Go in peace."

Lord God, you have forgiven us all our many sins for Jesus' sake. Keep us from ever downplaying our sin or downplaying your forgiveness. Help us to show our appreciation to you in our lives. Amen.

157. THE DEATH OF JOHN THE BAPTIST (MARK 6)

John the Baptist is put to death because he proclaimed God's Word.

Herod had sent men to arrest John. He had him bound in prison because Herod had married Herodias, the wife of his brother Philip. John had been telling him, "It is not lawful for you to have your brother's wife."

Herodias held a grudge against John and wanted to put him to death, but she could not, because Herod feared John. He knew that John was a righteous and holy man, so he kept him safe.

An opportune day came when it was Herod's birthday. He gave a banquet for his nobles, the military officers, and the prominent men of Galilee. When the daughter of Herodias came in and danced, she pleased Herod and his guests. The king said to the girl with an oath, "Whatever you ask of me, I will give you, up to half of my kingdom."

She went out and said to her mother, "What should I ask for?"

Herodias said, "The head of John the Baptizer."

The girl hurried right back to the king and made her request: "I want you to give me the head of John the Baptist on a platter right now."

The king was very sad. But because of his oaths and his dinner guests, he did not want to refuse her. The king sent an executioner at once and ordered him to bring John's head. He went, beheaded John in prison, brought his head on a platter, and gave it to the girl. Then the girl gave it to her mother.

When John's disciples heard about this, they came and took his body and laid it in a tomb.

Lord God, in this world your people suffer for proclaiming
your Word. Protect us, keep us strong in the truth
that we confess, and quickly send your Son Jesus
to end your people's suffering. Amen.

158. THE PARABLE OF THE SOWER AND THE SEED (MATTHEW 13)

Jesus tells a story to show that there are very different reactions to the gospel.

Jesus was sitting by the sea. A large crowd gathered around him. So he stepped into a boat and sat down, while all the people stood on the shore.

He told them many things in parables, saying: "Listen, a sower went out to sow. As he sowed, some seed fell along the path, and the birds came and ate it. Other seed fell on rocky ground, where it did not have much soil. Immediately the seed sprang up, because the soil was not deep. But when the sun rose, the seed was scorched. Because it had no root, it withered away. Other seed fell among thorns. The thorns grew up and choked it. But some seed fell on good ground and produced grain: some one hundred times, some sixty, and some thirty times more than was sown. Whoever has ears to hear, let him hear."

The disciples came and said to him, "Why do you speak to them in parables?"

He answered them, "To you it has been given to know the mysteries of the kingdom of heaven, but it has not been given to them. Even though they see, they do not see; and even though they hear, they do not hear or understand. But blessed are your eyes because they see and your ears because they hear. Amen I tell you: Many prophets and righteous people longed to see what you are seeing, but they did not see it. They longed to hear what you are hearing, but they did not hear it.

"So listen carefully to the parable of the sower. When anyone hears the word of the kingdom and does not understand it, the Evil One comes and snatches away what has been sown in his heart. This is the seed that was sown along the path.

"The seed that was sown on rocky ground is the person who hears the word and immediately receives it with joy, yet he is not deeply rooted and does not endure. When trouble or persecution comes because of the word, he immediately falls away.

"The seed that was sown among the thorns is the one who hears the word, but the worry of this world and the deceitfulness of wealth choke the word, and it produces no fruit.

"But the seed that was sown on the good ground is the one who continues to hear and understand the word. Indeed he continues to produce fruit: some a hundred, some sixty, and some thirty times more than was sown."

Lord God, we thank you that you have
worked faith in our hearts through your Word.
Give us a deeper understanding of that Word
and keep us from ever turning
our back on you. Amen.

159. THE CALMING OF THE STORM AND THE HEALING OF A DEMON-POSSESSED MAN (MARK 4-5)

Jesus shows his power over nature and hell.

When evening came, Jesus said to them, "Let's go over to the other side." After leaving the crowd behind, the disciples took him along in the boat, just as he was. Other small boats also followed him.

A great windstorm arose, and the waves were splashing into the boat, so that the boat was quickly filling up. Jesus himself was in the stern, sleeping on a cushion. They woke him and said, "Teacher, don't you care that we are about to drown?"

Then he got up, rebuked the wind, and said to the sea, "Peace! Be still!" The wind stopped, and there was a great calm. He said to them, "Why are you so afraid? Do you still lack faith?"

They were filled with awe and said to one another, "Who then is this? Even the wind and the sea obey him!"

They went to the other side of the sea, into the region of the Gerasenes. As soon as Jesus stepped out of the boat, a man with an unclean spirit came out to meet him.

Jesus said to him, "Come out of the man, you unclean spirit!"

There was a large herd of pigs there feeding on the hillside. The demons begged him, "Send us to the pigs so we may enter them." Jesus gave them permission. The unclean spirits went out and entered the pigs. Then the herd of about two thousand pigs rushed down the steep bank into the sea and drowned.

Those who were feeding the pigs ran and reported this in the city and the countryside. People came to see what had happened. When they saw the man who had been possessed by the legion of demons sitting there clothed and in his right mind, they were afraid. They began to plead with Jesus to leave their region.

As Jesus was getting into the boat, the man who had been demon-possessed begged to stay with Jesus. But Jesus would not let him. Instead, he told him, "Go home to your people, and tell them everything the Lord has done for you and how he had mercy on you."

The man left and began to proclaim in the Decapolis everything Jesus had done for him. And everyone was amazed.

Lord God, may your Son Jesus calm the storms of
this world with his power and calm the storms of doubt
in our hearts with his peace. Silence the powers
of hell which attack and accuse us. Amen.

160. THE DAUGHTER OF JAIRUS (MARK 6)

Jesus shows that he has the power to raise the dead.

When Jesus had again crossed over in the boat to the other side, a large crowd gathered around him near the sea. Then one of the synagogue rulers, named Jairus, came. When he saw Jesus, he fell at his feet and repeatedly pleaded with him, "My little daughter is near death. Please come and place your hands on her so that she may be healed and live." (She was twelve years old.)

Jesus went with him.

People from the synagogue ruler's house arrived, saying, "Your daughter is dead. Why bother the Teacher anymore?"

But when Jesus heard this report, he told the synagogue ruler, "Don't be afraid. Only believe." He did not allow anyone to follow him except Peter, James, and John the brother of James.

They went into the house of the synagogue ruler, and Jesus saw a commotion with people weeping and wailing loudly. When he entered, he said to them, "Why are you making a commotion and weeping? The child is not dead but sleeping."

They laughed at him.

But after he put everyone out, he took the father of the child, her mother, and those who were with him and went in where the child was. Grasping the hand of the child, he said to her, "Talitha, koum!" (When translated, that means, "Little girl, I say to you, arise!") Immediately the little girl stood up and began to walk around. They were completely and utterly amazed. Then he gave them strict orders not to let anyone know about this, and he told them to give her something to eat.

Lord God, your Son has conquered death for us.
When our last hour comes, remind us that by faith
in him, death is just a sleep. Wake us up on
the Last Day to live with you forever. Amen.

161. JESUS FEEDS THE FIVE THOUSAND AND WALKS ON WATER (MATTHEW 14)

Jesus miraculously provides for people's earthly needs.

Jesus withdrew in a boat to a deserted place to be alone. When the crowds heard this, they followed him on foot from the towns. When Jesus got out of the boat, he saw a large crowd. He had compassion on them and healed their sick.

When evening came, his disciples came to him and said, "This is a deserted place and the hour is already late. Send the crowds away, so that they can go into the villages and buy food for themselves."

But Jesus said to them, "They do not need to go away. You give them something to eat."

They told him, "We have here only five loaves and two fish."

"Bring them here to me," he replied. Then he instructed the people to sit down on the grass. He took the five loaves and the two fish. After looking up to heaven, he blessed them. He broke the loaves and gave them to the disciples. The disciples gave the food to the people. They all ate and were filled. They picked up twelve basketfuls of what was left over from the broken pieces. Those who ate were about five thousand men, not even counting women and children.

Immediately Jesus urged the disciples to get into the boat and to go ahead of him to the other side, while he dismissed the crowd. After he had dismissed the crowd, he went up onto the mountain by himself to pray. When evening came, he was there alone.

By then the boat was quite a distance from shore, being pounded by the waves because the wind was against it. In the fourth watch of the night, Jesus came toward them, walking on the sea. When the disciples saw him walking on the sea, they were terrified and cried out in fear, "It's a ghost!"

But Jesus spoke to them at once, saying, "Take heart! It is I! Do not be afraid."

Peter answered him and said, "Lord, if it is you, command me to come to you on the water."

Jesus said, "Come!"

Peter stepped down from the boat, walked on the water, and went toward Jesus. But when he saw the strong wind, he was afraid. As he began to sink, he cried out, "Lord, save me!"

Immediately Jesus stretched out his hand, took hold of him, and said to him, "You of little faith, why did you doubt?"

When they got into the boat, the wind stopped. Those who were in the boat worshipped him, saying, "Truly you are the Son of God!"

Lord God, give us each day our daily bread, and lead us
to realize that you are the source of our daily bread,
so that we receive it with thanksgiving. Strengthen

our faith to trust all of your promises to us,
especially your promise of forgiveness
and eternal life in your Son Jesus. Amen.

162. JESUS IS THE BREAD OF LIFE (JOHN 6)

Jesus explains that he is the Bread of Life that people must eat to live, since by believing in him we receive eternal life.

The next day, the crowd on the other side of the sea got into boats and went to Capernaum looking for Jesus. When they found him, they asked him, "Rabbi, when did you get here?"

Jesus answered them, "Amen, Amen, I tell you: You are not looking for me because you saw the miraculous signs, but because you ate the loaves and were filled. Do not continue to work for the food that spoils, but for the food that endures to eternal life, which the Son of Man will give you."

So they said to him, "What should we do to carry out the works of God?"

Jesus answered them, "This is the work of God: that you believe in the one he sent."

Then they asked him, "So what miraculous sign are you going to do, that we may see it and believe you? What miraculous sign are you going to perform? Our fathers ate the manna in the wilderness."

Jesus said to them, "Amen, Amen, I tell you: Moses did not give you the bread from heaven, but my Father gives you the real bread from heaven. For the bread of God is the one who comes down from heaven and gives life to the world."

"Sir," they said to him, "give us this bread all the time!"

"I am the Bread of Life," Jesus told them. "The one who comes to me will never be hungry, and the one who believes in me will never be thirsty. I have come down from heaven that everyone who sees the Son and believes in him may have eternal life. And I will raise him up on the Last Day."

So the Jews started grumbling about him. They asked, "Isn't this Jesus, the son of Joseph, whose father and mother we know? So how can he say, 'I have come down from heaven'?"

Jesus answered them, "Stop grumbling among yourselves. No one can come to me unless the Father who sent me draws him. And I will raise him up on the Last Day. I am the Bread of Life. Your fathers ate manna in the wilderness, and they died. This is the bread that comes down from heaven, so that anyone may eat it and not die. I am the living bread which came down from heaven. If anyone eats this bread, he will live forever. The bread that I will give for the life of the world is my flesh."

At that, the Jews argued among themselves, "How can this man give us his flesh to eat?"

So Jesus said to them, "Amen, Amen, I tell you: Unless you eat the flesh of the Son of Man and drink his blood, you do not have life in yourselves. The one who eats my flesh and drinks my blood has eternal life, and I will raise him up on the Last Day. For my flesh is real food, and my blood is real drink."

Many of his disciples said, "This is a hard teaching! Who can listen to it?"

But Jesus, knowing that his disciples were grumbling about this, asked them, "Does this cause you to stumble in your faith? What if you would see the Son of Man ascending to where he was before? The Spirit is the one who gives life. The flesh does not help at all. The words that I have spoken to you are spirit and they are life. But there are some of you who do not believe."

After this, many of his disciples turned back and were not walking with him anymore. So Jesus asked the Twelve, "You do not want to leave too, do you?"

Simon Peter answered him, "Lord, to whom will we go? You have the words of eternal life. We have come to believe and know that you are the Holy One of God."

Lord God, sometimes we focus on the earthly instead of on the heavenly. Sometimes we struggle with the truths of your Word. Forgive us our sins, and keep us trusting in Jesus as the food by which we receive eternal life. Amen.

163. PETER CONFESSES JESUS AS CHRIST BUT IS REBUKED FOR STANDING IN THE WAY OF THE CROSS (MATTHEW 16)

Peter proclaims that Jesus is the Christ, but he needs to learn that the Christ came to die on a cross.

Jesus came into the region of Caesarea Philippi. He asked his disciples, "Who do people say the Son of Man is?"

They said, "Some say John the Baptist, others say Elijah, and others Jeremiah or one of the prophets."

He said to them, "But you, who do you say that I am?"

Simon Peter answered, "You are the Christ, the Son of the living God."

Jesus replied, "Blessed are you, Simon son of Jonah, for flesh and blood did not reveal this to you, but my Father who is in heaven. And I tell you that you are Peter, and on this rock I will build my church, and the gates of hell will not overpower it. I will give you the keys of the kingdom of heaven. Whatever you bind on earth will be bound in heaven, and whatever you loose on earth will be loosed in heaven." Then he commanded the disciples not to tell anyone that he was the Christ.

From that time, Jesus began to show his disciples that he had to go to Jerusalem and suffer many things from the elders, chief priests, and experts in the law, and be killed, and on the third day be raised again.

Peter took him aside and began to rebuke him, saying, "May you receive mercy, Lord! This will never happen to you."

But Jesus turned and said to Peter, "Get behind me, Satan! You are a snare to me because you are not thinking the things of God, but the things of men."

Then Jesus said to his disciples, "If anyone wants to follow me, let him deny himself, take up his cross, and follow me. In fact whoever wants to save his life will lose it, and whoever loses his life for my sake will find it. After all, what will it benefit a person if he gains the whole world, but forfeits his soul? Or what can a person give in exchange for his soul?"

Lord God, we thank you for revealing Jesus to us as the Christ. We also thank you that he suffered and died to take away our sins. Strengthen us to follow him in carrying our crosses. Amen.

164. THE TRANSFIGURATION (MATTHEW 17)

Jesus shows the divine glory that he usually hid while on earth.

Six days later Jesus took with him Peter, James, and John the brother of James; and he led them up onto a high mountain by themselves. There he was transfigured in front of them. His face was shining like the sun. His clothing became as white as the light. Just then, Moses and Elijah appeared to them, talking with Jesus.

Peter said to Jesus, "Lord, it is good for us to be here. If you want, I will make three shelters here: one for you, one for Moses, and one for Elijah."

While he was still speaking, suddenly a bright cloud overshadowed them.

Just then, a voice came out of the cloud, saying, "This is my Son, whom I love; with him I am well pleased. Listen to him."

When the disciples heard this, they fell face down and were terrified. Jesus approached and as he touched them, he said, "Get up, and do not be afraid." When they opened their eyes, they saw no one except Jesus alone.

As they were coming down the mountain, Jesus commanded them, "Do not tell anyone what you have seen until the Son of Man has been raised from the dead."

Lord God, we thank and praise you that your glorious Son covered up his glory to live and die for us. Bring us one day to heaven where we will see our Savior in his glory. Amen.

165. THE PARABLE OF THE UNMERCIFUL SERVANT (MATTHEW 18)

Jesus tells us a story that shows that those who have been forgiven by God will want to forgive others.

The disciples approached Jesus and asked, "Who is the greatest in the kingdom of heaven?"

Jesus called a little child, had him stand in the middle of them, and said, "Amen I tell you: Unless you become like children, you will never enter the kingdom of heaven. Whoever humbles himself like this little child is the greatest in the kingdom of heaven. And whoever receives a little child like this one in my name receives me. See to it that you do not look down on one of these little ones, because I tell you that their angels in heaven always see the face of my Father who is in heaven. For the Son of Man came to save what was lost."

Then Peter asked Jesus, "Lord, how many times must I forgive my brother when he sins against me? As many as seven times?"

Jesus said to him, "Not seven times, but I tell you as many as seventy-seven times. For this reason the kingdom of heaven is like a king who wanted to settle accounts with his servants. When he began to settle them, a man who owed him ten thousand talents was brought to him. Because the man was not able to pay the debt, his master ordered that he be sold, along with his wife, children, and all that he owned to repay the debt.

"Then the servant fell down on his knees in front of him, saying, 'Master, be patient with me, and I will pay you everything!' The master of that servant had pity on him, released him, and forgave him the debt.

"But when that servant went out, he found one of his fellow servants who owed him one hundred denarii. He grabbed him and began choking him, saying, 'Pay me what you owe!'

"So his fellow servant fell down and begged him, saying, 'Be patient with me, and I will pay you back!' But he refused. Instead he went off and threw the man into prison until he could pay back what he owed.

"When his fellow servants saw what had happened, they were very distressed. They went and reported to their master everything that had taken place.

"Then his master called him in and said to him, 'You wicked servant! I forgave you all that debt when you begged me to. Should you not have had mercy on your fellow servant just as I had mercy on you?' His master was angry and handed him over to the jailers until he could pay back everything he owed.

"This is what my heavenly Father will also do to you unless each one of you forgives his brother from his heart."

Lord God, we have sinned against you many times,
but you have forgiven all of our sins through Jesus.
Make us forgiving towards all those
who sin against us. Amen.

166. THE TEN LEPERS (LUKE 17)

Jesus heals ten men of leprosy, but only one returns to thank him.

On another occasion, as Jesus was on his way to Jerusalem, he was passing along the border between Samaria and Galilee. When he entered a certain village, ten lepers met him. Standing at a distance, they called out loudly, "Jesus, Master, have mercy on us!"

When he saw them, he said, "Go, show yourselves to the priests." As they went away they were cleansed.

One of them, when he saw that he was healed, turned back, glorifying God with a loud voice. He fell on his face at Jesus' feet, thanking him. And he was a Samaritan. Jesus responded, "Were not ten cleansed? Where are the other nine? Was no one found to return and give glory to God except this foreigner?" Then he said to him, "Get up and go your way. Your faith has saved you."

Lord God, we thank you for all of your many blessings to us, the most important of which is forgiveness and life in your Son Jesus. Give us hearts which appreciate all of your gifts to us and which never forget to thank you. Amen.

167. THE WOMAN CAUGHT IN ADULTERY (JOHN 8)

Jesus shows his forgiveness and the hypocrisy of those who wish to condemn others.

Jesus came into the temple courts. And all the people kept coming to him. He sat down and taught them.

Then the scribes and Pharisees brought a woman caught in adultery and had her stand in the center. "Teacher," they said to him, "this woman was caught in the act of committing adultery. In the Law, Moses commanded us to stone such women. So what do you say?" They asked this to test him, so that they might have evidence to accuse him.

Jesus bent down and started writing on the ground with his finger. But when they kept on asking him for an answer, he stood up and said to them, "Let the one among you who is without sin be the first to throw a stone at her." Then he stooped down again and wrote on the ground.

When they heard this, they went away one by one, beginning with the older men. Jesus was left alone with the woman in the center. Jesus stood up and said to her, "Woman, where are they? Has no one condemned you?"

"No one, Lord," she answered.

Then Jesus said, "Neither do I condemn you. Go, and from now on do not sin anymore."

Lord God, Jesus has rescued us from the condemnation we deserve because of our sins. For this we thank and praise you. Give us power to keep from sinning. Amen.

168. DARKNESS VERSUS LIGHT (JOHN 8-9)

Jesus shows that he is the light of the world as he brings sight to a man born blind.

Jesus said, "I am the Light of the World. Whoever follows me will never walk in darkness, but will have the light of life."

So the Pharisees said to him, "You testify about yourself. Your testimony is not valid."

"Even if I testify about myself," Jesus replied, "my testimony is valid, because I know where I came from and where I am going. But the Father who sent me testifies about me. When you lift up the Son of Man, then you will know that I speak exactly as the Father taught me."

Many believed in him. So Jesus said to the Jews who had believed him, "If you remain in my word, you are really my disciples. You will also know the truth, and the truth will set you free. Everyone who keeps committing sin is a slave to sin. But a slave does not remain in the family forever. A son does remain forever. So if the Son sets you free, you really will be free. But you are looking for a way to kill me. You are doing the works of your father."

They said, "We have one Father: God."

Jesus replied, "If God were your Father, you would love me, because I came from God. You belong to your father, the Devil, and you want to do your father's desires. He was a murderer from the beginning and the father of lying. Whoever belongs to God listens to what God says. The reason you do not listen is that you do not belong to God. Amen, Amen, I tell you: If anyone holds on to my word, he will certainly never see death."

So the Jews said to him, "You have a demon. You are not greater than our father, Abraham, are you? He died. Who do think you are?"

Jesus answered, "Abraham was glad that he would see my day. He saw it and rejoiced."

The Jews replied, "You aren't even fifty years old, and you have seen Abraham?"

Jesus said to them, "Amen, Amen, I tell you: Before Abraham was born, I am." Then they picked up stones to throw at him. But Jesus was hidden and left the temple area.

Jesus saw a man blind from birth. His disciples asked him, "Rabbi, who sinned, this man or his parents, that he was born blind?"

Jesus answered, "It was not that this man sinned, or his parents, but that God's works might be revealed in connection with him. As long as I am in the world, I am the Light of the World."

After saying this, Jesus spit on the ground, made some mud with the saliva, and spread the mud on the man's eyes. "Go," Jesus told him, "wash in the pool of Siloam." So he went and washed, and came back seeing.

Now it was a Sabbath day when Jesus opened his eyes. So the Pharisees asked him how he received his sight.

"He put mud on my eyes," the man told them. "I washed, and now I see."

Some Pharisees said, "This man is not from God because he does not keep the Sabbath." They said to the blind man again, "What do you say about him?"

The man replied, "He is a prophet."

They ridiculed him and said, "We know that God has spoken to Moses. But this man—we do not know where he comes from."

"That's amazing!" the man answered. "You do not know where he comes from, yet he opened my eyes. If this man were not from God, he could do nothing."

They answered him, "You were entirely born in sinfulness! Yet you presume to teach us?" And they threw him out.

Jesus heard that they had thrown him out. When he found him, he asked, "Do you believe in the Son of God?"

"Who is he, sir," the man replied, "that I may believe in him?"

Jesus answered, "You have seen him, and he is the very one who is speaking with you."

Then he said, "Lord, I believe!" and he knelt down and worshipped him.

Jesus said, "I came into this world in order that those who do not see will see, and those who do see will become blind."

Some of the Pharisees who were with him heard this and asked, "We are not blind too, are we?"

Jesus told them, "If you were blind, you would not hold on to sin. But now that you say, 'We see,' your sin remains."

Lord God, we were trapped in the darkness of sin before your Son shined on us with his light of forgiveness and life. Keep us in the light of his truth all our days. Amen.

169. THE GOOD SHEPHERD (JOHN 10)

Jesus teaches us how he cares for his people like a shepherd.

"Amen, Amen, I tell you: Anyone who does not enter the sheep pen by the door, but climbs in by some other way, is a thief and a robber. The one who enters by the door is the shepherd of the sheep. The doorkeeper opens the door for him, and the sheep listen to his voice. He calls his own sheep by name and leads them out. When he has brought out all his own sheep, he walks ahead of them. The sheep follow him because they know his voice. They will never follow a stranger, but will run away from him, because they do not know the voice of strangers.

"Amen, Amen, I tell you: I am the door for the sheep. All who came before me were thieves and robbers, but the sheep did not listen to them. I am the door. Whoever enters through me will be saved. He will come in and go out, and find pasture.

"A thief comes only to steal and kill and destroy. I came that they may have life, and have it abundantly.

"I am the Good Shepherd. The Good Shepherd lays down his life for the sheep. The hired man, who is not a shepherd, does not own the sheep. He sees the wolf coming, leaves the sheep, and runs away. Then the wolf attacks the sheep and scatters them. Because he works for money, he does not care about the sheep.

"I am the Good Shepherd. I know my sheep and my sheep know me. And I lay down my life for the sheep. I also have other sheep that are not of this sheep pen. I must bring them also, and they will listen to my voice. Then there will be one flock and one shepherd. This is why the Father loves me, because I lay down my life so that I may take it up again. No one takes it from me, but I lay it down on my own. I have the authority to lay it down, and I have the authority to take it up again. This is the commission I received from my Father."

The Jews gathered around Jesus, asking, "How long will you keep us in suspense? If you are the Christ, tell us plainly."

Jesus answered them, "I did tell you, but you do not believe. The works I am doing in my Father's name testify about me. But you do not believe, because you are not my sheep, as I said to you. My sheep hear my voice. I know them, and they follow me. I give them eternal life, and they will never perish. No one will snatch them out of my hand. My Father, who has given them to me, is greater than all. No one can snatch them out of my Father's hand. I and the Father are one."

Again the Jews picked up stones to stone him for blasphemy, but he eluded their grasp.

Lord God, your Son is our Good Shepherd. He has laid
his life down for us and picked it back up again for us.
Thank you for bringing us to know him as our shepherd,
and keep us always following only his voice. Amen.

170. THE PARABLE OF THE GOOD SAMARITAN, AND MARY AND MARTHA (LUKE 10)

Jesus shows us that we should serve everyone, but that our first priority is be served by him in his Word.

An expert in the law stood up to test Jesus, saying, "Teacher, what must I do to inherit eternal life?"

"What is written in the law?" he asked him. "What do you read there?"

He replied, "Love the Lord your God with all your heart, with all your soul, with all your strength, and with all your mind; and, love your neighbor as yourself."

He said to him, "You have answered correctly. Do this, and you will live."

But he wanted to justify himself, so he asked Jesus, "And who is my neighbor?"

Jesus replied, "A man was going down from Jerusalem to Jericho. He fell among robbers who stripped him, beat him, and went away, leaving him half dead. It just so happened that a priest was going down that way. But when he saw the man, he passed by on the other side. In the same way, a Levite also happened to go there, but when he saw the man, he passed by on the other side. A Samaritan, as he traveled, came to where the man was. When he saw him, he felt sorry for the man. He went to him and bandaged his wounds, pouring oil and wine on them. He put him on his own animal, took him to an inn, and took care of him. The next day, when he left, he took out two denarii, gave them to the innkeeper, and said, 'Take care of him. Whatever extra you spend, I will repay you when I return.' Which of these three do you think acted like a neighbor to the man who fell among robbers?"

"The one who showed mercy to him," he replied.

Then Jesus told him, "Go and do likewise."

Jesus came into a village, and a woman named Martha welcomed him into her home. She had a sister named Mary, who was sitting at the Lord's feet and was listening to his word. But Martha was distracted with all her serving. She came over and said, "Lord, don't you care that my sister has left me to serve alone? Tell her to help me."

The Lord answered and told her, "Martha, Martha, you are worried and upset about many things, but one thing is needed. In fact, Mary has chosen that better part, which will not be taken away from her."

Lord God, you have given us the one thing which is truly needed—your Word, which gives us the good news of our Savior Jesus. Keep us from getting distracted by other things, and gather us and all your people around your Word each day. Help us to show love to everyone in need. Amen.

171. INVITATIONS TO THE BANQUET (LUKE 14)

When invited to a banquet, Jesus teaches the importance of humility, hospitality, and not rejecting his gospel invitation.

Jesus went into the house of a leader of the Pharisees to eat. When he noticed how they were selecting the places of honor, he told the invited guests a parable. "When you are invited by someone to a wedding banquet, do not recline in the place of honor, or perhaps someone more distinguished than you may have been invited by him. The one who invited both of you may come and tell you, 'Give this man your place.' Then you will begin, with shame, to take the lowest place.

"But when you are invited, go and recline in the lowest place, so that when the one who invited you comes, he will tell you, 'Friend, move up to a higher place.' Then you will have honor in the presence of all who are reclining at the table with you.

"Yes, everyone who exalts himself will be humbled, and whoever humbles himself will be exalted."

He also said to the one who had invited him, "When you make a dinner or a supper, do not invite your friends, or your brothers, or your relatives, or rich neighbors, so that perhaps they may also return the favor and pay you back. But when you make a feast, invite the poor, the crippled, the lame, the blind, and you will be blessed, because they cannot repay you. Certainly, you will be repaid in the resurrection of the righteous."

When one of those at the table with him heard these things, he said to Jesus, "Blessed is the one who will feast in the kingdom of God!"

Jesus said to him, "A certain man made a great banquet and invited many people. When it was time for the banquet, he sent out his servant to tell those who were invited, 'Come, because everything is now ready.' But they all alike began to make excuses.

"The first one told him, 'I bought a field, and I need to go and see it. I ask you to excuse me.'

"Another one said, 'I bought five yoke of oxen, and I am going to try them out. I ask you to excuse me.'

"Still another said, 'I just got married, and so I am unable to attend.'

"The servant arrived and reported these things to his master. Then the master of the house was angry and said to his servant, 'Go out quickly into the streets and alleys of the town, and bring in here the poor, the crippled, the blind, and the lame.'

"The servant said, 'Master, what you commanded has been done, and there is still room.'

"Then the master said to the servant, 'Go out into the highways and hedges, and urge them to come in, so that my house may be filled. Yes, I tell you that none of those men who were invited will taste my banquet.' "

Lord God, you have invited us to join you at your heavenly banquet. Help us to show humility in our lives and to show generosity towards all. Amen.

172. A LOST SHEEP, A LOST COIN, AND A LOST SON (LUKE 15)

Using three stories, Jesus shows God's love for the lost, a love which his people should share.

All the tax collectors and sinners were coming to Jesus to hear him. But the Pharisees and the experts in the law were complaining, "This man welcomes sinners and eats with them."

He told them this parable: "Which one of you, if you had one hundred sheep and lost one of them, would not leave the ninety-nine in the wilderness and go after the one that was lost until he finds it? And when he finds it, he joyfully puts it on his shoulders and goes home. Then he calls together his friends and his neighbors, telling them, 'Rejoice with me, because I have found my lost sheep!' I tell you, in the same way there will be more joy in heaven over one sinner who repents than over ninety-nine righteous people who do not need to repent.

"Or what woman who has ten silver coins, if she loses one coin, would not light a lamp, sweep the house, and search carefully until she finds it? And when she finds it, she calls together her friends and neighbors and says, 'Rejoice with me, because I have found the lost coin.' In the same way, I tell you, there is joy in the presence of the angels of God over one sinner who repents."

Jesus said, "A certain man had two sons. The younger of them said to his father, 'Father, give me my share of the estate.' So he divided his property between them. Not many days later, the younger son gathered together all that he had and traveled to a distant country. There he wasted his wealth with reckless living. After he had spent everything, there was a severe famine in that country, and he began to be in need. He went and hired himself out to one of the citizens of that country, who sent him into his fields to feed pigs. He would have liked to fill his stomach with the carob pods that the pigs were eating, but no one gave him anything.

"When he came to his senses, he said, 'How many of my father's hired servants have more than enough bread, and I am dying from hunger! I will get up, go to my father, and tell him, "Father, I have sinned against heaven and in your sight. I am no longer worthy to be called your son. Make me like one of your hired servants."'

"He got up and went to his father. While he was still far away, his father saw him and was filled with compassion. He ran, hugged his son, and kissed him. The son said to him, 'Father, I have sinned against heaven and in your sight. I am no longer worthy to be called your son.'

"But the father said to his servants, 'Quick, bring out the best robe and put it on him. Put a ring on his finger and sandals on his feet. Bring the fattened calf and kill it. Let us eat and celebrate, because this son of mine was dead and is alive again. He was lost and is found.' Then they began to celebrate.

"His older son was in the field. As he approached the house, he heard music and dancing. He called one of the servants and asked what was going on. The servant told him, 'Your brother is here! Your father killed the fattened calf, because he has received him back safe and sound.' The older brother was angry and refused to go in. His father came out and began to plead with him.

"He answered his father, 'Look, these many years I've been serving you, and I never disobeyed your command, but you never gave me even a young goat so that I could celebrate with my friends. But when this son of yours arrived after wasting your property with prostitutes, you killed the fattened calf for him!'

"The father said to him, 'Son, you are always with me, and all that I have is yours. But it was fitting to celebrate and be glad, because this brother of yours was dead and is alive again. He was lost and is found.'"

Lord God, we thank you that when we were lost
in sin and death, your Son sought and found us,
bringing us to faith in him. Help us to look for souls

who are still lost and to rejoice with him over all
who have been found. Amen.

173. THE RICH MAN AND POOR LAZARUS (LUKE 16)

Jesus tells a story that shows that this life is the only opportunity to gain salvation, and his Word is the only way to be saved.

Jesus said to his disciples, "There was a rich man who was dressed in purple and fine linen, living in luxury every day. A beggar named Lazarus had been laid at his gate. Lazarus was covered with sores and longed to be fed with what fell from the rich man's table. Besides this, the dogs also came and licked his sores. Eventually the beggar died, and the angels carried him to Abraham's side. The rich man also died and was buried. In hell, where he was in torment, he lifted up his eyes and saw Abraham far away and Lazarus at his side. He called out and said, 'Father Abraham, have mercy on me! Send Lazarus to dip the tip of his finger in water and cool my tongue, because I am in misery in this flame

"But Abraham said, 'Son, remember that in your lifetime you received your good things, and Lazarus received bad things. But now he is comforted here, and you are in misery. Besides all this, a great chasm has been set in place between us and you, so that those who want to cross from here to you cannot, nor can anyone cross over from there to us.'

"He said, 'Then I beg you, father, send him to my father's home, because I have five brothers—to warn them, so that they will not also come to this place of torment.'

"Abraham said, 'They have Moses and the Prophets. Let them listen to them.'

"'No, father Abraham,' he said, 'but if someone from the dead goes to them, they will repent.'

"Abraham replied to him, 'If they do not listen to Moses and the Prophets, they will not be convinced even if someone rises from the dead.' "

Lord God, we thank you that you have given us
your Word, and used it to bring us to faith in you.
When we die, take us to be with you forever
and to be comforted. Help us to make the most
of all the opportunities we have right now
to share that Word with others. Amen.

174. THE RAISING OF LAZARUS (JOHN 11)

Jesus shows his absolute power over death for his friend Lazarus of Bethany.

Now a man named Lazarus was sick. Mary and Martha, his sisters, sent a message to Jesus, saying, "Lord, the one you love is sick!"

When Jesus heard it, he said, "This sickness is not going to result in death, but it is for the glory of God, so that the Son of God may be glorified through it."

Jesus loved Martha and her sister and Lazarus. Yet when he heard that Lazarus was sick, he stayed in the place where he was two more days.

Then afterwards he said to his disciples, "Let's go back to Judea. Our friend Lazarus has fallen asleep, but I am going there to wake him up."

Then the disciples said, "Lord, if he has fallen asleep, he will get well."

Jesus had been speaking about his death, but they thought he was merely talking about ordinary sleep. So Jesus told them plainly, "Lazarus is dead. And I am glad for your sake that I was not there, so that you may believe. But let us go to him."

When Jesus arrived, he found that Lazarus had already been in the tomb for four days. When Martha heard that Jesus was coming, she went to meet him, while Mary was sitting in the house. Martha said to Jesus, "Lord, if you had been here, my brother would not have died. But even now I know that whatever you ask from God, God will give you."

Jesus said to her, "Your brother will rise again."

Martha replied, "I know that he will rise in the resurrection on the Last Day."

Jesus said to her, "I am the resurrection and the life. Whoever believes in me will live, even if he dies. And whoever lives and believes in me will never perish. Do you believe this?"

"Yes, Lord," she told him. "I believe that you are the Christ, the Son of God, who was to come into the world."

After she said this, Martha went back to call her sister Mary. She whispered, "The Teacher is here and is calling for you."

When Mary came to where Jesus was and saw him, she fell at his feet and said, "Lord, if you had been here, my brother would not have died."

When Jesus saw her weeping, and the Jews who came with her also weeping, he was deeply moved in his spirit and troubled.

He asked, "Where have you laid him?"

They told him, "Lord, come and see."

Jesus wept.

Then the Jews said, "See how he loved him!" But some of them said, "Could not he who opened the eyes of the blind man have kept this man from dying?"

Jesus was deeply moved again as he came to the tomb. It was a cave, and a stone was lying against it. "Take away the stone," he said. So they took away the stone.

Jesus looked up and said, "Father, I thank you that you heard me. I knew that you always hear me, but I said this for the benefit of the crowd standing here, so that they may believe that you sent me." After he said this, he shouted with a loud voice, "Lazarus, come out!"

The man who had died came out with his feet and his hands bound with strips of linen and his face wrapped with a cloth. Jesus told them, "Loose him and let him go."

Therefore many of the Jews who saw what Jesus did believed in him. But some of them went to the Pharisees and told them what Jesus had done. So the chief priests and the Pharisees called a meeting of the Sanhedrin. They asked, "What are we going to do, because this man is doing many miraculous signs? If we let him go on like this, everyone will believe in him. Then the Romans will come and take away our nation."

But Caiaphas, who was high priest that year, said to them, "It is better for us that one man die for the people than that the whole nation perish." He did not say this on his own, but, as high priest that year, he prophesied that Jesus was going to die for the nation, and not only for that nation, but also in order to gather into one the scattered children of God.

So from that day on they plotted to kill him.

Lord God, comfort us with the truth that all
who have died believing in your Son will rise to live
with you forever. When it is time for us to die,
bring our soul to be with you until you raise up
our body on the Last Day. Amen.

175. THE PARABLE OF THE PERSISTENT WIDOW AND THE PARABLE OF THE PHARISEE AND THE TAX COLLECTOR (LUKE 18)

Jesus uses stories to show the value of persistent prayer and the necessity of humble repentance.

Jesus told them a parable about the need to always pray and not lose heart: "There was a judge in a certain town who did not fear God and did not care about people. There was a widow in that town, and she kept going to him, saying, 'Give me justice from my adversary!' For some time he refused, but after a while he said to himself, 'Even though I do not fear God or care about people, yet because this widow keeps bothering me, I will give her justice so that she will not wear me out with her endless pleading.'"

The Lord said, "Listen to what the unjust judge says. Will not God give justice to his chosen ones, who are crying out to him day and night? Will he put off helping them? I tell you that he will give them justice quickly. However, when the Son of Man comes, will he find faith on the earth?"

Jesus told this parable to certain people who trusted in themselves (that they were righteous) and looked down on others: "Two men went up to the temple courts to pray. One was a Pharisee, and the other was a tax collector. The Pharisee stood and prayed about himself like this: 'God, I thank you that I am not like other people, robbers, evildoers, adulterers, or even like this tax collector. I fast twice a week. I give a tenth of all my income.'

"However the tax collector stood at a distance and would not even lift his eyes up to heaven, but was beating his chest and saying, 'God, be merciful to me, a sinner!'

"I tell you, this man went home justified rather than the other, because everyone who exalts himself will be humbled, but the one who humbles himself will be exalted."

Lord God, be merciful to me, a sinner. Do not treat me as my sins deserve, but instead forgive and bless me for Jesus' sake, and for his sake deliver me from all the evils of this world. Make me bold and persistent in prayer. Amen.

176. MARRIAGE AND FAMILY (MARK 10)

Jesus reasserts God's designs for marriage and speaks of the value of children.

Jesus went to the region of Judea beyond the Jordan. Crowds gathered around him again and, as he usually did, he taught them. Some Pharisees came to test him and asked, "Is it lawful for a man to divorce his wife?"

He replied, "What did Moses command you?"

They said, "Moses permitted a man to write a certificate of divorce and send her away."

But Jesus told them, "He wrote this command for you because of your hard hearts. But from the beginning of creation, 'God made them male and female. For this reason a man will leave his father and mother and be joined to his wife, and the two will become one flesh.' So they are no longer two but one flesh. Therefore, what God has joined together, let no one separate."

In the house his disciples asked him about this again. He said to them, "Whoever divorces his wife and marries another commits adultery against her. If she divorces her husband and marries another, she commits adultery."

Some people began bringing little children to Jesus so that he would touch them. But the disciples rebuked them. When Jesus saw this, he was indignant. He said, "Let the little children come to me! Do not hinder them, because the kingdom of God belongs to such as these. Amen I tell you: Whoever will not receive the kingdom of God like a little child will never enter it." And he took the little children in his arms, laid his hands on them, and blessed them.

Lord God, you love the little children. As we grow older, keep us from ever outgrowing our childlike faith in you. Help all husbands and wives to follow your good plans for marriage. Amen.

177. THE RICH YOUNG RULER, AND THE PARABLE OF THE VINEYARD (MATTHEW 19-20)

Jesus teaches that eternal life is a gift and not something that we can earn.

There was a man who came to him and said, "Teacher, what should I do that I may have eternal life?"

Jesus said to him, "If you want to enter life, keep the commandments."

"Which ones?" the man asked him.

Jesus said, "'You shall not murder. You shall not commit adultery. You shall not steal. You shall not give false testimony. Honor your father and mother.' And, 'You shall love your neighbor as yourself.'"

The young man said to him, "I have kept all these. What am I still lacking?"

Jesus told him, "If you want to be perfect, go, sell your possessions, and give to the poor, and you will have treasure in heaven. Then come, follow me."

But when the young man heard this, he went away sad, because he had many possessions. Jesus said to his disciples, "Amen I tell you: It will be very hard for a rich man to enter the kingdom of heaven. It is easier for a camel to go through the eye of a needle than for a rich man to enter the kingdom of God."

When the disciples heard this, they were greatly astonished and said, "Who then can be saved?"

Jesus looked at them and said, "With people this is impossible, but with God all things are possible."

Then Peter answered, "Look, we have left everything and followed you! What then will we have?"

Jesus said to them, "Amen I tell you: In the renewal, when the Son of Man sits on his glorious throne, you who have followed me will also sit on twelve thrones, judging the twelve tribes of Israel. Everyone who has left homes or brothers or sisters or father or mother or children or fields, because of my name, will receive a hundred times as much and will inherit eternal life.

"Many who are first will be last, and many who are last will be first. Indeed the kingdom of heaven is like a landowner who went out early in the morning to hire workers for his vineyard. After agreeing to pay the workers a denarius for the day, he sent them into his vineyard. He also went out about the third hour and saw others standing unemployed in the marketplace. To these he said, 'You also go into the vineyard, and I will give you whatever is right.' So they went. Again he went out about the sixth and the ninth hour and did the same thing. When he went out about the eleventh hour, he found others standing unemployed. He said to them, 'Why have you stood here all day unemployed?'

"They said to him, 'Because no one hired us.'

"He told them, 'You also go into the vineyard.'

"When it was evening, the owner of the vineyard said to his foreman, 'Call the workers and pay them their wages, starting with the last group and ending with the first.'

"When those who were hired around the eleventh hour came, they each received a denarius. When those who were hired first came, they thought they would receive more. But they each received a denarius too. After they received it, they began to grumble against the landowner: 'Those who were last worked one hour, and you made them equal to us who have endured the burden of the day and the scorching heat!'

"But he answered one of them, 'Friend, I am doing you no wrong. Did you not make an agreement with me for a denarius? Take what is yours and go. I want to give to the last one hired the same as I also gave to you. Can't I do what I want with my own money? Or are you envious because I am generous?'

"In the same way, the last will be first, and the first, last."

Lord God, we thank you for the money you have given us. Move us to be generous with our gifts towards others, and never let the things you have given us lead us away from you. Even more, we thank you for the gift of eternal life. Keep us from ever thinking of your gift to us as something we earn, but help us to serve you faithfully in appreciation for all you have done for us. Amen.

178. ZACCHAEUS, AND THE PARABLE OF THE MINAS (LUKE 19)

Jesus' love for Zacchaeus prompts Zacchaeus's love for others. Jesus also teaches that all his people should serve faithfully while they await his second coming.

Jesus entered Jericho and was passing through. A man named Zacchaeus was there. He was a chief tax collector, and he was rich. He was trying to see who Jesus was, but since he was short, he could not see because of the crowd. He ran on ahead and climbed up into a sycamore tree to see Jesus, because he was about to pass by that way. When Jesus came to the place, he looked up and said to him, "Zacchaeus, hurry and come down, for I must stay at your house today." He came down quickly and welcomed Jesus joyfully. When the people saw it, they were all grumbling because he went to be a guest of a sinful man.

Zacchaeus stood up and said to the Lord, "Look, Lord, I am going to give half of my possessions to the poor. And if I have cheated anyone out of anything, I will pay back four times as much."

Jesus said to him, "Today, salvation has come to this house, because he too is a son of Abraham. For the Son of Man came to seek and to save the lost."

Jesus went on to tell a parable, because he was near Jerusalem, and the people thought that the kingdom of God was going to appear at once. So he said, "A man of noble birth traveled to a distant country to receive a kingdom for himself and then to return. He called ten of his servants and gave them ten minas. 'Conduct business until I return,' he said to them.

"But his subjects hated him and sent a delegation after him, saying, 'We do not want this man to be king over us.'

"When he returned after receiving the kingdom, he summoned the servants to whom he had given the money. He wanted to find out what they had gained by conducting business.

"The first one came to him and said, 'Master, your mina has earned ten more minas.'

"He said to him, 'Well done, good servant! Because you were faithful in a very small matter, you will have authority over ten cities.'

"The second one came and said, 'Master, your mina has produced five more minas.'

"So he said to him, 'You will be over five cities.'

"And another one came and said, 'Master, here is your mina that I laid away in a piece of cloth. For I was afraid of you, since you are a demanding man.'

"He said to him, 'You wicked servant, I will judge you with your own words! You knew that I am a demanding man. Then why did you not put my money in the bank? Then, when I returned, I could have collected it with interest!'

"He said to those standing there, 'Take the mina away from him and give it to the one who has the ten minas.'

"But they said to him, 'Master, he already has ten minas!'

"'I tell you that to everyone who has, more will be given, but from the one who does not have, even what he has will be taken away. Now as for those enemies of mine who did not want me to be king over them, bring them here and kill them in front me.'"

Lord God, how joyful it makes me to know that
Jesus is my Savior and that I am forgiven in him.
Make me a faithful steward of all the time, the talents,
and the treasures that you have entrusted to me,
that I may use them to serve you. Amen.

PART 3

CHRIST'S DEATH AND RESURRECTION

After about a three-year public ministry, Jesus entered into Jerusalem on a mission. He was coming to die for the world and to rise again, and that is exactly what he did. None of this was a tragedy or an accident. This was God's plan to save us. In raising Jesus from the dead, God the Father confirms for us that Jesus is the Son of God, that all sins are paid for in him, and that he will raise all his believing people from the dead on the Last Day.

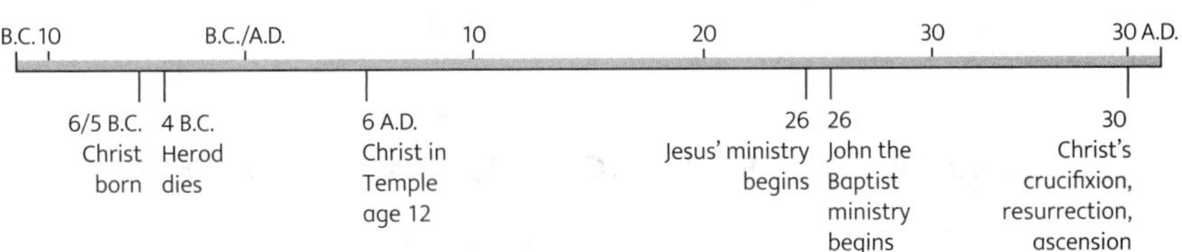

179. PALM SUNDAY (MATTHEW 21)

Jesus is praised by the people as he enters Jerusalem to die.

As they approached Jerusalem and came to Bethphage on the Mount of Olives, Jesus sent two disciples, telling them, "Go to the village ahead of you. Immediately you will find a donkey tied there along with her colt. Untie them and bring them to me. If anyone says anything to you, you are to say, 'The Lord needs them,' and he will send them at once."

This took place to fulfill what was spoken through the prophet: "Tell the daughter of Zion: Look, your King comes to you, humble, and riding on a donkey, on a colt, the foal of a donkey."

The disciples went and did just as Jesus commanded them. They brought the donkey and the colt, laid their outer clothing on them, and he sat on it. A very large crowd spread their outer clothing on the road. Others were cutting branches from the trees and spreading them out on the road. The crowds who went in front of him and those who followed kept shouting, "Hosanna to the Son of David! Blessed is he who comes in the name of the Lord! Hosanna in the highest!"

When he entered Jerusalem, the whole city was stirred up, asking, "Who is this?" And the crowds were saying, "This is Jesus, the prophet from Nazareth in Galilee."

Jesus entered the temple courts and drove out all those who were selling and buying in the temple. He overturned the tables of the money changers and the seats of those who were selling doves. He said to them, "It is written, 'My house will be called a house of prayer,' but you are making it a den of robbers!"

The blind and the lame came to him in the temple, and he healed them. But when the chief priests and the experts in the law saw the wonders he performed and heard the children calling out in the temple, "Hosanna to the Son of David!" they were indignant. They said to him, "Do you hear what they are saying?"

"Yes," Jesus told them, "Have you never read, 'From the lips of little children and nursing babies you have prepared praise'?"

Lord God, your Son, our Savior, Jesus rode into Jerusalem
as our humble but conquering king.
All praise to you for saving us. Amen.

180. THE PARABLE OF THE WICKED TENANTS (MATTHEW 21)

Jesus tells a story about the religious leaders who are rejecting him.

Jesus went into the temple courts. The chief priests and the elders of the people came to him while he was teaching. Jesus said to them, "Listen to another parable. There was a landowner who planted a vineyard. He leased it out to some tenant farmers and went away on a journey. When the time approached to harvest the fruit, he sent his servants to the tenants to get his fruit. The tenant farmers seized his servants. They beat one, killed another, and stoned a third. Then the landowner sent even more servants than the first time. The tenant farmers treated them the same way. Finally, he sent his son to them. 'They will respect my son,' he said.

"But when the tenant farmers saw the son, they said to each other, 'This is the heir. Come, let's kill him and take his inheritance!' They took him, threw him out of the vineyard, and killed him. So when the landowner comes, what will he do to those tenant farmers?"

They told him, "He will bring those wretches to a wretched end. Then he will lease out the vineyard to other tenants who will give him his fruit when it is due."

Jesus said to them, "Have you never read in the Scriptures: 'The stone the builders rejected has become the cornerstone. This was the Lord's doing, and it is marvelous in our eyes'? That is why I tell you the kingdom of God will be taken away from you and given to a people that produces its fruit. Whoever falls on this stone will be broken to pieces, and it will crush anyone on whom it falls."

When the chief priests and the Pharisees heard his parables, they knew that he was talking about them. Although they were looking for a way to arrest him, they were afraid of the crowds because the people regarded him as a prophet.

Lord God, your Son suffered and died for us.
Keep us from ever turning away from him.
Give us leaders who will point us always to him. Amen.

181. THE QUESTIONS OF THE PHARISEES AND SADDUCEES (MARK 12)

Jesus' enemies unsuccessfully attempt to trap Jesus in his words.

The Jewish leaders sent some Pharisees and some Herodians to Jesus to try to trap him in what he said. They came and said to him, "Teacher, is it lawful to pay a tax to Caesar or not?"

Jesus knew their hypocrisy. He said to them, "Why do you keep testing me? Bring me a denarius."

So they brought one.

He said to them, "Whose image and inscription is this?"

"Caesar's," they answered him.

Then Jesus told them, "Give to Caesar what is Caesar's, and to God what is God's." And they were amazed.

Next some Sadducees (who say that there will be no resurrection) came to him. They asked him a question: "Teacher, Moses wrote for us: 'If a man's brother dies and leaves behind a wife but no child, then his brother should take his wife and raise up children for his brother.' Now there were seven brothers. The first one took a wife and died without leaving children. The second one married her and died, leaving no children. The third one did the same. The seven left no children. Last of all, the woman also died. So when they rise in the resurrection, whose wife will she be, since all seven had her as a wife?"

Jesus said to them, "You are mistaken. You do not know the Scriptures or the power of God. When people rise from the dead, they do not marry, and they are not given in marriage, but they are like angels in heaven.

"But about the dead—that they are raised—have you not read in the book of Moses, in the passage about the burning bush, how God told him, 'I am the God of Abraham, the God of Isaac, and the God of Jacob'? He is not the God of the dead, but of the living. You are badly mistaken."

One of the experts in the law approached after he heard their discussion. When he saw that Jesus had answered them well, he asked Jesus, "Which commandment is the greatest of all?"

Jesus answered, "The most important is: 'Hear, O Israel, the Lord, our God, the Lord is one. Love the Lord your God with all your heart, with all your soul, with all your mind, and with all your strength.' The second is this: 'Love your neighbor as yourself.' There is no other commandment greater than these."

The expert in the law said to him, "Well said, teacher. To love him with all your heart, with all your understanding, and with all your strength, and to love your neighbor as yourself, is more important than all whole burnt offerings and sacrifices."

When Jesus saw that he had answered wisely, he said to him, "You are not far from the kingdom of God." After that, no one dared to ask him any more questions.

Jesus sat down opposite the offering box and was watching how the crowd put money into it. Many rich people put in large amounts. One poor widow came and put in two small bronze coins, worth less than a penny. He called his disciples together and said to them, "Amen I tell you: This poor widow put more into the offering box than all the others. For they all gave out of their surplus, but she, out of her poverty, put in everything—all that she had to live on."

Lord God, thank you for your blessings to us through our government. Thank you even more for your blessings to us through your Son Jesus, giving us forgiveness and eternal life. Help us to love you with all our heart. Help us to love our neighbor as ourselves. Help us to love you with generous offerings. Amen.

182. THE END OF THE WORLD (MATTHEW 24-25)

Jesus tells his disciples how to be ready for the end of the world.

Jesus was sitting on the Mount of Olives. The disciples came to him and said, "What will be the sign of your coming and of the end of the world?"

Jesus answered them, "Watch out that no one deceives you. Because many will come in my name, saying, 'I am the Christ,' and they will deceive many people. You will hear of wars and rumors of wars. See that you are not alarmed, because all these things must happen; but that is not yet the end. Nation will rise against nation, and kingdom against kingdom. There will be famines and earthquakes in various places. But all these things are only the beginning of birth pains. Then they will hand you over to be persecuted, and they will put you to death. You will be hated by all nations because of my name. Many will fall away from faith. Many false prophets will appear and deceive many people. Because lawlessness will increase, the love of many will grow cold. But whoever endures to the end will be saved. This gospel will be proclaimed throughout the whole world as a testimony to all nations, and then the end will come.

"Therefore when you see the abomination that causes desolation standing in the holy place, flee to the mountains. If those days were not shortened, nobody would be saved. But for the sake of the elect, those days will be shortened.

"At that time if anyone tells you, 'Look, here is the Christ,' do not believe it. For false Christs and false prophets will arise and will perform great signs and wonders so as to deceive even the elect, if it were possible. So if they tell you, 'Look! There he is in the wilderness,' do not go out there. Just as the lightning flashes from the east and shines as far as the west, so it will be when the Son of Man comes.

"Immediately after the misery of those days, the sun will be darkened, and the moon will not give its light; the stars will fall from the sky, and the powers of the heavens will be shaken. Then the sign of the Son of Man will appear in the sky. And at that time all the nations of the earth will mourn. They will see the Son of Man coming on the clouds of the sky with power and great glory. He will send out his angels with a loud trumpet call, and they will gather together his elect from the four winds, from one end of the heavens to the other.

"No one knows when that day and hour will be, not the angels of heaven, not even the Son, but only the Father.

"Just as it was in the days of Noah, so it will be when the Son of Man returns. In the days before the flood people were eating and drinking, marrying and giving in marriage, until the very day that Noah entered the ark. They did not realize what was coming until the flood came and took them all away. That is how it will be when the Son of Man returns.

"At that time the kingdom of heaven will be like ten virgins who took their lamps and went out to meet the bridegroom. Five of them were foolish, and five were wise. When the foolish ones took their lamps, they did not take any oil with them; but the wise took oil in their containers with their lamps. While the bridegroom was delayed, they all became drowsy and fell asleep. But at midnight there was a shout, 'Look, the bridegroom! Come out to meet him!' Then all those virgins got up and trimmed their lamps. The foolish ones said to the wise, 'Give us some of your oil because our lamps are going out.' But the wise answered, 'No, there may not be enough for us and for you. Instead, go to those who sell oil and buy some for yourselves.' But while they were away buying oil, the bridegroom came. Those who were ready went in with him to the wedding banquet, and the door was shut. Later, the other virgins also came and said, 'Let us in.' But he answered, 'Amen I tell you: I do not know you.' Therefore, keep watch, because you do not know the day or the hour."

Lord God, keep us always ready for your Son's return.
Make us strong in the faith and always
faithfully serving you. Amen.

183. THE LAST JUDGMENT (MATTHEW 25)

Jesus explains what will happen when he comes again to judge all people.

"When the Son of Man comes in his glory, and all the angels with him, he will sit on his glorious throne. All the nations will be gathered in his presence, and he will separate them one from another, as a shepherd separates the sheep from the goats. He will put the sheep on his right and the goats on his left. Then the King will say to those on his right, 'Come, you who are blessed by my Father, inherit the kingdom prepared for you from the foundation of the world. For I was hungry and you gave me food to eat. I was thirsty and you gave me something to drink. I was a stranger and you welcomed me. I was lacking clothes and you clothed me. I was sick and you took care of me. I was in prison and you visited me.'

"Then the righteous will answer him, 'Lord, when did we see you hungry and feed you, or thirsty and give you a drink? When did we see you a stranger and welcome you, or lacking clothes and clothe you? When did we see you sick or in prison and visit you?'

"The King will answer them, 'Amen I tell you: Just as you did it for one of the least of these brothers of mine, you did it for me.'

"Then he will say to those on his left, 'Depart from me, you who are cursed, into the eternal fire, which is prepared for the Devil and his angels. For I was hungry and you did not give me food to eat. I was thirsty and you did not give me anything to drink. I was a stranger and you did not welcome me, lacking clothes and you did not clothe me, sick and in prison and you did not take care of me.'

"Then they will also answer, 'Lord, when did we see you hungry or thirsty or a stranger or lacking clothes or sick or in prison and did not serve you?'

"At that time he will answer them, 'Amen I tell you: Just as you did not do it for one of the least of these, you did not do it for me.' And they will go away to eternal punishment, but the righteous to eternal life."

Lord God, we eagerly await your Son's return. By faith in him we know you will give us eternal life. Amen.

184. THE EVENTS OF MAUNDY THURSDAY, PART 1 (MARK 14)

Jesus eats his last supper with his disciples and institutes the Lord's Supper.

Judas Iscariot, one of the Twelve, went to the chief priests in order to betray Jesus to them. When they heard this, they were glad and promised to give him money. So he began to look for an opportunity to betray him.

On the first day of the Festival of Unleavened Bread, when the Passover lamb is sacrificed, his disciples asked him, "Where do you want us to go and prepare for you to eat the Passover?"

He sent two of his disciples and said to them, "Go into the city, and there a man carrying a jar of water will meet you. Follow him. Wherever he enters, tell the owner of the house that the Teacher says, 'Where is my guest room, where I may eat the Passover with my disciples?' He will show you a large upper room, furnished and ready. Make preparations for us there."

His disciples left and went into the city and found things just as he had told them; and they prepared the Passover.

When it was evening, he arrived with the Twelve.

While they were reclining and eating, Jesus said, "Amen I tell you: One of you will betray me, one who is eating with me."

They began to be sorrowful and said to him one by one, "Surely not I?"

He said to them, "It is one of the Twelve, one who is dipping bread with me in the dish. Indeed, the Son of Man is going to go just as it has been written about him, but woe to that man by whom the Son of Man is betrayed! It would have been better for that man if he had not been born."

While they were eating, Jesus took bread. When he had blessed it, he broke it and gave it to them, saying, "Take it. This is my body."

Then he took the cup, gave thanks, and gave it to them. They all drank from it. He said to them, "This is my blood of the new testament, which is poured out for many. Amen I tell you: I will certainly not drink again of the fruit of the vine until that day when I drink it anew in the kingdom of God."

Jesus said to them, "You will all fall away because of me. For it is written: 'I will strike the shepherd, and the sheep will be scattered.' But after I am raised, I will go ahead of you into Galilee."

But Peter said to him, "Even if all fall away, I will not."

Jesus said to him, "Amen I tell you: Today—this very night—before the rooster crows twice, you will deny me three times."

But Peter kept saying emphatically, "Even if I have to die with you, I will never deny you." And they all said the same thing.

Lord God, we thank you for the gift of Christ's body and blood which you give us to eat and to drink. Cause us

to be mindful of what we are receiving in this sacrament
and to receive it in true repentance, receiving
the forgiveness of our sins. Amen.

185. THE EVENTS OF MAUNDY THURSDAY, PART 2 (JOHN 13-17)

Jesus tells the disciples what will happen to them in the future and promises to send the Holy Spirit.

After Judas left, Jesus said, "Now the Son of Man is glorified, and God is glorified in him. Dear children, I am going to be with you only a little longer.

"A new commandment I give you: Love one another. Just as I have loved you, so also you are to love one another. By this everyone will know that you are my disciples.

"Do not let your heart be troubled. Believe in God; believe also in me. In my Father's house are many mansions. I am going to prepare a place for you. And if I go and prepare a place for you, I will come again and take you to be with me, so that you may also be where I am. You know where I am going, and you know the way. I am the Way and the Truth and the Life. No one comes to the Father, except through me. The one who has seen me has seen the Father. I am in the Father and the Father is in me.

"I will not leave you as orphans; I am coming to you. In a little while the world will see me no longer, but you will see me. Because I live, you also will live. In that day you will know that I am in my Father, and you in me, and I in you.

"I have told you these things while staying with you. But the Counselor, the Holy Spirit, whom the Father will send in my name, will teach you all things and remind you of everything I told you.

"I am the true vine, and my Father is the gardener. The one who remains in me and I in him is the one who bears much fruit. Without me you can do nothing. If anyone does not remain in me, he is thrown away like a branch and withers.

"This is my command: Love one another as I have loved you. No one has greater love than this: that someone lays down his life for his friends. You did not choose me, but I chose you and appointed you to go and bear fruit, fruit that will endure.

"If the world hates you, you know that it hated me first. If you were of the world, the world would love its own. However, because you are not of the world, but I have chosen you out of it, the world hates you. If they persecuted me, they will persecute you too. I have told you these things so that you will not fall away.

"Nevertheless, it is good for you that I go away. For if I do not go away, the Counselor will not come to you. But if I go, I will send him to you. When he, the Spirit of truth, comes, he will guide you into all truth. He will also declare to you what is to come.

"In a little while you are not going to see me anymore, and again in a little while you will see me, because I am going away to the Father. I have told you these things, so that you may have peace in me. In this world you are going to have trouble. But be courageous! I have overcome the world."

Jesus looked up to heaven and said, "Father, the time has come. Glorify your Son so that your Son may glorify you. I have glorified you on earth by finishing the work you gave me to do. Now, Father, glorify me at your own side with the glory I had at your side before the world existed.

"I revealed your name to the men you gave me out of the world. They learned the truth that I came from you. They believed that you sent me. I pray for them. I am no longer going to be in the world, but they are still in the world. Holy Father, protect them from the Evil One. Sanctify them by the truth. Your word is truth.

"I am praying not only for them, but also for those who believe in me through their message. Father, I want those you have given me to be with me where I am so that they may see my glory—the glory you gave me, because you loved me before the world's foundation."

Lord God, when we feel overcome by the world,
remind us that our Savior Jesus has overcome the world.
Give us your Holy Spirit through your Word and keep us
connected to your Son until you take us to the place
that you have prepared for us with you. Amen.

186. THE GARDEN OF GETHSEMANE (MATTHEW 26)

Jesus allows himself to be betrayed and arrested.

After they sang a hymn, they went out to the Mount of Olives. Then Jesus went with them to a place called Gethsemane. He told his disciples, "Sit here, while I go over there and pray." He took with him Peter and the two sons of Zebedee. He began to be sorrowful and distressed. Then he said to them, "My soul is very sorrowful, even to the point of death. Stay here, and keep watch with me."

He went a little farther, fell on his face, and prayed. He said, "My Father, if it is possible, let this cup pass from me. Yet not as I will, but as you will."

He came to the disciples and found them sleeping. He said to Peter, "So, were you not able to stay awake with me for one hour? Watch and pray, so that you do not enter into temptation. The spirit is willing, but the flesh is weak."

He went away a second time and prayed, "My Father, if it is not possible for this cup to pass from me unless I drink it, may your will be done." Again he returned and found them sleeping, because their eyes were heavy. He left them again, went away, and prayed a third time. He said the same words as before. Then he returned to his disciples and said to them, "Are you still sleeping and resting? Look, the hour is near, and the Son of Man is betrayed into the hands of sinners. Rise. Let us go. Look, my betrayer is near."

While Jesus was still speaking, suddenly Judas (one of the Twelve) arrived. With him was a large crowd with swords and clubs, who came from the chief priests and elders of the people. Now the betrayer had given them a sign: "The one I kiss is the man. Arrest him." Immediately he went to Jesus and said, "Greetings, Rabbi!" and kissed him.

Jesus said to him, "Friend, why are you here?"

Then they advanced, took hold of Jesus, and arrested him. Suddenly, one of the men with Jesus reached out his hand, drew his sword, and struck the servant of the high priest, cutting off his ear. Then Jesus said to him, "Put your sword back into its place, because all who take the sword will die by the sword. Do you not realize that I could call on my Father, and at once he would provide me with more than twelve legions of angels? But then how would the Scriptures be fulfilled that say it must happen this way?"

At that same time Jesus said to the crowd, "Have you come out to arrest me with swords and clubs as if I were a robber? Day after day I was sitting in the temple courts teaching, and you did not arrest me. But all this has happened so that the writings of the prophets would be fulfilled." Then all the disciples deserted him and fled.

Lord God, your Son willingly drank down
the cup of punishment for sin so that we will
never have to. For this we thank and praise you.
Keep us vigilant in prayer and protect us so
that we do not fall into temptation. Amen.

187. JESUS' TRIAL BEFORE THE JEWS, PETER'S DENIAL, AND JUDAS' DESPAIR (MATTHEW 26-27)

The Jewish leaders condemn Jesus to death even though he was innocent.

Those who had arrested Jesus led him away to Caiaphas, the high priest, where the experts in the law and the elders were assembled. Peter was following him at a distance and went as far as the courtyard of the high priest. He went inside and sat down with the guards to see how it would turn out.

The chief priests and the whole Sanhedrin were looking for false testimony against Jesus so that they could put him to death. They found none, even though many false witnesses came forward. Finally two came forward and said, "This fellow said, 'I am able to destroy the temple of God and rebuild it in three days.'"

The high priest stood up and said to him, "Have you no answer? What is this that these men are testifying against you?" But Jesus remained silent. Then the high priest said to him, "I place you under oath by the living God: Tell us if you are the Christ, the Son of God!"

Jesus said to him, "It is as you have said. But I tell you, soon you will see the Son of Man sitting at the right hand of power and coming on the clouds of heaven."

Then the high priest tore his robes and said, "He has spoken blasphemy! Why do we need any more witnesses? See, you have just heard the blasphemy! What do you think?"

They answered, "He is deserving of death!" Then they spit in his face and punched him. Some slapped him and said, "Prophesy to us, Christ! Who hit you?"

Meanwhile Peter was sitting outside in the courtyard. A servant girl came to him and said, "You were with Jesus the Galilean."

But he denied it in front of everyone, saying, "I don't know what you're talking about."

When Peter went out to the entryway, someone else saw him and said to those who were there, "This fellow was with Jesus of Nazareth."

Again Peter denied it with an oath and said, "I do not know the man."

After a little while those who stood by came and said to Peter, "Surely you are also one of them because even your accent gives you away."

Then he began to curse and to swear, "I do not know the man!" Just then the rooster crowed. And Peter remembered the word Jesus had spoken, "Before the rooster crows, you will deny me three times." And he went outside and wept bitterly.

Early in the morning, all the chief priests and the elders of the people reached the decision to put Jesus to death. When Judas, who had betrayed him, saw that Jesus was condemned, he felt remorse. He brought back the thirty pieces of silver to the chief priests and elders and said, "I have sinned by betraying innocent blood."

But they said, "What is that to us? That's your problem."

He threw the pieces of silver into the temple and left. Then he went out and hanged himself.

Lord God, we are sorry for our sins and trust in your Son
as our forgiveness. Keep us from ever denying him
or giving in to despair. Amen.

188. JESUS' TRIAL BEFORE THE ROMANS (JOHN 18-19)

Pilate condemns Jesus to death even though he was innocent.

Early in the morning, the Jews led Jesus from Caiaphas to the Praetorium. Pilate went out to them and said, "What charge do you bring against this man?"

They answered him, "If this man were not a criminal, we would not have handed him over to you."

Pilate told them, "Take him yourselves and judge him according to your law."

The Jews said, "It's not legal for us to put anyone to death." This happened so that the statement Jesus had spoken indicating what kind of death he was going to die would be fulfilled.

Pilate went back into the Praetorium and summoned Jesus. He asked him, "Are you the King of the Jews?"

Jesus answered, "Are you saying this on your own, or did others tell you about me?"

Pilate answered, "Am I a Jew? Your own people and chief priests handed you over to me. What have you done?"

Jesus replied, "My kingdom is not of this world. If my kingdom were of this world, my servants would fight so that I would not be handed over to the Jews. But my kingdom is not from here."

"You are a king then?" Pilate asked.

Jesus answered, "I am, as you say, a king. I came into the world to testify to the truth. Everyone who belongs to the truth listens to my voice."

"What is truth?" Pilate said to him.

After he said this, he went out again to the Jews and told them, "I find no basis for a charge against him. But you have a custom that I release one prisoner to you at the Passover. So do you want me to release the King of the Jews for you?"

Then they shouted back, "Not this man, but Barabbas!" (Barabbas was a rebel.)

Then Pilate took Jesus and had him flogged. The soldiers also twisted together a crown of thorns and placed it on his head. Then they threw a purple robe around him. They kept coming to him, saying, "Hail, King of the Jews!" And they kept hitting him in the face.

Pilate went outside again and said to them, "Look, I am bringing him out to you to let you know that I find no basis for a charge against him." So Jesus came out wearing the crown of thorns and the purple robe. Pilate said to them, "Behold the man!"

When the chief priests and guards saw him, they shouted, "Crucify! Crucify!"

Pilate told them, "Take him yourselves and crucify him, for I find no basis for a charge against him."

The Jews answered him, "We have a law, and according to that law he ought to die, because he claimed to be the Son of God."

When Pilate heard this statement, he was even more afraid. He went back inside the palace again and asked Jesus, "Where are you from?" But Jesus gave him no answer. So Pilate asked him, "Are you not talking to me? Don't you know that I have the authority to release you or to crucify you?"

Jesus answered, "You would have no authority over me at all if it had not been given to you from above. Therefore the one who handed me over to you has the greater sin."

From then on Pilate tried to release Jesus. But the Jews shouted, "If you let this man go, you are no friend of Caesar! Anyone who claims to be a king opposes Caesar!"

When Pilate heard these words, he brought Jesus outside. Pilate said to the Jews, "Here is your king!"

They shouted, "Away with him! Away with him! Crucify him!"

Pilate said to them, "Should I crucify your king?"

"We have no king but Caesar!" the chief priests answered.

So then Pilate handed Jesus over to them to be crucified.

Lord God, your Son is our only King. May he rule for us in the world with his power. May he rule for us in our hearts with his grace. May he rule for us face-to-face one day with his glory. Amen.

189. THE EVENTS OF GOOD FRIDAY (MATTHEW 27, LUKE 23, JOHN 19)

Jesus dies to pay for the sins of the world.

So they took Jesus away. Carrying his own cross, he went out to what is called the Place of a Skull, which in Aramaic is called Golgotha. There they crucified him with two others, one on each side, and Jesus in the middle.

Jesus said, "Father, forgive them, for they do not know what they are doing."

Pilate had a notice written and fastened on the cross. It read, "Jesus the Nazarene, the King of the Jews."

The chief priests said to Pilate, "Do not write, 'The King of the Jews,' but that 'this man said, "I am the King of the Jews."'"

Pilate answered, "What I have written, I have written."

When the soldiers crucified Jesus, they took his clothes and divided them into four parts, one part for each soldier. They also took his tunic, which was seamless, woven in one piece from top to bottom. So they said to one another, "Let's not tear it. Instead, let's cast lots to see who gets it." This was so that the Scripture might be fulfilled which says: "They divided my garments among them and cast lots for my clothing."

The rulers were ridiculing him, saying, "He saved others. Let him save himself, if this is the Christ!" The soldiers also made fun of him.

One of the criminals hanging there was blaspheming him, saying, "Aren't you the Christ? Save yourself and us!"

But the other criminal rebuked him. "Don't you fear God? We are punished justly, for we are receiving what we deserve for what we have done, but this man has done nothing wrong." Then he said, "Jesus, remember me when you come in your kingdom."

Jesus said to him, "Amen I tell you: Today you will be with me in paradise."

Jesus saw his mother and the disciple whom he loved standing nearby. He said to his mother, "Woman, here is your son!" Then he said to the disciple, "Here is your mother!" And from that time this disciple took her into his home.

From the sixth hour until the ninth hour, there was darkness over all the land. About the ninth hour Jesus cried out with a loud voice, saying, "My God, my God, why have you forsaken me?"

After this, knowing that everything had now been finished, and to fulfill the Scripture, Jesus said, "I thirst." A jar of sour wine was sitting there. So they put a sponge soaked in sour wine on a hyssop branch and held it to his mouth. When Jesus had received the wine, he said, "It is finished!" Jesus cried out with a loud voice, "Father, into your hands I commit my spirit!" Then, bowing his head, he gave up his spirit.

Suddenly, the temple curtain was torn in two from top to bottom. The earth shook and rocks were split. Tombs were opened, and many bodies of saints who had fallen asleep were raised to life. Those who came out of the tombs went into the holy city after Jesus' resurrection and appeared to many people. When the centurion and those guarding Jesus saw the things that had happened, they were terrified and said, "Truly this was the Son of God."

Since it was the Preparation Day, the Jews did not want the bodies left on the crosses over the Sabbath. They asked Pilate to have the men's legs broken and the bodies taken away. So the soldiers came and broke the legs of the first man crucified with Jesus, and then those of the other man. But when they came to Jesus and saw that he was already dead, they did not break his legs. Instead, one of the soldiers pierced his side with a spear. Immediately blood and water came out. These things happened so that the Scripture would be fulfilled, "Not one of his bones will be broken." Another Scripture says, "They will look at the one they pierced."

After this, Joseph of Arimathea, who was a disciple of Jesus, but secretly for fear of the Jews, asked Pilate to let him remove Jesus' body. When Pilate gave him permission, he came and took Jesus' body. Nicodemus, who earlier had come to Jesus at night, also came bringing a mixture of myrrh and aloes. There was a garden at the place where Jesus was crucified, and in the garden was a new tomb in which no one had ever been laid. So they laid Jesus there.

Lord God, your Son's death is our life, because
he has died in our place. We look to him,
who has finished all things for our salvation. Amen.

190. EASTER MORNING (JOHN 20)

Jesus rises from the dead in victory over sin and death.

Early on the first day of the week, while it was still dark, Mary Magdalene went to the tomb. She saw that the stone had been taken away from the tomb. So she left and ran to Simon Peter and the other disciple, the one Jesus loved. "They have taken the Lord out of the tomb," she told them, "and we don't know where they put him!"

So Peter and the other disciple went out, heading for the tomb. The two were running together, but the other disciple outran Peter and got to the tomb first. Bending over, he saw the linen cloths lying there, yet he did not go in.

Then Simon Peter, who was following him, arrived and went into the tomb. He saw the linen cloths lying there. The cloth that had been on Jesus' head was not lying with the linen cloths, but was folded up in a separate place by itself. Then the other disciple, who arrived at the tomb first, also entered. He saw and believed. (They still did not yet understand the Scripture that he must rise from the dead.)

Then the disciples went back to their homes.

But Mary stood outside facing the tomb, weeping. As she wept, she bent over, looking into the tomb. She saw two angels in white clothes sitting where the body of Jesus had been lying, one at the head and one at the feet. They asked her, "Woman, why are you weeping?"

She told them, "Because they have taken away my Lord, and I don't know where they have laid him."

After she said this, she turned around and saw Jesus standing there, though she did not know it was Jesus.

Jesus said to her, "Woman, why are you weeping? Who are you looking for?"

Supposing he was the gardener, she replied, "Sir, if you carried him off, tell me where you laid him, and I will get him."

Jesus said to her, "Mary."

She turned and replied in Aramaic, *"Rabboni!"* (which means, "Teacher").

Jesus told her, "Do not continue to cling to me, for I have not yet ascended to my Father. But go to my brothers and tell them, 'I am ascending to my Father and your Father—to my God and your God.' "

Mary Magdalene went and announced to the disciples, "I have seen the Lord!" She also told them the things he said to her.

Lord God, we thank and praise you for raising your Son from the dead, thereby declaring that the sins of the world have been paid for and forgiven. Use this truth to free us from all doubt and fear. Amen.

191. JESUS APPEARS TO THE EMMAUS DISCIPLES (LUKE 24)

Jesus appears to two believers and shows them how his death and resurrection were God's plan the whole time.

Now, on that same day, two of them were going to a village named Emmaus, about seven miles from Jerusalem. They were talking with each other about all of these things that had happened. While they were talking and discussing this, Jesus himself approached and began to walk along with them. But their eyes were kept from recognizing him. He said to them, "What are you talking about as you walk along?" Saddened, they stopped.

One of them, named Cleopas, answered him, "Are you the only visitor in Jerusalem who does not know the things that have happened there in these days?"

"What things?" he asked them.

They replied, "The things concerning Jesus of Nazareth, a man who was a prophet, mighty in deed and word before God and all the people. The chief priests and our rulers handed him over to be condemned to death. And they crucified him. But we were hoping that he was going to redeem Israel. Not only that, but besides all this, it is now the third day since these things happened. Also some women of our group amazed us. They were at the tomb early in the morning. When they did not find his body, they came back saying that they had even seen a vision of angels, who said that he was alive. Some of those who were with us went to the tomb. They found it just as the women had said, but they did not see him."

He said to them, "How foolish you are and slow of heart to believe all that the prophets have spoken! Did not the Christ have to suffer these things and to enter his glory?" Then beginning with Moses and all the prophets, he explained to them what was said in all the Scriptures concerning himself.

As they approached the village where they were going, he acted as if he were going to travel farther. But they urged him strongly, saying, "Stay with us, since it is almost evening, and the day is almost over."

So he went in to stay with them. When he reclined at the table with them, he took the bread, blessed it, broke it, and began giving it to them.

Suddenly their eyes were opened, and they recognized him. Then he vanished from their sight. They said to each other, "Were not our hearts burning within us while he was speaking to us along the road and while he was explaining the Scriptures to us?"

They got up that very hour and returned to Jerusalem. They found the Eleven and those who were with them assembled together. They were saying, "The Lord really has been raised! He has appeared to Simon." They themselves described what had happened along the road, and how they recognized him when he broke the bread.

Lord God, open God's Word to us by your Spirit.
Show us our risen Savior Jesus and chase away
our gloom and sadness. Amen.

192. JESUS APPEARS TO HIS DISCIPLES IN JERUSALEM (JOHN 20)

Jesus shows his disciples that he has risen from the dead.

On the evening of that first day of the week, the disciples were together behind locked doors because of their fear of the Jews. Jesus came, stood among them, and said to them, "Peace be with you!" After he said this, he showed them his hands and side. So the disciples rejoiced when they saw the Lord.

Jesus said to them again, "Peace be with you! Just as the Father has sent me, I am also sending you." After saying this, he breathed on them and said, "Receive the Holy Spirit. Whenever you forgive people's sins, they are forgiven. Whenever you do not forgive them, they are not forgiven."

But Thomas, one of the Twelve, the one called the Twin, was not with them when Jesus came. So the other disciples kept telling him, "We have seen the Lord!"

But he said to them, "Unless I see the nail marks in his hands, and put my finger into the mark of the nails, and put my hand into his side, I will never believe."

After eight days, his disciples were inside again, and Thomas was with them. Though the doors were locked, Jesus came and stood among them. "Peace be with you," he said. Then he said to Thomas, "Put your finger here and look at my hands. Take your hand and put it into my side. Do not continue to doubt, but believe."

Thomas answered him, "My Lord and my God!"

Jesus said to him, "Because you have seen me, you have believed. Blessed are those who have not seen and yet have believed."

Jesus, in the presence of his disciples, did many other miraculous signs that are not written in this book. But these are written that you may believe that Jesus is the Christ, the Son of God, and that by believing you may have life in his name.

Lord God, overcome our doubt and our fears
with the peace that comes from sins forgiven,
and that our Lord Jesus lives again. Amen.

193. JESUS APPEARS TO HIS DISCIPLES AT THE SEA OF GALILEE (JOHN 21)

Jesus again shows his disciples that he has risen from the dead.

After this, Jesus showed himself again to the disciples at the Sea of Tiberias. This is how he showed himself: Simon Peter, Thomas (called the Twin), Nathanael from Cana in Galilee, the sons of Zebedee, and two other disciples were together. Simon Peter said to them, "I'm going fishing."

They replied, "We'll go with you."

They went out and got into the boat, but that night they caught nothing. Early in the morning, Jesus was standing on the shore, but the disciples did not know it was Jesus.

Jesus called to them, "Boys, don't you have any fish?"

"No!" they answered.

He told them, "Throw your net on the right side of the boat and you will find some." So they cast the net out. Then they were not able to haul it in because of the large number of fish.

The disciple whom Jesus loved said to Peter, "It is the Lord!" When Simon Peter heard, "It is the Lord!" he tied his outer garment around him and jumped into the sea. But the other disciples came in the little boat, dragging the net full of fish, for they were not far from shore, about one hundred yards.

When they stepped out on land, they saw some bread and a charcoal fire with fish on it. Jesus said to them, "Bring some of the fish you just caught." So Simon Peter climbed aboard and hauled the net to land, full of large fish, 153 of them. Yet even with so many, the net was not torn.

Jesus said to them, "Come, eat breakfast."

None of the disciples dared ask him, "Who are you?" because they knew it was the Lord.

Jesus came, took the bread, and gave it to them, and also the fish. This was now the third time Jesus appeared to his disciples after he was raised from the dead. Jesus also did many other things. If every one of them were written down, I suppose the world itself would not have room for the books that would be written.

Lord God, in raising Jesus from the dead
you have assured us that all our sins really are forgiven.
Provide for us throughout this life until we get
to see the risen Jesus with our own eyes. Amen.

194. THE GREAT COMMISSION (MATTHEW 28)

Jesus sends his disciples throughout the world to gather more disciples with the means of grace.

The eleven disciples went to Galilee, to the mountain where Jesus had directed them. When they saw him, they worshipped him, but some hesitated because they were uncertain. Jesus approached and spoke to them saying, "All authority in heaven and on earth has been given to me. Therefore go and gather disciples from all nations by baptizing them in the name of the Father and of the Son and of the Holy Spirit, and by teaching them to keep all the instructions I have given you. And surely I am with you always until the end of the age."

Lord God, your Son rules over all things for our sake and
is always with us. As we go to share the gospel
with all nations, bless our proclamation and
gather many disciples for yourself. Amen.

195. JESUS ASCENDS AND THE APOSTLES WAIT (ACTS 1)

Jesus ascends into heaven, and a new apostle is added.

Jesus had given instructions to the apostles he had chosen: "Do not depart from Jerusalem, but wait for what the Father promised, which you heard from me. You will be baptized with the Holy Spirit not many days from now."

So when they were together with him, they asked, "Lord, is this the time when you are going to restore the kingdom to Israel?"

He said to them, "It is not for you to know the times or seasons that the Father has set by his own authority. But you will receive power when the Holy Spirit has come upon you, and you will be my witnesses to the ends of the earth."

After he said these things, he was taken up while they were watching, and a cloud took him out of their sight. They were looking intently into the sky as he went away. Suddenly, two men in white clothes stood beside them. They said, "Men of Galilee, why are you standing here looking up into the sky? This same Jesus, who has been taken up from you into heaven, will come back in the same way you have seen him go into heaven."

Then they returned to Jerusalem from the Mount of Olives. When they entered the city, they went to the upstairs room where they were staying. Peter and John were there, also James and Andrew, Philip and Thomas, Bartholomew and Matthew, James the son of Alphaeus, Simon the Zealot, and Judas the son of James. All of them kept praying together with one mind, along with the women, with Mary the mother of Jesus, and with his brothers. The group there numbered about 120 people.

Peter stood up among the brothers and said, "Gentlemen, brothers, the Scripture had to be fulfilled, which the Holy Spirit spoke long ago through the mouth of David about Judas, who became a guide for those who arrested Jesus. Judas was counted as one of us. Now this man acquired a field with what he was paid for his wicked act. When he fell headfirst, his middle burst open, and all his intestines spilled out.

"It is written in the book of Psalms: 'May his residence be deserted. Let there be no one dwelling in it.' And, 'Let someone else take his position.' Therefore it is necessary that one of the men who accompanied us during the entire time that the Lord Jesus went in and out among us become a witness with us of his resurrection."

They proposed two: Joseph, called Barsabbas, and Matthias. Then they prayed, "Lord, you know everyone's heart. Show us which of these two you have chosen to take the place in this apostolic ministry."

Then they assigned lots for them, and the lot fell to Matthias. So he was counted with the eleven apostles.

Lord God, your Son's ascension into heaven is the hope
and guarantee of our ascension into heaven one day.
Give us your Holy Spirit through your Word to comfort
and strengthen us until your Son returns to take us
to be with him forever. Amen.

PART 4

THE EARLY CHURCH

Jesus has already ascended into heaven, but still he is with his people, protecting and providing for them. Jesus has already finished his saving work, but now everyone needs to hear about it.

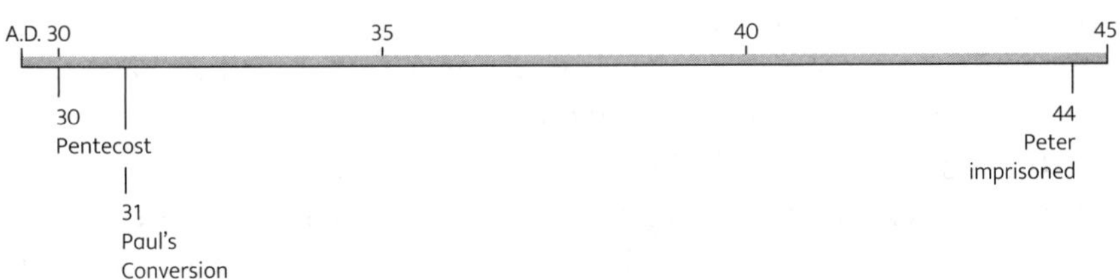

196. PENTECOST (ACTS 2)

Jesus sends the Holy Spirit on his apostles just as he had promised.

When the day of Pentecost came, they were all together in one place. Suddenly a sound like the rushing of a violent wind came from heaven, and it filled the whole house. They saw divided tongues that were like fire resting on each one of them. They were all filled with the Holy Spirit and began to speak in other languages fluently.

Now there were godly Jewish men from every nation in Jerusalem. When this sound was heard, a crowd came together and was confused, because each one heard them speaking in his own language. They said to each other, "Are not all these men Galileans? Then how is it that we hear them declaring in our own languages the wonderful works of God?" They were all amazed and perplexed. They kept saying to one another, "What does this mean?" But others mocked them and said, "They are full of wine."

Then Peter stood up with the Eleven and spoke to them: "Listen closely to my words. These men are not drunk, as you suppose. On the contrary, this is what was spoken by the prophet Joel: 'This is what God says will happen in the last days: "I will pour out my Spirit on all flesh. Your sons and your daughters will prophesy. Your young men will see visions. Your old men will dream dreams. Even on my servants, both men and women, I will pour out my Spirit in those days, and they will prophesy. And everyone who calls on the name of the Lord will be saved."' "

"Men of Israel, hear these words! Jesus the Nazarene was a man recommended to you by God with miracles that God did through him among you. This man, who was handed over by God's plan, you killed by having lawless men nail him to a cross. He is the one God raised up by freeing him from death, because death was not able to hold him.

"Indeed, David says concerning him: 'You will not abandon my life to the grave, nor will you let your Holy One see decay. You have made known to me the paths of life. You will fill me with joy in your presence.' The patriarch David both died and was buried, and his tomb is with us to this day. Since he was a prophet and knew that God had sworn to him with an oath that he would seat one of his descendants on his throne, he saw what was coming and spoke about the resurrection of Christ, saying that he was neither abandoned to the grave nor did his flesh see decay.

"This Jesus is the one God has raised up. We are all witnesses of that. After he was exalted to the right hand of God and after he received the promised Holy Spirit from the Father, he poured out what you are now seeing and hearing. David did not ascend into heaven, and yet he says: 'The Lord said to my Lord, "Sit at my right hand."' Therefore let all the house of Israel know for certain that God has made this Jesus, whom you crucified, both Lord and Christ."

When the people heard this, they were cut to the heart and said, "What should we do?"

Peter answered them, "Repent and be baptized, every one of you, in the name of Jesus Christ for the forgiveness of your sins, and you will receive the gift of the Holy Spirit. For the promise is for you and for your children and for all who are far away, as many as the Lord our God will call."

Those who accepted his message were baptized, and that day about three thousand people were added.

They continued to hold firmly to the apostles' teaching and to the fellowship, to the breaking of the bread, and to the prayers. Many wonders and signs were being done through the apostles. Day after day the Lord added to their number those who were being saved.

Lord God, we thank you that you poured out your
Holy Spirit on your apostles to lead them into all truth.
As we read your Word, written through them,
pour out the Holy Spirit on our hearts to preserve
and strengthen our faith. Amen.

197. PETER AND JOHN ON TRIAL (ACTS 3-4)

Jesus confirms the message of the apostles as he performs a miracle through them, but the apostles face opposition for their message.

Peter and John were going up to the temple. A man who was lame from birth was there. When he saw Peter and John, he asked them for a donation.

Peter said, "Silver and gold I do not have, but what I have I will give you. In the name of Jesus Christ the Nazarene, get up and walk!" Peter took him by the hand and raised him up. Immediately the man's feet and ankles were made strong. Jumping up, he stood and began to walk. He entered the temple courts with them, walking, jumping, and praising God. All the people saw him. They recognized him as the one who used to sit begging for money at the temple, and they were filled with amazement.

Peter addressed the people: "Why are you staring at us, as if by our own power we have made this man walk? The God of our fathers glorified his servant Jesus, whom you handed over. You killed the Author of Life, whom God raised from the dead. We are witnesses of this. It is the name of Jesus that has strengthened this man. This faith that comes through Jesus has given him this perfect health.

"Now brothers, I know that you acted in ignorance, just like your leaders. But in this way God fulfilled what he had foretold through the prophets: that his Christ would suffer. Therefore repent and return to have your sins wiped out. Jesus must receive heaven until the times when everything will be restored. God sent him to you first, to bless you by turning every one of you away from your wicked ways."

The priests and the Sadducees were very upset because Peter and John were proclaiming the resurrection from the dead in connection with Jesus. They arrested them and put them in jail. But many of those who had heard the message believed, and the number of the men increased to about five thousand.

The next day, the rulers, the elders, and the experts in the law assembled in Jerusalem. After they made Peter and John stand in front of them, they began to question them: "By what name did you do this?"

Then Peter, filled with the Holy Spirit, said to them, "If we are being questioned today for a kind act done for the lame man, let it be known to all of you that it was by the name of Jesus Christ the Nazarene, whom you crucified, whom God raised from the dead! By him this man stands before you healed. This Jesus is the stone that was rejected by you builders, which has become the cornerstone. There is salvation in no one else, for there is no other name under heaven given to people by which we must be saved."

When they saw the boldness of Peter and John and found out that they were uneducated men, they were astonished. But since they saw the man who had been healed standing there with them, they could not say anything in reply. After they had ordered them to leave, they asked, "What should we do? It is evident to all that a miraculous sign has been done through them, and we cannot deny it. However, in order that this may spread no further among the people, let us give them a strict warning not to speak any longer to anyone in this name."

Then they summoned them and commanded them not to speak at all in the name of Jesus.

But Peter and John answered them, "Decide whether it is right in the sight of God to listen to you rather than to God. For we cannot stop speaking about what we have seen and heard."

After they had threatened them further, they let them go. They found no way to punish them because all of the people were praising God for what had happened.

After Peter and John were released, they went to their friends and reported everything the high priests and the elders had said. When they heard this, they raised their voices to God and said, "Lord, give to your servants the ability to keep on speaking your word with all boldness as wonders take place through the name of your holy servant Jesus."

After they prayed, the place where they were gathered was shaken. Everyone was filled with the Holy Spirit, and they continued to speak the word of God with boldness.

Lord God, all healing and help comes from your Son. Grant us health and safety in his name. Eternal salvation also is found only in your Son. May we always be found in him by faith, and let nothing keep us from sharing the good news about him with others. Amen.

198. ANANIAS AND SAPPHIRA (ACTS 4-5)

God shows that he cannot be lied to or mocked.

The whole group of believers was one in heart and soul. No one claimed that any of his possessions was his own, but they held everything in common. There was not a needy person among them. For from time to time those who were owners of lands or houses sold them, brought the proceeds received from what was sold, and laid it at the apostles' feet. It was distributed to each one according to what anyone needed.

Now a man named Ananias, together with his wife Sapphira, sold a piece of property. With his wife's knowledge, he kept back part of the proceeds for himself. Then he brought a portion of it and laid it at the apostles' feet.

But Peter said, "Ananias, why has Satan filled your heart to lie to the Holy Spirit and to keep back part of the proceeds of the land? Was it not yours before it was sold? And after it was sold, was not the money at your disposal? How could you plan such a thing in your heart? You have not lied to men but to God."

When Ananias heard these words, he fell down and died. The young men wrapped up his body, carried him out, and buried him.

About three hours later, his wife came in, not knowing what had happened. Peter asked her, "Tell me, is this how much you got for the land?"

"Yes," she said, "that was the price."

Then Peter said to her, "How could you two agree to test the Spirit of the Lord? Look! The feet of those who buried your husband are standing at the door, and they will carry you out too!"

Instantly she fell down at his feet and died. The young men carried her outside and buried her beside her husband. Great fear gripped the whole church and all who heard about these things.

Many signs and wonders were done among the people through the hands of the apostles. With one mind, they all continued meeting in Solomon's Colonnade. More and more believers in the Lord were added to their group.

Lord God, nothing we think or say or do is hidden from you. Do not punish us as our sins deserve but forgive us for Jesus' sake. Keep us from ever testing you and your mercy by willful sin. Amen.

199. A LETTER BY JAMES (JAMES)

James, the half-brother of Jesus, writes a letter reminding Christians that their faith should show itself in their actions.

James, a servant of Jesus,

To the twelve tribes scattered abroad:

Greetings.

Consider it complete joy, my brothers, whenever you fall into trials, because you know that testing produces endurance. Blessed is the man who endures a trial patiently, because when he has stood the test, he will receive the crown of life. Let no one say when he is tempted, "I am being tempted by God," because God cannot be tempted by evil, and he himself tempts no one. But each person is tempted when he is enticed by his own desire. Desire gives birth to sin, and sin gives birth to death.

Do not be deceived, my dear brothers. Every good gift is from above, coming down from the Father of the lights, who does not change or shift like a shadow.

Let everyone be quick to listen, slow to speak, and slow to become angry. So after getting rid of all moral filthiness, receive with humility the word planted in you. It is able to save your souls.

Be people who do what the word says, not people who only hear it. If anyone hears the word and does not do what it says, he is like a man who looks at his face in a mirror, then goes away and immediately forgets what he looked like. But the one who looks into the law, and actually does what it says—that person will be blessed.

If anyone considers himself to be religious but does not bridle his tongue, this person's religion is worthless. Religion that is pure in the sight of God is this: to take care of orphans and widows and to keep oneself unstained by the world. If you really fulfill: "You shall love your neighbor as yourself," you are doing well. But if you show favoritism, you are committing a sin, since you are convicted by this law as transgressors. In fact, whoever keeps the whole law but stumbles in one point has become guilty of breaking all of it.

What good is it, my brothers, if someone says that he has faith but has no works? Such "faith" cannot save him, can it? If a brother or sister needs food and one of you tells them, "Go eat well," but does not give them what their body needs, what good is it? Such "faith," if it is alone and has no works, is dead. But someone will say, "You have faith, and I have works." Show me your faith without works, and I will show you my faith by my works.

Wasn't Abraham our father shown to be righteous by works? His faith was working together with his works, and by his works his faith was shown to be complete. Wasn't Rahab shown to be righteous by works? For just as the body without breath is dead, so also faith without works is dead.

Consider how a little flame can set a large forest on fire! And the tongue is a fire. It sets the whole course of life on fire, and is set on fire by hell. Every kind of animal has been tamed by mankind, but no one is able to tame the human tongue. It is a restless evil, full of deadly poison. Blessing and cursing come out of the same mouth. My brothers, these things should not be this way.

Don't you know that friendship with the world means hostility toward God? So whoever wants to be a friend of the world makes himself an enemy of God. Submit yourselves to God. Resist the Devil, and he will flee from you. Humble yourselves in the sight of the Lord, and he will lift you up.

Be patient until the coming of the Lord. See how the farmer waits for the harvest. You be patient too. You have heard of the patient endurance of Job and have seen what the Lord did in the end, because the Lord is especially compassionate and merciful.

Confess your sins to one another and pray for one another, in order that you may be healed. The prayer of a righteous person is able to do much because it is effective. If anyone among you wanders away from the truth and someone turns him back, let it be known that the one who turns a sinner from the error of his way will save his soul from death and will cover a multitude of sins.

Lord God, we are saved solely by faith in our Savior Jesus who lived and died and rose for us. Strengthen that faith so that we may live according to your will and do what pleases you. Keep us from all sins and help us show love to all people. Amen.

200. THE APOSTLES ARE ARRESTED AGAIN (ACTS 5)

The apostles suffer for speaking about Jesus but refuse to stop.

The high priest arrested the apostles and put them in the public prison. But during the night an angel of the Lord opened the doors of the prison, brought them out, and said, "Go, stand in the temple and keep on telling the people the whole message about this life." After they heard this, they entered the temple courts at daybreak and began to teach.

The high priest and his associates sent orders to the jail to have the apostles brought in. But when the officers arrived, they did not find them in the prison. They returned and reported, "We found the prison securely locked and the guards standing at the doors, but when we opened them, we found no one inside!"

Then someone came and reported to them, "Look! The men you put in prison are standing in the temple courts and teaching the people."

Then the captain went with the officers and brought the apostles in without force, because they were afraid that the people might stone them. They had them stand before the Sanhedrin. The high priest asked them, "Did we not give you strict orders not to teach in this name?"

But Peter and the apostles replied, "We must obey God rather than men. The God of our fathers raised Jesus, whom you arrested and killed by hanging him on a cross. God exalted him to his right hand as Prince and Savior, to give repentance to Israel and the forgiveness of sins. We are witnesses of these things, and so is the Holy Spirit, whom God has given to those who obey him."

When they heard this, they were furious and began making a plan to put them to death. But a Pharisee named Gamaliel said to them, "Men of Israel, keep away from these men and leave them alone! For if this undertaking is of human origin, it will fail. But if it is from God, you will not be able to stop them. Perhaps you might even be found to be fighting against God!"

They were convinced by him. They summoned the apostles, beat them, ordered them not to speak in the name of Jesus, and let them go.

The apostles left the Sanhedrin, rejoicing that they were considered worthy to suffer shame for the Name. Every day, in the temple courts and from house to house, they never stopped teaching and proclaiming the good news that Jesus is the Christ.

Lord God, spare us from opposition and mistreatment
for our faith. But when we are persecuted
by the world because of Christ's name,
keep us always faithful to him. Amen.

201. THE MARTYR STEPHEN (ACTS 6-8)

Stephen becomes the first New Testament Christian martyred for his faith.

The Twelve called together the whole group of disciples and said, "It is not right for us to neglect the word of God in order to wait on tables. Brothers, carefully select from among you seven men who are full of the Holy Spirit and wisdom. We will put them in charge of this service. But we will devote ourselves to prayer and the ministry of the word."

This proposal pleased the entire group. They chose Stephen, Philip, Procorus, Nicanor, Timon, Parmenas, and Nicholas. They had these men stand before the apostles, who prayed and laid their hands on them.

Now Stephen, full of grace and power, was doing great wonders among the people. Some men who were from what is called the Synagogue of the Freedmen came, dragged Stephen away, and brought him before the Sanhedrin. They presented false witnesses who said, "This man never stops making threats against this holy place and the law. We have heard him say that this Jesus of Nazareth will destroy this place and will change the customs Moses handed down to us."

Then the high priest asked, "Are these things true?"

Stephen said, "You are doing just what your fathers did. Which of the prophets did your fathers not persecute? They killed those who prophesied the coming of the Righteous One, and now you have become his betrayers and murderers."

When they heard these things, they were furious and gnashed their teeth at him. But Stephen, full of the Holy Spirit, gazed up into heaven and saw the glory of God and Jesus standing at the right hand of God. He said, "Look, I see heaven opened, and the Son of Man standing at the right hand of God."

But they screamed at the top of their voices, covered their ears, and rushed at him. They threw him out of the city and stoned him. The witnesses laid their cloaks at the feet of a young man named Saul.

While they were stoning Stephen, he called out, "Lord Jesus, receive my spirit!" Then he fell to his knees and cried out in a loud voice, "Lord, do not hold this sin against them." After he said this, he fell asleep.

Saul agreed with putting Stephen to death.

On that day a great persecution broke out against the church in Jerusalem, and all except the apostles were scattered throughout the countryside of Judea and Samaria. Saul was trying to destroy the church by going into one house after another, dragging off both men and women, and putting them in prison. Those believers who were scattered went around proclaiming the gospel message.

Lord God, defend your church from all who would do us harm. Finally, when our last hour comes, receive our spirit, for your Son has opened heaven for us and now is seated at your right hand. Amen.

202. PHILIP AND THE ETHIOPIAN EUNUCH (ACTS 8)

Philip explains the Scripture and baptizes a man who was on his way home to Africa.

An angel of the Lord said to Philip, "Go south to the road that goes down from Jerusalem to Gaza." So he went, and there was a man, an Ethiopian eunuch, a court official of Candace, Queen of the Ethiopians, who was in charge of all her treasury. He had come to Jerusalem to worship. He was on his way home, sitting in his chariot and reading the prophet Isaiah.

The Spirit told Philip, "Go over there and stay close to that chariot." Philip ran up to it and heard him reading Isaiah the prophet.

Philip asked, "Do you understand what you are reading?"

The man replied, "How can I unless someone explains it to me?" And he invited Philip to come up and sit with him.

Now the passage of Scripture the eunuch was reading was this: "He was led like a sheep to the slaughter, and as a lamb before its shearer is silent, so he does not open his mouth."

The eunuch said to Philip, "Who is the prophet talking about—himself or someone else?" Then Philip, starting with that very passage of Scripture, told him the good news about Jesus.

As they were traveling along the road, they came to some water, and the eunuch said, "Look, here is water. What is there to prevent me from being baptized?"

He ordered the chariot to stop. Then both Philip and the eunuch went down into the water, and Philip baptized him. When they stepped up out of the water, the Spirit of the Lord carried Philip away. The eunuch did not see him anymore, but went on his way rejoicing.

Philip, however, found himself at Azotus. And as he went from place to place, he preached the gospel in all the towns until he came to Caesarea.

Lord God, we thank you for your Word which shows us your Son, who was sacrificed for us. We thank you also for those you have given us who help explain your Word to us. Finally, we thank you for your gift of baptism through which you have washed away our sins and claimed us as your own. Amen.

203. THE CONVERSION OF SAUL (ACTS 9)

God turns an unbeliever into a believer, an enemy of the gospel into an apostle of it.

Meanwhile, Saul was still breathing out murderous threats against the disciples of the Lord. He went to the high priest and asked him for letters to the synagogues of Damascus, so that if he found any men or women belonging to the Way, he might bring them to Jerusalem as prisoners.

As he was approaching Damascus, suddenly a light from heaven flashed around him. He fell to the ground and heard a voice saying to him, "Saul, Saul, why are you persecuting me?"

He asked, "Who are you, Lord?"

He replied, "I am Jesus, whom you are persecuting. Get up and go into the city, and you will be told what you need to do."

The men traveling with him stood there speechless. They heard the voice but did not see anyone. They raised Saul up from the ground, but when he opened his eyes, he could not see anything. They took him by the hand and led him into Damascus. For three days he could not see, and he did not eat or drink.

There was a disciple in Damascus named Ananias. The Lord said to him in a vision, "Get up and go to the street called Straight, and at the house of Judas ask for a man from Tarsus named Saul."

Ananias answered, "Lord, I have heard from many people about this man and how much harm he did to your saints in Jerusalem. And he has authority here from the chief priests to arrest all who call on your name."

The Lord said to him, "Go! This man is my chosen instrument to carry my name before the Gentiles and kings and the people of Israel. Indeed, I will show him how much he must suffer for my name."

Ananias left and entered the house. Laying his hands on Saul, he said, "Brother Saul, the Lord Jesus, whom you saw on your way here, has sent me so that you may see again and be filled with the Holy Spirit."

Immediately something like scales fell from his eyes, and he could see again. He got up and was baptized. And after taking some food, he regained his strength.

Saul stayed with the disciples in Damascus for several days. Immediately he began to proclaim Jesus in the synagogues, saying, "He is the Son of God."

All who heard him were amazed and said, "Isn't this the one who raised havoc in Jerusalem among those who call on this name? Didn't he come here to bring them as prisoners to the chief priests?" But Saul continued to get stronger and kept confounding the Jews who lived in Damascus by proving that Jesus is the Christ.

After many days had passed, the Jews conspired to kill him, but Saul was informed of their plot. They were watching the gates both day and night in order to kill him. But his disciples took him at night and let him down through an opening in the wall by lowering him in a basket.

When Saul came to Jerusalem, he tried to join the disciples, but they were all afraid of him because they did not believe that he was a disciple. But Barnabas took him and brought him to the apostles. He described to them how Saul had seen the Lord on the road and that the Lord had spoken to him, and how in Damascus he had preached fearlessly in the name of Jesus.

Saul stayed with them, coming and going freely in Jerusalem and speaking boldly in the name of the Lord. Then the church throughout Judea, Galilee, and Samaria enjoyed peace as it was strengthened. It grew in numbers as it lived in the fear of the Lord and in the comfort of the Holy Spirit.

Lord God, we were by nature dead in sin and
your enemies, but you have raised us to a new life of faith.
Through your Holy Spirit continue to bring more
and more people to faith in your Son. Amen.

204. THE CENTURION CORNELIUS (ACTS 10-11)

The Holy Spirit makes Gentiles part of the people of God without them having to follow the Old Testament Law.

At Caesarea there was a man named Cornelius, who was a centurion. He was devout and God-fearing, as was his entire family.

One day he saw a vision in which an angel of God came to him and said, "Cornelius, send men to Joppa to get a man named Simon, who is called Peter. He is staying as a guest with Simon the tanner."

When the angel had left, Cornelius called two of his servants. After explaining everything to them, he sent them to Joppa.

The next day, as they were on their way, Peter went up on the roof to pray. He fell into a trance. He saw heaven opened and a large sheet being let down to earth by its four corners. In it were all kinds of animals.

A voice said to him, "Kill and eat!"

But Peter said, "Certainly not, Lord, for I have never eaten anything unclean."

Yet the voice came to him a second time: "What God has made clean, you must not continue to call unclean."

This happened three times, and then the object was taken up to heaven.

The men who were sent by Cornelius arrived while Peter was still deep in thought about the vision. The Spirit said to him, "See, three men are looking for you! Get up and go with them, because I have sent them."

So Peter left with them. The following day, he arrived in Caesarea. Peter went inside and found many people gathered there. He said to them, "You understand how unlawful it is for a Jewish man to associate with anyone who is not a Jew. But God showed me that I should no longer continue to call anyone unclean. May I ask why you sent for me?"

Cornelius replied, "I was praying in my house when a man in shining clothes suddenly stood in front of me. He said, 'Cornelius, send to Joppa and call for Simon, who is called Peter. He is staying as a guest in the house of Simon the tanner. When he comes, he will speak to you.' So I sent for you immediately. We are all here to listen to everything that the Lord has instructed you to say."

Then Peter began to speak: "Now I really am beginning to understand that God does not show favoritism, but in every nation, anyone who fears him and does what is right is acceptable to him. He sent his word to the people of Israel, proclaiming the good news of peace through Jesus Christ, who is Lord of all. God anointed Jesus of Nazareth with the Holy Spirit and with power. We are witnesses of all the things he did in the country of the Jews, yet they killed him by hanging him on a cross. But God raised him on the third day and caused him to be seen by the witnesses God had already chosen—by us. He commanded us to preach to the people that he is the one appointed by God as judge of the living and the dead. Everyone who believes in him receives forgiveness of sins."

While Peter was still speaking, the Holy Spirit came on all who were listening to the message. All the circumcised believers who had come with Peter were amazed that the gift of the Holy Spirit had been poured out even on the Gentiles. For they heard them speaking in other languages and praising God.

Then Peter gave directions that they be baptized in the name of Jesus Christ.

The apostles and brothers throughout Judea heard that the Gentiles had also received the word of God. When Peter went up to Jerusalem, those who insisted on circumcision criticized him, saying, "You went to visit men who were uncircumcised and ate with them!"

So Peter began to explain everything to them, point by point. When they heard these things, they had no further objections, and they praised God, saying, "So then, God has granted repentance that results in life also to the Gentiles!"

Lord God, even though we were not born as your people,
you have made us yours by faith. We praise you
that you call people from every nation to be your own,
and we ask that you would continue
to do that throughout the world. Amen.

205. PETER IS RESCUED (ACTS 12)

God sends an angel to miraculously rescue Peter.

At about that time, King Herod had James, the brother of John, put to death with the sword. When he saw that this pleased the Jews, he proceeded to arrest Peter. Herod put him in prison and handed him over to four squads of four soldiers each to guard him. The church earnestly offered up prayer to God for him.

The very night before Herod was going to bring him out for trial, Peter was sleeping between two soldiers. He was bound with two chains, while sentries were in front of the door, guarding the prison.

Suddenly an angel of the Lord stood near him, and a light shined in the cell. The angel woke Peter up by striking him on the side, saying, "Quick, get up!" The chains fell from his wrists.

Then the angel said to him, "Follow me." Peter went out, following the angel, but he did not realize that what the angel was doing was really happening. He thought he was seeing a vision. When they had passed through the first and second guard posts, they came to the iron gate that leads into the city. It opened all by itself for them. They went outside, walked down one street, and immediately the angel left him.

When Peter came to himself, he said, "Now I know for sure that the Lord sent his angel and rescued me from the hand of Herod."

He went to the house of Mary, the mother of Mark. Many had gathered there and were praying. When Peter knocked at the entrance gate, a servant girl named Rhoda came to answer. She recognized Peter's voice and was so overjoyed, she did not open the gate. Instead she ran in and announced that Peter was standing in front of the gate.

They told her, "You are out of your mind!"

Meanwhile, Peter kept on knocking. When they opened the door and saw him, they were astonished. Peter described to them how the Lord had brought him out of prison. He said, "Tell these things to the brothers." Then he left and went on to another place.

At daybreak, there was no small commotion among the soldiers about what had become of Peter. After Herod searched for him and did not find him, he questioned the guards and ordered that they be executed.

Then Herod, dressed in his royal robes and seated on his throne, delivered a public address. The crowd shouted, "It's the voice of a god and not of a man!" Immediately an angel of the Lord struck him down because he did not give the glory to God. He was eaten by worms and died.

But the word of God continued to grow and increase.

Lord God, we thank you for your angels which
watch over us. Send them to guard and
protect us whenever we are in danger. Amen.

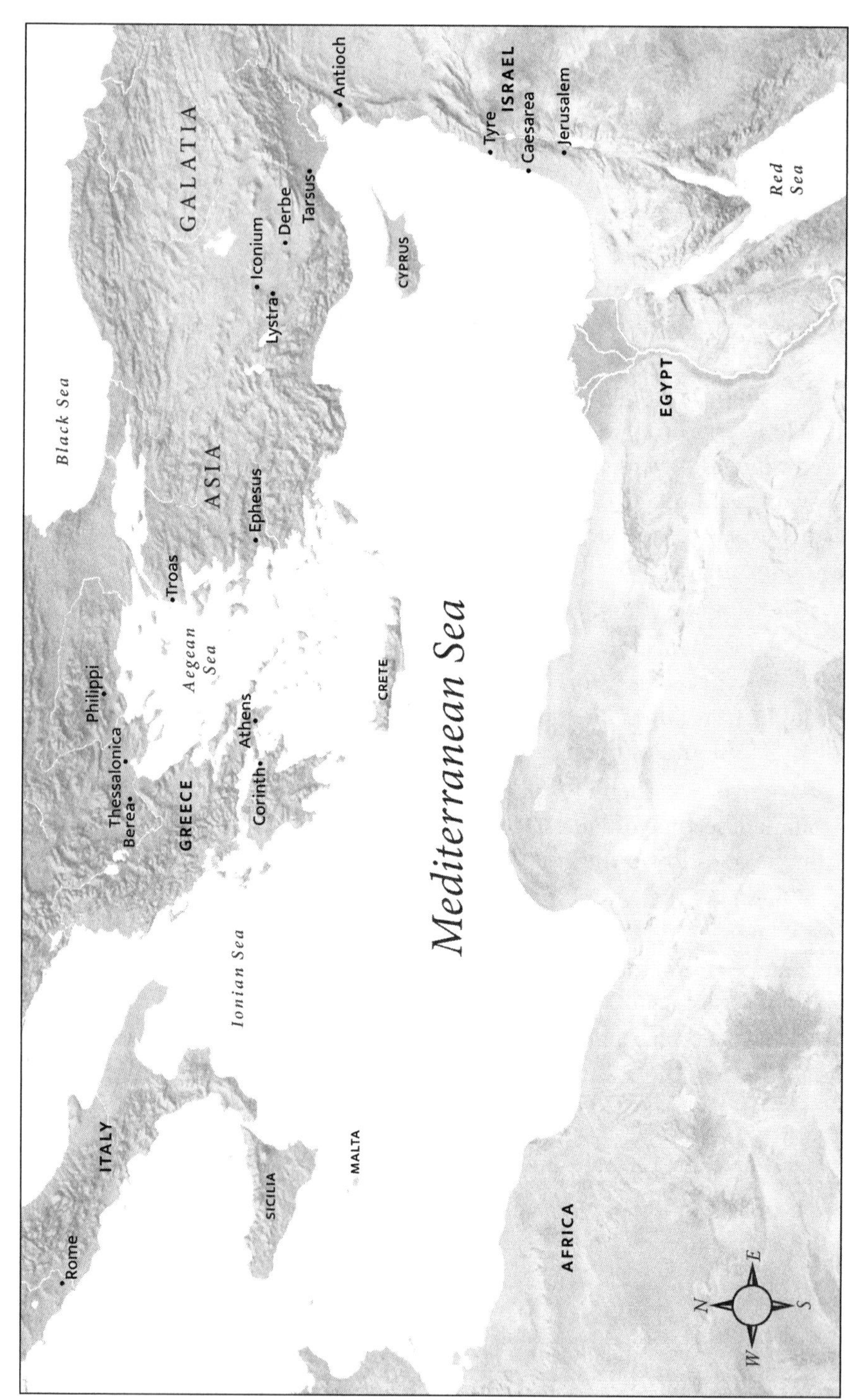

MEDITERRANEAN WORLD AT THE TIME OF PAUL

PART 5

TO THE ENDS OF THE EARTH (ACTS AND THE EPISTLES)

Just as Jesus promised, the gospel went out to all the world, both through the travels of apostles like Paul and also through the letters his apostles wrote to churches, to give them a greater understanding of the truth. While enemies attempted to stop the spread of the gospel, nothing could stop God from getting his saving message out throughout the world.

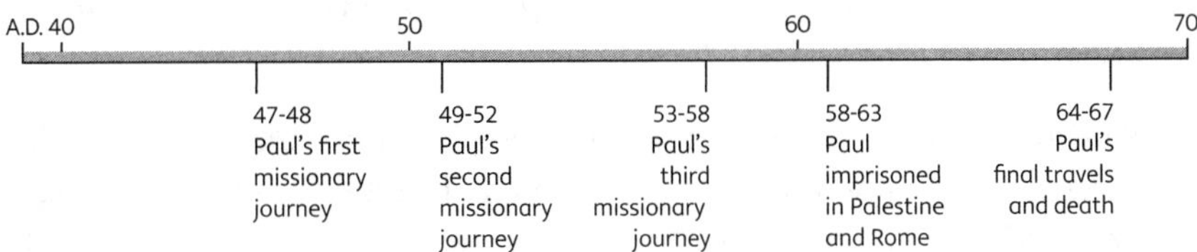

206: PAUL'S FIRST MISSIONARY JOURNEY: CYPRUS (ACTS 13)

Paul, Barnabas, and John Mark begin their missionary journey.

Now in the church at Antioch there were some prophets and teachers: Barnabas, Simeon, Lucius, Manaen, and Saul. While they were worshipping the Lord and fasting, the Holy Spirit said, "Set apart for me Barnabas and Saul for the work to which I have called them." Then, after they had fasted and prayed and laid their hands on them, they sent them off.

So they were sent out by the Holy Spirit and went down to Seleucia. From there they sailed to Cyprus. When they arrived at Salamis, they proclaimed the word of God in the Jewish synagogues. They also had John as their assistant.

When they had traveled through the whole island as far as Paphos, they came across a sorcerer, a Jewish false prophet whose name was Bar-Jesus. He was with the proconsul, Sergius Paulus. The proconsul summoned Barnabas and Saul and wanted to hear the word of God.

The sorcerer opposed them and tried to turn the proconsul away from the faith. But Saul, also called Paul, said, "You are full of every kind of deceit and fraud, you son of the Devil, you enemy of all righteousness! Will you never stop twisting the straight paths of the Lord? Now look! The hand of the Lord is against you. You will be blind, and for a time you will be unable to see."

Immediately mist and darkness came over him, and he went around looking for someone to lead him by the hand. When the proconsul saw what happened, he believed. He was amazed at the teaching of the Lord.

Lord God, we thank you that you call pastors
to proclaim your gospel on our behalf.
Bring your gospel also to all people everywhere. Amen.

207. PAUL'S FIRST MISSIONARY JOURNEY: ANTIOCH IN PISIDIA (ACTS 13)

Paul begins by speaking to the Jewish people, showing them from the Scriptures that Jesus is the promised Savior.

Paul and his companions set sail from Paphos and came to Perga. John, however, left them and returned to Jerusalem. But they went on from Perga and arrived at Antioch in Pisidia. They went into the synagogue on the

Sabbath day. The leaders of the synagogue sent a message to them, saying, "If you have a word of encouragement for the people, say it."

Then Paul stood up and said, "Men of Israel and you who fear God, listen. The God of the people of Israel chose our fathers and made them a great people. He gave land to his people as an inheritance. He raised up David as their king. From this man's descendants God brought the Savior Jesus to Israel, in keeping with his promise.

"Sons of Abraham's family, this message of salvation has been sent to you. The people of Jerusalem did not recognize him, and by condemning him they fulfilled the statements of the prophets. Though they found no grounds for a death sentence, they asked Pilate to have him executed. When they carried out everything that was written about him, they took him down from the cross and laid him in a tomb. But God raised him from the dead, and for many days he was seen by those who had come up with him from Galilee to Jerusalem. These same individuals are now his witnesses to the people.

"We are preaching to you the good news about the promise that was made to our fathers. God has fulfilled this promise for us, their children, by raising up Jesus. That God would raise him from the dead never again to be subject to decay, God said in this way: 'You will not let your Holy One see decay.' For David fell asleep and saw decay. But the One God raised did not see decay.

"Through this Jesus forgiveness of sins is being proclaimed to you. In this Jesus, everyone who believes is justified."

As Paul and Barnabas were leaving, the people kept begging them to speak again on the next Sabbath. Many of the Jews and devout converts to Judaism followed Paul and Barnabas.

On the next Sabbath almost the whole city gathered to hear the word of God. But when the Jews saw the crowds, they were filled with envy and began to contradict what Paul was saying by slandering him.

Then Paul and Barnabas responded fearlessly, "It was necessary that God's word be spoken to you first. But since you reject it and consider yourselves unworthy of eternal life, look: We are now turning to the Gentiles! For this is what the Lord has instructed us: 'I have made you a light for the Gentiles, that you may bring salvation to the end of the earth.'"

When the Gentiles heard this, they were rejoicing and praising the word of the Lord. All who had been appointed for eternal life believed.

And the word of the Lord was being carried through the whole region. But the Jews stirred up persecution against Paul and Barnabas and expelled them from their district. So they shook the dust off their feet against them and went to Iconium.

Lord God, you have kept your promise in sending
our Savior Jesus and raising him from the dead.
He is our light and our salvation. Raise us up
into eternal life in him. Amen.

208. PAUL'S FIRST MISSIONARY JOURNEY: ICONIUM, LYSTRA, DERBE, AND RETURN (ACTS 14)

When speaking to uneducated Gentiles, Paul begins his proclamation of the gospel by speaking about what is known of God from creation.

In Iconium, Paul and Barnabas entered the Jewish synagogue and spoke. A great number of both Jews and Greeks believed, but the Jews who refused to believe stirred up the Gentiles and poisoned their minds against the brothers.

Paul and Barnabas stayed there a long time, speaking boldly for the Lord, who confirmed the message of his grace by granting them the ability to perform miraculous signs. But the people of the city were divided. Some sided with the Jews and some with the apostles.

When there was a plot by both Gentiles and Jews, together with their rulers, to mistreat and stone them, they found out about it and fled to Lystra. There they kept on preaching the good news.

In Lystra there was a man who had never walked because he was lame from birth. When he was listening to Paul as he was speaking, Paul looked at him closely and saw that he had faith so that he could be healed. Paul said in a loud voice, "Stand up on your feet!" And the man jumped up and began to walk.

When the crowds saw what Paul had done, they raised their voices, saying in the Lycaonian language, "The gods have come down to us in human form." Barnabas they called Zeus, and Paul they called Hermes, because he was the main speaker. The priest of Zeus brought bulls and garlands because he wanted to offer sacrifices.

But when the apostles Paul and Barnabas heard about this, they tore their clothes and rushed into the crowd, shouting, "Men, why are you doing these things? We too are men. We are preaching the good news to you so that you turn from these worthless things to the living God, who made the heaven, the earth, the sea, and everything in them. In past generations he allowed all the nations to go their own ways. Yet he did not leave himself without testimony of the good he does. He gives you rain from heaven and crops in their seasons. He fills you with food and fills your hearts with gladness." Even though they said these things, they had a hard time stopping the crowds from sacrificing to them.

Then some Jews came from Antioch and Iconium and persuaded the crowds to stone Paul. When they thought he was dead, they dragged him out of the city. But after the disciples had gathered around him, he stood up and went into the city.

The next day, he left with Barnabas for Derbe. After they preached the good news in that city and had gathered many disciples, they returned to Lystra, Iconium, and Antioch, strengthening the souls of the disciples and encouraging them to continue in the faith. They told them, "We must go through many troubles on our way to the kingdom of God." They had elders elected for them in every church. When they had passed through Pisidia, they came to Pamphylia. When they had spoken the Word in Perga, they went down to Attalia.

From there they sailed back to Antioch, where they had been entrusted to the grace of God for the work they had just completed. When they arrived and called the church together, they reported everything God had done with them and how he had opened the door of faith for the Gentiles.

Lord God, we must go through many troubles on our way
to your kingdom. Sustain us with your kindness
to us in this life and even more so
with your grace to us in Jesus. Amen.

209. THE LETTER TO THE GALATIANS (GALATIANS)

Shortly after visiting the congregations of Galatia, Paul learns that false teachers had entered the congregations, claiming that one must be circumcised to be part of the people of God. Paul explains that justification is by faith alone and not by any works.

Paul, an apostle—not from men, nor through a man, but through Jesus Christ,

To the churches of Galatia:

Grace to you and peace from God our Father and the Lord Jesus Christ.

I am amazed that you are so quickly deserting Christ for a different gospel, which is really not another gospel at all. There are, however, some who are trying to disturb you by perverting the gospel of Christ.

I want you to know, brothers, that the gospel I preached is not of human origin. I received it through a revelation from Jesus Christ. Those who were important added nothing to my gospel. They saw that I had been entrusted with the gospel for the uncircumcised. And because James, Cephas, and John perceived the grace that was given to me, they gave me the right hand of fellowship.

We know that a person is not justified by the works of the law but through faith in Jesus Christ. So we also believed in Christ Jesus. Indeed, I live by faith in the Son of God, who loved me and gave himself for me. If righteousness is through the law, then Christ died for nothing!

Abraham "believed God, and it was credited to him as righteousness." Understand, then, that those who believe are the children of Abraham. So those who have faith are blessed along with Abraham, the man of faith.

In fact, those who rely on the works of the law are under a curse. For it is written, "Cursed is everyone who does not continue to do everything written in the law." Clearly no one is declared righteous before God by the law, because "The righteous will live by faith." The law does not say "by faith." Instead it says, "The one who does these things will live by them." Christ redeemed us from the curse of the law by becoming a curse for us. As it is written, "Cursed is everyone who hangs on a tree." He redeemed us in order that the blessing of Abraham would come to the Gentiles through Christ Jesus, through faith.

Then what about the law? It was our chaperone until Christ, so that we might be justified by faith. But now that this faith has come, we are no longer under a chaperone.

You are all sons of God through faith in Christ Jesus. Indeed, as many of you as were baptized into Christ have clothed yourselves with Christ. There is not Jew or Greek, slave or free, male or female, for you are all one in Christ Jesus. And if you belong to Christ, then you are Abraham's descendants and heirs according to the promise.

As long as the heir is a young child, he is no different from a slave, under guardians until the day set by his father. So also, when we were younger children, we were enslaved under the basic principles of the world. But when the set time had fully come, God sent his Son to be born of a woman, so that he would be born under the law, in order to redeem those under the law, so that we would be adopted as sons. And if you are a son, then you are also an heir of God through Christ.

Why are you turning back again to the basic principles? Do you want to be enslaved by them all over again? It is for freedom that Christ has set us free. Stand firm, then, and do not allow anyone to put the yoke of slavery on you again. You who are trying to be declared righteous by the law are completely separated from Christ. You have fallen from grace. In Christ Jesus neither circumcision nor uncircumcision matters. Rather, it is faith working through love that matters.

Walk by the spirit, and you will not carry out what the sinful flesh desires. Those who belong to Christ Jesus have crucified the sinful flesh with its passions and desires. If we live by the spirit, let us also walk in step with it.

But far be it from me to boast, except in the cross of our Lord Jesus Christ. In Christ Jesus circumcision or uncircumcision does not matter. What matters is being a new creation. Peace and mercy on those who follow this, namely, on the Israel of God.

The grace of our Lord Jesus Christ be with your spirit, brothers. Amen.

Lord God, we thank you that we are righteous
in your sight solely by faith in your Son who lived
and died for us. Keep us from ever looking
to anything else besides him for our salvation. Amen.

210. THE JERUSALEM COUNCIL (ACTS 15)

The question of whether circumcision was necessary for salvation comes up in other regions too, so the apostles meet together to officially address the issue.

Some men came down from Judea and began to teach the brothers: "Unless you are circumcised according to the law handed down by Moses, you cannot be saved." Because this brought about a serious argument between Paul and Barnabas and these men, they appointed Paul and Barnabas and some other men from the church to go up to Jerusalem, to see the apostles and the elders concerning this controversy.

When they arrived at Jerusalem, they were welcomed by the church, and they reported everything God had done through them. But some of the believers from the party of the Pharisees stood up and said, "It is necessary to circumcise the Gentiles and to command them to keep the Law of Moses."

The apostles and the elders gathered together to look into this matter. After much discussion, Peter said, "Brothers, you know that some time ago God made a choice among you, that through my mouth the Gentiles would hear the message of the gospel and believe. God, who knows the heart, testified on their behalf by giving them the Holy Spirit, exactly as he gave him to us. He showed that there is no distinction between us and them, cleansing their hearts by faith. Now then, why are you putting on the necks of the disciples a yoke which neither our fathers nor we have been able to bear? We believe that we are saved in the same way they are—through the grace of our Lord Jesus."

The whole assembly fell silent and listened to Barnabas and Paul, who reported all the wonders God had done among the Gentiles through them.

After they finished speaking, James responded, "Brothers, listen to me. Simon has reported how God has visited the Gentiles to take from them a people for his name. The words of the prophets agree with this, as it is written: 'After these things I will return and rebuild David's fallen tent. I will rebuild its ruins, and I will restore it, so that the rest of mankind may seek the Lord—even all the Gentiles who are called by my name, says the Lord who does these things.' Long ago he made these things known. So it is my judgment that we should not cause extra difficulty for those among the Gentiles who are turning to God. Instead we should write a letter telling them to abstain from things polluted by idols, from sexual immorality, from what is strangled, and from blood. For Moses is being read in the synagogues every Sabbath."

Then the whole church thought it would be best to choose men from their group to send to Antioch along with Paul and Barnabas. They wrote this letter for them to deliver:

> From the apostles and the elders,
>
> To the Gentile brothers in Antioch:
>
> Greetings.
>
> We heard that there were some who came from us without our authorization and caused you distress by unsettling your minds with what they said. So it seemed best to us to choose some men to send to you, along with our dear friends Barnabas and Paul. It seemed best to the Holy Spirit and to us to put no greater burden on you than these essentials: You are to abstain from food sacrificed to idols, from blood, from what has been strangled, and from sexual immorality. If you carefully avoid these things, you will do well.
>
> Farewell.

After they were sent on their way, they went down to Antioch and delivered the letter. The people read it and rejoiced over its encouraging message.

Lord God, our sinful pride always wants us
to look to ourselves and to our own actions as if

they were the source of our salvation, but salvation is found only in your Son. Keep us from trusting in ourselves for anything. Grant that our trust may always lie in Jesus, our perfect Savior. Amen.

211. PAUL'S SECOND MISSIONARY JOURNEY: PHILIPPI (ACTS 15-16)

Paul, this time with Silas, sets out on another missionary journey, and brings the gospel into Europe.

Paul said to Barnabas, "Let's visit the brothers in every town where we have preached the word of the Lord." Barnabas wanted to take Mark along with them. But Paul did not think it was a good idea to take him along, since he had deserted them. They had such a sharp disagreement that they parted company. Barnabas took Mark and sailed to Cyprus, but Paul chose Silas and went through Syria and Cilicia, strengthening the churches.

Paul arrived in Derbe and in Lystra, where there was a disciple named Timothy, who was the son of a believing Jewish woman, but his father was a Greek. Paul wanted Timothy to accompany him, so he circumcised him on account of the Jews who lived in those places.

They went through Phrygia and Galatia, because they were prevented by the Holy Spirit from speaking the word in the province of Asia. They tried to go into Bithynia, but the Spirit of Jesus did not allow them. So they went down to Troas. A vision appeared to Paul during the night. A Macedonian man was urging him, "Come over to Macedonia and help us!" As soon as he had seen the vision, we immediately made plans to proceed to Macedonia, because we concluded that God had called us to preach the good news to them.

We went to Philippi, which is a leading city in Macedonia and a Roman colony. We stayed in this city for a number of days.

Once, a slave girl met us. She had a spirit that foretold the future, and she made a large profit for her owners by fortune-telling. As she followed Paul and us, she kept crying out, "These men are servants of the Most High God, who are proclaiming to you the way to be saved." When she kept doing this for many days, Paul became so annoyed that he turned to the spirit and said, "I command you in the name of Jesus Christ to come out of her!" And it came out at that very moment.

When her owners saw that their hope of making money was gone, they seized Paul and Silas and dragged them before the authorities. They said,

"These men are throwing our city into a state of confusion. They are Jews, and they are teaching customs that are not lawful for us to practice, since we are Romans."

The magistrates ordered them to be beaten with rods. After they had beaten them severely, they threw them into prison and ordered the jailer to guard them securely. The jailer threw them into the inner prison and fastened their feet in the stocks.

About midnight Paul and Silas were praying and singing hymns to God, and the prisoners were listening to them. Suddenly there was such a violent earthquake that the foundations of the prison were shaken. Instantly all the doors were opened, and everyone's chains came loose. When the jailer woke up and saw that the prison doors were opened, he drew his sword and was about to kill himself, because he thought that the prisoners had escaped. But Paul shouted with a loud voice, "Don't harm yourself, because we are all here!"

The jailer called for lights, rushed in, and fell down trembling in front of Paul and Silas. Then he brought them outside and asked, "Sirs, what must I do to be saved?"

They said, "Believe in the Lord Jesus and you will be saved, you and your household." They spoke the word of the Lord to him and to everyone in his home. At the same hour of the night, he took them and washed their wounds. Without delay, he and all his family were baptized. He rejoiced, because he and his whole household had come to believe in God.

At daybreak the magistrates sent officers, saying, "Release those men!" The jailer reported these words to Paul: "The magistrates have sent orders that you should be released. Go in peace."

But Paul said, "They beat us publicly without a trial, even though we are Roman citizens, and now they are releasing us secretly? Absolutely not! Let them come themselves and escort us out!"

The magistrates were afraid when they heard that Paul and Silas were Roman citizens. So they came and apologized to them. After Paul and Silas came out of the prison, they went to the brothers, encouraged them, and then left.

Lord God, rescue us from all hopelessness and despair with the assurance that we are saved through faith in your Son. Give us hearts which sing of your love even in our darkest times. Amen.

212. PAUL'S SECOND MISSIONARY JOURNEY: THESSALONICA, BEREA, ATHENS, CORINTH, AND RETURN (ACTS 17-18)

Paul continues to preach the gospel in Europe, including to Jews who carefully examined the Scriptures and to Athenians who liked discussing philosophical ideas.

Paul and Silas came to Thessalonica. As was his custom, Paul went to the Jews, and on three Sabbath days he led them in a discussion from the Scriptures, proving that the Christ had to suffer and rise from the dead. Some of them were persuaded and joined Paul and Silas, as did a great number of God-fearing Greeks. But the Jews became jealous and started a riot. They searched for Paul and Silas in order to bring them out to the mob.

That night, the brothers sent Paul and Silas away to Berea. When they arrived, they went into the synagogue. Now the Bereans were more noble-minded than the Thessalonians. They received the word very eagerly and examined the Scriptures every day to see if these things were so. Many of them believed, along with more than a few prominent Greek women and men. But when the Jews in Thessalonica learned that the word of God was being proclaimed by Paul in Berea, they also went there to agitate the crowds. Then the brothers sent Paul to the seacoast, but Silas and Timothy stayed there. Those who escorted Paul brought him to Athens. When they left, they received instructions for Silas and Timothy to join Paul as soon as possible.

While Paul was waiting for them in Athens, he was very distressed to see that the city was full of idols. Some of the Epicurean and Stoic philosophers debated with him. Some said, "What is this seed picker trying to say?" Others said, "He seems to be proclaiming foreign gods." They said this because Paul was preaching the good news about Jesus and the resurrection.

They brought him to the council of the Areopagus, saying, "You seem to be bringing in some ideas that are strange to our ears, so we want to know what these things mean." (All the Athenians enjoyed listening to something new.)

Then Paul stood up and said, "Men of Athens, I see that you are very religious. As I was observing your objects of worship, I even found an altar on which had been inscribed, 'To an unknown god.' Now what you worship as unknown—this is what I am going to proclaim to you. The God who made the world and everything in it does not live in temples made with hands. Neither is he served by human hands, as if he needed anything, since he himself gives all people life and breath and everything they have. From one man, he made every nation of mankind. He determined where they would live. He did this so they would seek God and perhaps find him, though he is not far from us. As your own poets have said, 'Indeed, we are his offspring.' Therefore, since we are God's offspring, we should not think that the divine being is like an image formed by human skill. Although God overlooked the times of ignorance, he is now commanding all people everywhere to repent, because he has set a day on which he is going to judge the world by the man he appointed. He provided proof of this to everyone by raising him from the dead."

When they heard about the resurrection from the dead, some of them started to scoff. But others said, "We want to hear you again on this subject." So Paul left the council. However, some men became followers of Paul and believed.

After this, Paul went to Corinth. Silas and Timothy came down from Macedonia. Paul was testifying to the Jews that Jesus was the Christ, but when they opposed Paul, he shook out his clothes and said to them, "Your blood be on your own heads! From now on, I will go to the Gentiles!" And many of the Corinthians, when they heard, believed and were baptized.

One night the Lord spoke to Paul in a vision: "Do not be afraid. Keep on speaking, and do not be silent. For I am with you. No one will lay a hand on you to harm you. I have many people in this city." He stayed there a year and six months, teaching the word of God.

Then Paul sailed for Syria. When he landed at Caesarea, he went up and greeted the church. Then he went down to Antioch.

Lord God, we thank you for your Word. Make us diligent in our study of your Word, believing everything you have told us there. May Jesus our risen Savior protect us from all danger that threatens body and soul. Amen.

213. A LETTER TO THE THESSALONIANS (1 THESSALONIANS)

Shortly after founding the congregation in Thessalonica, Paul writes a letter back to them explaining to them again what they can look forward to on the Last Day.

Paul,

To the church of the Thessalonians:

Grace and peace to you from God our Father and the Lord Jesus Christ.

We always give thanks to God for all of you in our prayers. We know that God has chosen you, because our gospel did not come to you with mere words, but with power, with the Holy Spirit, and with deep conviction. You welcomed the word during a time of great affliction with the joy from the Holy Spirit. You turned to God from idols to serve the living and true God. You patiently wait for his Son from heaven, whom he raised from the dead—Jesus, the one who is going to rescue us from the coming wrath.

When you received God's word, which you heard from us, you did not receive the word of men but (as it really is) the word of God, which is now at work in you who believe. You became imitators of God's churches in Judea which are in Christ Jesus, because you suffered the same things from your own countrymen as they did from the Jews who killed the Lord Jesus and who severely persecuted us.

Brothers, after we were separated from you, we made every effort to see you again. You are our glory and our joy. So we sent Timothy to encourage you in your faith, so that no one will be shaken by these trials. Now Timothy has returned to us from you and has told us the good news about your faith and love. Because of this, brothers, in all our distress and affliction, we have been encouraged. For now we really live, if you are standing firm in the Lord. May God our Father himself and our Lord Jesus direct our way to you. And may the Lord increase your love and make it overflow for each other and for all people, just as ours does for you.

We do not want you to be uninformed, brothers, about those who have fallen asleep, so that you do not grieve in the same way as the others, who have no hope. If we believe that Jesus died and rose again, then in the same way God will bring with him those who have fallen asleep through Jesus. For the Lord himself will come down from heaven with a loud command and with the trumpet call of God, and the dead in Christ will rise first. Then we who are alive will be caught up in the clouds together with them, to meet the Lord in the air. And so we will always be with the Lord. Encourage one another with these words.

The Lord will come like a thief in the night. When people are saying, "Peace and security," destruction will suddenly come on them. But you, brothers, are not in the dark so that this day takes you by surprise like a thief, for you are all sons of the light and sons of the day. We do not belong to the night or the darkness. So then let us not sleep like everyone else, but rather let us remain alert and sober, putting on faith and love as a breastplate, and the hope of salvation as a helmet. You see, God did not appoint us for wrath, but for obtaining salvation through our Lord Jesus Christ. He died for us, so that whether we are awake or asleep, we may live together with him.

Rejoice always. Pray without ceasing. In everything give thanks. For this is God's will for you in Christ Jesus. Do not extinguish the Spirit. Do not treat prophecies with contempt. But test everything. Hold on to the good. Keep away from every kind of evil.

May the God of peace himself sanctify you completely, and may your whole spirit be kept blameless at the coming of our Lord Jesus Christ. The one who calls you is faithful, and he will do it.

The grace of our Lord Jesus Christ be with you.

Lord God, you have given us hope even in the face of death, because Jesus has risen again and will raise us up to be with him. Help us to stay alert and sober, living as the sons of the light which you have made us to be by faith. Amen.

214. ANOTHER LETTER TO THE THESSALONIANS (2 THESSALONIANS)

Not long after writing 1 Thessalonians, Paul writes a second letter to the believers in Thessalonica, explaining that they had not missed out on Judgment Day, since that will not happen until the man of sin, also known as the Antichrist, has been revealed.

Paul,

To the church of the Thessalonians:

Grace to you and peace from God our Father and the Lord Jesus Christ.

We always thank God for you, brothers, because your faith is growing more and more, and the love that each and every one of you has for one another is increasing. We ourselves boast in regard to your patient endurance and faith in all your persecutions and in the trials that you are enduring. This is evidence of God's righteous verdict that resulted in your being counted worthy of God's kingdom, for which you also suffer. Certainly, it is right for God to repay trouble to those who trouble you, and to give relief to you, who are troubled along with us. When the Lord Jesus is revealed from heaven with his powerful angels, he will exercise vengeance in flaming fire on those who do not obey the gospel of our Lord Jesus. Such people will receive a just penalty: eternal destruction away from the presence of the Lord and from his glorious strength, on that day when he comes to be glorified among his saints, and to be marveled at among all those who have believed, because our testimony to you was believed.

We ask you, brothers, not to be disturbed by a message which says that the day of the Lord has already come. Let no one deceive you in any way, because that day will not come until the man of sin is revealed. He opposes and exalts himself above God, so that he sits in the temple of God, displaying himself as God. You know what is holding him back, so that he may be revealed in his own time. In fact, the mystery of this lawlessness is already at work, but only until the one who is now holding him back moves out of the way. Then the lawless one will be revealed, whom the Lord Jesus will consume with the breath of his mouth and destroy when he appears in splendor at his coming. The coming of the lawless one will be in accordance with the work of Satan, with false signs and wonders, and with unrighteousness that deceives those who are perishing, because they refused to love the truth and so be saved.

But we always thank God for you, brothers, because God chose you from the beginning for salvation by the sanctifying work of the Spirit and faith in the truth. For this reason he also called you through our gospel so that you would obtain the glory of our Lord Jesus Christ. So then, brothers, stand firm and hold on to the teachings that were passed along to you. May our Lord Jesus Christ himself and God our Father, who loved us and in his grace gave us eternal encouragement and good hope, encourage your hearts and establish you in every good work and word.

Finally, brothers, pray for us so that the word of the Lord may spread quickly and be glorified just as it was among you. Pray also that we may be rescued from evil people. The Lord is faithful. He will establish you and protect you from the Evil One.

Avoid every brother who is walking idly. Imitate us, because we were not idle among you. We never ate anyone's bread without paying for it. Instead, we worked night and day, so that we would not be a burden to any of you. This was not because we lacked authority, but to provide an example for you to imitate. In fact, this was our command to you: If anyone does not want to work, he should not eat. We hear that some among you are idle. We command and urge these people to work quietly and eat their own bread.

But do not grow weary of doing good. And if anyone does not obey our word in this letter, do not associate with him, in order that he may be put to shame. Yet do not consider him an enemy, but admonish him as a brother.

The grace of our Lord Jesus Christ be with you all.

Lord God, we praise you that you have delivered us
from the lies and power of the man of sin by proclaiming

your pure gospel to us. Strengthen our faith in Jesus, so that we place all confidence in him and let no one enslave us to the idea that we are saved by what we do. Deliver those who are still under the man of sin's power to the freedom found in the gospel of Jesus. Amen.

215. PAUL'S THIRD MISSIONARY JOURNEY: EPHESUS (ACTS 19)

The Good News Paul proclaims in Ephesus overcomes the idolatry and superstition of the people.

Paul traveled to Ephesus. He entered the synagogue and spoke boldly for three months, leading discussions and trying to persuade them about the kingdom of God. But when some became hardened and refused to believe, even slandering the Way in front of the crowd, he left them. He took the disciples with him and led discussions every day in the lecture hall of Tyrannus. This went on for two years, with the result that all who lived in the province of Asia heard the word of the Lord. God was doing extraordinary miracles through Paul. Many of those who had become believers came forward, confessing and admitting their actions. And a large number of those who had practiced magic arts collected their books and burned them in front of everyone. They added up the cost of the books and found it to be fifty thousand pieces of silver. In this way the word of the Lord was growing and gaining strength.

After all this had happened, Paul resolved in his spirit to go to Jerusalem by traveling through Macedonia and Achaia. "After I have been there," he said, "I must also see Rome." After sending Timothy and Erastus to Macedonia, he stayed in the province of Asia for a while.

During that time there was more than a minor disturbance about the Way. A silversmith named Demetrius, who made silver shrines of Artemis, brought in no little income for the craftsmen. He called them together, along with the workers in similar trades, and said, "Men, you know that our prosperity comes from this income. You also see and hear that not merely in Ephesus but throughout almost the entire province of Asia, this Paul has persuaded and turned away a large number of people. He says that gods made by hands are not gods at all! Not only is there danger that our trade may be discredited, but also that the temple of the great goddess Artemis may be considered worthless."

When they heard this, they were filled with rage and began to shout, "Great is Artemis of the Ephesians!" The city was filled with confusion. They rushed to the theater, dragging along Paul's traveling companions. Paul wanted to enter the public assembly, but the disciples would not let him.

The assembly was in confusion. Most of them did not even know why they had come together. They made Alexander come out of the crowd. It was the Jews who pushed him forward. Alexander motioned with his hand and wanted to make his defense to the assembly. But when they recognized that he was a Jew, a single cry rose from all of them. For about two hours, they kept shouting, "Great is Artemis of the Ephesians!"

After the town clerk had quieted the crowd, he said, "Men of Ephesus, who does not know that the city of the Ephesians is the keeper of the temple of the great Artemis and of her image that fell from heaven? Therefore, since these things cannot be denied, you need not do anything rash. These men here are neither temple robbers nor blasphemers of our goddess. If Demetrius and his fellow craftsmen have a complaint against anyone, the courts are open. Let them press charges. We are in danger of being charged with rioting today, because we will not be able to give any reason for this disorderly mob." After he had said this, he dismissed the assembly.

Lord God, your Son is our only God and Savior.
Free us from all superstition and idolatry. Amen.

216. A LETTER TO THE CORINTHIANS, PART 1 (1 CORINTHIANS 1-6)

Paul writes a letter to the believers in Corinth, reminding them that their faith rests not on the skill of the one preaching to them but on the message preached to them—Christ crucified.

Paul, called to be an apostle of Jesus Christ by the will of God,

To the church of God in Corinth:

Grace to you and peace from God our Father and the Lord Jesus Christ!

I always thank my God for you because of the grace of God given to you in Christ Jesus. You were enriched in him in every way, because the testimony about Christ was established in you. He will also keep you strong until the end, so that you will be blameless on the day of our Lord Jesus Christ. God is faithful.

I heard that there are rivalries among you. Each of you says, "I belong to Paul," or "I belong to Apollos." Is Christ divided? Was Paul crucified for you? Or were you baptized into the name of Paul?

The message of the cross is foolishness to those who are perishing, but to us who are being saved, it is the power of God. Since the world through its wisdom did not know God, God in his wisdom decided to save those who believe, through the foolishness of the preached message. Jews ask for signs, Greeks desire wisdom, but we preach Christ crucified—which is offensive to Jews and foolishness to Greeks, but to those who are called, both Jews and Greeks, Christ is the power of God and the wisdom of God. We preach Christ crucified, because the foolishness of God is wiser than men, and the weakness of God is stronger than men.

When I came to you, I did not come with superior speech or wisdom in order to proclaim to you the testimony of God. For I had no intention of knowing anything among you except Jesus Christ, and him crucified. My message and my preaching were not marked by persuasive words of human wisdom, but by a demonstration of the Spirit and of power, so that your faith would not rest on human wisdom, but on God's power.

We do speak wisdom among those who are mature, but it is not a wisdom of this world. "What no eye has seen and no ear has heard and no human mind has conceived—that is what God has prepared for those who love him." But God revealed it to us through his Spirit. We also speak about these things, not in words taught by human wisdom, but in words taught by the Spirit, combining spiritual truths with spiritual words.

When one says, "I belong to Paul," and another, "I belong to Apollos," are you not being merely human? What is Apollos? And what is Paul? They are ministers through whom you believed, and each served as the Lord gave him his role. I planted, Apollos watered, but God was causing the growth. Think of us as servants of Christ and stewards of God's mysteries.

There is sexual immorality among you. Hand such a man over to Satan for the destruction of the flesh, so that the spirit may be saved on the day of the Lord Jesus. A little yeast leavens the whole batch of dough. Purge out the old yeast, for our Passover lamb has been sacrificed, namely, Christ! So let us keep celebrating the festival, not with old yeast, not with the yeast of malice and wickedness, but with the unleavened bread of sincerity and truth.

Do not be deceived. Neither the sexually immoral, nor idolaters, nor adulterers, nor males who have sex with males, nor thieves, nor the greedy, nor drunkards, nor the verbally abusive, nor swindlers will inherit the kingdom of God. And some of you were those types of people. But you were washed, you were sanctified, you were justified in the name of our Lord Jesus Christ and by the Spirit of our God.

"All things are permitted for me"—but not all things are beneficial. Flee from sexual immorality! Your body is a temple of the Holy Spirit, who is within you, whom you have from God? You are not your own, for you were bought at a price. Therefore glorify God with your body.

Lord God, we could not be saved or come to know you apart from Christ, our crucified Savior. Place our trust solely in him and not in human wisdom. And get rid of all immorality among us. Amen.

217. A LETTER TO THE CORINTHIANS, PART 2 (1 CORINTHIANS 8-11)

Paul continues his letter to the Corinthians, teaching them about gospel freedom and the Lord's Supper.

Concerning the eating of food from idol sacrifices, we know that an idol is not anything real. There is one God, the Father, and one Lord, Jesus Christ. However, that knowledge is not in everyone. Instead some, who are still affected by their former habit with the idol, eat the food as something sacrificed to an idol, and their conscience, being weak, is defiled.

Food will not bring us closer to God. We do not lack anything if we do not eat, nor are we better off if we do. And be careful that this right of yours does not somehow become a stumbling block to the weak. For if someone sees you dining in an idol's temple, will not the conscience of this man, weak as he is, be emboldened to eat food from an idol sacrifice? You see, the weak person is being destroyed by your knowledge. Therefore, if food causes my brother to sin, I will never eat meat again.

Am I not free? Am I not an apostle? Have I not seen Jesus, our Lord? Although I am free from all, I enslaved myself to all so that I might gain many more. To the Jews, I became like a Jew so that I might gain Jews. To those who are without the law, I became like a person without the law so that I might gain those who are without the law. To the weak, I became weak so that I might gain the weak. I have become all things to all people so that I may save at least some.

Let him who thinks he stands be careful that he does not fall. No testing has overtaken you except ordinary testing. But God is faithful. He will bring about the outcome that you are able to bear it.

Therefore, flee from idolatry. The cup of blessing that we bless, is it not a communion of the blood of Christ? The bread that we break, is it not a communion of the body of Christ? Because there is one bread, we, who are many, are one body, for we all partake of the one bread. What the Gentiles sacrifice, "they sacrifice to demons, and not to God," and I do not want you to become partners of demons. You cannot drink the cup of the Lord and the cup of demons. You cannot partake of the table of the Lord and of the table of demons. Or are we trying to provoke the Lord to jealousy?

"Everything is permitted"—but not everything is beneficial. Let no one seek his own good, but that of others. Whether you eat or drink, or do anything else, do everything to the glory of God. Do not give offense to Jews, or Greeks, or God's church, just as I also try to please all people in all things, by not seeking what is best for me but for the many, so that they may be saved.

I hear that when you come together in an assembly, there are divisions among you. For when you eat, each one goes ahead and takes his own supper, and so one person goes hungry while another is drunk. Do you despise God's church and humiliate those who have nothing?

I received from the Lord what I also delivered to you: The Lord Jesus, on the night when he was betrayed, took bread, and when he had given thanks, he broke it and said, "This is my body, which is for you. Do this in remembrance of me." In the same way, after the meal, he also took the cup, saying, "This cup is the new testament in my blood. Do this, as often as you drink it, in remembrance of me." For as often as you eat this bread and drink the cup, you proclaim the Lord's death until he comes.

Therefore whoever eats the bread or drinks the cup of the Lord in an unworthy manner will be guilty of sinning against the Lord's body and blood. Instead, let a person examine himself and after doing so, let him eat of the bread and drink from the cup. For if anyone eats and drinks in an unworthy way because he does not recognize the Lord's body, he eats and drinks judgment on himself. Therefore, my brothers, when you come together to eat, wait for one another.

Lord God, you have given us freedom from sin through
the gospel of your Son. You have also given us freedom in
how we live our lives. Help us to make use of
or give up our freedom for the sake of others. Thank you
for Holy Communion in which you forgive us all our sins.
Cause us to receive it always in a worthy manner,
humbly trusting in Jesus for our forgiveness. Amen.

218. A LETTER TO THE CORINTHIANS, PART 3 (1 CORINTHIANS 12-16)

Paul continues his letter to the Corinthians, discussing the loving way to use spiritual gifts and the resurrection of the dead.

No one can say, "Jesus is Lord," except by the Holy Spirit. There are various kinds of gifts, but the same Spirit. For just as the body is one and has many members, so also is Christ. If the whole body were an eye, where would the sense of hearing be? But God has arranged the members in the body as he desired. The eye cannot say to the hand, "I have no need for you." God put the body together so that there might not be any division, but that the members might all have the same concern for one another.

If I speak in the tongues of men and of angels but do not have love, I gain nothing. Love is patient. Love is kind. Love does not envy. It does not brag. It is not arrogant. It does not behave indecently. It is not selfish. It is not irritable. It does not keep a record of wrongs. It does not rejoice over unrighteousness but rejoices with the truth. It bears all things, believes all things, hopes all things, endures all things.

Keep on pursuing love, and eagerly seek spiritual gifts, but especially prophecy. For the person who speaks in a tongue speaks to God, not to people. No one understands him. However, the person who prophesies speaks to people things that edify, encourage, and comfort. I would rather speak five words with my understanding, in order to instruct others, than ten thousand words in a tongue. So when you come together, let all things be done in a way that builds people up.

Brothers, I am going to call your attention to the gospel I preached to you: Christ died for our sins in accordance with the Scriptures. He was buried. He was raised on the third day in accordance with the Scriptures. He appeared to the Twelve. After that he appeared to over five hundred brothers at the same time, most of whom are still alive. Last of all, he appeared also to me.

Now if Christ has been raised from the dead, how is it that some among you say that there is no resurrection? If the dead are not raised, not even Christ has been raised. And if Christ has not been raised, your faith is futile; you are still in your sins.

But Christ has been raised from the dead, the firstfruits of those who have fallen asleep. For as in Adam they all die, so also in Christ they all will be made alive. Christ as the firstfruits and then Christ's people, at his coming. Otherwise, why do we live in danger every hour? What good did it do if the dead are not raised?

But someone will object, "With what kind of body are they going to come?" What you sow is not made alive unless it dies. And what you sow is not the body that will be, but a bare seed. But God gives it a body of the kind he wanted it to have. That is the way the resurrection of the dead will be. What is sown is perishable; it is raised imperishable. It is sown in dishonor; it is raised in glory. It is sown as a natural body; it is raised as a spiritual body.

"The first man, Adam, became a living natural being." The last Adam became a life-giving spirit. The first man is of the earth, made of dust. The second man is the Lord from heaven. As was the man made of dust, so are the people who are made of dust, and as is the heavenly man, so the heavenly people will be. And just as we have borne the image of the man made of dust, let us also bear the image of the heavenly man.

We will not all sleep, but we will all be changed. For this perishable body must put on imperishability. Then what is written will be fulfilled: "Death is swallowed up in victory. Death, where is your sting? Grave, where is your victory?" The sting of death is sin, and the power of sin is the law. But thanks be to God, who gives us the victory through our Lord Jesus Christ!

Therefore, my dear brothers, be steadfast, immovable, always abounding in the Lord's work, because you know that your labor is not in vain in the Lord.

The grace of the Lord Jesus Christ be with you. Amen.

Lord God, we thank you for all the gifts that
you have given your people. Bind us together
in a spirit of unity so that we use these gifts not selfishly
for ourselves but lovingly for each other. Raise us up
in glory on the Last Day when Jesus returns. Amen.

219. PAUL'S THIRD MISSIONARY JOURNEY: BACK TO JERUSALEM (ACTS 20-21)

Paul heads back to Jerusalem, leaving final instructions with the church leaders.

Paul left to go to Macedonia. After he had spoken many words of encouragement to the people, he came to Greece and stayed there three months.

Because a plot was made against him by the Jews just as he was about to set sail for Syria, he decided to go back through Macedonia. We sailed from Philippi and came to Troas, where we stayed seven days.

On the first day of the week, when we were gathered together, Paul spoke to the people. Since he intended to leave the next day, he continued talking until midnight. Seated in a window was a young man named Eutychus. He was sinking into a deep sleep as Paul kept on talking for a long time. When he was sound asleep, he fell down from the third story and was picked up dead. Paul went down, bent over him, and said, "Do not be alarmed. He is alive!" They brought the boy home alive and were greatly comforted.

We went on ahead and sailed to Miletus. From Miletus, Paul sent to Ephesus and called for the elders of the church. When they came, he said to them, "You know how I lived the whole time I was with you. I served the Lord with all humility, with tears, and with the trials that came to me. You know how I did not hesitate to proclaim to you anything that would be beneficial for you. I have solemnly testified to both Jews and Greeks about repentance toward God and faith in our Lord Jesus Christ.

"Now I am going to Jerusalem, compelled by the Spirit, not knowing what will happen to me there, except that the Holy Spirit keeps warning me in town after town that chains are waiting for me. However, I consider my life as of no great value, so that I may testify to the gospel of God's grace. None of you will ever see my face again. Therefore I solemnly declare to you today that I am innocent of the blood of all of you, for I did not hesitate to proclaim to you the whole counsel of God.

"Keep watch over yourselves and over the whole flock in which the Holy Spirit has placed you as overseers, to shepherd the church of God, which he purchased with his own blood. I know that after my departure savage wolves will come in among you. Even from your own group men will rise up, twisting the truth in order to draw away disciples after them. Therefore be on the alert! Remember that for three years, night and day, I never stopped warning each one of you with tears. And now I entrust you to God and to the word of his grace, which has power to build you up." After Paul said these things, he knelt down with all of them and prayed. They all wept very much.

We headed straight to Cos, and the next day to Rhodes, and from there to Patara. We sailed to Syria and put in to port at Tyre. We located the disciples there. Through the Spirit, they kept telling Paul not to go to Jerusalem. When our time there came to an end, we left and went on our way.

When we completed our voyage from Tyre, we came to Caesarea. We entered the house of Philip and stayed with him. After we had stayed there for a number of days, a prophet named Agabus came down from Judea. He took Paul's belt, tied his own feet and hands with it, and said, "This is what the Holy Spirit says: 'This is the way the Jews at Jerusalem will bind the man who owns this belt and will deliver him into the hands of the Gentiles.' "

When we heard this, both we and the local residents urged Paul not to go up to Jerusalem. Then Paul answered, "What are you doing, weeping and breaking my heart? For I am ready not only to be bound but also to die in Jerusalem for the name of the Lord Jesus."

Since he could not be persuaded, we said nothing more except, "May the Lord's will be done." We got ready and went up to Jerusalem.

Lord God, your Son has delivered us from death,
and your messengers have brought us that good news.
Continue to give your church faithful shepherds
and protect us from all false teaching. Amen.

220. ANOTHER LETTER TO THE CORINTHIANS, PART 1 (2 CORINTHIANS 1, 3-5)

Paul writes another letter to the believers in Corinth, explaining to them that even if he appeared unimpressive, the gospel he proclaimed was powerful and life-giving.

Paul, an apostle of Christ Jesus by the will of God,

To the church of God that is in Corinth:

Grace to you and peace from God our Father and the Lord Jesus Christ.

Blessed be the God and Father of our Lord Jesus Christ, the Father of mercies and God of all comfort, who comforts us in all our trouble, so that we can comfort those in any trouble with the same comfort with which we ourselves are comforted by God. For as many promises as God has made, they have always been "Yes." God is the one who makes both us and you to be strong in Christ. He anointed us. He sealed us as his own and gave us the Spirit as the down payment in our hearts.

Do we need letters of recommendation? You yourselves are our letter, written on our hearts, read by everyone. It is clear that you are a letter from Christ, delivered by us, written not with ink but with the Spirit of the living God, not on stone tablets, but on tablets that are hearts of flesh.

Such is the confidence we have through Christ before God. Not that we are competent by ourselves; rather, our competence is from God. He also made us competent as ministers of a new testament (not of letter, but of spirit). For the letter kills, but the spirit gives life. If the ministry that brought death (which was engraved in letters on stone) came with glory, how will the ministry of the spirit not be much more glorious?

Therefore, since we have this ministry, we do not operate in a deceitful way, and we do not distort the word of God. Instead, by proclaiming the truth clearly, we commend ourselves to everyone's conscience in the sight of God. Indeed, we do not preach ourselves, but Jesus Christ as Lord, and ourselves as your servants for Jesus' sake. For the God who said, "Light will shine out of darkness," is the same one who made light shine in our hearts to give us the light of the knowledge of the glory of God in the person of Jesus Christ.

We hold this treasure in clay jars to show that its extraordinary power is from God and not from us. We always carry around in our body the death of the Lord Jesus, so that the life of Jesus may also be revealed in our body. We believe, and therefore we speak. For we know that the one who raised the Lord Jesus will also raise us with Jesus and bring us (together with you) into his presence.

Therefore we are not discouraged. Our momentary, light trouble produces for us an eternal weight of glory that is far beyond any comparison. We are not focusing on what is seen, but on what is not seen. For the things that are seen are temporary, but the things that are not seen are eternal.

If the tent that is our earthly home is destroyed, we have a building from God, an eternal home in heaven. The one who prepared us for this very purpose is God, who gave us the Spirit as the down payment. Therefore we walk by faith, not by sight. And for this reason we make it our goal to please him, for we must all appear before the judgment seat of Christ.

The love of Christ compels us, because we came to this conclusion: One died for all; therefore, all died. And he died for all, so that those who live would no longer live for themselves but for him, who died in their place and was raised again. So then, if anyone is in Christ, he is a new creation. The old has passed away. The new has come! God reconciled us to himself through Christ and gave us the ministry of reconciliation. That is, God was in Christ reconciling the world to himself, not counting their trespasses against them. And he has entrusted to us the message of reconciliation. Therefore, we are ambassadors for Christ. God is making an appeal through us. We urge you, on Christ's behalf: Be reconciled to God. God made him, who did not know sin, to become sin for us, so that we might become the righteousness of God in him.

Lord God, all your promises to us are true in Jesus,
through whom you have reconciled the world to yourself.
Preserve us throughout all our trials here and bring us
to our eternal home. Amen.

221. ANOTHER LETTER TO THE CORINTHIANS, PART 2 (2 CORINTHIANS 6-13)

Paul continues his second letter to the Corinthians, further explaining that his gospel is true despite his own weak appearance.

Do not be yoked together with unbelievers. For what does a believer share in common with an unbeliever? God said, "I will be your Father, and you will be my sons and daughters." So since we have these promises, let us cleanse ourselves from everything that defiles.

Make room for us in your hearts. We have wronged no one. Even if I caused you sorrow with my letter, I do not regret it. I rejoice, because this sorrow resulted in repentance. Yes, you were made sorry in a godly way. So you were not harmed in any way by us. In fact, godly sorrow produces repentance, which leads to salvation, leaving no regret. On the other hand, worldly sorrow produces death. Look what godly sorrow produced in you! In every way you proved yourselves to be pure in this matter. If I made any boast about you, I have not been put to shame. I rejoice because I have complete confidence in you.

But just as you overflow in every way, also overflow in this gracious gift. For you know the grace of our Lord Jesus Christ. Although he was rich, yet for your sakes he became poor, so that through his poverty you might become rich. So then, each one should give as he has determined in his heart, not reluctantly or under pressure, for God loves a cheerful giver. And he who provides seed to the sower and bread for food will provide and multiply your seed for sowing, and will increase the harvest of your righteousness. You will be made rich in every way so that you may be generous in every way, which produces thanksgiving to God through us. Thanks be to God for his indescribable gift!

Now I myself, Paul, appeal to you by the humility and gentleness of Christ. You are looking at things only according to the outward appearance. Indeed, even if I may boast some more about our authority, which the Lord has given for building you up and not for tearing you down, I will not be put to shame. We do not dare to classify ourselves with some of those who speak highly of themselves. It is not the one who commends himself who is approved, but the one whom the Lord commends.

I am jealous about you, with a godly jealousy, because I promised to present you as a pure virgin to one husband, Christ. But I am afraid that somehow your minds might be led astray from Christ. If someone comes and preaches another Jesus or a different "gospel," you put up with it all too well. The "super-apostles" are false apostles, deceitful workers, masquerading as apostles of Christ. And no wonder, for Satan himself masquerades as an angel of light.

If it is necessary that I boast, I will boast of the things that show my weakness. I was given a thorn in my flesh, a messenger of Satan, to torment me, so that I would not become arrogant. Three times I pleaded with the Lord about this, that he would take it away from me. And he said to me, "My grace is sufficient for you, because my power is made perfect in weakness." Therefore I will be glad to boast all the more in my weaknesses, so that the power of Christ may shelter me. For whenever I am weak, then am I strong.

I ought to be commended by you, because I was not inferior to the "super-apostles" in any way, even if I am nothing. The signs of an apostle—signs and wonders and miracles—were performed among you with all perseverance.

Are you thinking that we are trying to defend ourselves to you all this time? We are speaking in the sight of God in Christ. Dear friends, all these words are for your strengthening. For I am afraid that when I arrive, I may not find you as I want you to be. We are praying for your complete restoration.

The grace of the Lord Jesus Christ, and the love of God, and the fellowship of the Holy Spirit be with you all.

Lord God, we are weak and powerless on our own,
but make us strong in you. Restore us in repentance,
and work in us to give generously of what you have
given us, knowing that we have true and
eternal riches in Christ. Amen.

222. A LETTER TO THE ROMANS, PART 1 (ROMANS 1-4)

Paul writes to the believers in Rome, because he hopes to visit them soon on his way to Spain. In preparation for this visit he proclaims the gospel which he is not ashamed to proclaim: the righteous will live by faith.

Paul, a servant of Christ Jesus, called to be an apostle, set apart for the gospel. This gospel is about his Son—who in the flesh was born a descendant of David, who in the spirit was declared to be God's Son by his resurrection from the dead—Jesus Christ, our Lord. Through him we received the call to be an apostle to bring about faith among all the Gentiles, including you.

To all those loved by God in Rome, called to be saints:

Grace to you and peace from God our Father and the Lord Jesus Christ.

I have often planned to come to you but have been prevented from doing so. I have an obligation both to Greeks and non-Greeks. That is why I am eager to proclaim the gospel also to you who are in Rome. I am not ashamed of the gospel, because it is the power of God for salvation to everyone who believes—to the Jew first, and also to the Greek. For in the gospel a righteousness from God is revealed by faith, for faith, just as it is written, "The righteous will live by faith."

God's wrath is being revealed from heaven against all unrighteousness. Therefore, you are without excuse. Indeed, all people who have sinned without law will also perish without law, and all the people who have sinned in connection with law will be judged by law. All—both Jews and Greeks—are under sin. No one is righteous, not even one. For this reason, no one will be declared righteous in his sight by works of the law. Through the law we become aware of sin.

But now, completely apart from the law, a righteousness from God has been made known. This righteousness from God comes through faith in Jesus Christ to all who believe. In fact, there is no difference, because all have sinned and fall short of the glory of God and are justified freely by his grace through the redemption that is in Christ Jesus. What happens to boasting then? It has been eliminated. For we conclude that a person is justified by faith without the works of the law.

If Abraham had been justified by works, he would have had a reason to boast. But what does Scripture say? "Abraham believed God and it was credited to him as righteousness." Now to a person who works, his pay is not counted as a gift but as something owed. But to the person who does not work but believes in the God who justifies the ungodly, his faith is credited to him as righteousness.

Now then, does this blessing apply only to the circumcised? Faith was credited to Abraham as righteousness. Was he circumcised or uncircumcised at that time? He was not circumcised but uncircumcised. He received the mark of circumcision as the seal of the righteousness by faith that was already his while he was uncircumcised. So Abraham is the father of all the uncircumcised people who believe. He is also the father of the circumcised people who also walk in the footsteps of the faith our father Abraham had.

Indeed, the promise that he would be the heir of the world was not given to Abraham or his descendants through the law but through faith.

If people are heirs by the law, faith is empty and the promise is nullified, for law brings wrath. For this reason, the promise is by faith, so that it may be according to grace and may be guaranteed to all of Abraham's descendants—to the one who has the faith of Abraham. He is the father of us all. As it is written: "I have made you a father of many nations."

Abraham believed that he would become the father of many nations, just as he was told. He did not weaken in faith, even though he considered his own body and Sarah's womb to be dead. He did not waver in unbelief with respect to God's promise, but grew strong in faith, being fully convinced that God was able to do what he had promised. This is why "it was credited to him as righteousness."

Now the statement "it was credited to him" was not written for him alone, but also for us who believe in the one who raised our Lord Jesus from the dead. He was handed over to death because of our trespasses and was raised to life because of our justification.

Lord God, we thank you for your wonderful gospel, that we are justified by faith in your Son. Make us eager to share this good news with all people. Amen.

223. A LETTER TO THE ROMANS, PART 2 (ROMANS 5-8)

Paul continues his letter to the Romans, speaking of the victory we have in Jesus.

Just as sin entered the world through one man and death through sin, so also death spread to all people because all sinned. But if by the trespass of the one man, death reigned, it is even more certain that those who receive the gift of righteousness will reign in life through the one man Jesus Christ! So then, just as one trespass led to a verdict of condemnation for all people, so also one righteous verdict led to justification for all people. Just as through the disobedience of one man the many became sinners, so also through the obedience of one man the many will become righteous.

Then shall we keep on sinning? Absolutely not! We died to sin. How can we go on living in it? All of us who were baptized into Christ Jesus were baptized into his death, so that just as he was raised from the dead, we too would also walk in a new life. Our old self was crucified with him so that we would not continue to serve sin. Therefore do not let sin reign. Thanks be to God that you were set free from sin. The wages of sin is death, but the undeserved gift of God is eternal life in Christ Jesus our Lord.

We have been released from the law so that we serve in the new way of the Spirit. Then is the law sin? Absolutely not! I would not have recognized sin except through the law. For example, I would not have known about coveting if the law had not said, "You shall not covet."

The law is spiritual, but I am unspiritual, sold as a slave to sin. Good does not live in me, that is, in my sinful flesh. The desire to do good is present with me, but I am not able to carry it out. So I fail to do the good I want to do. Instead, the evil I do not want to do, that is what I keep doing. What a miserable wretch I am! Who will rescue me from this body of death? I thank God through Jesus Christ our Lord!

There is no condemnation for those who are in Christ Jesus. For what the law was unable to do, because it was weakened by the flesh, God did, when he sent his own Son in the likeness of sinful flesh to deal with sin.

The mind-set of the sinful flesh is hostile to God. It does not submit to God's law. Those who are in the sinful flesh cannot please God. But you are not in the sinful flesh but in the spirit, if God's Spirit lives in you. Those who are led by the Spirit of God are sons of God. For you did not receive a spirit of slavery but the Spirit of adoption by whom we call out, "Father," testifying that we are God's children. If we are children, we are also heirs—heirs of God and fellow heirs with Christ, since we suffer with him, so that we may also be glorified with him.

Our sufferings at the present time are not worth comparing with the glory that is going to be revealed to us. It was for this hope we were saved. We eagerly wait for it with patient endurance. And we know that all things work together for the good of those who love God, for those who are called according to his purpose, because those God foreknew, he also predestined to be conformed to the image of his Son. And those he predestined, he also called. Those he called, he also justified. And those he justified, he also glorified.

If God is for us, who can be against us? He who did not spare his own Son, but gave him up for us all—how will he not also graciously give us all things? Who will bring an accusation against God's elect? God justifies! Who is the one who condemns? Christ Jesus is at God's right hand, interceding for us! What will separate us from the love of Christ? Will trouble or distress or persecution or famine or nakedness or danger or sword? No! For I am convinced that neither death nor life, neither angels nor rulers, neither things present nor things to come, nor powerful forces, neither height nor depth, nor anything else in creation, will be able to separate us from the love of God in Christ Jesus our Lord.

Lord God, every day we struggle with sin, but you have rescued us from all condemnation through Jesus Christ. Empower us to fight sin in our lives. Give us endurance through all the difficulties of this life, knowing the eternal glory you have prepared for us and that nothing can separate us from your love for us in Jesus. Amen.

224. A LETTER TO THE ROMANS, PART 3 (ROMANS 9-11)

Paul continues his letter to the Romans, explaining that even for his fellow Jewish people salvation is only by faith in Jesus.

I have great sorrow. I almost wish that I myself could be separated from Christ in place of my brothers, the Israelites. Theirs are the adoption as sons, the glory, the covenants, the giving of the law, the worship, the promises, the patriarchs. From them came the Christ.

This does not mean that God's word has failed, because not all who are descended from Israel are really Israel, and not all who are descended from Abraham are really his children. On the contrary, "Your line of descent will be traced through Isaac." This means that it is not the children of the flesh who are God's children, but it is the children of the promise who are counted as his descendants. It does not depend on human desire or effort, but on God's mercy.

Gentiles, who were not pursuing righteousness, have obtained righteousness by faith. But Israel, while pursuing the law as a way of righteousness, did not reach it. Why? Because they kept pursuing it not by faith, but as if it comes by works. They have a zeal for God, but not knowledge. Since they sought to establish their own righteousness, they did not submit to the righteousness from God.

To everyone who believes, Christ is the end of the law, resulting in righteousness. If you confess with your mouth that Jesus is Lord and believe in your heart that God raised him from the dead, you will be saved. So there is no distinction between Jew and Greek, because the same Lord is Lord of all, who gives generously to all who call on him. Yes, "Everyone who calls on the name of the Lord will be saved."

But not all obeyed the gospel. Faith comes from hearing the message, and the message comes through the word of Christ. Did they not hear? Of course, they did. "The sound of their voice went out to all the earth." Yet Isaiah says, "I was found by those who were not looking for me." About Israel he says, "All day long I stretched out my hands to a people who disobey and oppose me."

So did God reject his people? Absolutely not! I myself am an Israelite. God did not reject his people whom he foreknew. Elijah was pleading with God against Israel: "Lord, they have killed your prophets and torn down your altars. I am the only one left, and they are trying to take my life." But what did God's answer tell him? "I have reserved for myself seven thousand men who have not bowed the knee to Baal." In the same way at the present time there is a remnant chosen by grace. Now if it is by grace, then it is not the result of works—otherwise grace would no longer be grace.

So did they fall permanently? Absolutely not! Rather, by their trespass, salvation came to the Gentiles to make the Israelites jealous. As long as I am an apostle to the Gentiles, I am going to speak highly of my ministry. Perhaps I may make my own people jealous, and so save some of them.

If some of the branches were broken off, and you—a wild olive branch—were grafted in among them, do not boast that you are better than the branches. You are not supporting the root. The root is supporting you. Branches were broken off because of unbelief, and you remain in place by faith. Do not be conceited, but stand in awe. For if God did not spare the natural branches, he will not spare you. So take note of God's kindness and his severity.

And if they do not remain in unbelief, those branches will be grafted in again. There has been a hardening of part of Israel until the full number of Gentiles has come in. And in this way all Israel will be saved. For just as you were once disobedient to God, but now have been shown mercy due to their disobedience, so also now they have become disobedient, so that by the mercy shown to you they may be shown mercy too. God imprisoned all in disobedience so that he may show mercy to all.

Oh, the depth of the riches and wisdom and knowledge of God! To him be the glory forever! Amen.

Lord God, if left to ourselves we would surely turn away
from and abandon you. Keep us in the faith,
for you have graciously chosen us for yourself in Jesus.
We pray for your people Israel that many of them
may return to the Savior promised to them. Amen.

225. A LETTER TO THE ROMANS, PART 4 (ROMANS 12-16)

Paul continues his letter to the Romans, now showing them some of the effects that the good news of salvation will have on the way they live.

Therefore I urge you, brothers, by the mercies of God, to offer your bodies as a living sacrifice. Do not continue to conform to the pattern of this world, but be transformed by the renewal of your mind.

I tell everyone among you not to think of yourself more highly than you ought. Though we are many, we are one body in Christ. We have different gifts, according to the grace God has given us.

Be devoted to one another with brotherly love. Be joyful in hope. Endure trials patiently. Persist in prayer. Share with the saints who are in need. Be quick to welcome strangers as guests.

Bless those who persecute you; bless, and do not curse. Do not pay anyone back evil for evil. Do not be overcome by evil, but overcome evil with good.

Everyone must submit to the governing authorities. The authorities have been established by God. Therefore the one who rebels against the authority is opposing God's institution, and those who oppose will bring judgment on themselves. Rulers are God's servant, a punisher to bring wrath on the wrongdoer. Therefore submit, not only because of wrath, but also because of conscience. For this reason you also pay taxes. Pay what you owe to all of them.

Do not owe anyone anything except to love one another. For the commandments are summed up in this statement: "Love your neighbor as yourself." And do this since you understand the present time. It is already the hour for you to wake up from sleep, because our salvation is nearer now than when we first believed. The night is almost over, and the day is drawing near. So let us walk decently as in the daytime, not in sin. Clothe yourselves with the Lord Jesus Christ, and do not give any thought to satisfying the desires of your sinful flesh.

Accept a person who is weak in faith, and do not pass judgment on things that are just a difference of opinion. One person believes it is right to eat anything. Another person who is weak eats only vegetables. The one who eats everything should not look down on the person who does not do so, and the one who does not eat everything should not judge the person who does, because God has accepted him.

Not one of us lives for himself, and not one dies for himself. Whether we live or die, we belong to the Lord. Therefore, let us stop passing judgment on one another. The kingdom of God does not consist of eating and drinking, but of righteousness and peace and joy in the Holy Spirit. Do not tear down God's work for the sake of food. Everything is pure, but it is wrong for a person to eat if it causes anyone to stumble. The one who has doubts is condemned if he eats, because everything that does not proceed from faith is sin. We who are strong have an obligation to bear with the weaknesses of those who are not strong, and not just to please ourselves.

Accept one another as Christ also accepted you. Christ became a servant of those who are circumcised for the sake of God's truth, to confirm the promises made to the patriarchs, so that the Gentiles would glorify God for his mercy.

I have written a letter to you because of the grace God has given me to be a public minister of Christ Jesus to the Gentiles. I am to do the priestly work of proclaiming the gospel of God so that the Gentiles would be an acceptable offering. I have fully proclaimed the gospel of Christ from Jerusalem all the way around to Illyricum, but I have longed for many years to come to you. So when I go to Spain, I hope to visit you on my way. And I know that when I come to you, I will arrive with the full blessing of Christ.

Greet one another with a holy kiss. All the churches of Christ greet you.

But watch out for those who cause divisions and offenses contrary to the teaching that you learned. Keep away from them.

The God of peace will soon crush Satan under your feet. The grace of our Lord Jesus Christ be with you. Amen.

Lord God, we thank you for the peace and protection
you provide us through the government. Help us
to obey all the authorities you have placed over us.
Move us to love all people and serve them,
for your Son has loved and served us. Amen.

226. PAUL IS ARRESTED (ACTS 21-23)

Paul is arrested when he gets back to Jerusalem.

When we arrived in Jerusalem, the brothers gave us a warm welcome. Paul reported in detail each of the things God had done among the Gentiles through his ministry. When they heard this, they praised God.

Jews from the province of Asia saw Paul in the temple. They stirred up the whole crowd and seized him, shouting, "Men of Israel, help! This is the man who teaches everyone everywhere against our people and our law and this place."

The whole city was stirred up, and the people rushed together as a mob. They seized Paul, dragged him out of the temple, and immediately the gates were shut. While they were looking for a way to kill him, a report went up to the commander of the cohort that all Jerusalem was in an uproar. He immediately took soldiers and centurions and ran down to them. When they saw the commander and the soldiers, they stopped beating Paul.

Then the commander approached Paul, arrested him, and gave an order that he should be bound with two chains. He asked who Paul was and what he had done.

Paul said, "I beg you, allow me to speak to the people."

When the commander had given him permission, Paul stood on the steps and motioned with his hand to the people. When they were all silent, Paul addressed them in Hebrew: "Brothers, listen to my defense. I am a Jew, born in Tarsus of Cilicia, but brought up in this city and trained at the feet of Gamaliel, according to the strict ways of the law of our fathers. I am just as zealous for God as all of you are today. I persecuted this Way to the death, tying up and throwing both men and women into prisons. I was going to Damascus to bring back those who were there as prisoners to Jerusalem so that they could be punished.

"While on the way, a very bright light from heaven suddenly flashed around me. I fell to the ground and heard a voice saying to me, 'Saul, Saul, why are you persecuting me?' I answered, 'Who are you, Lord?' He said to me, 'I am Jesus the Nazarene, whom you are persecuting. I will send you far away to the Gentiles.'"

Then they raised their voices, shouting, "Rid the earth of this fellow, for he is not fit to live!"

When they started shouting, the commander ordered that Paul be brought into the barracks. He directed that Paul be interrogated by whipping, in order to learn why the people were shouting at him like this. As they stretched him for the whipping, Paul asked the centurion standing by, "Is it legal for you to whip a man who is a Roman citizen and who has not been found guilty by a proper trial?"

When the centurion heard this, he went to the commander and said, "This man is a Roman citizen!"

The commander came and asked him, "Tell me, are you a Roman citizen?"

He answered, "Yes, I was born a citizen."

Immediately, those who were about to interrogate him moved away from him.

The next day, since the commander wanted to find out exactly why Paul was being accused by the Jews, he untied him and ordered the Sanhedrin to meet. Then he brought Paul down and had him stand before them.

When Paul realized that some of them were Sadducees and the others were Pharisees, he shouted out in the Sanhedrin, "Gentlemen, I am a Pharisee. I am on trial concerning the hope for the resurrection of the dead!"

When he said this, a dispute broke out between the Pharisees and the Sadducees, and the assembly was divided. (For the Sadducees say there is no resurrection or spirit, but the Pharisees believe in them.) There was a great uproar, and some of the Pharisees stood up and protested strongly: "We find nothing wrong with this man. What if a spirit spoke to him?" The uproar became so great that the commander was afraid Paul would be torn to pieces by them. He commanded the soldiers to take him away from them by force, and bring him into the barracks.

The following night the Lord stood next to Paul and said, "Take courage! As you have solemnly testified about me in Jerusalem, so you must also testify in Rome."

Lord God, you use even the sufferings of your people
to proclaim your word and to grow your church.
Keep your people safe from all persecution, keep them
faithful when opposed for their faith, and use
all things to bring your word to more people. Amen.

227. PAUL ON TRIAL (ACTS 23-25)

After being kept under guard for several years, Paul appeals his case to Caesar.

The Jews formed a conspiracy, saying that they would not eat or drink until they had killed Paul. There were more than forty who took part in this plot. But when the son of Paul's sister heard about the ambush, he went and told the commander. So the commander called two of the centurions and said, "Get two hundred soldiers ready, along with seventy cavalry and two hundred spearmen to go as far as Caesarea at the third hour of the night. Also provide mounts so that they can put Paul on one and bring him safely to Felix the governor."

So the soldiers took Paul and brought him to Antipatris during the night. The governor said, "I will give you a hearing when your accusers arrive." Then he ordered that Paul should be kept under guard in Herod's palace.

Five days later a lawyer named Tertullus brought formal charges against Paul to the governor, saying, "We have found this man to be a public menace, one who stirs up riots among all the Jews throughout the world, and a ringleader of the Nazarene sect. He even tried to desecrate the temple, so we arrested him." The Jews also joined in the attack, asserting that these things were so.

When the governor motioned to him to speak, Paul replied, "They cannot prove to you the accusations they are now making against me. But I do confess to you that I worship the God of our fathers according to the Way. I believe everything written throughout the Law and in the Prophets. I have the same hope in God that these men have, that there is going to be a resurrection of both the righteous and the unrighteous."

Then Felix, because he was rather well informed about the Way, adjourned the proceedings. He ordered the centurion to guard Paul, but to let him have some freedom and not to prevent any of his friends from taking care of his needs.

After two years had passed, Felix was succeeded by Festus.

The leaders of the Jews brought formal charges against Paul and asked Festus for the favor of transferring Paul's case to Jerusalem. Their plan was to ambush and kill Paul along the way. However, Festus replied that Paul was being held in custody at Caesarea and that he himself intended to go there soon. When he arrived, the Jews who had come down from Jerusalem brought many serious charges that they could not prove. Paul said in his defense, "I have not committed any offense against the Jewish law, against the temple, or against Caesar."

But since Festus wanted to do the Jews a favor, he said to Paul, "Are you willing to go up to Jerusalem and stand trial before me there on these charges?"

But Paul said, "I have done nothing wrong to the Jews, as also you yourself know very well. If there is nothing to the charges they are making against me, no one can hand me over to them. I appeal to Caesar!"

Festus answered, "You have appealed to Caesar. To Caesar you will go!"

Lord God, your Son Jesus is our Way, our Truth,
and our Life. Keep his name holy in the world and
keep our reputation in the world clear as well. Amen.

228. PAUL'S JOURNEY TO PRISON IN ROME (ACTS 27-28)

After God protects Paul throughout his dangerous journey, Paul arrives at Rome and preaches the gospel in the capital of the world.

When it was decided that we would sail for Italy, Paul and some other prisoners were handed over to a centurion named Julius. After boarding a ship from Adramyttium, we put out to sea.

We sailed slowly for a number of days and arrived with difficulty off Cnidus. Since the wind did not permit us to go further, we sailed on the sheltered side of Crete. With difficulty we came to Fair Havens.

Since so much time had passed and the voyage was now dangerous, Paul advised them, "Men, it looks to me as if the voyage is going to end with disaster." But the centurion paid more attention to the pilot than to Paul. Since that harbor was unsuitable to winter in, the majority decided to put out to sea, hoping to reach Phoenix and winter there. When a gentle south wind began to blow, they thought they could carry out their plan. They raised the anchor and sailed close to Crete.

But before long, a hurricane-like wind rushed down from the island. Since the ship was caught in it and could not head into the wind, we gave way to it and were driven along. Because we were tossed around so violently by the storm, they began to throw the cargo overboard. On the third day, they threw the ship's gear overboard. When neither sun nor stars appeared for many days and the violent storm kept pressing down on us, finally all hope that we would be saved was disappearing.

Paul stood up and said, "Men, you should have followed my advice and not set sail from Crete. But now I urge you to keep up your courage, because there will be no loss of life among you. Only the ship will be lost. In fact, last night an angel of God stood beside me and said, 'Do not be afraid, Paul. You must stand before Caesar. And surely God has graciously given you all those who are sailing with you.' However, we must run aground on some island."

When the fourteenth night came, they struck a sandbar and ran the ship aground. The bow stuck fast and would not move, while the stern began to break up from the pounding of the waves.

The soldiers' plan was to kill the prisoners so that no one would swim away and escape. But the centurion wanted to save Paul and kept them from carrying out their plan. He ordered those who could swim to jump overboard first and make their way to land. The rest were to follow on planks and other pieces from the ship. In this way, all of them were brought safely onto land.

Once we were safely on shore, we learned that the island was called Malta. The natives showed us extraordinary kindness. They built a fire and welcomed us all. As Paul gathered a bundle of sticks, a viper came out and fastened itself on his hand. However, Paul shook the snake off into the fire and was not harmed. The people expected him to swell up or suddenly fall down dead. But after they had waited for a long time and saw nothing unusual happen to him, they changed their minds and said he was a god.

In the nearby vicinity was an estate that belonged to a man named Publius, the chief official of the island. He welcomed us and entertained us hospitably as his guests. The father of Publius happened to be sick in bed, suffering from a fever. Paul went to him and healed him.

After three months, we set sail in an Alexandrian ship that had wintered at the island. So we came to Rome.

When we entered Rome, Paul was allowed to live by himself with a soldier who guarded him. Three days later, Paul called together the leaders of the Jews. From morning till evening he explained and testified about the kingdom of God. He also tried to convince them about Jesus, both from the Law of Moses and the Prophets. Some were convinced by what he said, but others continued in their unbelief.

For two whole years Paul stayed in his own rented house and welcomed all who came to visit him. He was preaching the kingdom of God and teaching about the Lord Jesus Christ with all boldness and without anyone stopping him.

Lord God, all health and healing come from you.
Keep us safe from all disaster and spare us from illness.
When we face danger and disease, comfort us
with the knowledge that you are still taking care of us
through all. Give us the wisdom to see all
the opportunities you give us to share your good news,
and the courage to take advantage of them. For nothing
can keep you from spreading the gospel of Jesus. Amen.

MORE EPISTLES

Although the New Testament records no further history of what happened after Paul was placed under house arrest in Rome, from his later letters, or epistles as they are called, we know that he was released, travelled around spreading the gospel, and was eventually arrested again and martyred. Yet God's Word could not be stopped, and we still have the messages God gave his people through Paul, as well as the messages God gave his people through other writers as well, teaching us and encouraging us still today.

229. A LETTER TO THE EPHESIANS (EPHESIANS)

While under house arrest in Rome, Paul writes a letter to the believers in Ephesus, reminding them of the great blessings Christ gives his church.

Paul, an apostle of Christ Jesus,

To the saints who are in Ephesus:

Grace to you and peace from God our Father and the Lord Jesus Christ.

Blessed be the God and Father of our Lord Jesus Christ, who has blessed us in Christ with every spiritual blessing. He chose us in Christ before the foundation of the world. In love he predestined us to be adopted as his sons through Jesus Christ. In him we also have redemption through his blood, the forgiveness of sins. In him, when you believed, you were sealed with the Holy Spirit, the down payment of our inheritance.

This is why I never stop giving thanks for you. I pray that you may know just how great his power is for us who believe. It is as great as the mighty strength God worked in Christ when he raised him from the dead and seated him at his right hand. God also placed all things under his feet and made him head over everything for the church, his body.

You were dead in your trespasses and sins. Formerly, we all carried out the desires of the sinful flesh. Like all the others, we were by nature objects of God's wrath. But God, because he is rich in mercy, made us alive with Christ and seated us with him in the heavenly places. Indeed, it is by grace you have been saved, through faith—and this is not from yourselves, it is the gift of God— not by works, so that no one can boast.

For we are God's workmanship, created in Christ Jesus for good works, which God prepared in advance so that we would walk in them.

Remember that at one time, you Gentiles were separated from Christ. But now in Christ Jesus, you have been brought near by the blood of Christ. So you are no longer foreigners but members of God's household. You have been built on the foundation of the apostles and prophets, with Christ Jesus himself as the Cornerstone. This mystery was not made known to past generations as it has now been revealed. This mystery is that in Christ Jesus the Gentiles are fellow heirs, members of the same body, and people who also share in the promise through the gospel.

Walk in a manner worthy of the calling with which you have been called. Make every effort to maintain the unity of the Spirit in the bond of peace. There is one body and one Spirit. There is one Lord, one faith, one baptism, one God and Father of all. Christ himself gave the apostles, the prophets, the evangelists, the pastors and teachers, for the purpose of training the saints for the work of serving, in order to build up the body of Christ, until we all reach unity in faith and knowledge.

So take off the old self, which is corrupted by its deceitful desires, and put on the new self, which has been created to be like God in righteousness and true holiness. Speak truthfully. Do not let any unwholesome talk come from your mouths. Say only what is beneficial. Get rid of bitterness, anger, quarreling, and slander. Be kind and compassionate to one another, forgiving one other, just as God in Christ has forgiven us. For you were once darkness, but now you are light in the Lord. Walk as children of light.

Wives, submit to your husbands as to the Lord. For the husband is the head of the wife, just as Christ is the head of the church, his body.

Husbands, love your wives, in the same way as Christ loved the church and gave himself up for her to make her holy, by cleansing her with water in connection with the Word so that she would be holy. In the same way, husbands have an obligation to love their wives as their own bodies.

Children, obey your parents in the Lord, for this is right.

Fathers, do not provoke your children to anger, but bring them up in the training and instruction of the Lord.

Finally, put on the full armor of God, so that you can stand against the Devil: the belt of truth, the breastplate of righteousness, the shield of faith, the helmet of salvation, and the sword of the Spirit, which is the word of God.

Grace be with all who have an undying love for our Lord Jesus Christ. Amen.

Lord God, you have raised us from the spiritual death of sin to spiritual life in Christ. Give your people unity in Jesus, and work in us through your Spirit to put on the new self and live as your people. Amen.

230. A LETTER TO THE COLOSSIANS (COLOSSIANS)

While under house arrest in Rome, Paul writes a letter to the believers in Colossae, reminding them that Christ is enough, and so they do not need anything else to be right with God.

Paul, an apostle of Christ Jesus by the will of God,

To the holy and faithful brothers in Christ at Colossae:

Grace to you and peace from God our Father.

We always thank God, the Father of our Lord Jesus Christ, when we pray for you, because we have heard of your faith in Christ Jesus and the love that you have for all the saints.

The Father rescued us from the domain of darkness and transferred us into the kingdom of the Son he loves, in whom we have redemption, the forgiveness of sins.

He is the image of the invisible God, the firstborn over all creation, for all things were created through him and for him. He is also the head of the body, the church. He is the firstborn from the dead. For God was pleased to have all his fullness dwell in him, and through him to reconcile all things to himself by making peace through the blood of his cross.

At one time, you were alienated from God and hostile in your thinking as expressed through your evil deeds. But now Christ reconciled you in his body of flesh through death, in order to present you holy, blameless, and faultless before him.

Therefore, just as you received Christ Jesus as Lord, continue to walk in him, by being rooted and built up in him, and strengthened in the faith just as you were taught, while you overflow in faith with thanksgiving. See to it that no one takes you captive through philosophy and empty deceit, which are in accord with human tradition but not in accord with Christ. For all the fullness of God's being dwells bodily in Christ, and you have been brought to fullness in him. Christ is the head over every ruler and authority. You were buried with Christ in baptism, and in baptism you were also raised with him through the faith worked by the God who raised Christ from the dead.

Even when you were dead in your trespasses, God made you alive with Christ by forgiving us all our trespasses. God erased the record of our debt. He took it away by nailing it to the cross.

Therefore, do not let anyone judge you in regard to food or drink, or in regard to a festival or a New Moon or a Sabbath day. These are a shadow of the things that were coming, but the body belongs to Christ. If you died with Christ to the basic principles of the world, why do you submit to its rules, as if you were still living in the world? While such rules have the appearance of wisdom, they have no value at all in checking the self-indulgence of the sinful flesh.

Because you were raised with Christ, seek the things that are above, where Christ is seated at the right hand of God. Set your mind on things above, not on earthly things. For you died, and your life is hidden with Christ in God. When Christ, who is your life, appears, then you also will appear with him in glory.

So put to death whatever is worldly in you, since you have put off the old self with its practices, and put on the new self, which is continually being renewed in knowledge, according to the image of its Creator. As God's elect, holy and loved, clothe yourselves with compassion. Bear with one another and forgive each other, just as Christ forgave you. And put on love, which ties things together in perfect unity. Let the peace of Christ control your hearts, and be thankful.

Let the word of Christ dwell in you richly, as you teach and admonish one another with all wisdom, singing psalms, hymns, and spiritual songs, with gratitude in your hearts to God. And everything you do, whether in word or deed, do it all in the name of the Lord Jesus, giving thanks to God the Father through him.

Be persistent in prayer, and as you pray, be alert and thankful. Walk in wisdom in the way you act toward those on the outside, making the most of your opportunity. Let your speech always be gracious, seasoned with salt, so that you know how you are to answer each person.

Grace be with you. Amen.

Lord God, our life is hidden with Christ. Set our hearts only on heavenly things. Prevent us from being enslaved to human rules. Assure us that we have everything we need physically and spiritually in your Son. Amen.

231. A LETTER TO PHILEMON (PHILEMON)

While under house arrest in Rome, Paul writes a letter to Philemon, encouraging him to forgive his runaway slave, Onesimus, who now is a fellow believer.

Paul, a prisoner of Christ Jesus,

To Philemon, our dear friend and coworker:

Grace to you and peace from God our Father and the Lord Jesus Christ.

I always thank my God as I remember you in my prayers, because I hear about your love and faith that you have toward the Lord Jesus and for all the saints.

For that reason, even though I have plenty of boldness in Christ to order you to do what is proper, I am appealing to you, instead, on the basis of love. I am appealing to you on behalf of my child Onesimus. I became his father while I was in chains. There was a time when he was useless to you, but now he is useful both to you and to me. I have sent him (who is my very heart) back to you. Welcome him. I wanted to keep him with me, so that he might serve me in your place while I am in chains for the gospel. But I did not want to do anything without your consent, so that your kindness would not be the result of compulsion, but of willingness. Perhaps this is why he was separated from you for a while: so that you would have him back forever, no longer as a slave, but as more than a slave, as a dear brother. He certainly is dear to me, but he is even more of a dear brother to you, both in the flesh and in the Lord.

So if you consider me your partner, welcome him as you would welcome me. And if he has wronged you in any way or owes you anything, charge it to me. Refresh my heart in Christ. Confident of your obedience, I write to you, knowing that you will do even more than I ask.

The grace of the Lord Jesus Christ be with your spirit. Amen.

Lord God, you have forgiven us so many sins
through Christ's sacrifice for us. Move our hearts
to forgive those who sin against us. Amen.

232. A LETTER TO THE PHILIPPIANS (PHILIPPIANS)

Towards the end of his house arrest in Rome, Paul writes to the believers in Philippi, expressing the joy that he has in Jesus regardless of the circumstances.

Paul,

To all the saints in Christ Jesus who are in Philippi:

Grace to you and peace from God our Father and the Lord Jesus Christ.

I thank my God every time I remember you. Every time I pray for you, I always pray with joy because of your fellowship in the gospel. He who began a good work in you will carry it on to completion until the day of Christ Jesus.

I want you to know, brothers, that the things which happened to me actually took place to advance the gospel. It has become clear throughout the whole palace guard that I am in chains because of Christ. And, through my chains, the majority of the brothers have become confident to speak the word of God fearlessly. Christ is being proclaimed, and in this I rejoice.

Yes, and I will continue to rejoice, because Christ will be magnified in my life or death. For me to live is Christ, and to die is gain. Yet which should I prefer? I desire to depart and be with Christ, which is better by far. But it is more necessary for your sake that I remain. And since I am convinced of this, I know that I will remain for your progress and joy in the faith.

Conduct yourselves in a way that is worthy of the gospel of Christ, contending for the gospel, not frightened by the adversaries. This is a sign of your salvation. For it has been graciously granted to you on behalf of Christ, not only to believe in him, but also to suffer for him, having the same kind of struggle I am experiencing.

So make my joy complete by being united. Do nothing out of selfish ambition, but in humility consider one another better than yourselves. Look carefully to the interests of others. Indeed, let this attitude be in you, which was also in Christ Jesus. Though he was by nature God, he did not consider equality with God as a prize to be displayed, but he emptied himself by taking the nature of a servant. When he was born in human likeness, and his appearance was like that of any other man, he humbled himself and became obedient to the point of death—even death on a cross. Therefore God also highly exalted him, so that at the name of Jesus every knee will bow, and every tongue will confess that Jesus Christ is Lord, to the glory of God the Father.

If anyone else thinks that he has grounds for confidence in the flesh, I have more: circumcised on the eighth day, of the people of Israel, a Pharisee, in regard to the law—blameless. But these things I consider a loss because of Christ. For his sake, I have lost all things and consider them rubbish, so that I may gain Christ and be found in him, not having a righteousness of my own, which comes from the law, but the righteousness that comes from God by faith. I do this so that I may know him and the power of his resurrection and the fellowship of his sufferings, being conformed to his death, in the hope that in some way I may arrive at the resurrection from the dead. Not that I have already reached the goal, but forgetting the things that are behind and straining toward the things that are ahead, I press on toward the goal.

Brothers, join together in imitating me. To be sure, many walk as enemies of the cross of Christ. They are thinking only about earthly things. But our citizenship is in heaven. We are eagerly waiting for a Savior from there, the Lord Jesus Christ. He will transform our humble bodies to be like his glorious body. So then, my brothers, my joy and crown, keep standing firm in the Lord.

Rejoice in the Lord always! I will say it again: Rejoice! The Lord is near. Do not worry about anything, but by prayer let your requests be made known to God, and the peace of God, which surpasses all understanding, will guard your hearts and your minds in Christ Jesus. I have learned to be content in any circumstances in which I find myself. Christ strengthens me.

The grace of the Lord Jesus Christ be with your spirit. Amen.

Lord God, you bless us in life and in death through Jesus.
Make us joyful in all circumstances and
strengthen us in Christ. Amen.

233. A LETTER BY PETER (1 PETER)

Peter writes a letter to persecuted Christians, encouraging them with the fact that after suffering with Christ, believers will have glory with Christ.

Peter, an apostle of Jesus Christ,

To the elect, scattered throughout Asia:

Grace and peace be multiplied to you.

Blessed be the God and Father of our Lord Jesus Christ! He gave us a new birth into a living hope through the resurrection of Jesus Christ from the dead, into an inheritance that is undying, undefiled, and unfading. Through faith you are being protected by God's power for the salvation that is ready to be revealed at the end of time. Because of this you rejoice, even though you have been grieved by trials. The prophets studied carefully concerning this salvation, trying to find out what the Spirit was indicating when he predicted the sufferings of Christ and the glories that would follow. They were serving you when they wrote about these things.

Therefore, conduct your pilgrimage in reverence. You know that you were redeemed from your empty way of life not with silver or gold, but with the precious blood of Christ, a lamb without blemish or spot. Through him you are believers in God, who raised him from the dead. You have been born again, not from perishable seed but from imperishable, through the living and enduring word of God. Therefore rid yourselves of all evil. Like newborn babies, crave the pure milk of the word so that by it you may grow up with the result being salvation.

As you come to him, the Living Stone, rejected by men but chosen by God, you also, like living stones, are being built as a spiritual house to be a holy priesthood, in order to bring spiritual sacrifices that are acceptable to God through Jesus Christ, the cornerstone. You are a chosen people, a royal priesthood, a holy nation, the people who are God's own possession.

At one time you were not a people, but now you are the people of God.

If you suffer for doing good, this is favorable with God. Christ also suffered for you, leaving you an example. He did not commit a sin when he suffered. Instead, he entrusted himself to him who judges justly. He carried our sins in his body on the tree so that we would be dead to sins and alive to righteousness. By his wounds you were healed.

Do not be afraid, but regard the Lord Christ as holy, always prepared to give a reason for the hope that is in you with gentleness and respect.

It is better to suffer for doing good than for doing evil. Christ also suffered once for sins in our place, the righteous for the unrighteous, to bring you to God. He was put to death in flesh but was made alive in spirit, in which he also went and made an announcement to the spirits in prison. These spirits disobeyed long ago, when God's patience was waiting while the ark was being built. In this ark a few souls were saved by water. And corresponding to that, baptism now saves you—not the removal of dirt but the guarantee of a good conscience before God through the resurrection of Jesus Christ. He is at the right hand of God, with powers made subject to him.

Therefore, because Christ suffered in flesh, arm yourselves with the same mindset. The one who has suffered in flesh is done with sin. No longer live for human desires but for God's will. The gospel was preached that they might be judged in flesh and live in spirit.

Dear friends, do not be surprised by the fiery trial, as if something strange were happening to you. Instead rejoice whenever you are sharing in the sufferings of Christ, so that you may rejoice when his glory is revealed. If you are insulted in connection with the name of Christ, you are blessed, because the Spirit of glory and of God rests on you. If you suffer for being a Christian, do not be ashamed, but praise God in connection with this name.

Humble yourselves under God's powerful hand so that he may lift you up at the appointed time. Cast all your anxiety on him, because he cares for you. Be alert. The Devil prowls around like a roaring lion, looking for someone to devour. Resist him by being firm in the faith. After you have suffered a little while, the God who called you into his eternal glory in Christ Jesus will himself restore you.

Peace to all of you who are in Christ Jesus.

Lord God, your Son suffered in this world for our sins
and now we suffer as his people. Encourage us through
these sufferings with the eternal glory we will share
through Christ, for you have made us your people. Amen.

234. ANOTHER LETTER BY PETER (2 PETER)

Peter writes a letter to clarify that, even though Jesus has not returned yet, he certainly will return.

Simon Peter, an apostle of Jesus Christ,

To those who have faith in the righteousness of our God and Savior, Jesus Christ:

Grace and peace be multiplied to you in the knowledge of God and of Jesus our Lord.

His divine power has given us everything we need for life and godliness through the knowledge of him who called us by his own glory and excellence. For this very reason, add to your faith moral excellence, knowledge, self-control, patient endurance, godliness, brotherly affection, and love. Be eager to make your calling and election sure for yourselves. For if you do these things, you will never stumble. In fact, in this way you will be richly supplied with an entrance into the eternal kingdom of our Lord and Savior Jesus Christ.

We were not following cunningly devised fables when we made known to you the powerful appearance of our Lord Jesus Christ. We were eyewitnesses of his majesty. For he received honor and glory from God the Father, when the voice came, saying, "This is my Son, whom I love; with him I am well pleased."

We also have the completely reliable prophetic word. You do well to pay attention to it, as to a lamp shining in a dark place, until the day dawns and the Morning Star rises in your hearts. No prophecy of Scripture comes about from someone's own interpretation. In fact, no prophecy ever came by the will of man, but men spoke from God as they were being carried along by the Holy Spirit.

There will be false teachers among you. They will secretly bring in destructive heresies, even denying the Master who bought them, bringing swift destruction on themselves. God did not spare angels when they sinned but handed them over to chains of darkness by casting them into hell. God did not spare the ancient world, but preserved Noah, when he brought a flood. God condemned Sodom and Gomorrah to destruction, turning them into ashes. He rescued righteous Lot, who was tormented in his righteous soul by the lawless deeds he saw. Then the Lord knows how to deliver the godly out of temptation and to keep the unrighteous under guard until the day of judgment, in order to punish them.

In the last days scoffers will come with their mocking, following their own lusts. They will say, "Where is this promised coming of his? For all things continue as they have from the beginning." What they are intentionally forgetting is that the heavens came into existence long ago by the word of God, and the former world perished when it was flooded with water. And now, by that same word, the heavens and earth have been stored up for fire, kept until the day of judgment. Do not forget: For the Lord, one day is like a thousand years, and a thousand years are like one day. The Lord is not slow to do what he promised. Instead, he is patient for your sakes, not wanting anyone to perish, but all to come to repentance.

The day of the Lord will come like a thief. The heavens will pass away with a roar, the elements will be dissolved as they burn with great heat, and the earth and what was done on it will be burned up. Therefore, since all these things will be destroyed, what kind of people ought you to be, living in holiness and godliness, as you look forward to and hasten the coming of the day of God? We look forward to new heavens and a new earth, in which righteousness dwells.

Dear friends, since you already know these things, be on your guard so that you do not fall from your own firm position by being led astray through the error of the wicked. Instead grow in the grace and knowledge of our Lord and Savior Jesus Christ. To him be the glory, both now and forever. Amen.

Lord God, we long for your Son's return.
Through your Word keep us prepared for his coming.
May that Word, always true and reliable,
be our guide throughout our life. Amen.

235. A LETTER TO TIMOTHY (1 TIMOTHY)

Now released from house arrest, Paul writes a letter to his younger colleague Timothy, giving him instruction for carrying out his ministry.

Paul, an apostle of Christ Jesus,

To Timothy, my true child in the faith:

Grace, mercy, and peace from God our Father and Christ Jesus our Lord.

Remain in Ephesus so that you may command certain men not to teach any different doctrines. Some have turned aside into meaningless talk. They want to be teachers of the law, although they do not comprehend what they are saying. The law is good as long as one uses it correctly, keeping in mind that the law is not laid down for a righteous person, but for lawless people.

I give thanks to Christ Jesus that he appointing me into his ministry, even though formerly I was a blasphemer. But I was shown mercy. This saying is trustworthy: "Christ Jesus came into the world to save sinners," of whom I am the worst. But I was shown mercy that in me, the worst sinner, Christ Jesus might demonstrate his unlimited patience as an example for those who are going to believe in him, resulting in eternal life.

I urge that prayers be made for all people. This is good and pleasing in the sight of God our Savior, who wants all people to be saved and to come to the knowledge of the truth. For there is one God and one mediator between God and mankind, the man Christ Jesus, who gave himself as a ransom for all.

I want the men in every place to pray without anger or argument. Likewise, I also want women to adorn themselves with modesty and self-control. A woman should learn in a quiet manner with full submission. And I do not permit a woman to teach or to have authority over a man. Instead, she is to continue in a quiet manner.

If anyone aspires to become an overseer, he desires a noble task. It is necessary, then, for the overseer to be above reproach.

I wanted you to know how it is necessary to behave in God's household, which is the church of the living God. He was revealed in flesh, was justified in spirit, was seen by messengers, was preached among the nations, was believed on in the world, was taken up in glory.

If you point out these things to the brothers, you will be a good servant of Christ Jesus, nourished by the words of the faith and the good doctrine. Pay no attention to worldly and absurd myths, but train yourself for godliness. For bodily training is beneficial to an extent, but godliness is beneficial in all things, because it holds promise both for life now and for the life to come. For this reason we work hard and are insulted. We have put our hope in the living God, who is the Savior of all people, especially of those who believe.

Insist on these things and continue teaching them. Let no one look down on your youth. Instead, be an example for the believers. Devote yourself to the reading of Scripture, to encouraging, and to teaching. Pay close attention to yourself and to the doctrine. Persevere in them, because by doing this you will save both yourself and those who listen to you.

If anyone teaches different doctrines and does not devote himself to the sound words of our Lord Jesus Christ and to godly teaching, he is puffed up with conceit and understands nothing. Separate yourselves from such people.

Godliness with contentment is great gain. For we brought nothing into the world, and we certainly cannot take anything out. But if we have food and clothing, we will be satisfied. Those who want to get rich fall into temptation and a trap and desires which plunge them into complete destruction. For the love of money is a root of all sorts of evils. By striving for money, some have wandered away from the faith.

But you, man of God, flee from these things and pursue righteousness. Fight the good fight of faith. Take hold of eternal life. Keep this command until the appearing of our Lord Jesus Christ.

Instruct those who are rich in this present age not to put their hope in the uncertainty of riches, but rather in God, who richly supplies us with all things. Instruct them to do good, to be rich in good works, to be generous and willing to share.

Timothy, guard what has been entrusted to you. Grace be with you. Amen.

Lord God, your mercy is so great that it even forgives sinners like us. We thank you for pastors who share your message of forgiveness with us. Equip them to carry out their ministry, and preserve the Word you have given us. Amen.

236. A LETTER TO TITUS (TITUS)

Paul writes a letter to another younger colleague in the ministry, Titus.

Paul, a servant of God and an apostle of Jesus Christ,

To Titus, my true child in our common faith:

Grace and peace from God our Father and Christ Jesus our Savior.

The reason I left you in Crete was so that you would set in order the things that were left unfinished and appoint elders in every city, as I directed you. Such a man is to be blameless. He must cling to the trustworthy message as it has been taught, so that he will be able both to encourage people by the sound teaching and to correct those who oppose him.

For there are many who are rebellious, whose words are empty, and who deceive, especially those of the circumcision party. The mouths of these people must be stopped, because they are ruining whole households by teaching what they should not teach, for the sake of dishonest gain. Correct them sharply so that they may be sound in the faith.

Speak what is appropriate for sound doctrine. Encourage older men to be temperate, worthy of respect, self-controlled, and sound in faith, love, and patient endurance. Encourage older women to be reverent in their behavior, not slanderers, not enslaved to much wine, but teachers of what is good, so that they can train the younger women. Encourage younger men to be self-controlled. Encourage slaves to submit to their masters in everything, to demonstrate complete trustworthiness, so that they may show the teaching of God our Savior to be attractive in every way.

For the grace of God has appeared, bringing salvation to all people. It trains us to reject ungodliness and worldly lusts and to live self-controlled, upright, and godly lives in this present age, while we wait for the blessed hope, that is, the glorious appearance of our great God and Savior, Jesus Christ. He gave himself for us to redeem us from all lawlessness and to purify for himself a people who are his own chosen people, eager to do good works. Keep telling people these things.

Remind them to be subject to rulers and authorities, to obey, to be ready to do any good work, to speak evil of no one, to be peaceable, to be gentle, and to display every courtesy toward all people.

For at one time we ourselves were also enslaved by many kinds of evil desires and pleasures. But when the kindness and love of God our Savior toward mankind appeared, he saved us—not by righteous works that we did ourselves, but because of his mercy. He saved us through the washing of rebirth and the renewal by the Holy Spirit, whom he poured out on us abundantly through Jesus Christ our Savior, so that, having been justified by his grace, we might become heirs in keeping with the hope of eternal life.

I want you to insist on these things, so that those who believe in God are intent on keeping busy with good works. Avoid foolish controversies, because these are useless. Reject a divisive person after a first and second warning. He condemns himself.

Grace be with you all. Amen.

Lord God, your grace has come to us in the coming
of our Savior Jesus, and it has been poured out
on us in baptism. Train us to reject all worldliness
and to live lives of self-control. Amen.

237. ANOTHER LETTER TO TIMOTHY (2 TIMOTHY)

Paul, now imprisoned again in Rome and soon to be executed for his service to Christ, writes his final letter, again to his younger colleague Timothy.

Paul, an apostle of Christ Jesus,

To Timothy, my child, whom I love:

Grace, mercy, and peace from God the Father and Christ Jesus our Lord.

I thank God as I constantly remember you in my prayers. I remember your sincere faith, which first lived in your grandmother Lois and your mother Eunice, and also lives in you.

Fan into flame the gift of God which is in you. Do not be ashamed of the testimony about our Lord or of me his prisoner. Instead, join with me in suffering for the gospel while relying on the power of God. He saved us, not because of our works, but because of his own purpose and grace, revealed through the appearance of our Savior Christ Jesus, who abolished death and brought life and immortality to light through the gospel. This gospel is why I am suffering these things. But I am not ashamed, because I know the one in whom I have believed, and he is able to guard what I have entrusted to him until that day.

Hold fast to the pattern of sound words that you heard from me. Entrust the things you heard from me to faithful men who will also be able to teach others.

Remember Jesus Christ, risen from the dead, a descendant of David, in accordance with my gospel, for which I am chained like a criminal. But the word of God is not chained. For this reason I endure all things for the sake of the elect, so that they also may obtain the salvation that is in Christ Jesus, along with eternal glory. This saying is trustworthy: If we have died with him, we will also live with him. If we endure, we will also reign with him. If we deny him, he will also deny us. If we are faithless, he remains faithful, because he cannot deny himself.

Remind people of these things, as you charge them not to fight about words, which does no good and only ruins those who listen. Present yourself to God as one who is approved, correctly handling the word of truth.

But know this: In the last days there will be terrible times. For people will be lovers of themselves, lovers of money, haters of what is good, lovers of pleasure rather than lovers of God, holding to an outward form of godliness but denying its power. Turn away from such people. They will not get very far, because their foolishness will be quite clear to everyone.

But you have faithfully followed my teaching, my way of life, my faith, my steadfast endurance, my persecutions—the Lord rescued me from all of them. Everyone who wants to live a godly life in Christ Jesus will be persecuted, while evil people will go from bad to worse, deceiving and being deceived. Continue in the things you have learned and about which you have become convinced. You know from whom you learned it. From infancy you have known the Holy Scriptures, which are able to make you wise for salvation through faith in Christ Jesus. All Scripture is God breathed and is useful for teaching, for rebuking, for correcting, and for training in righteousness, so that the man of God may be complete, well equipped for every good work.

I solemnly charge you in the presence of God and Christ Jesus: Preach the word, whether it is convenient or not. Correct, rebuke, and encourage. For there will come a time when people will not put up with sound doctrine. Instead, because they have itching ears, they will accumulate for themselves teachers in line with their own desires. As for you, keep a clear head in every situation. Bear hardship. Do the work of an evangelist. Fulfill your ministry.

You see, I am already being poured out like a drink offering, and the time of my departure has come. I have fought the good fight; I have finished the race; I have kept the faith. From now on, there is reserved for me the crown of righteousness. The Lord, the righteous Judge, will give it to me on that day, and not only to me but also to everyone who loved his appearing. The Lord will rescue me from every evil work and will bring me safely into his heavenly kingdom. To him be the glory forever and ever. Amen.

The Lord be with your spirit. Grace be with you. Amen.

Lord God, you have taught us your Word. Equip us
through that same Word for whatever we face in life,
and give us one day the crown of righteousness you have
reserved for us through Jesus' life and death for us. Amen.

238. A LETTER TO THE HEBREWS, PART 1 (HEBREWS 1-8)

Writing through an unnamed author, God shows believers that Jesus is the fulfillment of the Old Testament, so there is no need to go back to Old Testament ways.

In the past, God spoke by the prophets. In these last days, he has spoken by his Son. The Son is the exact imprint of the divine nature, superior to the angels. For to which of the angels did God ever say: "You are my Son"?

God did not place the coming world under the control of angels, but has testified: "What is man? You made him lower than the angels for a little while. You crowned him with glory. You put everything in subjection under his feet." At the present time, we do not yet see everything in subjection to him. But we look to Jesus, who was made lower than the angels for a little while, now crowned with glory.

Since the children share flesh and blood, he also shared flesh and blood, so that through death he could destroy the one who had the power of death (that is, the Devil) and free those held in slavery by death. He was not helping angels but Abraham's offspring. For this reason, he had to become like his brothers in every way, in order that he could pay for the sins of the people.

Therefore, focus your attention on Jesus. Jesus is worthy of greater glory than Moses. Moses was faithful as a servant within God's house. But Christ is faithful as a Son over God's house. We are his house, if we hold on firmly.

Therefore, as the Holy Spirit says, "Do not harden your hearts, as your fathers tested and tried me, and so I swore in my wrath, 'They will never enter my rest.'" There remains a Sabbath rest for the people of God. Therefore, let us make every effort to enter that rest, so that no one will fall into the same pattern of disobedience.

Therefore, since we have a great high priest who has gone through the heavens, namely, Jesus the Son of God, let us hold on to our confession. We do not have a high priest who is unable to sympathize with our weaknesses, but one who has been tempted in every way, just as we are, yet without sin. So let us approach the throne of grace with confidence.

Every high priest is chosen from the people to represent the people to God. No one takes this honor on himself, but he is called by God. In the same way, Christ did not take the glory of becoming a high priest on himself, but God said to him, "You are a priest forever, like Melchizedek."

In the days of his flesh, he offered prayers and was heard. After he was brought to his goal, he became the source of eternal salvation for everyone who obeys him, because he was designated by God as a high priest. We have this hope as an anchor for the soul, sure and firm. It goes behind the inner curtain, where Jesus entered ahead of us on our behalf, because he became a high priest forever like Melchizedek.

This Melchizedek, the one who met Abraham as he was returning from the defeat of the kings, is without genealogy, without beginning of days or end of life, and, resembling the Son of God, he remains a priest forever. Our Lord, like Melchizedek, became a priest, not on the basis of physical descent, but on the basis of an endless life. There were many priests, because death prevented them from continuing in office. But because this one endures forever, he has a permanent priesthood. So he is able to save forever those who come to God through him, because he always lives to plead on their behalf. Unlike the other high priests, he does not need to offer sacrifices on a daily basis, first for his own sins and then for the sins of the people. He sacrificed for sins once and for all when he offered himself.

We have the kind of high priest who has taken his seat at the right hand of the throne of the Majesty in heaven. He is the minister in the Holy Place, the true sanctuary—a ministry that is as much superior as the covenant that he mediates is better. If that first covenant were without fault, there would have been no reason to look for a second. But because God found fault with the people, he said, "I will make a new covenant with Israel. It will not be like the covenant I made with their forefathers. For I will not remember their sins any longer."

Lord God, your Son Jesus became a human being just like us to take our place. He is our priest, whose sacrifice has restored our relationship with you. May we approach you boldly and confidently as your forgiven people. Amen.

239. A LETTER TO THE HEBREWS, PART 2 (HEBREWS 8-13)

The anonymous letter continues, encouraging believers to continue to trust Jesus and not leave him for Old Testament ways.

Only the high priest would enter the second section of the tent, once each year, and not without blood, which he offered for himself and for the sins the people. This tent is a picture pointing to the present time. When Christ appeared as the high priest of the good things that were coming, he entered once into the Most Holy Place and obtained eternal redemption, not by the blood of goats, but by his own blood. Now if the blood of goats and bulls sanctifies, how much more will the blood of Christ cleanse our consciences? Without the shedding of blood, there is no forgiveness. But Christ was offered only once to take away the sins of many, and he will appear a second time to bring salvation.

The law is only a shadow of the good things to come, not the actual things. It will never be able to make perfect those who offer sacrifices. If it could, would they not have stopped bringing sacrifices? Instead, these sacrifices reminded them of their sins year after year. We have been sanctified once and for all through the sacrifice of Jesus Christ.

We have confidence to enter the Most Holy Place through the blood of Jesus. So let us hold on firmly to the confession of our hope. Let us also consider how to spur each other on to love. Let us not neglect meeting together, as some have the habit of doing. Rather, let us encourage each other, and all the more as you see the Day approaching.

For if we deliberately keep on sinning after we have received the full knowledge of the truth, there no longer remains any sacrifice for sins. Instead, there is a certain fearful expectation of judgment. You need patient endurance so that you may receive what was promised. For in just a little while "the one who is coming will come, and my righteous one will live by faith, but if he shrinks back, my soul takes no pleasure in him." Now we are not those who shrink back, but those who have faith.

Faith is being sure about what we hope for, being convinced about things we do not see. By this faith the ancients were commended. By faith we know the universe was created by God's word. By faith Abel offered a better sacrifice than Cain. By faith Enoch was taken up, commended as one who "pleased God." (Without faith it is impossible to please God.) By faith Noah built an ark. By faith Abraham obeyed when called to go to a place that he was going to receive as an inheritance, without knowing where he was going. By faith Moses chose to be mistreated with God's people rather than enjoy sin, because he was looking ahead to his reward. By faith Rahab did not perish with the unbelievers. All of these were commended by faith, yet they did not receive what was promised, because God had planned that they would not reach the goal apart from us.

Therefore, since we are surrounded by such a great cloud of witnesses, let us get rid of the sin that so easily ensnares us. Let us run with endurance the race laid out for us. Let us keep our eyes fixed on Jesus, the author of our faith and the one who brings it to its goal. In view of the joy set before him, he endured the cross, and has taken his seat at the right hand of God's throne. Carefully consider him who endured such hostility, so that you do not grow weary and lose heart.

Endure suffering as discipline. God is dealing with you as sons. No discipline seems pleasant when it is happening, yet later it yields a harvest of righteousness. Therefore strengthen your weak hands and feeble knees.

Remember your leaders, who spoke the word of God to you. Consider the outcome of their way of life and imitate their faith. Jesus Christ is the same yesterday and today and forever.

Now may the God of peace—who brought back from the dead our Lord Jesus, that great Shepherd of the sheep, in connection with his blood, which established the eternal testament—equip you with every good thing to do his will, as he works in us what is pleasing in his sight through Jesus Christ. To him be glory forever and ever. Amen.

Grace be with you all. Amen.

Lord God, through faith in your Son, who died for us,
all our sins are forgiven. Help us to persevere in our faith,
always looking ahead to the goal ahead of us,
the eternal life we have in him. Amen.

240. A LETTER BY JUDE (JUDE)

Jude, the half-brother of Jesus, writes a letter warning God's people against following false teachers.

Jude, a servant of Jesus Christ,

To those who are called, who are loved in God the Father and kept for Jesus Christ:

Mercy, peace, and love be multiplied to you.

Dear friends, although I was very eager to write to you concerning the salvation we share, I felt it was necessary for me to urge you to continue to contend for the faith. For certain individuals slipped in secretly, ungodly people who turn the grace of our God into a license for sin and deny our only Lord, Jesus Christ.

I want to remind you that after the Lord rescued his people out of the land of Egypt, he later destroyed those who did not believe. And the angels who left their place—God has kept them in everlasting chains under darkness for judgment. Like Sodom and Gomorrah and the cities around them, who indulged in extreme sexual immorality and pursued homosexual perversion, they serve as an example of those who are going to suffer the punishment of eternal fire. In the very same way, these dreamers are defiling the flesh, despising authority, and blaspheming glorious ones. These people do not understand what they are blaspheming. Woe to them! They have gone the way of Cain. They have abandoned themselves for hire to the error of Balaam. They perished in Korah's rebellion.

These people are filthy stains on your feasts. They are clouds without rain. They are trees without fruit. They are wild waves of the sea piling up the foam of their own shame. They are wandering stars for whom the gloom of darkness has been reserved for eternity. The Lord is going to come with tens of thousands of his holy ones, to execute judgment against all of them and to convict every soul concerning all their ungodly deeds and words that ungodly sinners spoke against him. But remember the words that were spoken earlier by the apostles. They said to you, "In the last time there will be scoffers who follow their own ungodly lusts." These are the people who cause divisions. They are worldly because they do not have the Spirit.

But you, dear friends, continue to build yourselves up in your most holy faith as you keep praying in the Holy Spirit. Keep yourselves in God's love as you continue to wait for the mercy of our Lord Jesus Christ, which results in eternal life. Show mercy to those who are wavering. Save others by snatching them out of the fire. Show mercy to still others with fear, hating even the clothing that is stained by the flesh.

Now to him who is able to keep you from stumbling and to present you faultless in the presence of his glory with great joy, to the only God, our Savior, be glory, majesty, power, and authority through Jesus Christ our Lord, before all time, now, and to all eternity. Amen.

Lord God, defend your church from all false teachers.
Keep us, your people, strong in the truth and in our trust
in our Savior Jesus. Amen.

241. A LETTER BY JOHN (1 JOHN)

The Apostle John teaches the importance of truth and love—the gospel truth of our Savior Jesus, and God's love to us which we reflect in our love for each other.

That which was from the beginning, which we have heard, which we have seen with our eyes, which our hands have touched, we proclaim to you: eternal life. We are proclaiming what we have seen and heard also to you, so that you may have fellowship with us. Our fellowship is with the Father and his Son Jesus Christ.

God is light. In him there is no darkness at all. If we say we have fellowship with him but still walk in darkness, we are lying. But if we walk in the light, we have fellowship with one another, and the blood of Jesus Christ, his Son, cleanses us from all sin. If we say we have no sin, we deceive ourselves, and the truth is not in us. If we confess our sins, he is faithful and just to forgive us our sins and cleanse us from all unrighteousness.

My children, I write these things to you so that you will not sin. If anyone does sin, we have an Advocate before the Father: Jesus Christ, the Righteous One. He is the atoning sacrifice for our sins, and not only for ours but also for the whole world.

We know that we have known him if we keep his commands. The one who says, "I know him," but does not keep his commands is a liar, and the truth is not in him. Everyone who denies the Son does not have the Father. But the one who confesses the Son has the Father as well.

See the kind of love the Father has given us that we should be called children of God. We are children of God now, but what we will be has not yet been revealed. We know that when he is revealed we will be like him, and we will see him as he really is.

Everyone who commits sin commits lawlessness. Sin is lawlessness. He appeared to take away our sins. In him there is no sin. Anyone who remains in him does not sin. The one who continues to sin is of the Devil. The Son of God appeared to destroy the works of the Devil.

Love one another. Everyone who hates his brother is a murderer, and no murderer has eternal life. This is how we have come to know love: Jesus laid down his life for us. Let us love not only with word, but also in action.

This is how we set our hearts at rest: If our hearts condemn us, God is greater than our hearts, and he knows everything. If our hearts do not condemn us, we have confidence before God, because we believe in his Son, Jesus Christ, and love one another just as he commanded us. We know that he remains in us from the Spirit he has given to us. Do not believe every spirit, but test the spirits to see if they are from God, for many false prophets have gone out into the world.

Let us love one another, because God is love. This is love: not that we have loved God, but that he loved us and sent his Son to be the atoning sacrifice for our sins. If God loved us so much, we also should love one another. Whoever remains in love remains in God and God in him. In this way his love has been brought to its goal among us, so that we may have confidence on the day of judgment, because in this world we are just like Jesus. Love drives out fear, because fear has to do with punishment.

We love because he first loved us. If anyone says, "I love God," but hates his brother, he is a liar. This is love for God: that we keep his commands. And his commands are not burdensome. This is the victory that has overcome the world: our faith. God has given us eternal life in his Son.

Anyone who has been born of God does not go on sinning. But the one who was born of God protects him, and the Evil One cannot take hold of him. The Son of God has come and has given us understanding so that we may know Jesus Christ, the true God and eternal life.

Lord God, you have shown us love in giving your Son to be our Savior. May we keep that truth pure and show that love to others. Amen.

242. ANOTHER LETTER BY JOHN (2 JOHN)

The Apostle John writes to a church and her members, rejoicing that they have remained in love and truth, and warning them to stay away from false teachers.

The Elder,

To the chosen lady and her children, whom I love in the truth:

Grace, mercy, and peace will be with us from God the Father and from Jesus Christ, the Father's Son, in truth and love.

I was overjoyed to find out that some of your children are walking in the truth, in keeping with the command we received from the Father. And now, let us love one another. And this is love: that we walk according to his commands. This is the command: Just as you have heard from the beginning, keep on walking in it.

Many deceivers who do not confess Jesus Christ as coming in the flesh have gone out into the world. Such a person is a deceiver and an antichrist. Watch yourselves so that you do not lose what we have labored for but receive a full reward.

Anyone who does not remain in the teaching of Christ does not have God. The one who remains in this teaching has both the Father and the Son. If someone comes to you and does not bring this teaching, do not receive him into your house. Do not even wish him well. For the one who wishes him well shares in his wicked works.

I hope to be with you so that our joy may be made complete.

Lord God, we thank you for all your believers that you preserve in their faith by your Word. Protect us from all false teaching and by your love for us continue to work in us that we may love others. Amen.

243. A THIRD LETTER BY JOHN (3 JOHN)

The Apostle John writes a letter to Gaius, encouraging him to partner with those who teach the truth.

The Elder,

To dear Gaius, whom I love in the truth:

Dear friend, I pray that you are doing well in every way. I was overjoyed when brothers came and testified to your truthfulness because you are walking in the truth. I have no greater joy than when I hear that my children are walking in the truth.

You are being faithful in what you are doing for the brothers even though they are strangers. You will do well to send them off in a manner worthy of God. They went out for the sake of the Name, accepting nothing from the Gentiles. We have an obligation to support such men, so that we may be coworkers for the truth.

Do not imitate what is evil, but what is good. The one who does what is good is from God. The one who does what is evil has not seen God.

I hope to see you soon. Peace to you.

Lord God, we thank you for the fellow believers
with whom you have united us together in your truth.
Bless our church and the work we do together
to proclaim your truth and show your love. Amen.

PART 6

JOHN'S VISIONS (REVELATION)

Last of all the books of the New Testament is the book of Revelation, where Jesus gives the Apostle John a series of visions which depict the present age, Judgment Day, and the age to come. Because visions use a lot of symbolic imagery to depict truth, sometimes the details of the visions can be rather difficult to interpret, and yet the overall picture of the images is clear: In this world God's people suffer for Christ's name, but they remain faithful to Jesus, because in the end he will destroy his people's enemies and bring all his believing people into eternal life. Simply put, the message is that Jesus will win.

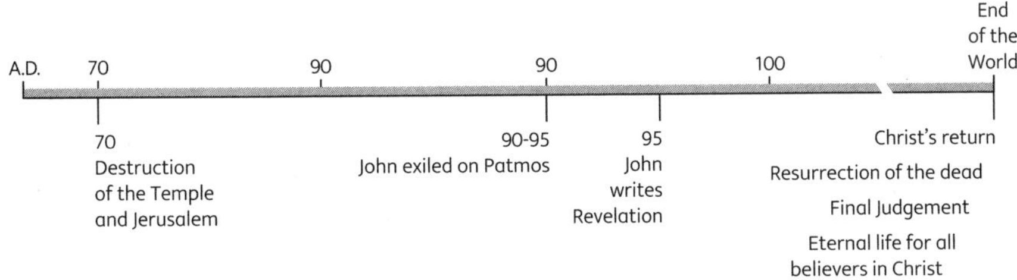

244. THE FIRST VISION: THE SEVEN LETTERS (REVELATION 1-3)

Exiled to the island of Patmos, John is given seven visions depicting the present and the future. This first vision has individual messages of comfort and warning for seven churches.

The revelation that Christ expressed by means of symbols to his servant John.

John,

To the seven churches in the province of Asia:

Grace to you and peace from him who is, who was, and who is coming, and from the seven spirits before his throne, and from Jesus Christ, the firstborn from the dead and the ruler of the kings of the earth.

I, John, was on the island called Patmos because of the word of God. I saw seven gold lampstands, and among the lampstands was one like a son of man. He was clothed with a robe that reached to his feet and a gold sash. His head and hair were white like snow. His eyes were like blazing flames. His voice was like the roar of many waters. He held seven stars in his right hand. A sharp two-edged sword was coming out of his mouth. His face was shining as the sun.

When I saw him, I fell at his feet like a dead man. He placed his hand on me and said, "Do not be afraid. I am the First and the Last—the Living One. I was dead and, see, I am alive forever and ever! I also hold the keys of death and hell. So write what you have seen, both those things that are and those that will take place after this. The seven stars are the messengers of the seven churches, and the seven lampstands are the seven churches."

To Ephesus write:

I know your patient endurance. You have endured hardships on account of my name. But you have forsaken your first love. Repent and do the works you did at first. Otherwise I will remove your lampstand. The one who is victorious will eat from the tree of life.

To Smyrna write:

I know your suffering and your poverty—but you are rich. Do not fear anything that you are about to suffer. Look, the Devil is about to throw some of you into prison and you will suffer. Be faithful until death, and I will give you the crown of life. He who is victorious will not be hurt at all by the second death.

To Pergamum write:

I know you live where the throne of Satan is. And I know that you hold fast to my name. But you have some people there who hold to the teaching of Balaam. Therefore, repent! If not, I will come and fight against them with the sword of my mouth. To the one who is victorious I will give some of the hidden manna.

To Thyatira write:

I know your works. You are doing more now than you did at first. But you allow that woman Jezebel to deceive my servants. Look, I am going to throw her and those with her into great suffering, if they do not repent of her works. To the rest of you, who do not hold to this teaching, hold fast to what you have until I come. To the one who is victorious I will give the morning star.

To Sardis write:

I know your works. You have a reputation for being alive, but you are dead. Repent! If you do not wake up, I will come like a thief. Yet you have a few people who have not defiled their clothes. The one who is victorious will be clothed in white. I certainly will not erase his name from the Book of Life.

To Philadelphia write:

I know your works. Look, I have set before you an open door, which no one can shut. I know that you have little strength, and yet you have kept my word and have not denied my name. I am coming soon. Hold on to what you have so that no one takes your crown. The one who is victorious I will make a pillar in the temple of my God.

To Laodicea write:

You are neither cold nor hot. So, because you are lukewarm, I am about to spit you out. You say, "I am rich. I need nothing." But you do not know that you are poor. So repent. Look, I stand at the door knocking. If anyone hears my voice and opens the door, I will go in with him and dine with him. To the one who is victorious I will give the right to sit with me on my throne.

Lord God, we thank you that your Son is present
among your people, upholding those who share
with us your Word. Keep us faithful until death
so that we may receive the crown of life
he has won for us. Amen.

245. THE SECOND VISION: THE SEVEN SEALS (REVELATION 4-7)

The second vision shows us the Lamb of God being worshipped by a multitude and opening up the seals which show the signs of the end and the end itself.

A throne was in heaven, and the one sitting there looked like jasper and ruby. Around the throne were twenty-four elders dressed in white garments, with gold crowns on their heads. Near the throne were four living creatures, full of eyes. The first living creature was like a lion, the second like an ox, the third like a man, and the fourth like a flying eagle. Each one of the four living creatures had six wings, and the wings were full of eyes. Day and night they keep saying: "Holy, holy, holy, Lord God Almighty."

I saw a scroll in the right hand of him who sat on the throne, sealed with seven seals. No one was able to open the scroll. I began to weep bitterly because no one was worthy to open the scroll. Then one of the elders said to me, "Look! The Lion from the tribe of Judah, the Root of David, has triumphed and is able to open the scroll."

I saw a Lamb standing near the throne. The Lamb seemed to have been slain. He had seven horns and seven eyes (these are the seven spirits of God). The Lamb came and took the scroll. The four living creatures and the twenty-four elders sang a new song: "You are worthy to take the scroll and to open its seals, because you were slain, and you bought us for God with your blood."

I heard many angels saying: "Worthy is the Lamb who was slain to receive power and riches and wisdom and strength and honor and glory and blessing."

When the Lamb opened the first of the seven seals, there was a white horse, and its rider held a bow. He went out conquering.

When the Lamb opened the second seal, another horse, a fiery red one, went out. Its rider was given power to take peace away from the earth.

When the Lamb opened the third seal, there was a black horse. Its rider had a scale in his hand. And I heard a voice say, "A quart of wheat for a denarius."

When he opened the fourth seal, there was a pale green horse. Its rider was named Death, and the Grave followed closely behind him. They were given power to kill people.

When the Lamb opened the fifth seal, the souls of those who had been slaughtered because of the word of God called out, "Lord, how long until you judge and exact justice for our blood?" A white robe was given to each one of them. And they were told to rest a little longer until their number would be complete.

When the Lamb opened the sixth seal, there was a great earthquake. The sun became black. The moon became like blood. The stars fell to the earth. The sky was removed like a scroll being rolled up. Every mountain and island was moved from its place. The kings of the earth hid in caves and kept saying to the mountains, "Hide us from the wrath of the Lamb."

After this I saw four angels holding back the four winds so that the wind could not blow on the earth.

And I saw another angel who had the seal of the living God. He called out to the four angels who were given power to harm the earth, "Do not harm the earth until we have placed a seal on the foreheads of God's servants." And I heard the number of those sealed: 144,000 from all the tribes of Israel.

After these things there was a great multitude that no one could count, from every nation, tribe, people, and language, clothed with white robes. They said: "Salvation comes from our God, who sits on the throne, and from the Lamb."

One of the elders said, "These people dressed in white robes are the ones who are coming out of the great tribulation. They have washed their robes and made them white in the blood of the Lamb. Because of this they are in front of the throne of God, and they serve him day and night in his temple. He who sits on the throne will spread his tent over them. They will never be hungry or thirsty ever again. The sun will never beat upon them, for the Lamb will be their shepherd. He will lead them to springs of living water. And God will wipe away every tear from their eyes."

Lord God, you alone are holy, and your Son is our only Savior. We long for your Son's coming that we may serve and worship him forever in perfect holiness. Amen.

246. THE THIRD VISION: THE SEVEN TRUMPETS (REVELATION 8-11)

The third vision shows us the damage done by false teachers and false teachings leading up until the end.

When the Lamb opened the seventh seal, there was silence in heaven for about half an hour. And I saw the seven angels who stand before God, and seven trumpets were given to them.

The seven angels, who had the seven trumpets, prepared to sound them. The first sounded his trumpet, and hail and fire mixed with blood were thrown on the earth. A third of the earth was burned up.

Then the second angel sounded his trumpet, and something like a great mountain burning with fire was thrown into the sea. A third of the sea became blood.

Then the third angel sounded his trumpet, and a huge star fell from the sky. It fell on a third of the rivers and on the springs of water. The name of the star was Wormwood, and a third of the waters became wormwood.

Then the fourth angel sounded his trumpet, and a third of the sun was struck, as well as a third of the moon, and a third of the stars, so that a third of them became dark.

Then the fifth angel sounded his trumpet, and I saw a star that had fallen out of heaven to the earth, and the key to the pit of the abyss was given to him. He opened the pit of the abyss, and out came locusts. They were told to harm only those people who do not have God's seal on their foreheads. In those days people will seek death but will certainly not find it. They will long to die, but death will escape them.

The locusts looked like horses ready for battle. Their faces looked like human faces. They had hair that looked like women's hair, and their teeth were like lions' teeth. They had breastplates that appeared to be made of iron. They had tails with stingers like those of scorpions. They have the angel of the abyss over them as their king.

Then the sixth angel sounded his trumpet, and I heard a voice speak from the altar, "Release the four angels." And the four angels who had been prepared for this hour, day, month, and year were let loose so that they could kill a third of the people. The number of soldiers on horseback was two hundred million. They had breastplates that were fiery red, hyacinth-blue, and sulfur-yellow. The heads of the horses were like the heads of lions, and out of their mouths came fire and smoke and sulfur. As a result of these three plagues, a third of mankind was killed.

Then I saw another powerful angel coming down out of heaven. He was clothed with a cloud and he had in his hand a little scroll, which had been opened. And when he cried out, the seven thunders spoke using their own voices. When the seven thunders had spoken, I was about to write. But I heard a voice from heaven, saying, "Seal up the things the seven thunders said, and do not write them down."

The voice that I heard from heaven also spoke to me again, saying, "Go, take the scroll and eat it. It will make your stomach bitter, but in your mouth it will be as sweet as honey." I took the little scroll out of the angel's hand and ate it. It was as sweet as honey in my mouth, but when I had eaten it, my stomach was made bitter. And they said to me, "It is necessary that you prophesy again."

Then the seventh angel sounded his trumpet, and there were loud voices in heaven, saying: "The kingdom of the world has become the kingdom of our Lord and of his Christ, and he will reign forever and ever."

The twenty-four elders, who were sitting on their thrones before God, also fell on their faces and worshipped God, saying: "We thank you, Lord God Almighty, because you have taken your great power and reigned."

And God's temple in heaven was opened and the Ark of his Covenant was seen in his temple.

Lord God, all the world belongs to you and
your anointed Son. Rule in our hearts through
your gospel about him and ward off all
who attack us with falsehoods and lies. Amen.

247. THE FOURTH VISION: THE SEVEN VISIONS (REVELATION 12-14)

The fourth vision shows us the attacks that Satan, godless government, and the Antichrist make against the church, but God gives his people the victory.

A sign appeared in the sky: a woman cried out in pain as she gave birth. Another sign appeared in the sky: a huge red dragon that had seven heads and ten horns. The dragon stood before the woman so that he could devour the child as soon as it was born.

She gave birth to a son, who will shepherd all the nations with an iron rod. Her child was snatched up to God. Then the woman fled into the wilderness, where she has a place prepared by God that she might be fed there for 1,260 days.

There was also a war in heaven. Michael and his angels fought the dragon with his angels. The dragon—the ancient serpent, the Devil, Satan, the one who leads the whole earth astray—was thrown down to the earth, and his angels were thrown down with him.

I heard a voice in heaven saying: "Now have come the salvation and the power and the kingdom of our God and the authority of his Christ, because the accuser has been thrown down."

When the dragon was thrown down to the earth, he pursued the woman. Wings were given to the woman so that she might fly to her place in the wilderness, where she is to be fed away from the presence of the serpent. The dragon was angry about what had happened to the woman, and he went away to make war against the rest of her children.

I saw a beast rising out of the sea. He had ten horns and seven heads with blasphemous names. The beast was like a leopard, and his feet were like those of a bear, and his mouth was like the mouth of a lion. The dragon gave the beast his power and authority, and the whole world followed the beast. The beast also spoke blasphemies against God. He was also given permission to wage war against the saints and to overcome them. All those who make their home on the earth will worship the beast—those whose names have not been written in the Book of Life. Here patient endurance and confidence are needed by the saints.

Then I saw another beast coming up out of the earth. He had two horns like the Lamb, and he spoke like the dragon. He exercises all the authority of the first beast on his behalf. He causes the earth to worship the first beast. He performs great miracles. This beast caused whoever did not worship the beast to be killed. He makes all people receive a mark on their foreheads, in order that no one may buy or sell unless he has the mark. His number is 666.

Then I looked, and there was the Lamb standing on Mount Zion, and with him 144,000 who had his name written on their foreheads. They were singing a new song. No one was able to learn that song except the 144,000, who had been purchased from the earth. They continually follow the Lamb wherever he goes. And they are blameless.

Then I saw another angel flying in the middle of the sky. He had the everlasting gospel to proclaim to every nation, tribe, language, and people. He said: "Fear God and give him glory, because the hour of his judgment has come."

Another angel said, "Fallen, fallen is Babylon the Great."

Another angel said, "If anyone worships the beast and receives a mark on his forehead, he will also drink from the wine of God's wrath."

Here patient endurance is needed by the saints. And I heard a voice from heaven say, "Write: Blessed are the dead who die in the Lord from now on."

"Yes," says the Spirit, "because they will rest from their labors, for their works follow them."

Then I looked, and there was a white cloud, and seated on the cloud was one like a son of man. He had a gold crown on his head and a sharp sickle in his hand. And the one sitting on the cloud swung his sickle over the earth, and the earth was harvested.

Lord God, rescue us from all who would threaten us,
body or soul. Grant that we fall asleep in Jesus and
receive all eternal blessings and salvation in him. Amen.

248. THE FIFTH VISION: THE SEVEN BOWLS (REVELATION 15-16)

The fifth vision shows us manifestations of God's wrath against sin leading up until the final judgment.

Then I saw another great and remarkable sign in heaven: seven angels with seven plagues—the last plagues, because in them God's wrath is completed.

And I saw those who had won the victory over the beast. They held the harps of God, and they were singing the song of Moses, God's servant, and the song of the Lamb. They said: "Great and marvelous are your works, Lord God Almighty."

After these things I looked, and the sanctuary of the Tent of the Testimony was opened in heaven. The seven angels who hold the seven plagues came out of the sanctuary. They were clothed with clean bright linen, and they wore gold sashes around their chests.

One of the four living creatures gave the seven angels the seven gold bowls full of the wrath of God. And the sanctuary was filled with smoke from the glory of God and from his power. No one was able to enter the sanctuary until the seven plagues of the seven angels were completed.

I heard a loud voice from the temple say to the seven angels, "Go and pour out the seven bowls of God's wrath on the earth."

The first angel poured out his bowl on the earth. Painful sores came on the people who had the mark of the beast.

The second angel poured out his bowl on the sea. It became blood, and every living creature in the sea died.

The third angel poured out his bowl on the rivers and the springs of water. They turned into blood. And I heard the angel of the waters say: "Because they poured out the blood of saints and prophets, you have given them blood to drink."

And I heard the incense altar, saying, "Yes, Lord God Almighty, true and just are your judgments."

The fourth angel poured out his bowl on the sun. It was allowed to burn people with fire. People were scorched by the fierce heat, but they did not repent.

The fifth angel poured out his bowl on the throne of the beast. The beast's kingdom was darkened. People gnawed their tongues in their torment, but they did not repent.

The sixth angel poured out his bowl on the great river, the Euphrates. Its water was dried up to prepare the way for the kings coming from the east. I saw three unclean spirits, like frogs, which came out of the mouth of the dragon, out of the mouth of the beast, and out of the mouth of the false prophet. They are demonic spirits which go out to the kings of the whole earth to bring them together for the battle on the great day of the Almighty God.

Look: I am coming like a thief. Blessed is the one who stays awake.

Then they brought them together to the place that is called Armageddon.

The seventh angel poured out his bowl on the air. And a loud voice came out of the temple from the throne, saying, "It is done." There were flashes of lightning, rumblings, and crashes of thunder. There was also a great earthquake of a kind that has not occurred since mankind has been on the earth.

And the great city split into three parts, and the cities of the nations collapsed. Babylon the Great was remembered by God, and he gave her the wine cup filled with his fierce wrath.

Lord God, when we were your enemies you sent your Son to save us and then made us your people by faith. We pray that you would bring those who are still your enemies to repentance. Prevent those who do not repent from carrying out any evil against us. Amen.

249. THE SIXTH VISION: CHRIST AND THE ANTICHRIST (REVELATION 17-19)

The sixth vision shows us that Jesus defeats the Antichrist forever.

I saw a woman sitting on a scarlet beast that had seven heads and ten horns. In her hand was a gold cup full of abominations and the filth of her sexual immorality. And on her forehead this name was written: Babylon the Great, the mother of the prostitutes. I saw that this woman was drunk from the blood of the saints and the blood of Jesus' martyrs. The seven heads are seven hills. The ten horns are ten kings who have not yet received a kingdom, but along with the beast they will receive authority like kings for one hour. They will wage war against the Lamb, but the Lamb will overcome them, because he is Lord of Lords and King of Kings. Those who are with him are the called, the elect, and the believing. The woman is the great city that rules over the kings of the earth.

After these things I saw another angel coming down out of heaven. He called out with a loud voice, saying: "Fallen, fallen, is Babylon the Great. All the nations have drunk from the wine of her adulterous desire and the kings of the earth committed adultery with her. Come out of her so that you will not share in her sins, and so that you will not receive any of her plagues. She will be burned in fire, because the Lord God who judges her is powerful. Rejoice over her, heaven, also you saints, apostles, and prophets, because God has judged her for the judgment you received from her."

After these things I heard what seemed to be an immense crowd in heaven, saying: "Alleluia! Salvation and glory and power belong to our God, for his judgments are true and just. He has condemned the great prostitute who corrupted the earth with her immorality, and he has avenged his servants' blood that was shed by her hand."

A second time they said, "Alleluia! Her smoke goes up forever and ever."

Then the twenty-four elders and the four living creatures bowed down and worshipped God, saying, "Amen! Alleluia!"

And from the throne came a voice that said, "Praise our God, all you his servants, small and great."

And I heard what seemed to be the roar of a large crowd saying: "Alleluia! For the Lord our God, the Almighty, reigns. Let us rejoice and be glad and give him glory, because the wedding of the Lamb has come. His bride has made herself ready, and she was given bright, clean, fine linen to wear." (The fine linen is the "not guilty" verdicts pronounced on the saints.)

The angel said to me, "Write: Blessed are those who are invited to the wedding supper of the Lamb." He also said to me, "These are the true words of God." And I bowed down at his feet to worship him. But he said to me, "Do not do it! I am a fellow servant with you and your brothers, who have the testimony about Jesus. Worship God."

I saw heaven standing open, and there was a white horse! Its rider is called Faithful and True, and he judges and makes war in righteousness. His eyes are like blazing flames, and on his head are many crowns. He has a name written on him, which no one knows except he himself. He is also clothed in a garment that had been dipped in blood, and his name is the Word of God. The armies in heaven, which were clothed with white, clean, fine linen, were following him on white horses. Out of his mouth comes a sharp sword with which to strike down the nations. He will shepherd them with an iron staff. He himself is going to trample the winepress of the fierce anger of the Almighty God. On his garment this name is written: King of Kings and Lord of Lords.

Then I saw the beast and the kings of the earth and their armies gathered together to make war against the rider on the horse and his army. The beast was captured along with the false prophet who performed miracles on his behalf. These two were thrown alive into the Lake of Fire, which burns with sulfur. The rest were killed with the sword that comes out of the mouth of the rider on the horse. And all the birds gorged themselves on their flesh.

Lord God, you have clothed us in your Son's righteousness
and declared us innocent of all sin by faith in him.
You have also rescued us from all those who
would enslave us to the idea that our righteousness
must come from ourselves. Continue to defend us
by your gospel truth, and rescue those who are still under
the power of that lie, so that they may know fully
the freedom of forgiveness with us. Amen.

250. THE SEVENTH VISION: CHRIST AND SATAN, THE HEAVENLY CITY, AND CHRIST'S RETURN (REVELATION 20-22)

The seventh vision shows us that Jesus defeats the Devil forever, that God's people have a perfect, eternal home to look forward to, and that Jesus will come back soon for his people.

I saw an angel coming down from heaven. He had the key to the abyss. He seized the dragon, bound him for a thousand years, threw him into the abyss, locked it, and set a seal on it, so that he could no longer deceive the nations until the thousand years come to an end. After this he must be released for a short time.

Then I saw the souls of those who had been beheaded because of their testimony about Jesus. They lived and reigned with Christ a thousand years. (The rest of the dead did not live until the thousand years came to an end.) This is the first resurrection. Blessed is the one who has a share in the first resurrection. The second death has no power over them. Instead they will be priests of Christ and will reign with him for a thousand years.

When the thousand years come to an end, Satan will be released from his prison. He will go out to deceive the nations to gather them for battle. They came and surrounded the camp of the saints. Fire came down from God and devoured them. And the Devil was thrown into the lake of fire and sulfur forever and ever.

Then I saw a great white throne and the one who sat on it. The earth and the sky fled from his presence. Death and Grave gave up the dead that were in them, and they were judged, each one according to what he had done. Death and Grave were thrown into the Lake of Fire. The Lake of Fire is the second death. If anyone's name was not found written in the Book of Life, he was thrown into the Lake of Fire.

Then I saw a new heaven and a new earth. (The first heaven and the first earth had passed away.) And I saw the Holy City, the New Jerusalem, coming down out of heaven from God, prepared as a bride adorned for her husband.

A loud voice said, "Look! God's dwelling is with people. God himself will be with them, and he will be their God. He will wipe away every tear from their eyes. There will be no more death or sorrow or crying or pain, because the former things have passed away."

The one who was seated on the throne said, "Look, I am making everything new!"

One of the angels said, "Come, I will show you the bride, the wife of the Lamb."

He showed me the Holy City, Jerusalem, coming down out of heaven from God. It has the glory of God. It has a large, high wall. It has twelve gates. Twelve names are engraved on the gates, the names of the twelve tribes of Israel. The city's wall also has twelve foundations, and on them are the twelve names of the Lamb's twelve apostles.

I did not see a temple in the city, because the Lord God Almighty and the Lamb are its temple. The city does not need the sun or moon, because the glory of God has given it light, and the Lamb is its lamp.

The angel showed me the river of the water of life, which was as clear as crystal, flowing from the throne of God and the Lamb. In the middle of the city's street was a tree of life. The tree yields fruit every month, and its leaves are for the healing of the nations.

There will no longer be any curse. The throne of God and of the Lamb will be in the city. His servants will worship him. They will see his face. His name will be on their foreheads. And they will reign forever and ever.

I, Jesus, have sent my angel to give you this testimony. I am the Root and the Offspring of David, the bright Morning Star. I give this warning to everyone who hears the words of this book: If anyone adds to them, God will add to him the plagues that are written in this book. And if anyone takes away from the words of the book of this prophecy, God will take away his share in the Tree of Life and in the Holy City, which are written in this book.

The one who testifies about these things says, "Yes, I am coming soon."

Amen. Come, Lord Jesus!

The grace of the Lord Jesus Christ be with all the saints. Amen.

Lord God, you defeated our enemy the Devil for us
when Jesus died to take all our sin and guilt away.
Protect us from all his temptations and attacks.
Bring us to the perfect home you have prepared for us.
Quickly bring about your Son's return. Amen.

EPILOGUE

Many years ago, there was a movie named *The Greatest Story Ever Told.* This movie told the story of the life of Jesus Christ. *The Greatest Story Ever Told* would also be a fitting title for the section of this book which is based on the life of Jesus in the Four Gospels. But this is equally fitting as a title for this whole book, which tells the story of God's plan of salvation from Eden to Eternity. It begins with the story of creation and the fall into sin. Then it traces the promise of a Savior across thousands of years until Jesus was born in Bethlehem. This book devotes the most attention to Jesus' three-year ministry and to the three days of his suffering and death which won forgiveness of sins and salvation for all people. It then tells the story of the beginning of the spread of the gospel of salvation throughout the world. It ends with a glorious vision of the new heavens and the new earth, where God's people will enjoy an eternal life of happiness with him. This is truly the greatest story ever told.

This book can also be called *The Story of God's Love.* Although there are many stories of sin and sorrow and death in the Bible, the focus is always on God's love—love which would not give up on the people he created, no matter how often they turned away from him. The story of God's love is truly the greatest story ever told.